Humanism, Reform and the Reformation

Humanism, Reform and the Reformation

The Career of Bishop John Fisher

edited by Brendan Bradshaw and Eamon Duffy

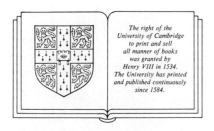

The right of the
University of Cambridge
to print and sell
all manner of books
was granted by
Henry VIII in 1534.
The University has printed
and published continuously
since 1584.

Cambridge University Press

Cambridge

New York   New Rochelle   Melbourne   Sydney

Published by the Press Syndicate of the University of Cambridge
The Pitt Building, Trumpington Street, Cambridge CB2 1RP
32 East 57th Street, New York, NY 10022, USA
10 Stamford Road, Oakleigh, Melbourne 3166, Australia

© Cambridge University Press 1989

First published 1989

Printed in Great Britain at
the University Press, Cambridge

British Library cataloguing in publication data
Humanism, reform and the Reformation: the
career of Bishop John Fisher.
1. Catholic church. Fisher, John,
Saint, 1469–1535. Biographies
I. Bradshaw, Brendan. II. Duffy, Eamon.
282'092'4

Library of Congress cataloguing in publication data
Humanism, reform and the Reformation.
Papers from a 1985 symposium sponsored by Cambridge
University and held in Queens' College.
1. Fisher, John, Saint, 1469–1535 – Congresses.
I. Bradshaw, Brendan. II. Duffy, Eamon. III. Cambridge
University.
BX4700.F34H85   1988   282'.092'4   [B]   88–4351

ISBN 0 521 34034 9

GG

Contents

Preface

This volume originated in the commemoration at Cambridge in 1985 of the 450th anniversary of the death of John Fisher, organised by members of the Faculties of Divinity and History, and sponsored by the University and Christ's, Queens', St John's and Trinity Colleges, with all of which Fisher had a particular connection. The bulk of the volume consists of papers originally read at a symposium held in Queens' College, under the chairmanship of Professor Geoffrey Elton. We wish to record our special indebtedness to Sir Geoffrey, whose astringent criticism and omniscience in the sources contributed much to the direction of discussion at the symposium, and thereby to the subsequent shaping of the volume. We wish also to thank all those students of the period who attended the symposium and whose expertise helped ensure its success. The symposium was possible because of the generous hospitality of Queens' College, and the financial support of Christ's, St John's, and Trinity.

On any reckoning John Fisher occupied a central place not only in the development of Cambridge University, but of English theology in its most turbulent era, a view perhaps reflected in the placing of his image, with that of Cranmer, above the entrance to the Cambridge Divinity School. Yet he has been regarded as largely the possession of Roman Catholic piety. The editors hope that the essays in this volume, in exploring the significance of Fisher's multifaceted career, will do something to direct scholarly attention to one of the most remarkable and complex figures of early Tudor England.

Abbreviations

DNB	*Dictionary of National Biography* (reference by name)
Documents	*Documents Relating to the University and Colleges of Cambridge* . . ., published by direction of the (University) Commissioners, 3 vols. (London, 1852)
Emden, *Cambridge*	A. B. Emden, *A Biographical Register of the University of Cambridge to 1500* (Cambridge, 1963)
Emden, *Oxford*	A. B. Emden, *A Biographical Register of the University of Oxford to 1500*, 3 vols. (Oxford, 1959)
Emden, *Oxford, 1501–40*	A. B. Emden, *A Biographical Register of the University of Oxford, 1501–40* (Oxford, 1974)
EW	*The English Works of John Fisher*, I, ed. J. E. B. Mayor, Early English Text Society, extra series, 27 (1876)
Grace Books A, B	*Grace Book A*, ed. S. M. Leathes; *Grace Book B*, ed. M. Bateson, 2 vols., Cambridge Antiquarian Society, Luard Memorial series, I–III (Cambridge, 1897, 1903–5)
Lewis, *Fisher*	J. Lewis, *The Life of Dr John Fisher*, 2 vols. (London, 1855)
Life	'Vie du bienheureux martyr Jean Fisher, cardinal, évêque de Rochester (+ 1535)', ed. F. Van Ortroy, *Analecta Bollandiana*, 10 (1891), 121–365; 12 (1893), 97–283 – references by volume and page; also, less accessibly, in book form (Brussels, 1893), and in modernised English, ed. P. Hughes (London, 1935)
LP	*Calendar of Letters and Papers, Foreign and Domestic, of the Reign of Henry VIII*, ed. J. S. Brewer, J. Gairdner and R. H. Brodie (London, 1862–1932)
Mayor, *Statutes*	*The Early Statutes of St John's College Cambridge*, ed. J. E. B. Mayor (Cambridge, 1859)
Opera	*R. D. D. Ioannis Fischerii, Roffensis in Anglia Episcopi, Opera* (Würzburg: G. Fleischmann, 1597)
PL	*Patrologiae cursus completus* . . . (Series Latina), ed. J. P. Migne, 221 vols. (Paris, 1844–64)
RCHM Cambridge	*Royal Commission on Historical Monuments, England, City of Cambridge*, 2 parts (London, 1959)
Reg. Fisher	Register of John Fisher as bishop of Rochester, Kent Archives Office, Rochester Diocesan Records, DRc/R7, fos. 6/40–182v

STC	*A Short-Title Catalogue of Books Printed in England, Scotland and Ireland and of English Books Printed Abroad, 1475–1640*, 2nd edn, ed. W. A. Jackson, F. S. Ferguson and K. F. Pantzer, 2 vols. (London, 1976–86)
VCH Cambs	*The Victoria History of the Counties of England: A History of the County of Cambridge and the Isle of Ely*, III, ed. J. P. C. Roach (London, 1959)
VCH Oxford	*The Victoria History of the County of Oxford*, III, ed. H. E. Salter and M. D. Lobel (London, 1954)
Venn	J. and J. A. Venn, *Alumni Cantabrigienses* (Cambridge, 1922–7)
Willis and Clark	R. Willis and J. W. Clark, *The Architectural History of the University of Cambridge and of the Colleges of Cambridge and Eton*, 4 vols. (Cambridge, 1886)

Bishop John Fisher, 1469–1535: the man and his work

BRENDAN BRADSHAW

The circumstances of John Fisher's death have impeded the study of his life in three ways. Firstly, his execution as a leading opponent of the Henrician ecclesiastical revolution has disposed historians of a Whiggish disposition to classify him without much more ado as a conservative medieval churchman. Accordingly they pass over his career as possessing little significance for the march of progress. The insidious influence of Whiggery largely explains the continuing marginalisation of Fisher even in the most recent accounts of the early Tudor period.[1] Secondly, obsession with the martyrdom has introduced an extraordinary imbalance in the treatment of Fisher's career within the Catholic historiographical tradition. The near contemporary early *Life* set the trend, devoting two thirds of its pages to the last eight years of the bishop's career, the period of his struggle against the royal divorce and the royal ecclesiastical supremacy.[2] That pattern has continued to characterise biographical studies of Fisher: the tail wags the dog – if the metaphor does not seem inappropriate to the circumstances. The career is passed over as quickly as may be; only the extraordinary episode at the end is treated with the scholarly respect that the whole deserves.[3] Thirdly, the incidental association of Fisher in death with Thomas More, the most beguiling of all Catholic martyrs, has proved a distraction. From the beginning, historical interest in the two has been totally disproportionate. As is well known, a 'More industry' began to form in the aftermath of More's death in the circle of his highly talented humanist household. It continues to flourish.[4] By contrast the publication of works by or about Fisher has always been desultory.[5] To that extent interest in More, no doubt to the saint's immortal embarrassment, has served to obscure the inherent interest and significance of Fisher's career, and has contributed to the latter's continuing marginalisation.

If Fisher's life and works are to be rescued from the twilight region to which posterity has consigned them, the great need is for specialist studies, undertaken by scholars with the necessary technical and conceptual equipment. Happily the need has come under increasing notice in the past two decades – largely as a spin-off from the More industry.[6] The point has now been reached where something between a report on work in progress and an

1

interpretative synthesis can be attempted. That is the purpose of the present essay. It attempts to provide an introduction to Fisher's life and works, drawing on the fresh insights and additional knowledge which current scholarship is providing. It does so within the framework of a biographical sketch: the career is unfolded in chronological sequence and related to a context that is intended to reveal its inner significance as well as enable the personality to emerge from the dusty records.

I

John Fisher was born in Beverley in Yorkshire: the date of birth was 1469 – calculated on the basis of a declaration of age made by Fisher when applying for a papal licence for ordination in 1491.[7] His father was a merchant in a relatively modest way of business who died when John was eight years old, leaving four children. John's mother, Agnes, then married William White, by whom she had five more children. Practically nothing else is known of Fisher's early years. Three of Agnes's children were to enter religion – Richard and Elizabeth White, as well as John Fisher – which may suggest a household of lively piety. A warm family atmosphere in those years seems to be reflected also in the close family ties maintained by Fisher later on: his brother Robert acted as his steward while he was bishop of Rochester and attended to him during his last imprisonment; two of his three Tower Works were addressed to his half-sister, the nun, Elizabeth;[8] and the early *Life* contains a delightful vignette of a family Christmas at Rochester in which the bishop lavishly provides the festive fare and then seeks refuge from the merry-making in his study.[9] The formative influence of Fisher's Yorkshire boyhood is reflected in later events in one other way, in his assiduous promotion of the Northern presence at Cambridge, a policy which he defended not only by appeal to the need to redress an existing imbalance but by appeal to the claims of kin-piety.[10]

Fisher went up to Cambridge in 1483. Fourteen was rather young even by contemporary practice. None the less it seems that he was already destined for the ministry: his college, Michaelhouse – soon to be absorbed into a new foundation, Trinity – possessed a distinctly theological orientation.[11] Fisher's arrival in Cambridge and Michaelhouse at this precise time had significant implications for his intellectual formation which are only now beginning to be explored. William Melton, his tutor, seems to have exerted a strong influence, as a passing recollection in a treatise years later suggests. And Melton emerges from present research not only as a pastorally minded churchman but as representative of a degree of openness to humanistic scholarship at Cambridge unsuspected hitherto.[12] However that may be, Fisher's Cambridge career offers the spectacle of a glittering and precocious success. As such it provides the first indication of those personal qualities that made him so formidable a figure to his contemporaries: considerable intellectual ability combined with practical sagacity and administrative capacity, and high moral seriousness.

The first step in his triumphal progress was election into a fellowship at Michaelhouse on proceeding MA in 1491.[13] This, in turn, opened the way for ordination to the priesthood the same year, four years under the canonical age. University office came in 1494 when Fisher was elected senior proctor by the members of the Regent House. In that year also comes the first evidence that Fisher had begun to attract interest in higher quarters: in an entry in the Proctor's Book, detailing the expenses of a trip to Greenwich, the 25-year-old senior proctor notes laconically, 'dined with the lady mother of the king . . . supped with the [lord] chancellor'. As is well known, Fisher was to turn contact with the Lady Margaret Beaufort to the spectacular advantage of the University, though not, at least directly to his own. The more immediate effect, however, was to withdraw him temporarily from Cambridge in order to reside in the household of the Lady Margaret as her personal confessor. By 1501 Fisher's Cambridge career had resumed. In that year he was elected vice-chancellor of the University and gained the highest of the University's academic degrees, the doctorate in divinity, for which he presented himself at the first opportunity on completion of the stipulated ten-year intermission from the award of an MA. The University had two further distinctions to bestow and they followed in rapid succession. In 1503 he was appointed the first Lady Margaret reader in theology: appropriately, if not inevitably, since the readership represented the first major benefaction of the Lady Margaret to the University, secured through the instrumentality of Fisher; it heralded an important new phase of development at Cambridge of which Fisher was to be the chief architect and the Lady Margaret the chief patron. Then in 1504 he was elected chancellor of the University for the first time. He was still only 35.

In that year also Fisher was elevated to the see of Rochester. Against the background of his Cambridge career what is notable about Fisher's episcopal career in the first instance is its failure to follow along predictable lines. The failure is all the more striking in the light of the favourable auspices that attended his elevation: he was the personal choice of King Henry VII himself, prompted by the influential councillor and royal secretary, Bishop Richard Fox of Winchester, with the powerful Lady Margaret lending her approbation.[14] Given Fisher's obvious talents and these resources of patronage, Rochester − the poorest and one of the smallest of English dioceses − should have marked for him, as it did for most of his late medieval predecessors there, the first rung of a ladder leading to one of the plum episcopal appointments, to a rich abbacy *in commendam* and, in view of his administrative capacity, to high government office.[15] This did not happen. Fisher's 31-year-long pontificate was spent as bishop of Rochester. It is entirely reasonable to suppose that it would not have been so had he wished it other-wise. His example in this regard shines all the more brightly in an age more notorious than most for prelatical careerism: rightly, it served as an inspiration to Carlo Borromeo, the model bishop of the Counter Reformation, in constructing his own model of the apostolic bishop wedded to his see.[16] A complementary aspect of Fisher's episcopate has been brought to light by research in the Rochester diocesan archives. These reveal him as a resident, pastoral bishop: the bulk of the surviving records find Fisher in his diocese attending to his episcopal duties.[17] In this regard he may have been less of an exception than is generally supposed. Recent work suggests that residence, at least part-time, and care of the cure, was more common among late medieval bishops, even among late medieval episcopal careerists, than the traditional jaundiced view of the late medieval English Church allows.[18]

Where Fisher's apostolate is undoubtedly and significantly novel is in the zeal which he displays for a preaching ministry. This has two aspects. One concerns the creation of a preaching clergy which, as will appear, was central to his continuing concern with Cambridge. The other relates to his personal practice. At a time when the episcopal office was conceived in juridical-institutional terms, identified with the twin powers of jurisdiction and sacramental orders, when, in effect, the ministry of preaching tended to be off-loaded on to the friars, and bishops were ready to admit to having never set foot in a pulpit, Bishop Fisher emerged as the foremost preacher in England.[19] A relatively substantial body of his published sermons survive and has earned for him a secure place in the history of English pulpit oratory. Formally they belong to a scholastic tradition, highly structured and analytical. But they achieve an often powerful rhetorical effect by means of an imaginative manipulation of imagery, deployed by way of simile or allegory to illuminate and develop the argument.[20] In content they hold a special interest since they constitute the earliest stratum of Fisher's literary remains and as such provide the best access, in the absence of a substantial body of personal correspondence or journals, to his religious outlook and to the nature of his pastoral concerns in the period before his embroilment in Reformation polemics.

To judge by the topoi that dominate his sermons – the vanity and transitoriness of life, the 'four last things' (death, judgement, hell, or heaven), repentance for sin, the passion of Christ, the economy of salvation – Fisher's mind seems set in the medieval mould at its most austerely transcendental.[21] Nevertheless, they also convey a peculiarly contemporary resonance. This is for two related reasons. One is the highly dramatic soteriological perspective to which Fisher constantly reverts: the critical dilemma posed by mankind's propensity for sin and the catastrophic eschatological consequences of sinning – hence the importunate call to repentance which is the leitmotiv of his sermons.[22] The other is the correspondingly dramatic perspective which he brings to bear on the state of the Church in his own times, under threat, as he believes, from the infidel without but, more lamentably, under threat from a decadent clergy within who have lost the evangelical spirit and have ceased to proclaim Christ's call of repentance to a sinful humanity.[23] These intense preoccupations, it would seem, provide the inner dynamisms of Fisher's career, of his personal pastoral ministry, of his preaching, and of his wider activities as a churchman and University chancellor. At the same time they serve to situate Fisher's religious consciousness within a wider thought world, that of the reforming impulse of the pre-Reformation Church. This impulse received various practical expressions. It comprehended the concerns and aspirations of the Christian humanists of the circle of Erasmus, the evangelical revivalism of the Dominican friar Savonarola, and the revived Augustinianism of theologians such as Martin Luther.[24] In the context of the severe penitential preaching of Savonarola at Florence and the anguished wrestling of the Wittenberg theologian with the problem of human sinfulness *coram Deo*, John Fisher's transcendental penitential religion seems very much in touch with the spirit of his age.

II

Like his elevation to Rochester in 1504, Fisher's election as chancellor of Cambridge the same year initiated a lifelong tenure: he was re-elected annually until 1514, when he was elected for life.[25] In its own way this latter turn of events was as remarkable as the permanent occupancy at Rochester – and no less revealing. As we now know, the fifteenth century saw a change in the pattern of office-holding in regard to the senior post at the two English Universities whereby the resident, medieval working-chancellor was transformed into a chancellor-patron, habitually an absentee prelate, well placed to advance the interests of the University, most especially in the corridors of government and at court.[26] Fisher can be set in this new mould down to 1509. Then death dealt his potential as patron a double blow by removing first Henry VII, who had lent such a ready ear to his claims to Rochester, and then, within months, the Lady Margaret Beaufort, the *fons et origo* of the benefactions he had secured for Cambridge. He was never again to possess such access to influence and munificence. Ironically his devotion to the interests of the University complicated his relationship with the young Henry VIII from the start, as he fought to secure the recognition of an unsigned and undated codicil to the Lady Margaret's will which assigned a large part of her estate to the foundation of a new college at Cambridge at the expense of the other legatees, most especially of the crown.[27] Realistically appraising his situation in 1514, Fisher urged the University to look for a chancellor elsewhere and suggested Wolsey, whose meteoric rise in Church and state was well under way. When Wolsey declined – perhaps anticipating a call from his own University which never came – Cambridge elected Fisher as chancellor for life, a gesture all the more remarkable for the fact that life tenure, although not unprecedented, was still a rarity in 1514.[28]

In the circumstances, this final vote of confidence on the part of the University – for as such it must be seen – provides an impressive climax to an unfaltering series that began with Fisher's election as senior proctor in 1495. Behind it lies an equally impressive record of achievement. Most conspicuously there was Fisher's success in directing the pious charity of the Lady Margaret Beaufort away from the votive chantry foundations of medieval tradition to a more practical form of University endowment, thereby precipating a major expansion of the University's facilities: a readership (soon to become a chair) in theology (1503), a University preachership (1504), and two new colleges, the large and well-endowed Christ's College (1505–6) and St John's, incorporated in 1511 and, despite the legal wrangle over the Lady Margaret's will, steadily accumulating the resources on which its future greatness was to be built.[29] Fisher's achievement is not to be measured, of course, in sheer quantitative terms, as a purely material contribution to the expansion of the University. It must also be assessed as a contribution towards educational reform in the context of a European-wide movement associated with Renaissance humanism.[30] In this context Fisher's designs can seem disappointing if approached with expectations of radical innovation or from the perspective of an ideal of educational reform based on Renaissance aspirations towards the revival of classical literature. Close analysis of the early statutes of Christ's and of the successive versions drafted by Fisher for St John's reveals, in the first, a considerable degree of adherence to traditional forms – the extent of his involvement here is hard to unravel in any case – and that the forward-looking provisions in the second were anticipated or, at least, foreshadowed elsewhere, or were adopted from the scheme devised contemporaneously by Richard Fox for Corpus Christi, Oxford. Similarly, while Fisher's commitment to the *bonae litterae* cannot be gainsaid, the practical promotion of such studies could not be claimed to be the central feature of his programme of reform at Cambridge: St John's, and more so Christ's, continued to provide an essentially scholastic training, albeit by means of a reformed curriculum and pedagogical method; the *bonae litterae* were assigned an ancillary role directed towards the improvement of standards of biblical study and of homiletics.[31] However, to disparage Fisher's contribution on that account would be to miss the real achievement. Even though the developments which he engineered were not notably innovative in specific detail, they were firmly progressive in their thrust towards the ideal of a collegiate University, evangelically orientated in theology and in its training, and committed to promoting the three biblical languages.[32] His activities provided an impulse towards the realisation of that ideal that was unprecedented in scale and was not to be equalled by any later individual contribution. Here it must be remembered that his achievement lay not only in advancing the programme of development in material terms. He was also concerned with expansion of the University's specifically academic resources, with the acquisition of books, the grooming of likely young scholars, and with attracting foreign scholars to the University. Thus, Erasmus's three years at Cambridge (1511–14)[33] represented a major coup – recognised more in the aftermath than at the time, it seems – for the University and particularly for Queens', where Fisher, as former president of the College (1505–8), arranged for Erasmus to stay. Against that background, Fisher's election as chancellor for life gains added significance. It points to an aspect of his achievement at Cambridge that has received little notice: his ability to retain the confidence of the University establishment while committing himself to the advancement of reform. Fisher's leadership must in large part explain, as Erasmus maintained, the relative tranquillity which marks this phase of reform at Cambridge by comparison with the explosive tensions generated elsewhere, at Oxford, for instance, to travel no further afield or, indeed, at Cambridge itself in the succeeding generation.[34] The quiet evolution over which Fisher presided in the first quarter of the sixteenth century marks a crucial phase in the process by which the University overtook her elder sister in academic performance and in reputation. That, perhaps, is the best measure of Fisher's achievement as University chancellor.

Before leaving this phase of Fisher's career, the complexity of the personality that emerges from it, by contrast with the various historiographical stereotypes, deserves attention. First, the other-worldly man of God turns out to be a remarkably capable man of affairs, determined, resourceful, adaptable – as his rescue of the Lady Margaret's posthumous foundation at St John's shows – and possessed of the political skills as chancellor to lead the University firmly in the direction of reform while retaining the confidence of a conservative academic establishment.[35] Then, again, the Catholic polemicist of later years – the embodiment, as it is supposed, of conservative medieval churchmanship[36] – emerges here as a committed reformer: frankly critical of the *status quo ante*; responsive to the winds of change blowing in from the continent; supportive of promoters of the humanist cause against the obscurantists (applauding Agricola's new style *Dialectica*, effusive in his admiration for Reuchlin's Hebrew scholarship, sympathetic towards Erasmus in his troubles over the New Testament); and plunging into the study of Greek and Hebrew with boyish enthusiasm in middle age.[37] Yet Fisher's humanistic enthusiasms, in turn, lend credence to a distorting stereotype. This sets the reforming chancellor within the charmed circle of Erasmians. It is, however, abundantly clear that Erasmus's anthropocentric

Christian philosophy could find little resonance in Fisher, given the transcendental and charismatic quality of his religious outlook.[38] His humanistic affinities must be sought elsewhere. His effusive admiration for Reuchlin's Hebrew scholarship, which Erasmus did not share, points to a more congenial alternative, though one with which the bishop's orthodox admirers find no less difficulty in coming to terms. It was as the intellectual successor of Pico della Mirandola that Fisher hailed Reuchlin.[39] And it is in terms of the religious syncretism promoted by Pico in turn-of-the-century Italy that Fisher's transcendental religion and his humanistic enthusiasms can be most satisfactorily reconciled. For Giovanni Pico envisaged an intellectual synthesis that would not only preserve the philosophical heritage of medieval scholasticism, accommodated to the modes of the new humanistic rhetoric, but would assimilate the charismatic tradition of Hebrew Cabbalistic scholarship as well.[40] Furthermore, towards the end of his brief career, Pico set out to align this comprehensive intellectual synthesis with an aspiration towards practical religious reform well attuned to Fisher's eschatological spirit. This was the reform purveyed by the penitential preaching of Girolamo Savonarola at Florence – whose orthodoxy, despite excommunication and execution, Fisher is found upholding as late as 1526.[41] To distance Fisher from the thought-world of Erasmian Christian humanism, therefore, is not to push him back into the mould of conservative, medieval churchmanship. It is rather to place him within the ambit of a Renaissance world in which his career as a penitential preacher and as reforming University chancellor achieves ideological coherence.

III

In 1519, as Fisher entered his fifties, his career took a new turn. In that year he made his first forays into the field of religious controversy. He was to emerge as a leading controversialist on the European scene in the 1520s. Lying behind this development was the spread of his reputation to the continent in the 1510s as a bishop who, for a rarity, conformed with the humanist ideal, a reputation which – despite the ideological distance between them – Erasmus's rhapsodies on the theme of the 'saintly and learned' bishop of Rochester in correspondence at this time did much to cultivate.[42] The connection between Fisher's growing reputation and his new role is highlighted by the circumstances in which he entered the fray in 1519. The occasion was not, as might be supposed, the early stirrings of Lutheran heresy – which had yet to penetrate beyond Germany – but a celebrated controversy provoked by the French humanist, Jacques Lefèvre dÉtaples, when he debunked the medieval cult of the Magdalene as unscriptural. Fisher, by his own account, was not disposed to take more than a mild scholarly interest in the affair. What brought him to a different frame of mind, and to contribute

8

three volumes in defence of the traditional understanding of the Magdalene, was the persuasion of two distinguished foreign ecclesiastics, Cardinal Campeggio, then papal legate in England, and Bishop Poncher of Paris.[43] Their interest in involving Fisher is clear: they sought to overtop the moral authority of the pious humanist Lefèvre with that of the bishop of Rochester. Whatever the success of the strategy on that occasion – the controversy petered out in 1521[44] – it was inevitably repeated as the battle of the books with the protestants got under way: according to Vitoria in 1534 Fisher was the only bishop in the opening phase of the theological debate who was intellectually equipped to respond to the reformers in kind.[45] He did not stint himself. Between 1522 and 1527, when he indicated his intention of withdrawing from controversy, he expended well over half a million words on five volumes of Latin polemic: a tract against the humanist Velenus defending the historicity of the tradition associating the apostle Peter with Rome (1522); three works against Luther, including the first comprehensive rebuttal of his doctrine, the *Assertionis Lutheranae Confutatio* (1523); and a blockbuster of some 220,000 words against the eucharistic doctrine of the Swiss reformer, Oecolampadius in 1527.[46] There were also two pamphlets in English originating in keynote sermons at Paul's Cross: the first on the occasion of the burning of heretical books organised by Wolsey in 1521; the second – by royal command – on the abjuration of Robert Barnes and other heretics in 1526.[47]

Fisher did not, of course, withdraw from polemical controversy in 1527. He simply transferred his energies to a religious issue of more specifically English concern. The moral stature he had by now attained is reflected in the fact that, when Henry VIII embarked upon his quest for a divorce in the spring of 1527, almost his first move was to attempt to secure the support of the bishop of Rochester.[48] The earliest extant opinion on the case is provided in a letter from Fisher to Wolsey, firmly negative in its conclusion. As the controversy developed, the bishop of Rochester emerged as the chief protagonist on Queen Catherine's side, and disappointment quickly turned the king's admiration for 'the saintliest bishop in christendom' to venom. The history of Fisher's defence of the queen's cause is difficult to document because of the vicissitudes suffered by the contemporary documents, not least in consequence of a ruthless royal censorship. Only one published work from Fisher's pen is known to survive, *De Causa Matrimonii*, smuggled out of England – probably in the Spanish ambassador's diplomatic bag – and printed in Alcalá in 1530.[49] However, meticulous research in the English archives has now succeeded in uncovering and co-ordinating a substantial body of evidence.[50] Six tracts by Fisher on the royal divorce have either been recovered or their substantial content reconstructed from other sources: he himself estimated that he had written 'seven or eight' such works when interrogated on the matter in the Tower in 1534. These and a sheaf of letters provide the evidence from which the history of Fisher's involvement in the divorce controversy can, at last, be reconstructed. They tell the story of a characteristically relentless campaign on Fisher's part, waged by means of a steady stream of letters and tracts which begin as early as the spring of 1527 and continue, in the aftermath of his dramatic intervention at the legatine trial in 1529, until the tide of events by the spring of 1533 rendered further argument otiose – and provided the bishop with a cause of even more fundamental import to defend.[51]

Before addressing the intellectual issues raised by this corpus of polemical writings for the interpretation of Fisher's career, its sheer bulk deserves to be emphasised. The tally stands at a minimum of fourteen separate works in Latin and two English pamphlets, amounting to some 800,000 words. Fisher's total literary output over the period stands higher still: a Latin treatise on prayer dates from 1520; a treatise on Christian living appeared in 1532 – it had originated in two sermons delivered twelve years before; at the same time the bishop was occupied with two major works of biblical scholarship, a massive psalm commentary – never completed – which can be reliably dated to c. 1525, and a study of the Septuagint.[52] Fisher's literary productivity at this time seems all the more remarkable in the light of his personal circumstances. His authorial role was performed, it must be remembered, in conjunction with a host of other duties which took a heavy toll of time and energy: the administrative and sacramental routines attaching to episcopal office, to which, as the evidence shows, Fisher continued to be scrupulously attentive;[53] the calls of his preaching ministry; his increasing involvement in the inquisitorial campaign against the heretics; not least, the claims of public worship and of private devotion.[54] Moreover, the bishop, now in his fifties, was advancing into old age, according to contemporary standards, and was not in robust health in any case. The sheer scale of Fisher's polemical output, therefore, testifies to considerable intellectual vitality, whatever its implications otherwise.

The content is generally considered less flattering, revealing, it is supposed, the cast of mind of a conservative, medieval churchman, stubbornly resistant to progress. In assessing the religious mentality which Fisher's polemical works reflect, a fundamental, if seldom acknowledged, difficulty presents itself. A systematic intellectual analysis of the massive polemical corpus was not undertaken until very recently and still awaits completion.[55] Pending the outcome of that Herculean task, the theological and ideological underpinning of Fisher's polemics remains problematic, and pronouncements concerning the outlook which informs them can only be tentative and provisional. Nevertheless, a variety of considerations can be adduced to undermine the image of the diehard conservative and to advance instead a view of Fisher as a religious controversialist more credibly at one with that of the reforming chancellor of Cambridge. Firstly, the reactionary image seems heavily indebted to an outmoded teleological conception of the religious controversies of the period, according to which the defenders of orthodoxy are taken to represent the forces of reaction and set over against an alignment of humanists, protestants and Erastian politicians, who are taken to represent the forces of progress. The fact is that the alignment of forces produced in the course of Fisher's polemical battles is not amenable to categorisation in such simplistic terms. The bishop's humanist opponents in 1519–20, Lefèvre and Clichtove, became his allies in the subsequent debate with the protestants;[56] and in dissociating themselves from the protestant Reformation they conformed to a pattern observable among the leading lights of humanism generally, including their doyen, Desiderius Erasmus. Then, again, in rejecting the king's claim on the issue of the royal divorce, Fisher found himself in the unlikely company of the arch-heresiarch, Martin Luther, and his English evangelist, William Tyndale.[57] All of this serves to highlight the inadequacies of a confessionally determined explanatory model of reactionaries and progressives and, in particular, its inapplicability in Fisher's case.

Discarding the teleological framework, therefore, a more positive assessment of Fisher's stance as a religious controversialist emerges when the causes which he espoused are considered on their own merits. Turning first to the debates which revolved upon issues of critical scholarship, it is worthy of note that in two cases out of three the advance of knowledge has served to vindicate Fisher's position: on the historicity of the Petrine Roman tradition, now long undisputed;[58] and on the exegesis of the crucial Levitical prescription against marriage to a brother's wife – the case, argued by the supporters of Henry VIII, for elevating this to the status of immutable divine law can be dismissed, in the light of modern critical exegesis and hermeneutics, as fundamentalism of the crassest kind.[59] The third case, where time has told against Fisher's view, is particularly illuminating, though not in the way generally assumed. The issue here was the authenticity of the figure at the centre of the widespread medieval cult of St Mary Magdalene. Against Fisher's defence of the medieval Magdalene, the weight of modern scholarship comes down on the side of the view argued by Jacques Lefèvre and his supporters in 1519–21 that the romantic penitent represented, in fact, a conflation of three distinct New Testament figures: the repentant sinner (unnamed) who wiped the feet of Jesus with her hair (Luke 7:36–50); Mary, called the Magdalene, a demoniac healed by Jesus and numbered among the women who ministered to him and the disciples (Luke 8:1–3); and Mary, the sister of Martha and Lazarus who entertained Jesus at their home in Bethany (Luke 11:38–42). The debate holds special interest intellectually as an early instance of the impact of critical humanist methods and attitudes on credulous medieval piety.[60] As a reflection of Fisher's frame of mind, therefore, his blasts against the demythologisers may seem especially damning. Closer examination of the episode shows that this is not the case. What needs to be emphasised in the first instance in this connection is the scholarly arrogance and eccentricity that marked Lefèvre's original statement of his case.[61] Not only did he insist on dividing the Magdalene of the medieval cult into her three New Testament components, he also insisted on subdividing the New Testament Magdalene, in turn, into two distinct figures of the same name, so that, for instance, according to Lefèvre, two persons of that name watched by Jesus on Calvary.[62] What needs emphasising on the other hand is the open-minded attitude which Fisher brought to bear on the issue. Pressed to interest himself in the debate by Campeggio and Poncher, he approached it personally inclined to the hypothesis of conflation and with deep respect for Lefèvre's piety and scholarship – only to be jolted by the humanist's apparently mindless iconoclasm into an indignant rebuttal.[63] The final modifying consideration is the intellectual power with which his case was argued – acknowledged by modern scholarship, despite its sympathy for the progressive Lefèvre – which succeeded in isolating with characteristic acuity the fundamental issue raised by the debate: the relationship between scholarship and the teaching authority invested in the Church in establishing the truths of religion. Ironically, it was Fisher's correct understanding of the problem that impelled him, against his original intuition, towards the wrong conclusion, i.e. that the magisterium, expressing itself in devotional practice, had authenticated the medieval cult and, therefore, the figure who was its object. Precisely because of the negative outcome, however, Fisher's behaviour in this instance goes furthest towards illuminating the complexity of his intellectual outlook. It highlights the ambiguity that necessarily attended a devoted man of the Church, responsive to the reforming potential of the new humanist learning, yet deeply conscious of his episcopal role as a custodian of the Catholic tradition. Here, surely, may be glimpsed a major source of the inner tension to which the Holbein sketch of the late 1520s gives such miraculous expression.

Turning to the strictly theological debates in which Fisher engaged with Luther and Oecolampadius, the findings that have begun to emerge from the systematic analysis now in progress add depth to the picture just sketched in three ways. The first concerns the matter of tone. The restraint of Fisher's polemical style, his evident distaste for the vilificatory diatribe as a mode of argument, his failure to conform to the trend towards uninhibited invective, evident in the Reformation debates from the outset, together convey an impression distinctly at odds with that of an embattled reactionary.[64] They suggest an intellectual disposition more attuned to Pico's eirenic enterprise than to the intellectual pugilism of the Reformation debates – a disposition implied in another way by the picture in the early *Life* of Fisher, confronted with an early example of heretical defiance at Cambridge, breaking down in tears in the act of pronouncing sentence of excommunication against a member of his beloved University.[65] The second feature complements the first. It relates to the ideological thrust of Fisher's theology. No doubt this was undeviating in its conformity with medieval Catholicism. However, the significant feature is the moderation – once again – of his stance within that context. His approach on the crucial issue of ecclesiology provides the prime example.[66] On the one hand, he emerges here as an adherent of the late-medieval school of ecclesiology characterised as papal monarchism.[67] On the other hand, despite his trenchant defence of the doctrine of papal primacy *iure divino*, he notably fails to press the doctrine to its theoretical limits. The jurisdictional notion of papal monarchy which he elaborates is strikingly constitutionalist in character, inspired, it would seem, by a tradition of English political reflection. On the pope's magisterial authority he hesitates to assert a prerogative of infallibility, recognising, in fact, papal fallibility, and finding himself unable to resolve the dilemma of disagreement between pope and ecumenical council.[68] Over all, the thrust of Fisher's ecclesiological reflection can be described as synthetic rather than dialectical. In the vision that emerges, pope, college of bishops and theologians operate harmoniously in mutual service of the Mystical Body of Christ. The third significant feature of Fisher's theological polemics is their intellectual quality. As his contributions to the Reformation debate are subjected to comparative analysis, his achievement, for long only dimly grasped, appears in sharper relief. It has a twofold aspect. Fisher, it now appears, was probably the quickest to grasp the basic issues – the nature and function of the Church, and the status of human nature, in the economy of salvation. Correspondingly he was also a leading pioneer in developing a coherent polemic against the reformers, contributing a number of key arguments to the Catholic armoury.[69] It will be some time before Fisher's contribution to the Reformation debate can be authoritatively assessed. Meanwhile, however, attention may be drawn to an emerging picture of England as a major centre in moulding the Church's intellectual response to protestantism in the 1520s, and of the bishop-theologian of Rochester as the most influential figure in this development.

Fisher's role as a Catholic polemicist has lent a spurious credibility to the stock image of him as a deeply conservative, medieval churchman. Close attention to the actual content of the polemical writings reveals a more complex and a more interesting personality, one rooted in the medieval Catholic tradition to be sure, but open-minded, ideologically moderate by disposition, and of exceptional intellectual calibre. The figure discernible behind the polemical writings is not at odds with that of the reforming Chancellor of Cambridge, any more than is the latter with the penitential preacher and pastoral bishop. The personality coheres just as the careers overlap. The task of the historian is to comprehend the complexity of the living reality, not to diminish it by resort to simplistic categorisations.

IV

The final phase of Fisher's career assumes the aspect of a heroic tragedy. It finds the bishop at the forefront of resistance to the historical process which launched a Reformation in England greatly at variance with the one he himself had envisaged and striven to realise. The unfolding tragedy, and Fisher's place within it, is highlighted in a series of dramatic confrontations that mark the stages of a progressive – and eventually fatal – alienation between himself and his king. The first was the occasion in the long gallery in Windsor in June 1527 when Henry VIII's importunate solicitations on the matter of his proposed divorce met with no less urgent solicitations to the contrary from Fisher.[70] The second was set at the abortive trial of the case before the papal legates, Wolsey and Campeggio, at Blackfriars in June 1529, where Fisher emerged as the outspoken champion of an increasingly embattled queen – and added insult to injury by evoking John the Baptist's defence to the death of the marriage bond against the adulterous King Herod Agrippa.[71] The third marked the extending ramifications of the controversy and the new depths of menace it had begun to hold. It was the occasion of the Convocation of Canterbury over the winter and spring of 1530–1 when the king mulcted the clergy on a trumped-up charge of Praemunire, and sought to consolidate his victory by extracting an acknowledgement of royal ecclesiastical supremacy from the assembled clergy – only to have Fisher snatch away the fruits of victory by his success in modifying the acknowledgement by the addition of 'so far as the law of Christ allows' to the form of words.[72] The queen's champion had now emerged as the focus of resistance to anti-clerical bullying on the part of the parliamentary Commons and the regime. As the menace to queen and Church heightened, against the background of the 'Submission of the clergy' in May 1532, Fisher was prepared to advance the confrontation to a more desperate plane. Austerely apolitical throughout his career, he now actively sought to persuade the emperor to dispatch an invasionary force to assist dissenting elements in England.[73] However, the course of events in 1533 signalled the effective collapse of his cause. The act 'in restraint of appeals' asserted an unambiguous principle of royal ecclesiastical supremacy and at the same time gave the principle practical effect by rescinding judicial appeals in marriage cases to Rome. A cowed clergy under the king's new archbishop duly conceded the divorce. And Anne Boleyn was crowned queen on 1 June. The personal battle of wills and wits between Henry VIII and John Fisher remained to be resolved. In the spring of 1534 the king set out to reduce the recalcitrant bishop to submission to the new dispensation on oath. And the bishop set out to maintain his conscience intact. The course of that unequal struggle has been chronicled by biographers of both Fisher and Thomas More many times: the ingenious legal defence, entered before the royal commissioners at Lambeth in April 1534, and maintained through the deprivations and harassments of the fourteen long months of imprisonment, culminating in the denouement of the show trial and execution on Tower Hill on 22 June 1535.[74] That story need not be repeated here. Suffice it to say that the barbarous act of executing 'the saintliest bishop in christendom', already at death's door in any case, provided John Fisher with the opportunity of finally vindicating his conscience, and contributed in no small way to settling the reputation of Henry VIII as the most contemptible human specimen ever to sit upon the throne of England.

Consideration of the historical significance of Fisher's death returns the discussion to the point at which it began, with the historiographical tradition in which he is dismissed as the upholder of outmoded values against the onward march of progress.[75] That view may seem less inherently plausible in the light of the evidence of his career presented here. Addressing the substantive issue, it becomes necessary to draw attention, yet again, to the failure of this Whiggish view to comprehend the complexity of the historical reality. The question of the cause for which Fisher died comes to hinge on his refusal of the oaths to the succession and the royal ecclesiastical supremacy as prescribed by parliamentary statute. The first point to be made in this connection is that, contrary to a highly influential interpretation for long current, John Fisher did not die a victim to the onward march of a parliament which had discovered, through the enactment of the Reformation, the omnicompetence and sovereignty of statute. The issue was not the sovereignty claimed by parliament. It was rather the sovereignty claimed by the imperial monarch. The difference is crucial. Fisher expressed his willingness to swear loyalty to the succession as decreed by statute. However, that is not what the oath required him to do. It required him to swear to the validity of the marriage of Henry VIII and Anne Boleyn, hence to the succession as decreed by legitimate inheritance which statute simply endorsed.[76] Fisher's stance, therefore, was based on acceptance of the basic tenet of parliamentary sovereignty, namely that the ruler's mandate derives from the community mediated through their representatives in parliament. But that is precisely what the doctrine of imperial sovereignty rejected, holding, as the Act of Succession succinctly expressed it, that the ruler's mandate derives immediately from God and is transferred by inheritance: the monarch rules by an absolute divine right, not by the will of the community.[77] Fisher, therefore, was a victim not to the onward march of parliament, but to the onward march of imperial monarchy. Nor did he die a victim to the onward march of the nation; its sovereignty, now, for the first time, allegedly being asserted by means of the royal ecclesiastical supremacy against the universal jurisdiction claimed by the medieval papacy. Fisher's appeal to conscience is at the heart of the matter here.[78] In refusing the oaths to the succession and the supremacy he resolutely declined to express a view on the conflicting jurisdictional claims of the pope and the English monarch. As he explained, that was not the issue. The issue was rather the monarch's attempt to settle the dispute in his own favour by commanding adherence on oath to his ideology. The issue, therefore, concerned not the respective claims of the sovereign state and the universal Church but the respective claims of the sovereign state and the private individual. Specifically, the question was whether the jurisdiction of the state can so far constrain the liberty of the individual as to regulate the domain of conscience. That is precisely what the Henrician regime sought to do by using public law to extract submission on oath to its ideology. Whatever the other issues involved, the death of John Fisher was, in the first instance, a testimony to the liberty of conscience. That is the source of its perennial significance. As to those other issues, it may suffice to observe that the royal ecclesiastical supremacy, as an adjunct to imperial monarchy, did not prove a happy or an enduring constitutional experiment. By the reign of Elizabeth devout Anglicans of all shades of opinion had begun to discover in it a yoke as insupportable, to say no more, as the Roman one. It has long since been dismantled in practice.[79]

Fisher's response to the crisis that engulfed him between 1527 and 1534 brought into sharp relief two qualities that characterised his career as a whole and that between them provide a key to his historical significance. One was his capacity for leadership. Detailed study of his personal campaign against the succession and the supremacy brings once more into view those qualities that made him so formidable a chancellor of Cambridge: clarity and confidence of vision, tenacity of purpose, resourcefulness and decisiveness in action.[80] Promoters of the ecclesiastical revolution did not possess a monopoly of the brightest and best talents in early Tudor England. Conversely, opposition to it must not be presumed to indicate a limited intellectual or psychological responsiveness to the forces of modernity. The second quality is Fisher's highly attuned religious sensibility. In seeking to characterise its manifestations in the course of these final critical years, the notion of prophetic witness comes readily to mind. The outspoken condemnation of wickedness in the seat of power, the outraged defence of the sacred against secular profanity, the uncompromising testimony to divine truth, all of this is in the authentic mode of biblical prophecy. In that light it can be seen that the prophetic mode most aptly characterises the entire corpus of Fisher's surviving sermons: classically, for instance, as early as 1509, in the heavy moral censure of the funeral oration on Henry VII; but quite as emphatically in the urgent call to repentance that rings through the *œuvre*. Here surely resides the inner significance of Fisher's devotion to St John the Baptist, in whom the entire biblical tradition was seen to culminate, and the clue to Fisher's own religious self-identity.

By representing the crisis of 1527–34 as a conflict between modernising reformers and clerical conservatives, with Fisher prominently to the fore, historians of a Whiggish disposition have misconceived the issues that were involved and the mentality that Fisher and those of his kind brought to bear upon them. He, as much as his opponents, was a progressive and a reformer. His question was about the content of the reformation programme, not about the ideal as such. As much as any of his opponents in 1527–34, Fisher deserves the attention of historians as a significant figure in the history of English religious, intellectual and cultural development. His place in that history is at the centre, not on the margins. And he has the added claim to historical attention that future generations, as much as his own, ignore the witness of the prophet at their peril.

Notes

1 The treatment afforded Fisher by John Bass Mullinger in the 1880s provides a good example of the Whiggish approach. Despite a basic sympathy, Mullinger regarded Fisher as fatally flawed by a conservative medieval outlook: see his entry on Fisher in the *DNB* and Mullinger, *History of the University of Cambridge* (London, 1888), pp. 67–72. Here Mullinger comments (p. 71), apropos of Fisher's statutes for St John's, 'His [Fisher's] life presents us with more than one significant proof of how little mere moral rectitude of purpose avails to preserve men from pitiable superstition and fatal mistakes. As his faith in the past amounted to a foolish credulity, so his distrust of the future became an unreasoning dread.' As illustrations of the conventional historiographical treatment of Fisher in which he is presented as a conservative churchman of marginal significance, see Kenneth Pickthorn, *Early Tudor Government* (Cambridge, 1934), especially pp. 134–5, and J. D. Mackie, *The Earlier Tudors* (Oxford, 1952), especially pp. 362–3. In more recent times the tradition is well represented in the highly influential A. G. Dickens, *The English Reformation* (London, 1964), especially pp. 146–7. The image of Fisher was fixed along these lines for students of early English literature in the classic C. S. Lewis, *English Literature in the Sixteenth Century, Excluding Drama* (Oxford, 1954), especially pp. 161–4, on which see Duffy, 'The spirituality of John Fisher', below, pp. 205–7.
2 In Van Ortroy's edition of *Life* the account of these eight years occupies over 200 of the total 313 pages.
3 In the first modern biography, T. E. Bridgett, *Life of Blessed John Fisher, Bishop of Rochester* (London, 1888), the author disposes of Fisher's career as far as the divorce by chapter 7 (p. 141), with another fourteen chapters (and 349 pages) still to go. In the most recent scholarly biography, E. E. Reynolds, *St John Fisher* (2nd edn, Wheathampstead, 1972) the divorce and its aftermath occupy 55 per cent of the text. An exception, somewhat in the nature of the case, is the intellectual biography of Edward Surtz, *The Works and Days of John Fisher* (Cambridge, Mass., 1967). Surtz allows the divorce and the English Reformation only 50 of the 400 pages of text.
4 For a brief introduction to the plethora of early biographies, plays and editions of More's works, see R. W. Chambers, *Thomas More* (London, 1935), pp. 15–47.

The greatest single testimony to the continuing More industry is the modern critical edition of his writings, *The Yale Edition of the Complete Works of St Thomas More* (Yale University Press, New Haven and London, 1961–). Another sign of vigorous life is the recent surge of articles, monographs and biographies in a revisionist vein, see my 'The Controversial Sir Thomas More', *Journal of Ecclesiastical History*, 36 (1985), 535–69. A revealing comparison of the relative interest in More and Fisher in Roman Catholic circles is provided by the space devoted to them in the major Roman Catholic general work of reference in English, *The New Catholic Encyclopaedia* (1966), where More is given 11 columns and Fisher 2½. In the earlier edition (1909), More received 7 2/3 cols. and Fisher 3 cols. In the *Encyclopaedia Britannica*, More receives 4½ cols. to Fisher's 1¼ cols. The entries in the *DNB* extend to 30 cols. for More and 11 cols. for Fisher. It is also instructive to note a similar disproportion in the column inches devoted to the two in the great contemporary antiquarian compilations, Edward Hall's *The Triumphant Raigne of Kyng Henry the VIII* (1548), John Foxe's *Acts and Monuments* (1563), and Raphael Holinshed's *Chronicles* (1577).

5 A biography of Fisher was compiled in the reign of Elizabeth. However a printed version did not appear until 1655, Thomas Bailey, *The Life and Death . . . of John Fisher* (London, 1655); that edition was highly unsatisfactory because of editorial excisions and interpolations. A satisfactory text was not published until the critical edition of Francis Van Ortroy, *Analecta Bollandiana*, X (1891), 121–365; XII (1893), 97–283. Fisher's Latin writings, with the addition of his English sermons in Latin translation, appeared in an edition printed at Würzburg in 1597. The edition was not reprinted and Fisher's writings do not have a modern critical edition. Some of the English works were edited by John E. B. Mayor (ed.), *The English Works of John Fisher* (London, 1876). The correspondence of Fisher and Erasmus with English translations was produced by Jean Rouschausse (ed.), *Erasmus and Fisher: Their Correspondence* (Paris, 1968). Modern editions or translations of some of Fisher's devotional and polemical writings have been produced, but none of the major polemical works has been made available. The canonisation in 1935 saw a spate of biographical studies, the most authoritative of which is Richard L. Smith, *John Fisher and Thomas More* (London, 1935). Since then three biographies have appeared: R. L. Smith, *St John Fisher* (London, 1935); E. E. Reynolds, *St John Fisher*, 2nd edn (Wheathampstead, 1972); Michael Macklem, *God Have Mercy. The Life of John Fisher of Rochester* (Ottawa, 1967). A new departure in Fisher scholarship is represented by the intellectual biographies of Edward Surtz, *The Works and Days of John Fisher* (Cambridge, Mass., 1967), and Jean Rouschausse, *John Fisher, Vie et œuvre* (Angers and Nieuwkoop, 1972). A succinct summary of the bibliographical details is contained in Rouschausse, *Correspondence*, pp. 25–38.

6 In addition to the works of Surtz and Rouschausse cited above n. 5, Fisher's contribution to the debate over King Henry VIII's divorce suit has been studied by Virginia Murphy (see below, note 48). A study of Fisher's polemical writings, excluding writings on the divorce, is the subject of a recently completed (1988) Ph.D. project by Richard Rex, Trinity College, Cambridge. This essay is especially indebted to Rex's research, with which he has generously kept me in touch, and also, as will be clear, to the contributions to the present collection.

7 A. H. Lloyd, *Early History of Christ's College* (Cambridge, 1934), p. 391. Cf.

H. M. Langton, 'John Fisher', 1469–1535: A Papal Dispensation', *The Eagle*, 65 (1972–3), 80–3.

8 On Robert Fisher see Reynolds, *Fisher, passim*. The two works addressed to Elizabeth are *A Spirituall Consolation* and *The Wayes to Perfect Religion*, both published in *EW*, pp. 349–63, 364–87.

9 *Life*, XII, 267. The source is the 'Rastell Fragments', notes on Fisher compiled by William Rastell, biographer and son-in-law of Sir Thomas More.

10 Underwood, below, pp. 27–8.

11 Underwood, below, p. 26.

12 The allusion to Melton occurs in the preface to Book V of *De Veritate Corporis et Sanguinis Christi*. The reception of humanism at Cambridge is dealt with in Richard Rex's dissertation. Also, see Underwood, below, p. 26, and Rex, below, pp. 124–5.

13 The details of Fisher's Cambridge career are succinctly presented in Rouschausse, *Correspondence*, pp. 16–19. However, for scepticism regarding Fisher's supposed election as master of Michaelhouse, see Brooke, below, p. 50.

14 On the circumstances of Fisher's elevation, see Thompson, below, pp. 68–9. Cf. Brooke, below, p. 52 and note 13.

15 Thompson, below, p. 70, points out that eight of the fourteen bishops elevated to Rochester in the century preceding Fisher's arrival were subsequently promoted elsewhere, and six of the eight were promoted for a second time.

16 For Carlo Borromeo's regard for Fisher, see Scott, 'The Portraits of Bishop Fisher', *The Eagle*, 16 (1889–90), 326.

17 Thompson, below, pp. 70–1. Also Appendix 2.

18 Brooke, below, pp. 49, 54–1.

19 On conceptions of the episcopal office in the late-medieval church, see Francis Oakley, *The Western Church in the Later Middle Ages* (Ithaca and London, 1979), pp. 25–81, 157–77; Steven Ozment, *The Age of Reform, 1250–1550* (New Haven and London, 1980), pp. 135–81. For a discussion of the aversion of bishops and secular clergy generally towards preaching on the eve of the Reformation, see G. R. Elton, *Policy and Police* (Cambridge, 1972), pp. 232–7.

20 Most of the surviving sermons are published in *EW*, pp. 1–348. Two additions to the corpus are in Marie Denise Sullivan (ed.), '*Two Fruytfull Sermons* of St John Fisher', Ph.D. thesis, Notre Dame, Ind., 1961. The standard commentary is in J. W. Blench, *Preaching in England in the Late Fifteenth and Early Sixteenth Centuries* (Oxford, 1964), pp. 11–57, 129–36, 228–9, and *passim*. See further, Surtz, *Fisher*, pp. 255–73. For a discussion of Fisher's sermons in terms of style and content, see Duffy, below, pp. 205–25.

21 See the comments of Blench, *Preaching in England*, pp. 228–63; the transcendental quality of Fisher's sermons is emphasised by the almost total absence of concern with issues of social justice, concerning which a strong tradition existed in medieval pulpit oratory, G. R. Owst, *Literature and Pulpit in Medieval England* (rev. edn Oxford, 1961), pp. 548–93.

22 The most graphic expression of Fisher's alarming soteriological consciousness is the nightmarish scene that he conjures up to introduce his commentary on Psalm 51 ('Miserere Mei Deus'). Man hangs suspended in a deep pit while savage animals prowl at the bottom. His fate depends on the fragile bucket in which he

hangs (i.e. his body), on the thin cord which holds the bucket (his life) and on the person holding the cord at the mouth of the pit, i.e. God, whom man has grievously offended, *EW*, p. 90.

23 This theme finds graphic expression in Fisher's second sermon on Psalm 51, which is devoted to a consideration of ecclesiastical reform, *EW*, pp. 113–37; the *Life* contains a lengthy report of an address on the theme of ecclesiastical reform allegedly delivered at the synod convened by Wolsey as *legatus a latere* in the Lent of 1519. The critique of clerical abuses there presented corresponds generally with that contained in the sermon, *Life*, X, 255–9.

24 On the aspiration towards religious reform and renewal in its various manifestations, see Oakley, *Western Church*, pp. 219–60; H. A. Oberman, *Masters of the Reformation*, trans. Dennis Martin (Cambridge, 1981), pp. 45–112; Ozment, *Reform*, pp. 132–81, 290–317. Cf. W. D. J. Cargill Thompson, 'Seeing the Reformation in Medieval Perspective', *Journal of Ecclesiastical History*, 25 (1974), 297–308.

25 Brooke, below, pp. 52–8.

26 Ibid., pp. 53–4.

27 Underwood, below, pp. 35–6.

28 Brooke, below, pp. 52–4.

29 Underwood, below, pp. 36–7.

30 Donald J. Wilcox, *In Search of God and Self* (Boston, 1975), pp. 57–142; Quentin Skinner, *The Foundations of Modern Political Thought* (Cambridge, 1978), I, 241–3.

31 Underwood, below, p. 29–33.

32 On the significance of the development of the collegiate system, see James McConica (ed.), *The Collegiate University* (*The History of the University of Oxford*, III, Oxford, 1986), pp. 1–68.

33 On Erasmus's Cambridge sojourn see D. F. S. Thomson and H. C. Porter (eds.), *Erasmus and Cambridge* (Toronto, 1971 edn). Cf. Porter, below, pp. 83–4.

34 For a summary of Erasmus's comments on the achievement of Fisher at Cambridge, see Surtz, *Fisher*, pp. 190–2; for the exactly contemporary disturbances at Oxford, see Daniel Kinney (ed.), *In Defense of Humanism* (Yale Edition of the Complete Works of St Thomas More, XV, New Haven and London, 1986), especially pp. xxviii–xxxi, 129–50, also McConica, *The Collegiate University*, pp. 66–8. For the later disturbances at Cambridge, see J. A. Muller, *Stephen Gardiner and the Tudor Reaction* (Cambridge, 1926), pp. 121–4; cf. Peter Stein, 'Sir Thomas Smith: Renaissance Civilian', *Acta Juridica* (1978), pp. 79–89 at pp. 79–81.

35 The combination of piety and practicality may well explain the Lady Margaret Beaufort's admiration for Fisher. Her own career exhibits the same combination: Malcolm G. Underwood, 'Politics and Piety in the Household of Lady Margaret Beaufort', *Journal of Ecclesiastical History*, 38 (1987), 39–52. Another notable contemporary in whom the same combination is found is Margaret, Lady Hungerford: see M. A. Hicks, 'The Piety of Lady Hungerford', ibid., pp. 19–38. It is illuminating to consider such examples beside that of Henry VI, whose life notoriously and tragically exhibits the piety without the practicality: Christine Carpenter, 'Fifteenth Century Biographies', *Historical Journal*, 25 (1982), 729–34.

36 For a vigorous critique of this view of Fisher see Duffy, below, pp. 205–6.

37 All of this is well documented in the correspondence of Erasmus. See *The*

Correspondence of Erasmus (The Collected Works of Erasmus, Toronto, Buffalo and London, 1974–), ed. and trans. R. A. B. Mynors and D. F. S. Thomson, nos. 300 (Erasmus to Reuchlin, Aug. 1514), 324 (Erasmus to Reuchlin, 1 Mar. 1515), 432 (Fisher to Erasmus, 30 June 1516), 452 (Erasmus to Andreas Ammonio, 17 Aug. 1516), 456 (Erasmus to Henry Bullock, [22?] Aug. 1516), 456 (More to Erasmus, 31 Oct. 1516), 520 (William Latimer to Erasmus, 30 Jan. 1517), 562 (Reuchlin to Erasmus, 27 Mar. 1517), 948 (Erasmus to Petrus Mosellanus, 22 April 1519), 965 (Erasmus to William Blount, 15 May 1519).

38 Duffy, below, pp. 215–16, 223–6, explores the difference in religious ideology between Fisher and Erasmus. For a rather more sympathetic account of Erasmus's *philosophia Christi*, see my 'The Christian Humanism of Erasmus', *The Journal of Theological Studies*, n.s., 33 (1982), 411–47; Porter, below, pp. 92–6, attempts to develop the suggestion of Allen of a growing rift between Fisher and Erasmus in the 1520s, Erasmus's sympathy for the Reformation having exacerbated personal tensions. It seems fair to point out in this regard, first that Erasmus's *bête noire* increasingly in the 1520s was Luther, and secondly that the evidence indicates that the friendly contact between Erasmus and Fisher continued – culminating in Erasmus's *piam in memoriam* reference in the *De Ratione Concionandi* of 1535.

39 On Erasmus's lack of enthusiasm for Hebrew and Cabbalistic lore, see Porter, below, pp. 88–9. Fisher's celebration of Reuchlin as the successor of Pico is in *The Correspondence of Erasmus*, ed. and trans. Mynors and Thomson, no. 324 (Erasmus to Reuchlin, 1 Mar. 1515). Other references to Fisher's admiration for Reuchlin and Hebraic lore are found in ibid., nos. 432 (Fisher to Erasmus, 30 June 1516), 457 (Erasmus to Reuchlin, 27 Aug. 1516), 471 (Erasmus to Reuchlin, 29 Sept. 1516), 562 (Reuchlin to Erasmus, 27 Mar. 1517).

40 On Pico's quest for a synthesis between philosophy and rhetoric, see the famous debate between Pico and Ermolao Barbaro in which Pico defends scholasticism and Barbaro defends rhetoric, published with translation and commentary in Quirinus Breen, 'Mirandola on Philosophy and Rhetoric', *Journal of the History of Ideas*, 13 (1952), 384–426. The point of the debate is sometimes missed, as it is rather by Breen. It hinges on the (typically Renaissance) paradox, deliberately set up, of a brilliant rhetorical defence of scholastic philosophy on Pico's part matched by a brilliant dialectical defence of humanist rhetoric on the part of Barbaro. The laugh is on those who rely excessively (i.e. exclusively) on the one or the other. On Pico, Reuchlin and Christian Cabala, see Frances A. Yates, *The Occult Philosophy in the Elizabethan Age* (London, 1979), pp. 17–28.

41 Fisher's defence of Savonarola is in the *Assertionis Lutheranae Confutatio*, art. 33, cols. 637–8. The most recent account in English of Savonarola's religious ideology is Donald Weinstein, *Savonarola and Florence* (Princeton, 1970). The question of Fisher's relationship with Savonarola and with the Cabbalistic tradition is more fully explored in Richard Rex's dissertation (see above, note 6).

42 E.g. *The Correspondence of Erasmus*, ed. and trans. Mynors and Thomson, nos. 252 (Erasmus to Antoon Van Bergen, 6 Dec. 1512), 254 (Erasmus to Thomas Halsey, 8 Feb. 1512), 300 (Erasmus to Reuchlin, August 1514), 324 (Erasmus to Reuchlin, 1 Mar. 1515), 333 (Erasmus to Raffaele Riario, 1515), 334 (Erasmus to Grimani, 1515), 456 (Erasmus to Henry Bullock, [22?] Aug. 1516), 457 (Erasmus to

Reuchlin, 27 Aug. 1516), 948 (Erasmus to Petrus Mosellanus, 22 April 1519), 965 (Erasmus to William Blount, 15 May 1519). The epithets saintly and learned may seem a conventional form. However, Erasmus does not in fact apply the combination to any other English ecclesiastic, with the significant exception of Colet. Even his great patron, Archbishop Warham, is not praised in those terms.

43 For Fisher's account of the circumstances in which he became embroiled in the debate – which there is no reason to doubt – see *De Unica Magdalena*, in *Opera*, cols. 1395–6, and *Confutatio Secundae Disceptationis* (Paris, 1519), fo. ii. See also Rex, below, pp. 109–10.

44 On the course of the controversy, see Anselm Hufstader, 'Lefèvre d'Étaples and the Magdalen', *Studies in the Renaissance*, 16 (1969), 31–60.

45 *Comentarios a la secunda secundae de Santo Tomás*, ed. Vicente Beltrán de Heredia (Salamanca, 1932–5), I. 76 ('. . . multi insurgent haereses, et quasi nullus episcopus hactenus inventus est qui eis obviam eat. Solus unus episcopus est modo in Ecclesia, puta Roffensis, vir magnae doctrinae, qui scribat contra luteranos'). Quoted in Surtz, *Fisher*, p. 17 and n. 101.

46 Rex, below, pp. 110–12.

47 The sermon against Luther is in *EW*, pp. 311–48. The sermon against Barnes is included in the 1935 edn of *EW*. On the king's instruction to Wolsey to have Fisher preach at the abjuration of Barnes, see *LP*, IV, no. 995.

48 The history of the divorce debate has been unravelled in Virginia Murphy's unpublished Cambridge Ph.D. Dissertation, 'The Debate over Henry VIII's First Divorce: An Analysis of the Contemporary Treatises' (1984). What follows is based on Dr Murphy's research.

49 Published *apud* Michel de Eguia, Alcalá de Henares, August 1530, and was republished the same year.

50 The achievement is that of Virginia Murphy, above note 48.

51 See below, pp. 14–16.

52 I owe the information concerning the manuscript commentaries to Richard Rex, who studied them in connection with his Ph.D. dissertation.

53 See Appendix 2.

54 The early *Life* says that Fisher normally celebrated daily mass. He was also bound to recite the Divine Office daily. This involved mainly the recitation of thirty psalms, interspersed throughout the day, and the nine rather short *lectiones* which formed part of matins. According to the early *Life* Fisher tried to articulate every word of the breviary, which made it a very time-consuming exercise, scarcely less than three hours in all. Richard Rex has drawn to my attention a papal dispensation from part of the breviary granted to Fisher in 1534 to enable him to devote more time to polemical writing. The dispensation arrived too late to be of use, but it indicates something of the personal cost at which Fisher's literary output was produced: *Life*, X, 219–20.

55 Surtz and Rouschausse, above, note 5, surveyed the field. Gogan, below, pp. 131–54, represents the kind of specialist investigation that is required. The task of systematically analysing the entire corpus has been undertaken by Richard Rex.

56 See Anthony Levi, 'Humanist Reform in Sixteenth-Century France', *Heythrop Journal*, 6 (1965), 447–64. Cf. Heather Vose, 'A Sixteenth-century Assessment of the Gallican Church in the Years 1521–4 by Bishop Guillaume Briconnet of

Meaux', *Journal of Ecclesiastical History* (forthcoming). It is evident that a fundamental antipathy existed between Luther and the circle of Lefèvre in the matter of anthropology, crucial both to the humanist ideology and Luther's theology, Eugene F. Rice, Jr, 'The Humanist Idea of Christian Antiquity: Lefèvre d'Étaples and his Circle', in Werner L. Gundersheimer (ed.), *French Humanism, 1470–1600*, pp. 163–80. This was precisely the issue for Erasmus also: thus his choice of free will as the ground for his debate with Luther. His initial diatribe, *De Libero Arbitrio* (1524), and Luther's riposte, *De Servo Arbitrio* (1525), was followed by two further contributions by Erasmus: *Hyperaspistes* I (1526) and *Hyperaspistes* II (1527). The bulk and vigour of Erasmus's two rejoinders indicate the importance of the issue for him.

57 J. J. Scarisbrick, *Henry VIII* (London, 1968), pp. 518–19.
58 Oscar Cullmann, *Peter: Disciple–Apostle–Martyr*, trans. Floyd V. Filson (London, 1953), pp. 70–152. Cf. Henry Chadwick, *History and Thought of the Early Church* (London, 1982), chs. 2 and 3.
59 Martin Noth, *Leviticus: A Commentary*, rev. trans. (London, 1982), pp. 132–6.
60 Anselm Hufstader, 'Lefèvre d'Etaples and the Magdalen', in *Studies in the Renaissance*, 16 (1969), 31–60. Also Levi, above note 56.
61 For Fisher's account, see above note 43. See also Rex, below, pp. 119–20.
62 I am grateful to Richard Rex for information about the details of Lefèvre's exegesis.
63 Above, note 43.
64 On Fisher's polemical style, see Rex, below, pp. 124–5.
65 *Life*, X, 229–35.
66 Gogan, below, pp. 131–54, and Rex, below, pp. 118–19.
67 This is Rex's analysis and, despite Gogan's modifications, Fisher's fundamentally papalist ecclesiology can hardly be denied. On the papal monarchical tradition of late medieval ecclesiology, see Francis Oakley, *The Western Church in the Later Middle Ages* (Ithaca and London, 1979), pp. 157–78; Steven Ozment, *The Age of Reform, 1250–1550* (New Haven and London, 1980), pp. 135–82.
68 Gogan, below, pp. 134–5; Rex, below, pp. 118–19.
69 Rex, below, pp. 124–6.
70 The incident is recorded in *Life*, X, 296–8. It does not have other documentary support. However, the fact of confrontation between Fisher and the regime is well documented as early as the summer of 1527. By June 1527 Wolsey had made three overtures to Fisher on the king's behalf and been rebuffed each time with increasing firmness. Reporting to Henry VIII on his third interview with Fisher at Rochester, Wolsey anticipates the king's displeasure, 'verayley it may be thought, that having som conjecture or smelling of the matier, his said opinion procedith rather of affection, than of sinceritie of his learning, or scripture', *State Papers, Henry VIII*, I, 189 (*LP*, IV, 3231); Murphy shows that Fisher's written opinion, delivered to Wolsey in June, prompted a quest for a scholarly refutation and this precipitated the opening phase of the divorce debate as well as largely establishing its agenda: Murphy, 'The Debate over Henry VIII's First Divorce', above, note 48.
71 Ibid.
72 For a revisionist interpretation of the episode, see J. A. Guy, 'Henry VIII and the

praemunire Manoeuvres, 1530–1', *English Historical Review*, (1982), 481–503. A convincing rejoinder is in G. W. Bernard, 'The Pardon of the Clergy Reconsidered', *Journal of Ecclesiastical History*, 37 (1986), 258–82; a further exchange is at ibid., pp. 283–7.

73 Scarisbrick, below, p. 157.

74 E. E. Reynolds, *St John Fisher* (rev. edn, Wheathampstead, 1972), pp. 222–97.

75 This is a necessary corollary of the Elton interpretation of the Tudor constitutional revolution, on which see G. R. Elton, *Reform and Reformation* (London, 1977), pp. 191–5.

76 Fisher's position is set out in a letter from the Tower in December 1534, in which he explains his response to the Commissioners for the oath in the previous April. He was ready to swear to the succession: 'I dowted not but the prynce of eny realme with th' assent of his nobles and commons, myght appoynte for his succession royal, such an order as was seen unto his wysdom most accordyng.' However he was not prepared to swear the oath of succession as prescribed because it offended his conscience. The letter is reproduced in Lewis, *Fisher*, II, 330–2. The paraphrase in *LP*, VII, no. 1563 misrepresents Fisher to say that he had actually sworn to the substance of the act but not to the preamble. Characteristically, Cranmer pleaded that Fisher's offer be accepted, but significantly the king required recognition of the validity of his marriage: Reynold's, *Fisher*, pp. 227–30.

77 The Act of Succession is in *Statutes of the Realm*, III, 471–4, ch. 22. See especially the Preamble: '. . . the bishop of Rome and see Apostolic, contrary to the great and inviolable grants of jurisdictions given by God immediately to emperors, kings and princes in succession to their heirs, hath presumed in times past to invest who should please them to inherit in other men's kingdoms and dominions . . .'

78 *LP*, VII, nos. 136, 1563. He refused the oath as offensive to his conscience and he declined to explain why as that would put him in danger of the law.

79 The novelty of the ecclesiastical supremacy claimed by Henry VIII, against the background of Christian antiquity, the recoil from it within the English Church, and its withering away are the subject of Chadwick's thoughtful and thought-provoking study below. On the emerging dissatisfaction within the Elizabethan and Early Stuart Church, see also Patrick Collinson, *The Religion of Protestants* (Oxford, 1982), pp. 1–39, and W. D. J. Cargill Thompson, 'Sir Francis Knollys's Campaign against the *Jure Divino* Theory of Episcopacy', in Cargill Thompson, *Studies in the Reformation* (London, 1980), pp. 94–135.

80 Above, pp. 5–8.

John Fisher and the promotion of learning

MALCOLM UNDERWOOD

John Fisher was a pastor and theologian to whom his University remained central throughout life: it provided indeed the chief arena of his influence and patronage. His standing within it as promoter, in company with the Lady Margaret Beaufort, of two new colleges, and as chancellor for life, was in marked contrast to his modest preferment in Church and state. His political and diplomatic service was limited to rare appearances at the king's council, the reception of ambassadors, and a journey to the Field of the Cloth of Gold in the suite of the queen.[1] Richard Fox, who remained his constant friend and had first commended him to the king, was much more at the centre of affairs as councillor and keeper of the privy seal. Only after a long and busy civil career did Fox devote his main energies to Winchester and Oxford, where his new foundation of Corpus Christi College influenced Fisher's own plans for St John's College, Cambridge. Unlike Fox, Fisher was never bishop of a large and prestigious see, but held for life the poor see of Rochester, acquiring the reputation of a model bishop seldom away from his charge.[2] On the other hand he was the chief link between the household of the Lady Margaret Beaufort and Cambridge University; in this sphere his labours were momentous and were publicly recognised by the University in its grant of exequies to him in 1529.[3] He had directed the flow of the Lady Margaret's pious charity into the first successful endowed professorship, into the University preachership, and finally towards the foundations of Christ's and St John's. In the light of Fisher's fruitful partnership with the king's mother, his later breach with her grandson, Henry VIII, is a striking irony of history.

If Fisher's encouragement of learning at Cambridge relied mainly on the Lady Margaret's material resources, intellectually he owed a great deal to his master, William Melton of Michaelhouse, where Fisher became a fellow in 1491. Melton, like his pupil, came from Yorkshire, ending his career as chancellor of York. His formative influence is alluded to by Fisher in the preface to the fifth book of his *De Veritate Corporis*.[4] The context of the tribute paid there to Melton is important for understanding Fisher's attitude towards scholarship in general. Melton, he says, instilled in him as a young student the need to be attentive to every detail in Euclid: if he came to think the least figure or letter superfluous, he would not be able to grasp the mind of the master. Fisher goes on to apply this principle to the theological work he has in hand: if the disciple of Euclid needs to take such care, how much more the disciple of Christ when dealing with the precise words of the institution of a sacrament. Throughout his life this attention to detail characterised Fisher's scholarship and educational ideals. It shows itself in the ever more elaborate revisions of the statutes of St John's, and also in his determination that the traditional art of logic, sharpened in disputation, should be allied to new, more accurate, knowledge of classical and biblical languages. Like Fisher, Melton combined by the time of his death the old scholastic learning with an acquaintance with new authors and with the Church fathers. The list of books in his will in 1528 includes works of Aquinas, Scotus, John Andreas, Augustine, Jerome, Chrysostom, Valla, Erasmus, Pico della Mirandola, and a Greek New Testament. Melton also shared with his former pupil a concern for the reformation of the lives of the clergy, was a preacher of some note, and the author of tracts against Luther.[5]

Michaelhouse, the college of Melton and Fisher, was designed to train a small number of priest-fellows in theology and to maintain masses for its founder. These twin aims of providing a seminary and chantry were also to be expressed in the foundations of Christ's and St John's. The statutes of Michaelhouse, founded in 1327, placed no emphasis on the study of law or the service of secular society as well as the Church, as do for example those of Peterhouse and Gonville Hall. They laid stress rather on the plan of God for man's knowledge of the divine and on the importance of chantry duties, leaving it to the scholars to regulate precisely the balance between divine service and study. The importance of both elements was acknowledged about 1508 by the master, then John Fothede, Fisher's colleague in the service of the Lady Margaret and of the University. He wrote in alarmed tones to Fisher, as chancellor and visitor of the College, about the behaviour of a fellow of Michaelhouse who wished to continue to hold his fellowship with another post, although his income was too large to allow him to do so under the statutes of the college. Fothede stressed that if such conduct became general the learning of the house would decay and no one would be available to celebrate the masses of the founder.[6]

Other of Fisher's friends at Michaelhouse later worked with him in University affairs and some found preferment with the Lady Margaret. Mentioned with him in a conveyance to Michaelhouse in 1498 were Nicholas Metcalfe, his future archdeacon and head of St John's, and Robert Bekynsall, whom Fisher named to succeed him as head of Queens' College.[7] While still at Michaelhouse, Bekynsall, as bachelor of divinity, had received an exhibition from the Lady Margaret's household, and soon after becoming president of Queens' he was dispensed from University residence for her service. In 1508–9 he was her almoner and after her death became almoner to the queen. Fisher himself had not resided at Queens' while he was president but its fellows held neither his non-residence nor his nomination of his successor against him.[8] On the contrary they praised Fisher's 'multiiuga eruditio', and accepted Bekynsall gladly as his candidate and the servant of the Lady Margaret, whose influence had secured Queens' land in Essex. The college was too well aware of the benefits of close contact with the royal family to have any scruples about free election or conditions of residence.[9]

It is difficult to say whether Fisher gained intellectually from his brief headship of Queens', but we may note that the college already had features which Fisher would develop more fully at St John's. Fellows of Queens' had obligations to preach outside the college under two fifteenth-century benefactions, and the chantry duties attached to a third, the Duke of Gloucester's foundation, required two priests of ability who would proceed as doctors and preach the word of God.[10] The college also funded regular lectures within its walls, a feature earlier displayed by God's House long before its refoundation by Lady Margaret as Christ's College.[11] When we come to consider Fisher's organisation of preaching and lecturing at St John's, and his debt to Richard Fox and Corpus Christi College, Oxford, it is well to keep in mind these Cambridge antecedents. Fisher must already have been acquainted, at Michaelhouse and Queens', with the preaching, lecturing and dedication to theological study which were to be united at St John's on a grander scale.

To Queens' Fisher added his prestige, that of the Lady Margaret and of Erasmus, but left it no benefaction. With Michaelhouse he had older and stronger links and his name is listed among its benefactors, although the scale of his gift is uncertain.[12] The college figured formally as a guarantor in the statutes of Christ's and St John's. At Christ's the master's bond of office was to be held jointly by the heads of King's College and Michaelhouse, and at St John's disputes between a fellow and the master were to be referred to the heads of King's, Christ's and Michaelhouse. When Fisher came to establish his own chantry at St John's, parties to the agreement included the head of his old college, and Michaelhouse was given a right of distraint on the estates of St John's should the terms of the agreement be breached.[13] Three other benefactors, also founders of fellowships and scholarships in the new college, made similar provisions, so that Michaelhouse would actually receive their benefactions should St John's fail in its obligations.[14]

Behind old college ties lay regional ones. Fisher and the three other benefactors to St John's all gave preference to men from Yorkshire in their foundations. In 1529 Richard Croke would accuse Fisher of showing partiality to the men of his own country in the government of St John's. This, as we shall see, was inaccurate, but it is true that as a Northerner Fisher was at home both at Michaelhouse and in the Lady Margaret's household, where many of his colleagues came from either side of the Pennines. In the two new colleges which he and the Lady Margaret inspired, half the original foundation-places were to be taken by men from nine Northern counties. While this no doubt reflected the great need of the North, as was stated in the college statutes, the numerous private benefactions which swelled the foundation-places at St John's also testified to the region's influence. Long afterwards, Roger Ascham was to admit that the college in its early days owed most of its prosperity to the generosity of Northern men.[15]

Christ's College, which was so well endowed by the Lady Margaret during her lifetime that it did not need private founders to help it out, was the final fruit of her personal co-operation with John Fisher, although her legacy helped him to establish the second new college after her death. Her statutes of 1506 appointed Fisher visitor of Christ's for life, and injunctions which he gave the college in 1510 show him to have been mindful of her wishes in matters of college record-keeping and dress.[16] Christ's itself credited him with responsibility for its regulations, but it is difficult to be precise about his influence.[17] He is the most likely source for stipulations about academic exercises and the organisation of lectures contained in the statutes, especially as a similar hierarchy of lectors and sub-lectors was afterwards adopted at St John's. Yet the most striking academic feature, a college lecture based on the classical poets and orators, was borrowed from God's House without alteration. Apart from this lecture and the obligation to teach grammar, also carried over from God's House, Christ's was a school of arts and theology, staffed, like Michaelhouse, with fellows bound to enter the priesthood within a year of admission to their fellowships.[18] Lady Margaret's statutes envisaged it primarily as a chantry for herself and her relatives. After the worship of God the fellows were to devote themselves to the pursuit of study.

Christ's was a more conservative foundation than St John's, for which Fisher was first to provide statutes ten years later. While he desired St John's also to train men in the service of God, he did not attempt to compel them to enter the priesthood within a year of admission as fellows, although men already priests were by preference to be recruited. Eventually, in 1530, the bishop was to allow fellows of St John's a full six years' active study and teaching in the faculty of arts before obliging them to seek ordination as priests.[19] Two features peculiar to Christ's give us a hint of the fuller treatment they were to receive at St John's. The union of preaching duties with fellowships later established in the larger college was heralded in an amendment to the regulations of the University preachership, founded in 1504, by which preachers were to be chosen by preference from among the fellows of Christ's.[20] The basic provisions at Christ's for college lectures as well as for attendance by fellows and scholars at the University's lecture schools were to be worked out at St John's in much greater detail.

While the foundation of Christ's was being settled and Fisher was president of Queens', King Henry VII and his mother made several visits to Cambridge. In June 1505 the Lady Margaret visited the University schools. In April 1506 the king stayed at Queens' while Fisher lodged at Michaelhouse, and both the king and the Lady Margaret were in Cambridge again in the summer, she for nine days during August.[21] The oration attributed to Fisher, made before Henry VII, his mother and the Prince of Wales, which took as its main theme royal encouragement of learning at Cambridge, probably took place either in the summer of 1506 or in 1507. In July of the latter year the Lady Margaret was again in the town, a present being sent to Christ's College for her, and a gift of Damascus water was presented by the University to the king and his mother.[22] Fisher presided at the creation of twelve doctors in the church of the greyfriars in the presence of all three members of the royal family.[23] Taking an active part in the ceremonial academic exercises with Fisher – 'acutissimo theologo' – were various other masters including Geoffrey Blyth, Bishop of Lichfield.[24]

These episodes give us a glimpse of Fisher, the scholar-bishop, performing the important function of bringing the University into close regular contact with the dynasty. His oration before the royal family is that not only of a scholar fêting his University but of a subject praising his prince in true Renaissance fashion. He symbolises in his own person, he claims, the king's patronage of learning, for he was promoted to a bishopric, although lacking experience at court and benefices, as a demonstration of Henry's regard for letters. These expressions of loyalty are consonant with the image of Fisher the conservative theologian, supporter of the clerical establishment of Henry VII, in which he and many of his colleagues had successful careers. There was as yet no agonising decision to be made between the political establishment and the Church's authority and doctrine: to the builder of Cambridge colleges the two orders were complementary. When he came to preach at the month's mind of the Lady Margaret he portrayed her not simply as an exemplar of piety, but as a royal and noble example to the people, describing how all the estates of the realm mourned her. There was nothing of the social rebel about him: from his perspective it would be Henry VIII by his actions who would threaten the stability of the kingdom.

In the light of this basic conservatism it might seem remarkable that Fisher should be open to intellectual change. For, as we know there was another side: the experienced scholar, versed in the schoolmen, who toyed with the new learning and once wrote disarmingly to his friend Erasmus to thank him for tuition in Greek.[25] In fact this other side was a consequence of the same ideal that informed his conservatism: he was concerned, as a matter of vital importance for the wellbeing of mankind, that all learning, old and new, should be placed at the service of the Church. The same concern issued in a genuine wish to persuade and convert those whom he saw as trapped by heresy. In a sermon at St Paul's in 1526 he called upon anyone distracted by the Lutheran heresy to come to him secretly and 'break his mynde at length' in a discussion which would remain confidential.[26] This did not prevent him at other times taking a harsher attitude for the sake of the Church, endorsing, for instance, the condemnation of Bilney. If we are to understand his programme for learning at Cambridge, and in particular at St John's, we have to take account of the balance of old and new, both in his own outlook and in that of men with whom he came into contact.

As we saw in his tribute to Melton, his master, and as is evident from the schemes for Christ's and St John's, Fisher viewed traditional scholastic training in the arts as indispensable to theological study. Nor was he alone in seeking to retain some of the benefits of scholasticism alongside the new learning. Richard Croke, a former member of King's College and a Greek scholar of international repute, addressed the University in 1519 as 'professor of Greek and Latin and the Good Arts', at Fisher's request. His lecture exhorts his hearers to the study of classical literature, and does indeed stress its superiority over the traditional diet of the trivium and quadrivium, but he wishes it to be harnessed to a theological training from which the schoolmen are not to be excluded. He protests his respect for Mayronius, John Canonicus and Aquinas (the systematic study of whom was new at the time), and embraces the subtlety of Duns Scotus.[27] He desires only that culture which imparts brilliance to the rest. Scholars should *add* to the study of these authors the cultivation of classical ones, and correct classical diction. As to disputations, Croke is not their foe, but fears the harmful effects that might follow from scholars growing old in them without branching out into other methods of study. One recalls that Fisher himself, according to Erasmus, began to learn Greek in a modest way in 1516–17, when he was in his late forties.[28] Croke's call for an alliance between the classical authors and the schoolmen was in fact answered in detail by Cardinal Wolsey. In his statutes for Cardinal College in 1525, Wolsey prescribed classical texts to give a linguistic and rhetorical grounding but insisted on the importance of the schoolmen and scholastic method in the study of theology and for the defence of the faith.[29]

Croke's problem with the schoolmen was clearly cultural and stylistic rather than one of content, with which he had little concern. The same aversion can be seen in Fisher's famous clause in the statutes of 1530 for St John's, allowing the lecture on Hebrew to be replaced with one on the works of Duns Scotus, *if his books should be turned into better Latin.* There were evident stresses in trying to graft on to a tightly organised programme of logical disputations a discursive literary method with emphasis on philology. The stresses are reflected in the St John's statutes of 1516–18, where Fisher's directions for the study of Greek and Hebrew strike one as perfunctory beside the detailed plan for disputations. Two statutes, probably written between 1524 and 1530, which were never included in any of his codes but which he must have pondered, make the difficulties even clearer.[30] The first of these statutes expresses concern that the cultivation of 'bone littere' in the college has led to the other arts being despised and to a decline in the skill of disputation. The second appoints two lecturers in the college instead of one, because of the great number of youths flocking to its doors. Both statutes prescribe scholastic texts to take students through disputations in logic and philosophy. According to the second, it is essential that those proceeding to the higher arts and theology should be experienced in scholastic lore when they make trial of their learning and skill in college or outside.[31]

Fisher was fonder of the schoolmen than was his friend Richard Fox, whose statutes for Corpus Christi College, Oxford, in 1517 stressed the superiority of the fathers of the Church over later commentators, excluding from study Hugh of Vienna and Nicholas of Lyra. Fox appointed lecturers in Latin (Humanitas) and in Greek whose lectures were to be public, achieving the widest dissemination possible within Oxford. The public lecturer in Greek was to act as an 'examiner', testing students on lectures on the classics heard within the college. When Fisher attached to his expanded code of statutes made for St John's in 1524 some statutes for his private foundation in the college, these contained detailed provision both for examiners and for lecturers in Greek and Hebrew. The examiners were by preference to be fellows of Fisher's own foundation and were to drill students in Latin, logic, mathematics and philosophy, which were the subjects of lectures in the University schools. They were also to give additional lectures in college if necessary.

If the details of the scheme for examiners at St John's owed something to the contemporary establishment of Rede's lectures on the same subjects in the University, both examinerships and lectureships had a precedent in Fox's code. Fisher certainly made use of it, for a copy is bound up with his statutes of 1524, and in his code of 1530 he adopted the titles and lay-out of many of the Corpus statutes, just as Wolsey had done earlier. What Fisher did not adopt, either from Fox or Wolsey, was the principle of public lectures open to outsiders. His students, like Fox's, had to attend some lectures outside the college,[32] but there was no intention to provide instruction within it to any but students of St John's. Through combined college and University teaching these were to be made a learned elite, equipped for evangelism.

It was a key principle of the college that the elite should be evangelical as well as academic. This was to be achieved through a union of the study of the bible and preaching, and for this combination too Fisher owed something to Richard Fox. In the statutes for St John's of 1516–18 a quarter of the fellows were given the duty of preaching to the people in English. Senior fellows who had been designated preachers were, if not suited to the task, to engage in disputations or to employ their pens in interpreting scripture.[33] Fisher, like Fox, directed that a reading should be given at meals in accordance with the usual monastic and collegiate custom. Fisher followed the statutes of Christ's in permitting reading from the fathers as well as from the bible, but Fox restricted it to the bible and made this the occasion for *exposition* of the text by his fellows. Fisher may have borrowed this idea, because in his second code of 1524 he laid the same duty of exposition on the fellows of the college who were preachers. The title of the relevant chapter in his final complete code of 1530 combines that of his original statute on preaching with that of Fox on the reading and exposition of the bible: 'De his qui concionibus ad plebem exercitabunt sese, et de lectura biblie et eius expositione'.[34]

In another respect Fisher excelled Fox's scheme: he made St John's a *collegium trilingue*, providing for the study of Hebrew as well as of classical Latin and Greek, and during the 1520s he appointed Robert Wakefield, an expert in Hebrew from Louvain, to teach in the college.[35] Both Wakefield and Croke, however, later became embarrassments to Fisher, as active polemicists for the cause of Henry VIII in the matter of the royal divorce. In 1530, when Wakefield was sent by the king to teach Hebrew in Oxford, Fisher's third code of statutes allowed St John's to change the Hebrew lecture for one on the works of Duns Scotus. This alteration can be seen as a measure of the bishop's conservatism, but it was also probably due to his disappointment with Wakefield. The famous clause itself is not as rigid as appears at first sight. We have already noted the concern expressed by Fisher in this statute that Scotus should be adopted only if his Latinity could be improved, and this was at the heart of the matter both for Croke and Fisher. The name of Scotus came to evoke real horror only after the royal injunctions to the University in 1535, when he was seen as the symbol of all that was bad in the schoolmen. The clause was permissive, rather than directive: 'If it seems to the master and seniors that the Hebrew lecture is of little profit to its hearers' − which might arise in a new discipline with few practitioners − 'I will allow it to be changed into something more advantageous ['conducibilioris'], for example on John Scotus, if he shall be cast into better Latin.'[36]

The code for St John's of 1530, despite this sign of Fisher's loss of confidence in the new, contained a Renaissance leaven. Besides the regulations for a lecturer in Greek and an examiner in classics, there were to be declamations, or set speeches, according to the style of Seneca or Quintilian on Saturdays in term and vacation, and a lecturer in perspective was included among those teaching mathematics.[37] The idea that young students, 'discipuli', should deliver declamations is a rhetorical feature not found in the statutes either of Corpus Christi, Oxford, or of Cardinal College, where the *Declamationes* of Quintilian are mentioned only as one of the texts to be used by the professor of humanity. At St John's it was also to be one of the duties of the examiner in classics to 'set a speech to be rendered in other words'.[38]

Nevertheless, the successive codes of statutes for St John's as a whole strike one as less adventurous than those of Fox and Wolsey. This feeling of caution is emphasised by the slow development of detailed provisions for Greek and Hebrew teaching between 1516 and 1530. As we shall see, it is explained in part by the history of Fisher's own foundation in the college, a foundation to which the lectureships were bound. Apart from that, however, we miss in Fisher's statutes the detailed lists of classical authors which we find in those of his friends, and there is less emphasis on the study of patristics than we might expect from so able an expositor.

The statutes of 1530 were the fullest expression of Fisher's intentions for the college, and they constitute the last authentic code of his which we possess. Yet copies of statutes were being produced regularly until 1534, and for that year we have two independent records of attempted revisions. The first is contained in two letters written by the college to unnamed magnates, probably Cranmer and Cromwell, asking for access to Fisher in the Tower of London and mentioning amendments to the statutes by Cranmer which need Fisher's ratification. There is no evidence that permission for this inter-view was ever granted. The second record comes from the earliest biography of Fisher, compiled in its final form about 1577. The *Life* speaks of the visit of two fellows of St John's to Fisher while he stayed for a few days at his house at Lambeth Marsh before removing to the Tower. The fellows wished him, while there was still time, to set his seal to statutes which he had drawn up long before but never confirmed. The bishop, careful as ever, refused to endorse the statutes without further perusal; but time, as the fellows feared, was not to be granted to him. The *Life* continues with a reference to a code of statutes imposed by Cranmer and Cromwell which then superseded all statutes granted by Fisher, and which they drew up under the authority of a commission from the king.[39]

One further manuscript, incomplete and disbound, may represent a stage beyond the code of 1530.[40] Unlike any other code, including the royal code of 1545, it is written in an italic hand. It contains all the references to Fisher which were suppressed in the royal code as part of the obliteration of the disgraced bishop's name. It bears Fisher's signature but no seal or notarial attestation, suggesting, as both the *Life* and the college's letters indicated, that there had been no formal ratification. The italic manuscript omits the points of radical change apparent in the royal code of 1545: the constitution of the college is the same as that laid down in 1530, and it lacks the emphasis placed in 1545 on New Testament study and on original texts of Plato and Aristotle rather than on the schoolmen. Yet in less controversial points the italic manuscript anticipates word for word the code of 1545 and departs from that of 1530. The italic version seems in fact to have provided the exemplar for the royal code, subject to alteration at crucial points. One passage in which the italic version anticipates the royal code is especially striking. Hitherto the statutes of 1545 have been thought to be the first to mention play-acting in the college. The statute appointing examiners directs that in the short vacations scholars shall spend at least five days before term begins in 'composing songs ['carmina'], epistles or declamations, reading Greek poets, orators or historians ['historiographi'], and acting dialogues, comedies or tragedies, according to the judgement of the lecturer in humanity and the other examiners'.[41] The italic manuscript contains exactly the same passage, immediately following an exhortation to pray for Fisher's soul, and the ordering of the folios makes it clear that this statute was part of the private statutes for his own foundation, kept as a separate unit as in the code of 1530.

The italic version differs from both the code of 1530 and that of 1545 in an aspect central to the studies of the college: while use of the schoolmen remains unchallenged, the texts authorised are more varied than those named in 1530. Instead of the twice-weekly disputations in philosophy based on John (Duns) Scotus, the italic text mentions a list of questions from scholastic disputants compiled by Fisher and his friends as the basis for the problems to be discussed.[42] Elsewhere in the text authors besides Scotus are actually named: Thomas (Aquinas), Alexander (of Hales), Bonaventure and Peter Lombard. The use of other approved scholastic authors is left to the discretion of the governing body.

Whether or not these are the statutes which the course of events prevented Fisher from ratifying, the design would have remained that of 1530: a college enlightened by aspects of the new learning, which would help to train the clergy and so renew the Church. Within this framework Fisher's contribution was twofold. Firstly he gave preaching a higher priority than before, creating a class of preacher-fellows and making that office the principal route into the college for senior members of the university.[43] Secondly, a traditional feature – his own chantry foundation – provided the endowment for his boldest innovation, the praelectorships in Greek and Hebrew. This signal marriage of ancient piety with the new learning was not destined to endure. To understand more fully the nature of Fisher's chantry, and its eclipse, we must now turn from the bishop's relations with St John's as framer of its statutes to his role as its benefactor and patron.

In contrast to Fisher's personal austerity, his chantry, built on the north of the college chapel between 1525 and 1533, was undoubtedly splendid. It was celebrated in a letter of thanks to him from the college. With its fine columns and pinnacles it was said to exceed in space and height the chantry of Dr Thompson, master of Christ's, which lay opposite.[44] The altar cloths of the chantry chapel, of blue, yellow, red and white satin, were decorated with dolphins and wheat-ears, the punning 'fish-ear' of Fisher's own name. The motif was repeated on the stall ends of the choir in the body of the college chapel, and over the entrance to the chantry was the text 'faciam vos fieri piscatores hominum'.

Among the payments for building work to masons, carpenters and labourers are some of an entirely different kind: the allowances and stipends for the fellows of Fisher's own foundation.[45]. His plans for such a foundation, in addition to the main foundation of the college based on the Lady Margaret's estate, were included in the first statutes of 1516–18, given by Fisher in the name of her executors. His efforts to found and endow St John's and his personal outlay of £500 towards it were mentioned. Four fellows and two scholars were to be supported by the college in return for his generosity. If priests, they were to say masses for the bishop, his family ('parentes'), friends and benefactors, for the Lady Margaret and for her son Henry VII. If not priests, they were to say daily the *de profundis*. The master and fellows bound themselves and their successors upon oath to maintain these arrangements. Five of the students were to come from Yorkshire, Fisher's home county, the sixth from the diocese of Rochester, or failing that from Richmond, Yorkshire, in honour of the Lady Margaret. In all other respects they were to be treated on the same terms as the rest of the college: there was no mention at this stage of Fisher having control over selection of candidates.[46]

St John's was at this time a modest college, uncertain of its endowments. Between 1511 and 1520 the executors of the Lady Margaret, principally Fisher and Henry Hornby, shifted from one expedient to another, to obtain funds. The profits of some of the Lady Margaret's lands, previously put in trust to fulfil the conditions of her will, were withdrawn for the benefit of her grandson and heir, Henry VIII, sooner than her executors had expected. In 1513 Fisher had given the college his £500 to buy land, from which a pension of £25 annually was to be paid to him; but this pension remained unpaid. Its purpose is nowhere specified, but it may have been to enable Fisher to support his fellows and scholars himself. As things turned out, he allowed the college to devote the money directly to its own use in its time of need, limited by the obligations to support students on his behalf. Between 1512 and 1516 Fisher had also begun to stock the college library, apparently from bonds due from Joye, Wynkyn de Worde and Pynson. By 1521 he had personally given over £100 more in jewels and plate, and sufficient money to buy lands worth £60 a year.[47]

These years were trying for Fisher, but perhaps also for royal officials dealing with the legacy of the Lady Margaret, much of which had been diverted to pious uses such as the college. Fisher's contacts with the king's servants were not always happy, partly because of changes of personnel: it was a new and more aggressive royal auditor who, in 1515, insisted on reclaiming the king's inheritance without further delay. Fisher also later recalled that unnamed servants of the Lady Margaret had claimed her goods as a result of a misunderstanding about their share of her bequests and had slandered him to the king, which had made Henry, in the bishop's vivid phrase, 'a werray hevy lorde agaynst me'.[48] It must also be remembered that Fisher had no great personal influence at court: he relied upon Fox to get a licence to help endow the college soon after the Lady Margaret's death.[49] Nevertheless, the king had been generous enough to grant in compensation for the loss of the Lady Margaret's rents both a wardship, which gave the college temporary relief, and the royal hospital of Ospringe in the diocese of Canterbury. According to his own account, Fisher spent many days on the road between Ospringe, London and Canterbury before the title to the hospital and its property was assured to the college. By 1521 things were looking better. The college was sure of Ospringe, and others besides Fisher, mostly Northerners, were giving benefactions with which lands could be bought.

Nicholas Metcalfe, Fisher's archdeacon, had succeeded to the mastership of St John's in 1518 and he and the bishop were active in seeking further endowments. Under legal advice Fisher accepted the necessity for the dissolution of small religious houses to increase the lands of the college. One such small house was Higham priory, a scandalous community in his own diocese of Rochester, which he had made only half-hearted attempts to reform. The proceedings for its dissolution were begun with the sanction of the king and Wolsey, and the nuns living there resigned in 1521.[50] The bishop fully acquiesced in this solution, his concern for St John's being paramount. But he was not a man to be active in the mercenary and tedious course of a forcible dissolution. The king admonished him for not getting on with the removal of the nuns, and Fisher's agents were concerned lest the business be undertaken by laymen and the bishop's jurisdiction suffer. Metcalfe's part in the affair was important, for he had been left to negotiate with Cardinal Wolsey face to face. The cardinal had offered the college the choice of one of two nunneries or a thousand marks. Metcalfe made some unrecorded objection to the terms, and was threatened with the king's displeasure. Fisher was consulted through an intermediary and replied that Metcalfe must stand firm for a better offer – Higham and something in addition. He added characteristically that if, as a result, the college got nothing the scholars would be forced to live the more hardily, and he would commit the matter to God.[51] Eventually, two houses, Higham and an equally decayed nunnery at Broomhall in Berkshire, were secured and the fellows under new college statutes of 1524 could be awarded stipends as well as a subsistence allowance. Fisher gave personally towards a necessary licence in mortmain, and the cardinal received a payment from the college and was included among its benefactors.[52]

At the same time as these matters were in progress, Fisher was thinking about his own foundation in the college. He associated his brother Robert, steward at Rochester, in an agreement with the college in 1521 which effectively made it guardian of Fisher's will. All the bishop's gifts in money, plate and lands were mentioned. The lands were now clearly intended to support a separate foundation, members of which were to be appointed by Fisher who was to make ordinances for them. After his death the college was to appoint them, respecting the founder's wishes as to their counties of origin and paying them an extra stipend. Twenty pounds were to be shared among Fisher's brethren and servants for a time to be determined by his last will, and afterwards among eight fellows of the college not of his own foundation. The surplus of profits of the lands was to go towards endowing an anniversary for Fisher in such form as he would decide.[53] A fuller version of this agreement, made in April 1525, included the new educational features: praelectorships in Greek and Hebrew and examinerships. It also referred to statutes to be made for the foundation, which were drawn up and appended to the college code of 1524. The religious obligations mentioned in the first code were much more detailed in these private statutes. Two of the fellows of the foundation were always to be priests, and those not priests were to seek ordination within two years, their duty of saying masses meanwhile being undertaken by other priests in the college.[54] The examiners and Greek praelector were exhorted to pray for the bishop in their masses or, if they were not priests, in their daily prayers. The Hebrew praelector, who was invariably to be a theologian in priest's orders, was bound to celebrate masses for Fisher's soul four times a week. By the terms of the agreement the college still promised to provide money for Fisher's brethren and servants. Indeed, payments to the praelectors in Greek and Hebrew were to be deferred until the obligations to his family and household had been discharged. In addition, trental masses were to be said for Fisher by needy and deserving priests of the college. His declared intention was to support such people in this way at a time when, as he feared, popular support for priests and scholars would wane.

Fisher was to leave no will and so his statutes, and the agreement which secured them, constitute his only surviving testament, apart from a conditional bequest to St John's made in November 1525. By this the college was put in legal possession of a quantity of plate, vestments, and all the printed books in his studies at Rochester, subject to them being reserved for his own use while he lived.[55] His plans were now laid, both for the present and for the future. During his lifetime, while his chantry chapel was being built, the Fisher fellows and the examiners were paid out of the estates bought for his foundation. The praelectorships were never accounted for under that name, but Ralph Baynes and Robert Wakefield, both noted Hebraists, were receiving sums only a little lower than those set by the statutes for the eventual stipends of the praelectors.[56] As we contemplate the building of the chapel and tomb we must keep in mind that, while Fisher lived, his design was not complete: the chantry and the contribution to scholarship was part of a vision yet to be fulfilled. Not until his death, and after some of his dependants had been pensioned by the college, were all his works of charity set in motion.

The status of Fisher's foundation became a bone of contention as the political scene changed at the end of the 1520s. Fox, his old patron and friend, died in 1528, when rumours of a royal divorce had already begun to circulate. In June 1529 Fisher made his famous declaration against the dissolution of the king's marriage. Other issues were on the horizon: while insisting that the Lady Margaret's name be placed before his own in the exequies decreed for him by the University, Fisher would not refuse them outright, 'for I do not share the opinion of those who deny purgatory'.[57] The atmosphere was becoming tense, and it was now that Richard Croke, his erstwhile spokesman and a brilliant scholar, began to denounce him in the University. From their exchange it seems that Croke was residing at St John's, although his name does not appear among its records. His charges, as far as can be seen from Fisher's reply, were that the bishop had misused the Lady Margaret's money to further his own kindred and men from his locality, and that he ordered that Yorkshiremen be given a majority on the governing body of St John's.[58] In answer Fisher distinguished between Lady Margaret's foundation and his own. As to Northerners in general, he claimed that he was merely respecting her wishes in favouring nine Northern counties; it was only in his own foundation, stemming from his personal endowment, that men from Yorkshire were preferred. As to the assets of the Lady Margaret, he pointed out that her executors had left clear accounts of the disposal of her goods. He declared that he would leave behind him another account of all of her money that had come into his hands.[59]

When Fisher comes to speak of his own gifts to the college and of his duty towards his kin, he allows us precious insights into his dilemma as a benefactor. Had he wished to act dishonestly with the Lady Margaret's money, he says, he could have lavished it on his many brothers and nephews; no corner of the college would have been free of them. But who is he to speak about favouring relations when he has so frequently been criticised for not providing properly for them? He cannot, from his own funds, afford to provide adequately for those of his own region ('conterranei'), though scripture commands such care and condemns the lack of it. He is here voicing the predicament of a bishop who had eschewed the worldliness, in its widest sense, of a Wolsey or a Wykeham, and who had not been thanked because this very virtue entailed a lack of disposable wealth and therefore absence of largesse.

Croke's criticisms unleashed a personal defence the intensity of which suggests that they had touched a nerve. Had they any foundation? Fisher stated in the statutes for his foundation in 1524 that shortly before she died the Lady Margaret had given him a large sum of money which he had devoted, together with part of his episcopal income, to the needs of the college. In the wake of the exchange with Croke this statement was amplified in the code of 1530, where Fisher justified it by his wish to avoid the charge that he had misused the foundress's assets. Nevertheless, since no complete accounts of the money remained, it was not easy for people to tell the difference between his endowment and hers. A tradition persisted that the bishop had been in possession at his death not of Lady Margaret's money, but of some of her goods. The college later wrote to both the protestant protector Somerset and the Catholic Queen Mary mentioning that it had lost his books and the Lady Margaret's plate by his fall and execution.[60]

There was more definite evidence to support Croke's charge of personal influence on behalf of countrymen and family, though Fisher stressed in his reply that he thought such preferment perfectly legitimate within his own private foundation. At the same period as the controversy with Croke, Fisher was in fact trying to give his relatives and servants greater security: a college register contains forms of annuity for life drawn up in 1529 for Robert Fisher, Edward White another kinsman, and nine others.[61] A third version of the agreement for his foundation, dated 1525 but evidently contemporary with the forms of annuity, states that the pensions, which previously had not been given a fixed duration, were to be paid for life. As those pensioned died, the money formerly paid to them was to be assigned for the provision of trental masses until the sum set aside should rise to the value of eight pounds a year, when it was to be paid in stipends for the lecturers in Greek and Hebrew.[62] Fisher had thus placed the immediate needs of his dependants and family before a benefaction to priests to say mass for his soul, and before the establishment of his lectures with full stipends payable by the college.

Even outside the bishop's own foundation there was evidence of his influence. Robert Fisher, and relatives of Metcalfe, who was also a Yorkshireman, were often employed on college business, and this may have given the impression that real power in St John's was in the hands of a Yorkshire coterie. Richard Brandisby, of the same county, one of the fellows said to have visited Fisher in 1534, owed his place directly to the bishop. He was admitted to the college as the result of a promise made by Fisher to Richard's brother, John Brandisby, a student at Paris. Nicholas Metcalfe personally supported Richard for a scholarship in 1521, in preference to another candidate, and in due course he became a Fisher fellow.[63] To minds well disposed, occasional patronage of this kind might not seem very serious, especially in the light of provisions made for the kindred of the founder in some other colleges. However Croke and his patron had already parted company, Croke to defend the divorce, Fisher to oppose it. In his reply to Croke's charges Fisher returns to the attack: Croke does not lecture, eats in his own rooms away from the hall without leave, and gathers round him a clique whose discussions are carried on in secret. He and Wakefield are ingrates, whose stipends have been wasted.[64]

Fisher's growing feeling of isolation, and resentment at unorthodox elements in the University, are also apparent at the end of his reply which is addressed to a wider audience. He says that the chancellorship of the University begins to give him little pleasure: let some other have it to whom Luther's doctrines are pleasing. He hints at an attempt to oust him and recalls his offer of the office to Wolsey in 1513 who, however, had refused it. On that occasion the University had responded by conferring the honour upon Fisher for life, but his known opposition to the king now made him a dubious asset. Very soon a tangible sign of disaster appeared: Lord Cobham invaded one of the principal estates on which the bishop's own foundation at St John's rested, and revenues were withheld from the land for two years. When disgrace finally came all the revenues of the foundation were paid to the king, who scrupulously returned them to the college after Fisher's death.[65] Meanwhile, St John's continued loyal to its fallen patron. In a letter to him in prison, the society associated itself with his misfortunes 'as the body suffers with the head'.[66] The college's loyalty was inevitably mixed with a prudent concern for its own well-being, and Cranmer and Cromwell were approached not only to gain Fisher's approval for its statutes, but to secure the goods and books granted to it in 1525. His property, however, had been seized by the crown as that of a traitor, so St John's never succeeded in acquiring what had been one of the finest libraries in Europe.

Fisher's execution did not immediately extinguish his name and standing in the college. A crucial development took place in 1537 when Nicholas Metcalfe was summoned to London, and was subsequently deprived of the mastership.[67] As archdeacon of Rochester since 1512, Metcalfe had represented the bishop in the college and had acted as his agent for many purposes, including literary ones.[68] Most of the work involved in appropriating Broomhall priory devolved upon him. He was also the keeper of accounts for Fisher's foundation. The bishop was glad to have him at his side, although his errands made him a frequently non-resident master of the college. Despite Metcalfe's fall, however, the college kept up Fisher's fellowships and exequies for nine years. It was only in 1540 that his carved fishes in the college chapel were defaced, allegedly by Cromwell's order, and his arms removed from an empty tomb.[69] In 1545 the king issued his new statutes for the college, from which mention of Fisher's name and foundation were omitted, although, as we have seen, much of their wording was probably taken from a text which Fisher had considered.

Irony presides over the end of the bishop's design: the eternal seemed to have been destroyed by earthly hands. Learning, without the piety which had inspired it, was Fisher's memorial. It was left to Henry VIII to merge his foundation with that of the Lady Margaret, while the bishop's chantry itself was dissolved. Fisher himself seems at the end of his life to have been conscious of the fragility of all he had established. He warns his sister, Elizabeth, a nun at Dartford, to prepare herself carefully by prayer for her death, for the prayers of others cannot be relied upon and 'neither building of colleges, nor making of sermons, neither yet any other manner of business shall help you without this'.[70] Fortunately his own faith sustained him and he does not seem to have flinched in the eye of death.

Some irony, too, attaches to his academic legacy. His foundation produced many notable scholars, including some whose later views he would have repudiated. George Day, Fisher fellow 1529–34, the bishop's chaplain and the public orator at Cambridge, was the choice of Henry VIII and Cromwell as successor to Metcalfe. Day accepted the royal supremacy over the Church and became bishop of Chichester, but was no radical reformer of doctrine. He resigned the provostship of King's College when private masses were abolished, was imprisoned under Edward VI, and restored to his bishopric by Queen Mary. Ralph Baynes, paid as a lecturer by Fisher between 1527 and 1534, was more of his patron's mettle. He was exiled for adherence to the pope, returned in 1553, and was deprived of a bishopric by Queen Elizabeth. John Seton, author of the famous *Logic* and examiner in classics at St John's 1529–30, became chaplain to Gardiner, bishop of Winchester. He escaped to Rome as a recusant in 1561. At the other extreme was John Cheke, Fisher fellow in 1530, examiner 1532–4, who became a convinced protestant and tutor to Edward VI. Most interesting of all, perhaps, is John Redman, examiner 1532–3, later warden of the King's Hall Cambridge and master of Henry VIII's new foundation of Trinity College. Like Day he was the king's man, and conservative in eucharistic doctrine. The opening of an anonymous address to the University, probably delivered by Redman in 1549, compares the present state of Cambridge with its condition in his youth.[71] The author recalls the University sunk still in the obscurities of Scotus and Aquinas, and praises the recent growth of linguistic skills, shown especially in extempore speeches.

The traumatic break between Fisher and those of the generation of Redman, Cheke and Ascham who disowned the past was accentuated by the rigidity of some who espoused it during Mary's reign. Fisher's statutes for St John's were then restored; his foundation once more flourished briefly; but it was in a soil made bitter by the experiences of division and exile. It has been argued here that he, in company with others of his day, wished to harmonise old scholastic discipline and new literary training. From our perspective, his loyalty to kindred and dependants and the need to provide for them, for his own salvation and for that of his patrons and friends, laid what may appear as constraints upon his academic goals. Within the limits of his aims, however, he achieved the creation of an unparalleled collegiate base for the new learning in Cambridge. It was an achievement drawn from his piety and his long university experience, and fortified by his personal labours.

Notes

1 He was to have gone to the Lateran Council as one of the king's ambassadors but the idea was dropped at the last moment. For his commission see *LP*, I, nos. 2085 (p. 320), 3100 (p. 341); for his place in the queen's suite at the Field of the Cloth of Gold, *LP* III (1), 245.

2 Fisher discloses in his statutes for St John's in 1524 and 1530 that the Lady Margaret had intended to secure him a richer see but died before she could effect her purpose: Mayor, *Statutes*, pp. 238, 342.

3 Lewis, *Fisher*, II, 301 (doc. XXI).

4 *De Veritate Corporis et Sanguinis Christi* (P. Quentel, Cologne, March 1527), p. 235.

5 Melton's will is printed in *Testamenta Eboracensia*, V (Surtees Society, 79 (1884)), 251–63. On his exhortatory sermon printed by Wynkyn de Worde see A. G. Dickens, *The English Reformation* (London, 1964), p. 73. His tracts against Luther are referred to by Fisher as unpublished in the preface to *De Veritate*, Bk I, p. D.

6 St John's College Archives (henceforth SJC), D105.102, 6 November, no year. The fellow concerned was Robert Cutler who was made provost of Rotherham College in 1508.

7 Trinity College Archives, Michaelhouse Muniments, no. 121, 1 February 1498.

8 His episcopal register shows that during this period he was usually resident in his see: see Appendix 2.

9 For Fisher's relations with Queens', see W. G. Searle, *The History of Queens' College . . .*, 2 vols. (Cambridge, 1867–71), I, ch. 3, where his presidency is discussed and contemporary letters are printed.

10 Ibid., pp. 65, 81, 87.

11 For the history of college lectures at Queens' and other colleges during this period, see D. R. Leader, 'Teaching in Tudor Cambridge', *History of Education*, 13 (1984), 114–17.

12 The Otryngham Book lists 110s. and £10 given by 'dominus John Fysshere' towards new buildings: Michaelhouse Muniments, box 29B, Otryngham Book, p. 23. The earliest biography of Fisher mentions a gift of one hundred pounds in gold, but it is often unreliable in such details: *Life*, XII, 129.

13 All three versions of this agreement were printed by R. F. Scott in the St John's College magazine, *The Eagle*, 35 (1913), no. 162, 7–22.

14 A. F. Torry, *Founders and Benefactors of St John's College* (Cambridge, 1888), pp. 3–4.

15 W. A. Wright (ed.), *The Schoolmaster, English Works of Roger Ascham* (Cambridge, 1904), Bk II, p. 279.

16 SJC, D57.172.

17 Christ's paid the tribute when it granted Fisher an anniversary in 1525; H. Rackham (ed.), *Early Statutes of Christ's College Cambridge* (Cambridge, 1927), p. 127.

18 Rackham, *Early Statutes*, p. 81.

19 Mayor, *Statutes*, pp. 370, 376 (1516); 122, 124 (1530).

20 In both copies of the deed establishing the preachership this preference has been inserted above the main text: SJC, D5.16, 17.

21 SJC, the Lady Margaret's household accounts, 1505–6, D91.21, p. 28; 1506–7,

ibid., p. 126; account roll of the Lady Margaret's treasurer of household, 1506–7, D91.16, m.13; Cambridge University Library, Queens' College Archives, QC, Bk I, fo. 194b (note at head); extracts from the Queens' College accounts, Searle, *Queens' College*, I, 134, 136–7.

22 SJC, Lady Margaret's household accounts, 1507–8, D91.19, p. 27; *Grace Book B*, I, 219–20, 222. The oration, written out by Peter Meghen, is in the Bodleian Library, Bodley MS 13, fos. 22r–31v. The manuscript gives no indication of the orator's identity. It was printed by Thomas Hearne as the speech of 'a learned prelate', *The Itinerary of John Leland* (Oxford, 1710–12), II, 95–102. Lewis, *Fisher*, includes both an English abstract and the original text (I, 20–4; II, 263–72, doc. VIII). Gairdner thought the orator was John Blythe, chancellor of the University (1493–5) and that it was delivered before the king, the Lady Margaret and Prince Arthur: *Letters and Papers Illustrative of the Reigns of Richard III and Henry VII* (London, 1861–3), p. 422. J. B. Mullinger identified the speech with Fisher's 'little proposition' made before Henry in April 1506, recorded in E. Ashmole, *The Institution, Laws and Ceremonies of the Noble Order of the Garter* (London, 1672), p. 558; J. B. Mullinger, *The University of Cambridge from the Earliest Times to 1535* (Cambridge, 1873), pp. 449–52. The oration is, however, more than a 'proposition', which sounds like part of a scholastic exercise, and was perhaps a speech made by Fisher at the ceremonies recorded in the Clare College Master's Old Book at which the king, the Lady Margaret, and Prince Henry were present. The date given there is 1507, but both the king and his mother (the prince is not mentioned elsewhere) were also present at the academic ceremonies of 1506. It is not likely to have been delivered at the king's visit in April that year, since the Lady Margaret did not accompany him on that occasion. Other elements in the speech point to Fisher rather than to Blythe: the orator claims to have been made a bishop while lacking any benefices or service at court, while Blythe was archdeacon of Huntingdon and Richmond and master of the Rolls before being made bishop. He also mentions the king's renewal of work on King's College. This took place in 1508 or a little earlier, but not as early as 1493–5. Allusion is made to a large gift of money by the king to the University. The proctors' accounts record such a gift in 1506–7, but none figures earlier. The only powerful counter-indication is the absence of any references to Christ's College, whose charter was granted in May 1505 and statutes presented in October 1506, which surely should have figured in any recital of the king's beneficence. The explanation is perhaps that the foundation of God's House by Henry VI, which *is* mentioned in the speech, was more relevant to the theme, for Christ's itself was a completion of this foundation on the initiative not of the king but of the Lady Margaret.

23 Clare College Archives, Master's Old Book, safe C/1/7, fo. 53r.

24 William Woodruff, the master of Clare who was one of the doctors created on that occasion, preached in the household of the Lady Margaret at the Feast of the Assumption in August 1507; SJC, household accounts, D91.19, p. 30.

25 P. S. Allen (ed.), *Erasmi Epistolae*, II (Oxford, 1910), no. 592 (p. 598).

26 *EW*, p. 434.

27 R. Croke, *Orationes Duae* (Simon de Colines, Paris, 1520); summary in J. B. Mullinger, *The University of Cambridge*, pp. 533–4. In this summary the reference to John Canonicus appears as one to John Scotus Eriugena, a misreading or misinter-

pretation of the original printed text. I am most grateful to Richard Rex for point-ing out this error. Croke's wage from Fisher, 'ad mandatum episcopi', is in SJC, master's accounts, 1518–20, M3.5. The king was paying Croke more handsomely in 1520, *LP*, III (1), p. 409.

28 *Erasmi Epistolae*, III (Oxford, 1913), no. 653 (p. 75).

29 *Statutes of the Colleges of Oxford* (Royal Commission, London, 1853), II, 71, 127.

30 SJC, The Thin Red Book, C7.11, fos. 8–9. Fisher's sanction for new statutes was specifically required by his first code for St John's: Mayor, *Statutes*, p. 394.

31 For recent views on the eclipse of medieval logic after 1530, see N. Kretzman, A. Kenny, J. Pinborg (eds.), *The Cambridge History of Later Medieval Philosophy* (Cambridge, 1982), chs. 42, 43.

32 Those of the Lady Margaret professor of divinity.

33 Mayor, *Statutes*, p. 377.

34 Ibid., pp. 315, 96.

35 Wakefield's receipts for wages from Fisher, SJC, D56.140, 180; Fisher's permis-sion for him to go abroad, SJC, C7.11, fo. 219, printed in T. Baker, *History of St John's College*, ed. J. E. B. Mayor (Cambridge, 1869), I, 358. See also Edward Surtz, *The Works and Days of John Fisher* (Cambridge, Mass., 1967), pp. 143–8. In the preface to *De Veritate*, however, Fisher praises Corpus Christi College as a centre for the study of all three languages, *De Veritate*, p. C; also printed in *Let-ters of Richard Fox*, ed. P. S. Allen (Oxford, 1929), p. 152.

36 Mayor, *Statutes*, p. 252. If a lecture on Scotus was adopted, the Greek lecturer was to study Hebrew, to prevent knowledge of it being lost.

37 The absence of payments for any but the principal lecturer in the accounts prevents us from knowing further details.

38 Mayor, *Statutes*, p. 246.

39 Van Ortroy dismisses the account of the visit to Lambeth as a confusion with a visit to the Tower, which he accepts took place on the evidence of Thomas Baker from the college archives. The records do not say this, however, but merely men-tion visits to London, of which there were many: *Life*, XII, 133 and notes; cf. SJC, D106.14, D106.11, under miscellaneous expenses.

40 SJC, C1.40.14. These statutes are unlikely to have been devised in consultation with Cranmer: as well as the references to scholastic authors the original text car-ries some to the pope and court of Rome. It is possible that the *erasure* of the latter (fos. 7, 7v, 18v) took place at Cranmer's direction, but the text was extensively altered later to accord with the statutes of 1530 and the erased references were then rewritten. The names of students present in the college during the 1550s on the corners of many folios suggest that the work of wholesale alteration was done during the reign of Mary.

41 Clothes for players are mentioned in the college accounts for 1524–5 and 1527–8: SJC, D106.12, p. 146, D106.11, fo. 103. Plays performed in the college may have included one by Fisher himself: a letter of 1521 from the president to the master mentions the willingness of 'our company' to perform 'the play that my lord made', SJC, D105.47. I owe these references to Professor Alan Nelson of the University of California and the project for Records of Early English Drama.

42 SJC, C1.40.14, fo. 30v: '. . . idque ordine in huiusmodi questionibus quas nos

studio et opera nostra [*sic*] atque amicorum ex . . . [manuscript damaged] simis scholasticis disputatoribus decerpsimus'. Cf. Mayor, *Statutes*, pp. 110, 112.

43 But a readership could be held with a benefice worth £20, reinforcing the tendency to non-residence in poor parishes.

44 Baker and Mayor, *History of St John's College*, I, 343.

45 SJC, building accounts for the chantry, D106.6; extracts printed in *The Eagle*, 35 (1913), no. 162, 33–5.

46 Mayor, *Statutes*, pp. 398–9.

47 The money amounted to £1,600 or £1,700: SJC D106.5, fo. 4v; cf. list of benefactors in C7.2, fo. 43.

48 SJC, C7.11, fos. 38–40 (memorandum on the difficulties encountered in establishing the college). Parts of it are in the first person and clearly it was prepared by Fisher.

49 The duke of Devonshire had to encourage Nicholas Metcalfe to press harder for another licence in 1520, SJC, D105.53. At the same period Fisher's chaplain, Richard Sharpe, asked Metcalfe to solicit the king through the dean of St Paul's (probably still Colet), for a minor post for one of Fisher's servants, D105.253.

50 The story of the decline of the house and its dissolution is told fully in A. F. Allen, 'Higham Priory', *Archaeologia Cantiana*, 80 (1965), 186–99.

51 SJC, D10.12.5 (Richard Sharpe to Metcalfe); D105.163 (John Wylbor to Metcalfe).

52 Mayor, *Statutes*, p. 311.

53 SJC, D58.58, 6 March 1521, printed in Mayor, *Statutes*, pp. 346–8.

54 SJC, D58.59, 18 April 1525, and note 13 above. The Lady Margaret is affectionately referred to as like a second mother – 'cui non secus atque propriae genetrici fuerim obnoxius' – and Henry VII is commemorated for having, unprompted, made Fisher a bishop, Mayor, *Statutes*, p. 242.

55 This reservation later proved fatal to the bequest: see p. 40 below.

56 Payments to the lecturers, 1524–45, were as follows: to Robert Wakefield, £1, part of £4 per annum, Christmas 1524; £2 per annum during 1525 and 1526; 10s for one term, 1528 (Wakefield was on leave part of the time); to Ralph Baynes, £4 per annum, 1527–34, SJC, D106.6. Between 1534 and 1545, although rates of pay fluctuated, the Greek and Hebrew lectures were kept up on the foundation of the college, SJC, D106.14–17, and SB3.10–18.

57 Reproduced in Lewis, *Fisher*, II, 305–7 (doc. XXIII).

58 SJC, C7.11, fos. 49–50b, printed in J. Hymers (ed.), *The Funeral Sermon of Margaret Countess of Richmond* (Cambridge, 1840), pp. 210–16.

59 The executors' accounts were published, with omission of some details, in C. H. Cooper, *The Lady Margaret* (Cambridge, 1874), appendix, pp. 178–214. Either Fisher failed to draw up his promised account of her money, or it has not survived.

60 SJC, C7.12, pp. 183–8 and fos. 360–1. This can only refer to his conditional bequest of 1525. No items on the schedule to that gift exactly match any on lists of the Lady Margaret's plate, although some bear the same general description, e.g. the kind of cloth used in vestments, features of design in ornaments. Some items in the schedule certainly were Fisher's, for they are mentioned as stamped with his arms. The purpose of the letters to the protector and the queen was, of

course, to secure government aid, and it was in the college's interest to stress the part played by the Lady Margaret as a royal foundress.

61 SJC, C7.2, fos. 209–19. Payment of the last annuitant continued until 1564.
62 SJC, C.7.11, fos. 68–72, and note 13 above.
63 SJC, John Brandisby to Nicholas Metcalfe,? 1518, D105.245; John Smith, president, to Metcalfe, 14 December 1521, D105.49.
64 Hymers, *Funeral Sermon*, p. 215.
65 SJC, bursars' accounts, 1534–5, SB3.10.
66 Lewis, *Fisher*, II, 356–8 (doc. XXXIV), printed from the seventeenth-century copy in the college register of letters, C7.16, pp. 46–8.
67 SJC, D48.307, reproduced in *The Eagle*, 31 (1910), no. 152, 288–91.
68 Letters from Richard Sharpe and Thomas Bocher, official to the archdeacon of Rochester, to Nicholas Metcalfe, requesting and returning works used by Fisher between 1521 and 1523, were printed by C. J. Gray, 'Letters of Bishop Fisher', *The Library* (1913), 3rd series, IV, 133–45, from SJC, D105.41, 43, 44–5, 51.
69 SJC, bursars' accounts, 1540–1, D106.17, fos. 56, 66. Cromwell's name is not mentioned and figures only in informations for the *Life*, a source strongly hostile to the king's principal secretary: *Life*, X, 165.
70 *A Spirituall Consolation . . . by John Fyssher . . . to hys Sister Elizabeth, at suche tyme as hee was prisoner in the Tower of London*, *EW*, pp. 351–63, at p. 362.
71 The address, undated, is copied into the back of an account book, SJC, D107.3, fos. 235–57. It is not in Redman's hand, but contains autobiographical references to a career of theological study interrupted by royal service in the King's Hall and as head of Trinity College, which seem to fit no one else. In 1549 Redman was Lady Margaret professor for the second time; this is the likeliest date for the address.

The University chancellor[1]

CHRISTOPHER N. L. BROOKE

Between 1440 and 1550 Cambridge became a collegiate University: the centre of gravity in the teaching passed into the colleges, and the academic quarter, the special beauty of Cambridge – which stretches from Peterhouse and Queens' in the south to St John's in the north – was completed. It owed much to the fourteenth-century founders who had grouped Clare and Trinity Hall and Gonville Hall round the Old Schools – with other foundations not far away; it was completed by the landscape gardeners between the sixteenth and the eighteenth centuries who created the Backs, and canonised when Capability Brown laid out the Fellows' Garden at St John's and when his scheme to turn the rest of the Backs into a park was rejected. But the special and peculiar beauty of the academic quarter of Cambridge for many of us lies in the old red-brick courts set at the southern end by Andrew Doket, founder of Queens', and at the northern by John Fisher, founder of John's.[2]

It is common form to attribute Queens' to Queen Margaret of Anjou encouraged by her husband, Henry VI, and John's to the Lady Margaret Beaufort; quite rightly, for without their interest and their patronage the foundations could never have occurred. It is particularly the case that the Lady Margaret and Fisher are inseparable in their foundations, as Malcolm Underwood has shown in his penetrating studies of their work.[3] But we may wonder if the 17- or 18-year-old Queen Margaret really chose the red bricks, and note that they are alien to any of Henry VI's foundations;[4] and I am sure that throughout the early history of Queens' it is Doket, who cared nothing for the vicissitudes of Lancaster and York so long as every reign brought a new benefactor to his college, that we must see as the central figure in the foundation; and no one questions that, if Fisher had not first inspired the Lady Margaret with the idea, and then fought the lions in the arena at Ephesus to retain some vestige of her legacies, St John's College would not have been founded.[5] We touch here the edge of an exceedingly interesting problem, of the relative significance of the men who were inspired to found colleges by their work and experience within Oxford and Cambridge, and the great patrons who threw the bags of gold from afar. The distinction is too sharply drawn. Both were needed. In distributing the credit for the great

47

transformation of Cambridge over this period, let us at once observe that it was not the work of a single patron or group of patrons, and that the rise of the colleges was even more dramatically paralleled in Oxford (where they had been less conspicuous before); we must not hope too much from explanations local to the banks of the Cam. Then we may admit that Henry VI is a central figure, for he had a vision of a great college by the Cam, and he was deeply interested in pedagogy, as Roger Lovatt has taught us.[6] But I would still hold that if we wish to understand the process we must look most closely at Andrew Doket, founder-president of Queens', at John Fisher, fellow of Michaelhouse turned chancellor and bishop (I do not myself believe he was ever master of Michaelhouse, but he was certainly a fellow), and Thomas Wolsey, fellow and bursar of Magdalen turned founder of Cardinal College. To these I would add the unsung hero of the survival of the Cambridge colleges and the foundation of Trinity, John Redman, but that is a story for another day.[7]

I do not at all mean that Fisher conceived or carried through the revolution which converted Cambridge into a federation of colleges, still less the completion of the academic quarter. For the first, his interest in University preachers and professors came before the foundation of colleges; for the second, he helped the Lady Margaret to refound Christ's, which is not in the quarter at all, before he laid hands on the ancient religious house of the hospital of St John; and the Lady Margaret herself was a very determined character, by no means to be neglected.[8] Yet he remains the central figure in any attempt to unravel this very crucial era in Cambridge history.

It is, first and foremost, an academic story; and it is the academic element in the work of Fisher which I fancy is of greatest interest, as it was to Fisher himself – and this I leave in Malcolm Underwood's hands; for we have made a happy treaty which leaves the heart and substance of the thing to him.[9] Nor by the same token shall I speak more than occasionally of the great patroness. Nor shall I say much of the architectural evidence. No one who contemplates Willis and Clark or the volumes of the Royal Commission, or Pevsner, can say that this has been neglected, though in some measure it has been neglected by historians, and there is still a large gap between Willis and Clark and our current understanding of Cambridge history, which greatly interests me.[10] Let it suffice to say that if one studies the facade and the old court of Queens' so perfectly preserved, and then walks to St John's to see the beautiful facade and the first court, so mutilated in the eighteenth and nineteenth centuries, one can hardly be surprised to learn that the founder of John's had once been president of Queens'. It is sometimes alleged that the beauty of red brick Cambridge is due to the lack of building stone in the neighbourhood. This is not wholly false; but we cannot doubt that these two colleges at least – and St Catharine's too from a later age or Robinson from later still – reflect the personal taste of their founders.[11]

The academic and the architectural evidence are perhaps the greatest themes; my own is more modest. I wish to consider Fisher as chancellor – that is, to sketch the way in which we might trace his path between the royal court and other seats of patronage, and the Cambridge he loved and in which he had once lived; to trace some of the attitudes and activities which help to explain how the relations between the local and the distant benefactors worked.

I start with two difficulties. The statutes of the University of Cambridge made it abundantly clear in Fisher's day that the chancellor should be resident; only modest periods of non-residence were permitted.[12] Later chancellors doubtless avoided this difficulty until it was removed in 1570 by not reading the statutes. We can hardly believe that Fisher, once a very conscientious senior proctor and vice-chancellor, shared their ignorance. We are in danger of misunderstanding. I am not wanting to bark at his heels, to chip small fragments off the lofty reputation which we so rightly celebrate today. I am trying to understand him and his relation to the world in which he lived – in terms of the fifteenth century which witnessed his birth. He was a creative and a conservative figure. He has many characteristic features of the world in which he was born: Fisher and Wolsey represent the hatred of abuses and the ebullient delight in them which were equally at home in that world. But, if Fisher and Wolsey – for all their common academic background – were alien to one another, Fisher was close to many who represented the space between, and especially to Richard Fox, bishop of Winchester, founder of Corpus, Oxford, the one person he set above the Lady Margaret as his special patron and friend.[13] There is a region here to be explored.

My other difficulty is that the historians of Cambridge have neglected to provide the lists which should underpin our theme – a failing in which I rejoice, for it gives me some excuse to deliver this paper. There is indeed a list of the masters of Michaelhouse in the *VCH*, derived from A. E. Stamp's useful account of the college; but neither gives a critical discussion of Fisher's place.[14] Stamp makes it clear that Fisher and his mentor, William Melton – both undoubtedly fellows of Michaelhouse – do not occur as masters in the list in the Otryngham benefactors' book of the fifteenth and sixteenth centuries, though both are called master in the sixteenth-century *Life* of Fisher.[15] Malcolm Underwood and I are convinced, on the whole, that he was never master, though the college was important to him. The list of medieval chancellors in the *VCH* is worse – but at least it can in fair measure be revised by the simple process of reading Emden's great *Biographical Register*.[16] Emden leaves many problems unsolved, owing to gaps in the evidence; and it is only fair to the editors of the *VCH* to say that they wrote in the dark ages before Emden, when there was little on which to found such a list. For the thirteenth and fourteenth centuries it is a work of fiction: my favourite fourteenth-century chancellor is Anthony of Grant-chester, invented by Dr Caius out of the initials A. de G. on the draft statutes of Edmund Gonville – which were in their turn a misreading by a fifteenth-century scribe of A de B (ciphers, as we might say X of Y) on the original.[17] Most other names have more basis than this; few of the dates are right. For the fifteenth century things are better; but most of the dates are still wrong, and there is a punctuation of names of more than doubtful validity; Cardinal Morton would doubtless have been mortified to discover that he has been totally omitted. As in so many things, Fisher himself is the fulcrum: from Fisher on all is plain sailing and the list (so far as I have checked it) is correct.

By reconstructing an accurate list – always bearing in mind that there are many uncertainties and mighty little evidence about the relation of most early chancellors with the University – we can form a picture of the process by which the chancellor became a distant officer of state. The sixteenth century saw two remarkable additions to the tradition of the office, one lasting, one happily short-lived. The first is the tradition that the chancellor should be a leading figure in the royal court – a practice adumbrated in the fifteenth century, canonised in the sixteenth, especially by Lord Burghley, devoted servant of the queen and the University alike.[18] The other is that it became for a while one of the most dangerous offices in christendom – between 1535 and 1601 four chancellors out of eight died on the scaffold.

Down to the early fifteenth century the chancellors of Oxford and Cambridge were busy University administrators, elected for up to two years – occasionally re-elected – by the regent and non-regent masters, men of the stamp of Richard of Badow, first founder of Clare in the 1320s.[19] Signs of change – to cut a long story short – meet us in John Rickinghall in the 1410s and 1420s and John Langton in the 1430s and 1440s. Both clearly had powerful patrons. Rickinghall started under the wing of the disreputable Bishop Henry Despenser of Norwich and ended confessor to the much more reputable John duke of Bedford; he became bishop of Chichester. He was for a number of years master of Gonville Hall as well as chancellor – a new kind of pluralism.[20] Langton was the first man to combine the chancellorship with the mastership of Pembroke, enjoyed the favour of Henry VI and played a part in the foundation of King's. He combined a role in court, wide pluralism, and serious work for Cambridge.[21] He was succeeded by two royal clerks and an aristocrat, William Percy; and two of them were bishops of Carlisle while chancellor of Cambridge – why this particular bishopric was thought so appropriate an office for the chancellor of Cambridge I do not know; several combined the two in the fifteenth century. With Lawrence Booth we come to the first major name in this list, a member of a rapacious clan which filled many great offices in Church and state.[22] Booth has left an ambiguous reputation. He has acquired a certain guilt by association with his half-brother William, who as archbishop of York consecrated Lawrence bishop of Durham, and who was undoubtedly unscrupulous. Lawrence rose first by dedicated service to Queen Margaret of Anjou. Within a few months of the victory of Edward IV, Lawrence, as bishop of Durham, was Edward's confessor. But he must somehow have himself confessed to intrigue if not spying on the queen's behalf, for he was in total disgrace a year or two later – compelled to live in retirement in Cambridge. In the 1470s by a process equally mysterious he won back Edward's favour, was translated to his brother's see of York, and lies beside him in Southwell Minster. Meanwhile he was from 1450 till his death in 1480 master of Pembroke – absentee, one presumes, virtually throughout those years, save when in a political twilight compelled to live in the modest space of Pembroke Lodge.[23] Yet, for all the ambiguity of his public fame and his absenteeism, he was happily remembered in Pembroke, both as a benefactor and as an absentee master, for the experiment was continued in Thomas Rotherham and Richard Fox. The fellows of Pembroke found they did very well without a master and enjoyed the benefits of his patronage at court. But we have only to compare the relative modesty of Pembroke's endowment with the great wealth of Queens' at Doket's death in 1484 to see the actual difference between a non-resident master, however great, and a resident master who knew on which doors to knock.[24]

Meanwhile, both Lawrence Booth and Thomas Rotherham had periods as chancellor. Booth's was short, and he was succeeded by Robert Wodelarke, whose brief spells as chancellor remind us that the local man could still fill the office: for Wodelarke was Henry VI's provost of King's, who devoted his working life to shoring up the ramshackle edifice of a large college the king had so incompetently thrust upon him; and in his last years he founded a tiny college-chantry of his own, St Catharine's, which should be innocent of the uncertainties of lofty patronage and could never excite envy and malice by its wealth.[25] With Rotherham we enter the world of the future most completely.[26] Like Fisher a devout Yorkshireman, Rotherham became bishop of Rochester and chancellor of Cambridge in 1469, perhaps within a few months of Fisher's birth (but contrary to what is commonly asserted we cannot be sure that Fisher was born in that year – only that he *claimed* to be in his 22nd year or thereabouts in June 1491).[27] In 1475 Rotherham was for a spell chancellor of France and England and Cambridge all at once. In 1480 he succeeded Lawrence Booth as archbishop of York and master of Pembroke. His later career saw various vicissitudes, but he was firmly in office in Cambridge and York on the December day in 1491 when Fisher was ordained priest in York, on the title of his fellowship at Michaelhouse. Fisher went to York, following a common practice of seeking ordination in one's home country – and the immediate precedent set by William Melton five years before. It would be nice to add that he sought ordination at the hands of the chancellor of his university, Archbishop Rotherham; but David Smith, director of the Borthwick and custodian of Rotherham's register, has kindly verified for me the following facts: that Rotherham never ordained at all, but left it all to his suffragan, William bishop of Dromore, an Austin friar who went the rounds of the great churches of York and actually ordained Fisher priest in the Austin friars' church; and Rotherham was probably in Battersea at the time.[28] Where Fisher received his earlier orders, heaven knows; certainly not York, nor Ely.[29] None the less, Fisher was a loyal Yorkshireman who had evidently studied and meditated the career of Rotherham, his fellow-Yorkshireman, and perhaps noted the way he had rescued Lincoln College, Oxford, of which he was truly a founder.

Rotherham resigned the chancellorship finally in the early or mid 1490s, and perhaps as the result of the mysterious disgrace which led to his impeachment in 1495.[30] His successor, John Blythe, bishop of Salisbury, held office till 1498 or 1499. Thereafter the practice of annual or biennial elections was resumed, but the chancellors were still great men: Richard Fox, John Morton, George FitzHugh (master of Pembroke, but an aristocrat, pluralist, and royal chaplain as well), William Sever, later bishop of Durham.[31] In 1504–5, Fisher was elected to succeed him. The precise date is not known, nor whether his appointment to Rochester was in prospect or had taken place when he was chosen: the entry in the *Grace Book* which refers to him as 'cancellarium electum episcopum Roffensem' may suggest that he was bishop first; but the Latin is ambiguous, and, as the earliest date known for his episcopate is the papal provision of October 1504, we may presume that it had been in the wind a while before.[32] All that we know for sure is Fisher's own statement that it was Fox who suggested him to Henry VII;[33] and from the king's letter to his mother we know that Henry VII took the initiative and then tactfully enquired if Lady Margaret was ready for her favourite confessor to be consecrated bishop. It is likely enough that Fox had a hand in Fisher's election to both offices.

It is instructive to compare the chancellors of Cambridge with their brothers of Oxford.[34] After the sudden death of Duke Humphrey in 1447, his physician, Gilbert Kymer, remained in office till 1453. Then Oxford, which had practised the highest arts of sycophancy in its letters to Duke Humphrey, tried its first major experiment in an aristocratic chancellor. The masters discovered in their midst a likely young man called George Neville.[35] He already had some experience of office in the church, since he had been a canon of Salisbury at the age of ten and of York at fourteen – enjoying the rich prebend of Masham, the dream of many a seasoned pluralist before him. Neville was a BA when just 18 and his final acts for the MA were hastened through in 1452. The next year he was installed as chancellor, aged twenty. We may suspect that we are in the world of Gilbert and Sullivan – and the suspicion is not entirely unfounded, though there is evidence that young George had been a hard-reading man. More significantly, however, he was brother of Warwick the kingmaker. He had an ample concern for the University, and held the chancellorship for two spells, 1453–7 and 1461–72; he is better known for his ostentation and grandeur. He may have been resident – more probably partly resident – till he became bishop of Exeter in 1456; his translation to York in 1465 is celebrated for the thousands of sheep that were slaughtered for the feast at his installation. He has been closely studied in an Oxford thesis by Gillian Keir, which she generously lent me while I was preparing this paper, and she makes a good case for a serious interest in Oxford. I would conjecture that he was at least as interested as his two successors at York, Booth and Rotherham, were in Cambridge. If Rotherham refounded Lincoln College, Oxford, Neville had saved it from suppression by timely intervention with Henry VI. After his brother's fall he was disgraced, and in 1472 Edward IV instructed the regents that he was to be chancellor no more.[36]

Neville alternated with Thomas Chandler, who was warden of New College for most of his two reigns as chancellor, and a local man, like Wodelarke, with great friends afar: he had been a protégé of Bekynton and Waynflete. He was followed by two aristocratic bishops. In or about 1483 John Russell, bishop of Lincoln, became chancellor; and his appointment may well have been a quick manoeuvre by the University to curry favour with Richard III. He was the first 'life' chancellor, and he and his successor, John Morton, immediately made it apparent that they would accept only if exempted from residence: Russell was given a formal dispensation, Morton refused to take the formal oaths.[37] Fisher took neither of these courses, so far as we know. After a couple of short-lived bishops, William Warham, archbishop of Canterbury and ex-fellow of New College, took up the chancellorship, which he held almost as long as Fisher, refusing to be ousted by his rival from Magdalen, Thomas Wolsey.[38]

Behind the pattern we have been tracing lie two traditions, of residence and patronage. The pattern of patronage is the more obvious, and has come out as clearly as it will in what I have said – as clearly as it will, since we have very little except the formal record and a pile of begging letters by which to judge the intention of those who appointed such men as chancellors; and those who have striven to determine whether there was or was not a crisis of patronage in the late fourteenth and early fifteenth century have sunk in deep water.[39] What no one doubts is that patronage was needed, and even more eagerly sought, by the masters and scholars of the universities; and that the favour of the rich and the great was essential if colleges were to be founded, endowed and supplied with mortmain licences and other privileges. It was no easy matter to succeed in such enterprises, as that vast expanse of empty building site now covered with the stately lawns of King's still testifies: and who had greater resources or a stronger wish to succeed than King Henry VI? A sharper edge was put on the relationship of Oxford and Cambridge with kings and bishops and popes and other potentates by the problem of heresy from Wyclif on; and very likely it was the fear of heresy in Oxford which was a major factor in helping Cambridge, from being Oxford's little sister, to draw even in the fifteenth century.[40] In the end it was the growth of heresy in Cambridge which alienated the ageing Fisher – and yet kept him wedded to the office of chancellor in the hope, one presumes, that the tide would turn and he could lead it back into the pure Catholic fold.

Thus the role of chancellor as it had developed down to Fisher's time, and grown under his hand and his inspiration, depended on three assumptions: that the University and its students and scholars needed patronage; that its intellectual life and its doctrines and opinions were of great importance to England as a whole and to Christendom; and that these functions needed to be channelled and represented by a figure of national consequence, with ready access to the royal court and the corridors of power in Church and state alike. Fisher in his later years stood rather apart from the court; and so his successor, Thomas Cromwell, appears to mark a striking contrast. He was only briefly chancellor, from 1535 till his execution in 1540, but his reign was decisive: he opened a succession of leading lay royal ministers, concerned to preserve the role of Cambridge as an agent of the religious principles in favour at the court, and a safe place for the sons of ministers and gentry and all manner of folk to receive some part of their education; at the same time Cromwell himself was seriously interested in 'good letters', as well as a devoted patron of learned propaganda, and William Cecil (chancellor from 1559 to 1598) was deeply interested in the welfare of Cambridge. But we observe the change partly because these men have left rich archives, partly because they were laymen. In seventeenth-century Oxford, William Laud was to show that the tradition of Morton and Warham and Wolsey, who had combined the roles of prelacy and royal service, still survived; or, to put it another way, that Cromwell's work could be done by an archbishop.

Residence is a subtler problem. Historians sometimes talk as if there was some golden age in the past when the secular clergy of England had resided on their cures and even their archdeaconries. Much of my life has been spent in the cathedral chapters of the late eleventh and twelfth centuries, in the period, that is, when the English secular cathedral chapters of the old foundation were founded or refounded after the Norman Conquest; and I am sure no such golden age ever existed. The idea of dividing up the revenues of a church between the poor underpaid royal clerks goes back at least to Edward the Confessor's reign: St Martin-le-Grand in the City of London was founded – just like St Stephen's, Westminster, and St George's, Windsor, in the fourteenth century – to provide jobs, or anyway incomes, for the boys, and a grand chapel for the king when he happened to be visiting the city.[41] The early cathedral chapters, where we can document them, contained substantial groups of absentee pluralists. But at the same time there were reforms and reformers, plenty of folk who thought all this an abuse. In every century between the formation of the prebendal system in the eleventh or twelfth centuries and its destruction by the Victorian reformers there were men about who thought it mere abuse; and in the fourteenth and fifteenth centuries probably a large number, from the pope down, who denounced pluralism with one hand and fostered it with the other. The same Pope Urban V of the 1360s, who propounded the most effective measures ever taken by a medieval pope against pluralism, provided a pluralist cardinal to the prebend of Masham, later to be a handsome present for the fourteen-year-old George Neville. These attitudes are not simple. John Fisher the arch-reformer, who was not a pluralist before he became a bishop, none the less held a fat rectory in Yorkshire where residence must have been occasional at best;[42] as bishop he was dispensed from part of his residence to attend the court of the Lady Margaret, and was not at all dispensed (so far as I know), either to attend or to absent himself, from the supposedly residential office he held in Cambridge.

From the twelfth century to the nineteenth, three approaches to residence disputed for mastery in the counsels of the Church and the hearts of churchmen. First, there was candid non-residence, anyway as applied to posts which could perfectly well be managed by deputy, such as archdeaconries; and in this Fisher in a modest measure concurred, since he appointed his own archdeacon first master of St John's.[43] Malcolm Underwood tells me he seems actually to have resided mainly in London, and was in fact Fisher's Pooh-Bah or man of affairs. But he visited Rochester from time to time, and was certainly by no means so non-resident as were the cardinals, or that notable Cambridge humanist and diplomat Christopher Urswick, who held five archdeaconries in the course of a busy life spent serving Henry VII in almost all the courts of Europe.[44]

There were also the totally resident – or those at least who set such an ideal before their eyes. There were probably far more bishops than is realised who spent most of their days in their sees – though there were a few who never visited them at all, especially if they lay far to the North or far to the West. I know none from the later middle ages whose record can compare (of all unexpected candidates) with William of Wykeham – who even when in Westminster regularly seems to have returned to his palace in Southwark (which was in his diocese) to sleep – and who probably never strayed outside his see as far as Oxford to visit New College.[45] In any case the idea and ideal of residence was ever present in statutes and homilies and episcopal visitations.

Midway lived the large majority of mankind for whom – if they could arrange it and afford it – the natural life was one of part-time residence. The idea that every post should involve full-time employment is a modern heresy. The civil servant or the canon or the parish priest of the middle ages, if he was a conscientious man, reckoned to spend a few months on one task, a few months on another, and to do the rounds – that at least was his aspiration. These practices are exceedingly difficult to document, but they are reflected in countless careers and cathedral statutes. It is instructive to compare the statute of residence of Lichfield of the 1190s, which (characteristically of that period) demands a minimum residence of a quarter of the year for all – or that of St Paul's of the same era, which allows off one month in four but lists all manner of other alleviations – with the St Paul's statute of residence of the mid fourteenth century which assumes that most are totally non-resident and demands for a few a tough and expensive probation.[46] By the fourteenth century the perquisites of residence were great and a small number of canons prevented the majority from receiving them by such manoeuvres; but in turn the so-called residentiaries adopted their own system, which survives in some cathedrals, whereby a canon is expected to reside for only two or three months in the year.

Now we do not have any commentary known to me from the pen of John Fisher on these attitudes or practices, save a passing reference in one of his sermons, and the growing stringency of residence in successive versions of the St John's statutes.[47] *Econtra*, he presented non-residents to some benefices in the Lincoln diocese, as Margaret Bowker has shown, and his own archdeacon to the mastership of St John's.[48] We can be sure from what we do know that he aspired to total residence – on this principle the statutes of Christ's and St John's are categorical – and regarded the Urswicks of this world as an abuse; between him and Wolsey, the prince of pluralists, whom even Stigand, Edward the Confessor's archbishop, would have recognised as his master, there was little sympathy.[49] But he clearly had the strongest feeling for Richard Fox, to whom he owed much, to whose advice he seems frequently to have turned.[50] Fox was not *persona grata* in high places till 1485, and he became bishop of Exeter in 1487, so he had little time to cultivate the garden of pluralism.[51] But he had already amassed four canonries, which was not bad going; and once a bishop he demanded and achieved rapid translations – to Bath and Wells and Durham and Winchester, from which few men ever sought translation, for it was the richest see in the land. Only one bishop of Winchester was translated between John Stratford, who went to Canterbury in 1333, and Randall Davidson – the Laudian Richard Neile, who went to York in 1632.[52]

I tend to take a needlessly austere view of these translations because I am a native of the eleventh and twelfth centuries, when the prejudices of the early Church still lingered: the bishop was married to his see, and translation involved divorce and remarriage, and could be attempted only by papal dispensation. The papal dispensation survived till the Reformation, but the prejudice departed; none the less, the practice, which became hectic only in the late fourteenth century, involved a much less personal link with the diocese than had been assumed as normal in earlier times.[53] Fisher implies in one of his writings that the Lady Margaret intended to have arranged his translation to a richer see had she lived, which we can believe.[54] His supposed refusal of translation must be taken with a pinch of salt. But not more than a pinch — he was indeed a devoted pastor: we can hardly think he would have wished to follow Fox in all his manoeuvres; yet he clearly admired and loved him.

It is abundantly clear that when Fisher became chancellor of Cambridge he hoped to be occasionally resident: to serve the University by walking the corridors of power, maybe; to serve it by his intimacy with Margaret Beaufort, undoubtedly; to serve it by his prayers and watchfulness, beyond doubt. He cannot have hoped, as bishop of Rochester and queen mother's confessor, to be often or long in Cambridge. But a man who had devoted so much of the best years of his life already to Cambridge must have hoped to be a frequent visitor still: for he had been a student since the mid 1480s at latest; he was Master of Arts and (from 1501) Doctor of Divinity; he had been fellow of Michaelhouse; and was a devoted and active senior proctor and vice-chancellor.[55] Malcolm Underwood has convinced me that the proctor's account of 1494–5, with the dramatic entry 'I had lunch with the lady mother of the king' 'pransus eram apud dominam matrem regis', really is in Fisher's own hand.[56] he had been vice-chancellor from July 1501, the first Lady Margaret's reader from September 1502.[57] And if more evidence is needed, the close interest he took in two Cambridge colleges, and eventually in three, presupposes not only an involvement in Cambridge warm, devout and continuing, but a measure of residence too. At Christ's the Lady Margaret provided herself with two ample chambers and an oratory with direct access to the chapel, and now the heart and core of the Master's Lodge, similar to that which Fisher made for himself at Rochester; and she provided in her statutes that her confessor, the chancellor of Cambridge, might use them too.[58] There is in Christ's Chapel a mysterious gallery or mini-transept, unparalleled in college chapels and almost certainly part of the work of Margaret and Fisher, not an inheritance from the chapel of Godshouse. It is opposite the Lady Margaret's oratory; and it has been suggested that it was intended as a formal pew for the chancellor when both were present. We do not know if they ever visited Christ's together; probably they did, though not often. Much later, in St John's, Fisher provided for his chantry, which was intended (fruitlessly alas) to ensure that he was continuously resident in his relics after death.[59] But the chief evidence of his purposes comes from Queens'. Here by the river Andrew Doket had built the charming lodging, now connected to the old court by the cloister walks.[60] Jonathan Riley-Smith suggested a while ago that its original function was to house notable visitors, and especially the royal visitors who undoubtedly lodged in Queens' in the late fifteenth and early sixteenth centuries. The building is unique; no other plausible explanation of it has been offered; and the purpose would be entirely consonant with Doket's work as a brilliant entrepreneur of royal patronage.[61] It seems likely that it was this lodging which in its turn inspired Fisher with the desire to be president of Queens' – an office that Margaret promptly and characteristically demanded for him. From 1505 to 1508 he was president, and then resigned.[62] The first surviving Queens' account book throws some light on the interesting question of how resident Fisher actually was. First of all, he took his stipend – or rather the half-stipend evidently due to a man normally non-resident; and it was usually paid via the vice-president, who evidently managed the continuum of residence and administration. There were three notable feasts each year, when the exequies of Doket and two other benefactors were celebrated, and of these nine possible occasions in the three years, Fisher was present only once – and that, also significantly, was in 1507, when the accounts show other expenses incurred by the president acting on college business and by the college in his entertainment. In 1504–5 he made a first visit as president; and we know that he came in 1506, and again in 1507, when he probably made his famous oration to the king, glorifying Cambridge, founded by Henry's predecessor King Cantaber – an alumnus ('it was said', as he had the grace to admit) of Athens.[63] In these years he was doubtless much involved in the foundation of Christ's; and we may suppose that the flurry of activity in 1507–8 recorded in the accounts was partly the fruit of a wish to do the college some service before he retired.[64] From 1508 he had no further need of lodging by the Cam, for he had ample chambers for his modest needs at Barnwell Gate, in the newly founded, or refounded, Christ's College.

He was chancellor from 1504–5 till his death in 1535, save for a brief pause in 1514 when he resigned and advised the University to elect Thomas Wolsey. Fisher saw clearly then which way the wind of patronage and power was blowing, and probably already knew that he and Wolsey, and the king, were not soul-mates.[65] But Wolsey refused and the University bound Fisher again to the task. There is a moving passage in E. E. Reynolds' life of Fisher in which he describes the 'tall, gaunt figure of the bishop' of Rochester as a familiar sight on the roads that led from Rochester to Cambridge.[66] Perhaps it was; but I have found little evidence of it. The early *Life* speaks of his dividing his time between London, Cambridge and his diocese, but in a context which is very generalised and mainly reflects his early years; and it occurs only in the English version of the *Life*.[67] He came to Cambridge in 1516 to the opening of St John's,[68] and it is likely that he had paid other visits before in that cause; but his main function in the founding of the College had been to struggle and fight, as Margaret's executor, to see her will and his carried out – and the arena was the royal court and the courts of justice, not Cambridge. After 1516 there is only one substantial piece of evidence of a visit to Cambridge known to me, and that is embedded in a passage in the

Life which mainly refers to his support of the Lady Margaret's work in his very early years as chancellor. Pope Leo X, we are told, issued an indulgence, and one Peter de Valence, led astray by Luther's teaching, secretly added a rude comment to a copy set up on the 'schoolegate' ('in portis scholarum'). The chancellor in person presided over a three-day congregation, and, when Peter failed to confess, he uttered a stern and solemn censure on the culprit; but Peter was obdurate, though much disturbed in conscience – he fled the city and served Goodrich, the 'superintendent' or pseudo-bishop of Ely.[69] This is doubtless a biassed account and chronologically confused: the indulgence seems to belong to Leo X and to 1521, and Goodrich became bishop of Ely (pseudo-bishop in papal eyes) only in 1534; but Peter of Valence really was his chaplain and it is most probable that we have here a genuine reminiscence, if garbled and tendentious in part, of an event of 1521 or soon after.[70] On the evidence of his register – from which a skeleton itinerary has been constructed[71] – the records of parliament and convocation and the like, we can show that a great part of his life was spent in his diocese, and some of it in Lambeth Marsh (his London residence) and Westminster. There are gaps indeed which would allow for visits to Cambridge from time to time, but we simply cannot tell – with this one exception – whether he used them so.

The evidence on which F. W. Steer and Gervase Jackson-Stops raised doubts whether William of Wykeham ever visited New College are the hall books, which are complete, and show no scent of an exceeding for a visit by the founder; the itinerary based on his register allows for some gaps when he might have slipped off to Oxford – but there is assuredly no indication now surviving that he did.[72] So far as I know, none of the four colleges in which Fisher was specially involved has records comparable to those of New College. But we have some hint in the proctors' accounts in the *Grace Books*. In 1507–8, when we know he was visiting Queens', the bellringer was paid 18d. 'for his laborious work in carrying seats from the schools to the [church of the] Austin Friars . . . and then to the Church of [Great] St Mary's . . . and back to the schools at the time of the sermons of the Observant Friar and the lord Chancellor' – and for 'bellringing for the friar's 15 sermons 15d.'.[73] We might hope to have similar indications later on of the chancellor's visits, but none have been found. This is not such peremptory negative evidence as the New College hall books, for the proctors' accounts pass over the visit of 1516 in silence.[74] We must not deduce from this silence that Fisher never came again to Cambridge. We simply do not know. It is probable that we should have some hint if his visits were frequent; and the proctors' books and other evidence show clearly that the University normally communicated with him by letter.[75] It is a likely conjecture that he grew increasingly aware of the distance that separated him from the Cambridge of his youth and his dreams; and the fierce anger he showed against the heretics of Cambridge, and against the University for harbouring them, may well have deterred him from coming in person.[76] It would be strange, however, if he did not from time to time make his presence felt as the clouds gathered in the 1520s. But, when a new cloud of deeper hue came to alienate him from the king for his loyalty to Queen Catherine, he may well not have wished to compromise his University by too evident a display of his presence. This is conjecture: I am not at all trying to say that he did not visit Cambridge much after 1508, and only very rarely after 1516; but only that we do not know, we have little evidence that he did.

The John Fisher who met the Lady Margaret in 1494–5 and entered her service a few years later was an ambitious young man of visions and dreams. He encouraged Margaret to take over Godshouse and refound it – though with due observance to Henry VI. He followed the example of John Alcock (another Beverley man of an earlier generation) in suppressing a religious house and making a college of it – the suppression of St John's Hospital seems to me no less high-handed, and no less sensible and admirable a measure, than the suppression of St Radegund's, after what look like exemplary steps not to reform it, and convert it into Jesus.[77] Fisher showed other signs of a readiness to do away with religious houses which he thought less worthy than St John's – thus, we may think, encouraging Wolsey a little in his more violent measures – which were in their turn to put into the receptive minds of Cromwell and Henry the notion of the holocaust. In these and various other ways John Fisher appears as a man of his times; and I am sure he shared in the high-handed notions of his patroness, so long as he was convinced of the rightness of the aim. But to pursue this any distance would be petty. For, whether he was right or wrong to care little for the rights of the poor of St John's or the nuns of Higham,[78] whether he was right or wrong to grasp at absentee offices in Cambridge while insisting that everyone else should reside, these are after all only examples of the conventional activities of his age. When we see him sustaining Queens' and raising Christ's and St John's, urging Margaret on to the support of preachers and readers – and fighting with the relentless obstinacy which alone could have succeeded to save St John's from extinction – and when we set these in their place in the vision of the collegiate University which emerged from this world – then we may see very clearly that he remains the greatest of the benefactors of the University and of all the colleges of that age for his role in the creation of Cambridge as we know it.

Yet that is all very well. As academics, we wish to know more: what vision of the academic society had he; what were his academic values, his role in the preservation of old traditions and the formation of new? – but to this deeper study Malcolm Underwood has already pointed the way.

Notes

1 I owe much to the generous help of Malcolm Underwood at every point in the preparation of this paper – I could not otherwise have undertaken it. I am also very grateful to John Twigg for his help on Fisher as president of Queens'; to Richard Rex (below, n. 70), David Smith (see below, notes 15, 29, 42), Nigel Yates, County Archivist of Kent, and the County Archivist and staff of the East Sussex Record Office at Lewes, where Fisher's Rochester register was on temporary deposit, for their help – see also below, n. 15.

2 C. N. L. Brooke, *A History of Gonville and Caius College* (Woodbridge, 1985), pp. 41–6; C. N. L. Brooke and J. R. L. Highfield, *Oxford and Cambridge* (Cambridge, 1988), pp. 138–56; on the academic aspect of the changes of this century, see especially D. R. Leader, 'The Study of Arts in Oxford and Cambridge at the end of the Middle Ages', University of Toronto Ph.D. thesis, 1981, and Dr Leader's general study of the University of Cambridge, *A History of the University of Cambridge: I, The University to 1546* (Cambridge, 1988); on the architectural history, *RCHM Cambridge*, and Willis and Clark; on churches and chapels, C. N. L. Brooke, 'The Churches of Medieval Cambridge', in D. Beales and G. Best (eds.), *History, Society and the Churches. Essays in Honour of Owen Chadwick* (Cambridge, 1985), pp. 49–76. On Queens' and Doket, see J. Twigg, *History of Queens' College* (Woodbridge, Suffolk, 1987) and W. G. Searle, *The History of the Queens' College* . . ., 2 vols. (Cambridge, 1867–71), but the interpretation of Doket is my own.

3 See the following by M. G. Underwood: 'Records of the Foundress', *The Eagle*, 68 (Easter 1979), 8–23; 'Behind the Early Statutes', *The Eagle*, 69 (Easter 1983), 3–9; 'The Lady Margaret and her Cambridge Connection', *Sixteenth Century Journal*, 13 (1982), 67–82; 'Politics and Piety in the Household of Lady Margaret Beaufort', *Journal of Ecclesiastical History*, 38 (1987), 39–52; A general account, M. Jones and M. Underwood, 'Lady Margaret Beaufort', *History Today*, 35 (August 1985), 23–30. Also unpublished studies which Malcolm Underwood has kindly shown me.

4 According to *DNB* (T. F. Tout), Margaret was born on 23 March 1430; other scholars have assumed that the year was 1429. 1430 is undoubtedly correct: see C. N. L. Brooke and V. Ortenberg, *Historical Research*, forthcoming.

5 See esp. M. G. Underwood, all titles above, note 3, and above, pp. 35–6, 44–5, and references.

6 See R. Lovatt, 'John Blacman: Biographer of Henry VI', in R. H. C. Davis and J. M. Wallace-Hadrill (eds.), *The Writing of History in the Middle Ages: Essays Presented to Richard William Southern* (Oxford, 1981), pp. 415–44, esp. pp. 420–2.

7 On Redman see meanwhile Brooke and Highfield, *Oxford and Cambridge*, pp. 152–3; Brooke, *Gonville and Caius*, pp. 47, 52–3; A. B. Cobban, *The King's Hall within the University of Cambridge in the Later Middle Ages* (Cambridge, 1969); and especially above, pp. 41, 46 n. 71 (M. Underwood). For Fisher and Michaelhouse see below, n. 15.

8 See n. 3; M. Rubin, *Charity and Community in Medieval Cambridge* (Cambridge, 1986).

9 See above, pp. 25–46.

10 Willis and Clark; *RCHM Cambridge*; N. Pevsner, *The Buildings of England, Cambridgeshire*, 2nd edn (Harmondsworth, 1970); cf. Brooke, *Gonville and Caius*, pp. 44–6.

11 Cf. Brooke and Highfield, *Oxford and Cambridge*, pp. 108–13, 150–1, 215–16.

12 *Documents*, I, 311, c. 8; I have checked the texts by all the surviving statute books. The earliest statutes of the thirteenth century, discovered by M. B. Hackett in Rome and published in *The Original Statutes of Cambridge University* (Cambridge, 1970), ch. 7, give no residence rules for the chancellor; the version of *c.* 1304–37 in Markaunt's book (probably written *c.* 1417–18), does not allow absence of more than one month 'in uno termino' (Hackett, *Original Statutes*, p. 315; cf. pp. 240ff, 309–11). The definitive version current in Fisher's time, represented by the version of *c.* 1385 in the Old Proctor's Book and Gonville and Caius MS 706/692, and the Senior and Junior Proctors' Books of the late fifteenth century, and printed in *Documents*, I, 311, does not allow him to be absent more than a month 'citra cessatione magistrorum', which evidently means 'before the end of lectures in the Easter Term' (thus *Documents*, I, 311 n., evidently correctly: Caius MS 706/692, II, fos. 1v–2; Cambridge University Library, CUA, Coll. Admin. 7, fo. 45v (Markaunt); 3, fo. 18 (Old Proctor); 1, part II, fo. 2r–v (Senior Proctor); 2, fo. 57 (Junior Proctor); the variants are trivial and do not affect the sense). The Junior Proctor's Book is dated 1494–6 by Hackett (p. 290 n. – cf. ch. 11 as a whole) and may have been written when Fisher was senior proctor; the Senior Proctor is dated by Hackett *c.* 1496–1502 (p. 294 and n.) and both belong to the period of Fisher's most active administrative work in Cambridge.

13 See the dedicatory letter (1526) to Fox of his *De Veritate Corporis et Sanguinis Christi . . . Aduersus Iohannem Oecolampadium, Opera*, pp. 746–7; cf. Lewis, *Fisher*, I, 14–15.

14 *VCH Cambs*, III, 472–3; A. E. Stamp, *Michaelhouse* (privately printed, Cambridge, 1924), p. 50. Both are given as masters in *Life*, X, 205–8; but see n. 15.

15 Trinity College, Michaelhouse Muniments, Otryngham Book, p. 71, has a list of masters of Michaelhouse in a series of contemporary hands of the fifteenth and early sixteenth centuries. There is a minor erasure in a somewhat earlier entry; but it is clear that no erasure can explain Fisher's absence, and it seems almost inconceivable that a whole series of names could have been added before his disgrace without anyone noticing that he was missing – it would mean that the man who was throughout the last thirty years of his life the most famous product of Michaelhouse had been forgotten there. It is hard to believe that Fisher was master of Michaelhouse. He was certainly a fellow from 1490–1. Archivio Segreto Vaticano, Reg. Lat. 908, fo. 70r–v shows that he had been fellow for less than a year on 14 June 1491; in December that year he was ordained on the title of his fellowship: York, Borthwick Institute, Reg. 23 (Rotherham), fo. 429v. I owe these references to Miri Rubin, Malcolm Underwood and David Smith. See also Emden, *Cambridge*, p. 229.

16 *VCH Cambs*, III, 331–3; see below, pp. 233–4.

17 Brooke, *Gonville and Caius*, pp. 10–11.

18 H. C. Porter, *Reform and Reaction in Tudor Cambridge* (Cambridge, 1958), pp. 112–15 and *passim*; cf. Brooke, *Gonville and Caius*, pp. 70–3, 87–8, 91–3.

19 See A. C. Chibnall, *Richard de Badew and the University of Cambridge, 1315–1340* (Cambridge, 1963).

20 Brooke, *Gonville and Caius*, pp. 38–9; Emden, *Cambridge*, p. 23; C. Hall and C. Brooke, 'The Masters of Gonville Hall', *The Caian* (1983), p. 46.

21 Emden, *Cambridge*, pp. 351–2; cf. *VCH Cambs*, III, 376, for his role in the founding of King's.

22 On the Booths, see C. N. L. Brooke, 'The Earliest Times to 1485', in W. R. Matthews and W. M. Atkins (eds.), *A History of St Paul's Cathedral* (London, 1957), pp. 45, 63–4, 91–6; on Lawrence, 'the only Lancastrian bishop . . . promoted to a higher see' by Edward IV, see C. Ross, *Edward IV* (London, 1974), p. 318 (cf. pp. 45, 313); Emden, *Cambridge*, pp. 78–9; *DNB* (T. F. Tout); R. J. Knecht, 'The Episcopate and the Wars of the Roses', *University of Birmingham Historical Journal*, 6 (1958), 109, 115–16; R. L. Storey, *The End of the House of Lancaster* (London, 1966), pp. 181, 183.

23 Emden, *Cambridge*, pp. 78–9; cf. A. L. Attwater, *Pembroke College, Cambridge* (Cambridge, 1936), pp. 20–3; *VCH Cambs*, III, 348.

24 On Queens', see Twigg, *History of Queens' College*, pp. 6, 64–6; Searle, *Queens' College*, especially I, 87–101 for the benefactions of Richard III, lost to the College in 1485 – but Doket was so fortunate as to die in 1484.

25 Emden, *Cambridge*, pp. 645–6; A. B. Cobban, 'Origins; Robert Wodelarke and St Catharine's', in E. E. Rich (ed.), *St Catharine's College, Cambridge, 1473–1973* (Cambridge, 1973), pp. 1–32.

26 Emden, *Cambridge*, pp. 489–91; *DNB*.

27 See the papal dispensation in Archivio Segreto Vaticano, Reg. Lat. 908, fo. 70r–v.

28 York, Borthwick Institute, Reg. 23 (Rotherham), fo. 429v; for the bishop of Dromore's ordinations, see ibid., fos. 372–468 – references kindly provided by David Smith.

29 David Smith has kindly verified this for York; for Ely, I have checked Cambridge University Library, Ely Diocesan Records, G/1/6, fos. 223–52 (ordinations, 1486–1500).

30 Emden, *Cambridge*, pp. 489–91.

31 Ibid., pp. 239–41, 412–14, 231. Sever is a puzzle: see below, p. 234. He is not in Emden, *Cambridge*, who makes Thomas Ruthall chancellor in 1503, but *Grace Book B*, I, 184, to which he refers, specifically makes the bishop of Durham, i.e. Sever, chancellor.

32 *Grace Book B*, I, 203: see below, p. 234. The entry (by analogy with similar ones elsewhere in the *Grace Book*) probably means he was bishop before he was elected chancellor; the marginal note giving the date October 1504 may well refer to his papal provision to the see. But the Michaelmas term 1504 is the earliest, and perhaps the most likely, date for this entry referring to him as chancellor or chancellor elect, and we can safely date his election to 1504 or 1505.

33 See above, n. 13.

34 *VCH Oxford*, III, 38–9, compared with Emden, *Oxford*. For Kymer, Emden, *Oxford*, II, 1068–9.

35 For what follows see G. Keir, 'The Ecclesiastical Career of George Neville, 1432–1476', Oxford B.Litt. thesis, 1970; Emden, *Oxford*, II, 1347–9. He was probably born in Oct.–Nov. 1432, and so was only twenty when he took the chancellor's oath on 9 June 1453 (Keir, 'George Neville', p. 37).

36 Keir, 'George Neville', p. 52, citing M. R. James, *A Descriptive Catalogue of the*

Manuscripts in the Library of Corpus Christi College, Cambridge (Cambridge, 1912), II, 324.

37 Emden, *Oxford*, III, 1609–11 (Russell); II, 1318–20 (Morton).

38 Emden, *Oxford*, III, 1988–92.

39 G. F. Lytle, 'Patronage Patterns and Oxford Colleges c. 1300–c. 1530', in L. Stone (ed.), *The University in Society*, 2 vols. (Princeton, 1975), I, 111–49; cf. T. H. Aston, G. D. Duncan and T. A. R. Evans, 'The Medieval Alumni of the University of Cambridge', *Past and Present*, 86 (1980), pp. 68–84; and especially the cautious but penetrating study of Jean Dunbabin, 'Careers and Vocations', in J. I. Catto (ed.), *The History of the University of Oxford*, I, *The Early Oxford Schools* (Oxford, 1984), pp. 565–605. Professor Lytle's valuable study seems to convert perennial anxiety, and the fluctuations it engenders, into patterns of 'crisis'; and to depend on evidence too defective for his more ambitious purposes. For the begging letters, see *Epistolae Academicae*, ed. H. Anstey, 2 vols. (Oxford Historical Society, 1898–9), esp. nos. 123–5, 143–4, 152, 175, 180.

40 See J. A. Robson, *Wyclif and the Oxford Schools* (Cambridge, 1961), pp. 240–6. For numbers at Cambridge, see Aston, Duncan and Evans, 'Medieval Alumni', pp. 11–27. For what follows – especially on Cromwell as chancellor – see G. R. Elton, *Reform and Renewal: Thomas Cromwell and the Common weal* (Cambridge, 1973), pp. 31–7.

41 See C. N. L. Brooke and G. Keir, *London 800–1216, the Shaping of a City* (London, 1975), pp. 310–12 and references; and for cathedral residence, and what follows, K. Edwards, *The English Secular Cathedrals in the Middle Ages*, 2nd edn (Manchester, 1967), ch. 1; Brooke, 'The Earliest Times to 1485', pp. 38–57, esp. 52–4, 365, for the measures of Urban V; for early residence cf. also D. Greenway, 'The false *Institutio* of St. Osmund', in D. Greenway, C. Holdsworth, and J. Sayers (eds.), *Tradition and Change: Essays in Honour of Marjorie Chibnall* (Cambridge, 1985), pp. 91–2. For the prebendaries of Masham, see J. Le Neve, *Fasti Ecclesiae Anglicanae 1300–1541*, 12 vols., VI (London, 1963), 66–8.

42 York, Borthwick Institute, Reg. 23 (Rotherham), fo. 165v (cf. Reg. 25, fo. 64, for his successor – refs. kindly supplied by David Smith). He was presented to Lythe (Cleveland, North Yorks.) by Sir Ralph Bigod; his successor was presented by the Lady Margaret. It is valued in the *Taxatio . . . Papae Nicholai* of 1291, Record Commission, London (1802), p. 301, at £33 6s 8d; in the *Valor Ecclesiasticus* of 1535, Record Commission, 5 (1825), p. 90, at £34 4s 0d net (£59 gross). On the rectory of Lythe, see J. Graves, *The History of Cleveland* (Carlisle, 1808; repr. Stockton-on-Tees, 1972), pp. 307–8.

43 For Nicholas Metcalf as archdeacon, 1512–37, see Le Neve, *Fasti*, IV, 42; Reg. Fisher, fos. 60r–v, 63, 72v; cf. fo. 48; as master, Emden, *Cambridge*, p. 403, and above, pp. 37, 40.

44 Emden, *Cambridge*, pp. 605–6; cf. Brooke, *Gonville and Caius*, p. 27.

45 *Wykeham's Register*, ed. T. F. Kirby (London and Winchester, 1899), II, 621–9; G. Jackson-Stops, 'The Architecture of the College', in J. Buxton and P. Williams (eds.), *New College Oxford, 1379–1979* (Oxford, 1979), p. 157.

46 D. Wilkins, *Concilia Magnae Britanniae*, 4 vols. (London, 1737 edn), I, 500–1; Ralph de Diceto, *Opera Historica*, ed. W. Stubbs (Rolls Series, 1876), I, lxix–lxxiii. For what follows, Brooke, 'The Earliest Times to 1485', pp. 40–1, 60–4, 86–90.

47 *EW*, p. 77. Statutes of St John's allow absences, apart from college business or real necessity, of one month per quarter in 1516 (following the Lady Margaret's statutes for Christ's); 60 days a year in 1524; 28 days a year in 1530; Mayor, *Statutes*, pp. 352–3, 265, 14. For Christ's, *Early Statutes of Christ's College*, ed. H. Rackham (Cambridge, 1927), pp. 46–7 – the statute for St John's of 1516 is almost identical.

48 M. Bowker, *The Henrician Reformation* (Cambridge, 1981), pp. 45, 199; E. Miller, *Portrait of a College* (Cambridge, 1961), p. 8.

49 Emden, *Oxford*, III, 2077–80.

50 See above, n. 13.

51 Emden, *Oxford*, II, 715–19; Emden, *Cambridge*, pp. 239–41.

52 *Handbook of British Chronology*, 2nd edn, ed. F. M. Powicke and E. B. Fryde (Royal Historical Society, London, 1961), pp. 258–9.

53 Brooke, 'The Earliest Times to 1485', pp. 83–4.

54 Lewis, *Fisher*, II, 16 and n.; see, above, n. 13, for his contentment with his see.

55 Emden, *Cambridge*, pp. 229–30; *Grace Book B*, I, 67–78, 156, 162 (D.D. 5 July, Vice-Chancellor 15 July 1501). Humphrey Fitzwilliam was elected vice-chancellor on 13 October 1502, *Grace Book B*, I, 176; cf. Emden, *Cambridge*, p. 233. It is probably significant that the earliest surviving Register of Wills (1501–58) of the vice-chancellor's court opens when Fisher was vice-chancellor: Cambridge UL, CUA, Vice-Chancellor's Court.

56 *Grace Book B*, I, 68.

57 *Grace Book B*, I, 162; Emden, *Cambridge*, p. 229.

58 *Early Statutes of Christ's College*, ed. H. Rackham, pp. 52–3; cf. Willis and Clark, II, 212–18; *RCHM Cambridge*, I. 33.

59 Willis and Clark, II, 282–6; above, p. 34; Mayor, *Statutes*, pp. 254–6, gives the arrangements made for his trentals and exequies – never, sadly, put into effect.

60 Willis and Clark, II, 13–14; *RCHM Cambridge*, II, 176. Its limits of date are given as 1448 and 1494, but it is identical in style with the old court and surely mid fifteenth century in date.

61 Above, p. 47; cf. Twigg, *History of Queens' College*, pp. 130–1.

62 Twigg, *History of Queens' College*, pp. 13–19, 67; Searle, *Queens' College*, I, 131–43; for what follows, Cambridge UL, Queens' College Muniments, Book 1, fos. 173–96.

63 See below pp. 236, 237; Queens' College Muniments, Book 1, fo. 194r–v; *Grace Book B*, I, 203; Lewis, *Fisher*, I, 19, II, 267. For the date of Henry VII's visit, see above, p. 43 n. 22. Queens' College Muniments, Book 1, fo. 194, shows him present, in 1507, at John Aswell's exequies, the precise date of which I have not been able to ascertain.

64 Queens' College Muniments, Book 1, fos. 194v–196.

65 Emden, *Cambridge*, p. 229; cf. Lewis, *Fisher*, I, 44–7, II, 282–6.

66 E. E. Reynolds, *St John Fisher*, 2nd edn (Wheathampstead, 1972), p. 45.

67 *Life*, X, 252–3.

68 Lewis, *Fisher*, pp. 52–3; below, p. 241.

69 *Life*, X, 229–35; for 'schoolegate', see p. 230.

70 *Life*, X, 229–35; Van Ortroy's note, p. 229, suggests a date of 1525–30. But Richard Rex has suggested to me that it is much more likely to be related to the

excommunication of Luther by Leo X, which was published in England c. May–June 1521. For Peter of Valence, see C. H. and T. Cooper, *Athenae Cantabrigienses* (Cambridge, 1858), I, 155. He seems to have started his academic career in Gonville Hall (1521–4): see J. Venn, *Biographical History of Gonville and Caius College*, I (Cambridge, 1897), pp. 25–6: 'Peter Devall'.

71 See below, pp. 235–49.

72 See above, n. 45.

73 *Grace Book B*, I, 230.

74 *Grace Book B*, II, 39–50. There is a reference in a letter of Fisher dated from Rochester on 20 October of a year unknown – but possibly in the late 1510s – to the bishop's last visit to Cambridge; this could refer back to the visit of 1516, but there are too many conjectures involved in these dates to lay any weight on its evidence: see G. J. Grey, 'Letters of Bishop Fisher 1521–3', *The Library*, 3rd series, 4 (1913), 133–45, at 134–5.

75 *Grace Book B*, I and II, Index *s.v.* Fisher.

76 See above, pp. 39–40.

77 *VCH Cambs*, III, 421, 429–30; A. H. Lloyd, *The Early History of Christ's College, Cambridge* (Cambridge, 1934), especially chs. 16 and 19.

78 For the poor of St John's Hospital see especially Rubin, *Charity and Community in Medieval Cambridge* (Cambridge, 1986); for Higham, see above, p. 36: it was suppressed and granted to St John's – but only after what seem to have been prolonged efforts to reform it.

The bishop in his diocese

STEPHEN THOMPSON

The study of John Fisher's episcopate is of unusual interest. Its length alone was remarkable enough by medieval standards, being exceeded at Rochester by only one bishop, Hamo de Hethe (1319–52). More important still, Fisher was one of the few of any generation to be hailed in his own lifetime as a model bishop. The great humanist scholar Desiderius Erasmus commented in a letter to his friend Reuchlin in 1520, 'Episcopus ille anglus, quo non alius in ea gente vel eruditor vir, vel praesul sanctior.'[1] Erasmus was not alone in his opinion. In 1537 Reginald Pole, admittedly partisan, wrote to Henry VIII in his *De Unitate Ecclesiae*,

What other have you, or have you had for centuries, to compare with Rochester in holiness, in learning, in prudence and in episcopal zeal? You may be, indeed, proud of him, for, were you to search through all the nations of Christendom in our days, you would not easily find one who was such a model of episcopal virtues.[2]

Seventy years later Cardinal Borromeo was to keep a portrait of Fisher in his study and venerate it equally with that of St Ambrose, founder of his diocese of Milan.[3] In addition to this praise, we are fortunate enough to have detailed descriptions of him and appraisals of his life written by contemporaries and by one who had access to people who knew him. Even allowing for the fact that we are dealing with Fisher's friends, fellow-Catholics and defenders of the papal supremacy, the extent to which Fisher is praised, not for his controversial writings, nor for his stand against Henry, but simply for his holiness of life and devotion to his diocese, is remarkable. It should, of course, be added that, but for his execution, much of this material would not have been written, and that the terms which are employed are, for the most part, the staple of lives of the saints, which in turn were simply an embellishment of the ideal bishop St Paul depicts in his letter to Timothy:

Oportet episcopem esse irreprehensibilem: sobrium, pudicum, ornatum, prudentem, doctorem, modestum, non violentum, non percussorem, non litigiosum, non cupidum, sed modestum cum castitate.[4]

Further interest is added to the study of Fisher's episcopate by the fact that, along with Alcock of Ely and Longland of Lincoln, he is one of the few bishops in the early sixteenth century to have expressed his views on the subject of the pastoral role of the clergy.[5] Perhaps it comes as no surprise to find in Fisher a deep commitment to the divinely ordained hierarchical order in Church and state. At the same time it is also clear that this view went hand in hand with high ideals of pastoral service based on the Pauline model mentioned above. Indeed, Fisher tended to emphasise the episcopal role as shepherd rather than ruler and judge.[6] In his sermons on the Penitential Psalms he maintained that all clergy had to teach the laws of God to the people or they would be damned: the clergy must set a good example to the rest.[7] Again, in the preface to his *Assertionis Lutheranae Confutatio* of 1523, Fisher, in a rare dismissive moment, said there was no hope of saving Luther but, as a bishop, it was his duty to help weaker souls whose faith was in doubt (on a knife's edge, as he put it) and who could veer towards either the Fathers and the Church or Luther.[8] In the *Defence of the Sacred Priesthood* Fisher reiterated the need for a group of people set apart from the whole multitude who would bear responsibility for the masses. The priesthood – and, it followed, the episcopate – was a vocation and, in line with the Pauline model, Fisher saw that preaching and education in the broader sense was a fundamental part of the bishop's role, equal in importance to supervisory and sacerdotal duties.[9] A. H. Thompson, in his masterly study of the clergy of the late middle ages, acknowledges that such a 'benignant idea of a father in God and a shepherd of souls' existed in theory, but the prevailing aspect of episcopal paternity amongst the late medieval episcopate was the 'spirit of correction', not compassion.[10]

All of this serves to pose a number of basic questions. What was the relationship between Fisher's high episcopal reputation and the reality? How far did his own performance in his diocese match the high ideal of the episcopal office articulated so clearly in his commentaries and sermons? Finally, and bearing in mind A. H. Thompson's comments above, how did Fisher the pastor compare with his fellows on the bench? These are the questions to which this study is ultimately addressed. For clarity, Fisher's episcopate will be examined under seven aspects. A study of the diocese of Rochester itself is followed by an examination of Fisher's predecessors and successors in the bishopric in order to place him in some broader context. Then, using the diocesan registers and court books from Rochester (both comparatively full by late medieval standards), the study will examine Fisher's record of residence in the diocese, his use of patronage, his role in the supervision of the clergy and laity, his participation in those sacraments and duties reserved to bishops and, finally, his charitable works. In order to establish just how exceptional Fisher was as a diocesan, contemporary material from a wide range of other dioceses will also be used.

John Fisher was provided to the see of Rochester in October 1504 and consecrated in Lambeth Palace chapel on 24 November at the same time as William Barons of London, with bishops Smith and Nykke assisting

Archbishop Warham.[11] Fisher was then enthroned in his cathedral of Rochester by proxy on 24 April 1505 – not an unusual occurrence but one which is perhaps a little out of character with this particular bishop.[12] According to Harpsfield's life of More, Fisher owed his promotion to Margaret, mother of Henry VII, although Fisher himself attributed it to the prompting of Bishop Richard Fox, and it would seem that Henry had his mother's confessor in mind before he raised the matter with her; 'for none other cause, but for the great and singular virtue that I know and see in him, as well in cunning and natural wisdom, and specially for his good and virtuous living and conversation'.[13] The anonymous early *Life* of Fisher remarks that he was reluctant to accept the dignity. The refusal could have been something more than the traditional 'nolo episcopari' as the biography also mentions the fact that Fox had to persuade Fisher to take on the diocese,[14] and this receives some support from Fisher's own claim in 1527 that Fox had, in fact, recommended him from the start to Henry VII.[15] Whatever the circumstances, it was a natural promotion for a royal chaplain and confessor of some academic and theological distinction.

The diocese to which Fisher was appointed was, according to the *Valor Ecclesiasticus* of 1535, the poorest of English dioceses and also the smallest in terms of area. Only two dioceses had fewer parishes. The bishop could expect about £411 per annum. By comparison, the diocese of Ely was worth about £2,134, and the nearest in income to Rochester was Chichester, whose bishop received about £670 a year in 1533.[16] These dioceses were, however, either much larger than Rochester in terms of numbers of parishes or in area, or they covered particularly inaccessible terrain. In 1535 Rochester had only 123 parishes. This compares with 134 at Ely (60 per cent larger in area and prone to drastic flooding), 278 at Chichester (three times larger in area), 694 at York (sixteen times larger in area), and 1,736 parishes in Lincoln (fourteen times larger in area).[17] Further, the diocese of Rochester, in common with many southern province dioceses, had relatively small parishes, about 5 square miles each on average, compared to parishes of anything between 12 and 70 square miles in the three mountainous, sprawling dioceses of the Northern province. Rochester in Fisher's episcopate also had 20 religious houses, including the Benedictine cathedral priory. This was a high number considering the size of the diocese, although not all of them were either large or subject to episcopal visitation. By way of comparison, Chichester and Ely had only 11 religious houses each, York over 70 and Lincoln some 111 subject to episcopal jurisdiction. Rochester was, then, a small, accessible diocese with few parishes, but with a sufficient number of religious houses to indicate that a diligent bishop might spend a large proportion of his time dealing with regular clergy. The diocese did not cover any difficult terrain, although the existence of ports and proximity to the continent meant that in our period heresy took up more of the bishop's time than, for example, it did in Northern dioceses.[18] Although it had a low income, costs in hospitality resulting from royal and gentry visits were not likely to be particularly high, given the humble accommodation available and the proximity of the wealthy dioceses of London, Winchester and Canterbury.[19]

In view of the modesty of the promotion represented, it is probably no accident that appointees to Rochester tended to be theologians rather than canonists in the period 1400–1600. Fisher's immediate predecessor, Fitzjames, and his immediate successor, Hilsey, were both theologians, though neither had Fisher's academic ability nor his close connections with the court.[20] Fitzjames had an Oxford background, was an active preacher and served on diplomatic missions. Hilsey was an obscure Augustinian friar who came to prominence as an active preacher on behalf of the Reformation. Fisher was also unusual in another way. Eight out of fourteen bishops in the period 1400–1504 were translated to bigger, wealthier dioceses and six of these were subsequently translated to larger dioceses yet again. Eight out of twelve of Fisher's successors up to 1605 were also translated to larger dioceses. Alcock, for instance, was translated to Worcester in 1476 then Ely in 1486, Savage to London in 1496 then to York in 1500, Fitzjames to Chichester in 1503 then London in 1506. If Fisher was atypical in staying in the diocese for thirty years, there is at least an indication that he was offered other dioceses. The early *Life* mentions Lincoln (1514?) and Ely (1506? 1515?).[21] In the preamble to the 1516 statutes of St John's college, Fisher himself said that the Lady Margaret had wanted him to have a greater bishopric but she died before being able to realise her wish, and instead left him money for his new foundation.[22] It is, perhaps, easy to account for his refusal of Lincoln if he were offered it – it was an enormous diocese in which fulfilment of the Pauline ideals would prove very difficult. On the other hand, Ely contained his well-beloved Cambridge and was not a large diocese. Whatever the truth of these suggestions, it seems clear that Fisher was content with Rochester, which yielded a sufficient income to enable him to live in accordance with his own austere ideal without squandering his income on ornaments, splendid vestments, or other worldly goods.

What, then, of Fisher's fulfilment of his office? The major interest of a study of Fisher's episcopate lies, of course, in the extent to which he succeeded in putting the ideal that he preached into practice. Bearing in mind his association with Northern humanism and the significance of his academic connections with, and chancellorship of, Cambridge, a further question can be asked. Was he a reforming bishop and, if so, in what way?

The apostolic ideal clearly required a resident bishop, and canon law was specific in that it required bishops to visit their cathedral churches in Lent and Easter.[23] In the fifteenth century Gascoigne had thought episcopal residence necessary in order that hospitality could be maintained in a diocese, a view shared by some of Fisher's contemporaries.[24] Fisher's attitude to residence was embodied in his own statutes for St John's; it was, quite simply, 'suitable for the head to be united and associated with the rest of the members'.[25] In his sermons on the Penitential Psalms Fisher noted that when bishops were absent from their dioceses, souls fell to the devil.[26] In the early biography we are told that Fisher disliked being summoned away from his flock to state affairs,[27] and it is clear from the late Fr Surtz's treatment of Fisher's views on authority in the Church that, logically, there could be no defensible alternative to residence. We are fortunate in being able to reconstruct Fisher's itinerary in reasonable detail for all of his episcopate (see Appendix 2). This suggests that he was present in his diocese for about 90 per cent of the period December 1504 to 1534, after which he was imprisoned: of about 430 references to Fisher's whereabouts, about 350 refer to his diocese. The bishop made full use of his manors of Bromley and Halling and occasionally the convent of West Malling. After about 1515, and apart from visitation, parliament and Convocation periods, he confined himself more to Malling and especially to Rochester. Unlike the other bishops who held dioceses with monastic cathedral chapters, and unlike his predecessor, Fitzjames,[28] Fisher resided in his cathedral city in the palace which used to exist between the cathedral and the river. This was built in about 1450 by Bishop Low and fell into disuse and ruin after Fisher's episcopate.[29] The early *Life* says he had a special window knocked into the cathedral so that he could watch and hear mass when not himself celebrating.[30] However that may be, the extent to which a bishop did alter his manors can be taken as a measure of his attachment to the diocese. From slender evidence, it appears Fisher maintained his oft-frequented manors well. For example, in 1511, to the evident pride and satisfaction of his registrar, he had the wall around Lambeth Marsh palace rebuilt.[31] When, in 1534, royal commissioners ransacked his palace at Rochester, they found £300 which had traditionally been transferred from one bishop to the next for dilapidations and Fisher had added a further £100 to this.[32] The transfer of such funds was also common practice at Canterbury, London and Hereford, and its confiscation might well account for the complaints from Fisher's successor concerning the upkeep of buildings.[33]

Fisher allowed few distractions to keep him away from his diocese. Apart from parliament and convocation times, he seems to have visited London only to preach after the first years of his episcopate following the Lady Margaret's death. His visits to Cambridge, despite his interests there, were infrequent, and state events such as the Field of the Cloth of Gold (1520) and the visit of the Emperor Charles V (1522) were of short duration, [34] the latter taking him only to Canterbury and so causing him a minimum of inconvenience (and expense – that was largely Henry VIII's and Warham's headache).[35] Comparison suggests that Fisher's residence record was better than that of most of his contemporaries (Appendix 3), although it must be stressed that the calculation of residence can only be, at best, very approximate for most dioceses. Fisher was, however, mobile in his admittedly small diocese, unlike a number of older bishops who spent a lot of time in their dioceses but do not *seem* to have moved around very much, e.g. Audley of Salisbury or even Fox of Winchester after 1515. Although this does not necessarily mean that these bishops were neglectful of their duties, we can make one very obvious point: Fisher's continued residence and mobility in his diocese gave him ample opportunity for close supervision of his cure and reform of it when and where necessary.

Next after residence perhaps the most vital requirement for a bishop closely involved with his diocese was to appoint clergy of good quality. Indeed, as a reflection of this importance, appointments to benefices have left the greatest mark on most diocesan records. Rochester had 123 parishes but the bishop could appoint to only twenty of these, which included only three vicarages (Appendix 4). Nevertheless, a high proportion of the bishop's patronage was based on parochial, as opposed to prebendal, livings (Appendix 4, column 5) and this, combined with the fact that they commanded 20 per cent of all parochial patronage, meant that he was, like most bishops elsewhere, the single most influential patron in his diocese.[36]

In thirty-one years Fisher made a total of sixty-seven collations, nine of them *per lapsum*. Half of these were on behalf of graduates as compared with only 21 per cent of the 246 clergy he instituted for their patrons. In this respect Fisher was no different to many other bishops in other dioceses – graduates throughout the country sought out the bishops as the patrons who were most likely to give them good livings.[37] Fisher's appointees to rectories were probably no more or less reliable in appointing diligent curates to benefices than those of other bishops, although, because of their relatively low value – less than £20 per benefice on average – the Rochester livings did not attract the worst of the pluralists. Fisher used his patronage in a very conventional way to reward his diocesan administrators, such as Nicholas Metcalfe, who resided at Hoo vicarage for a couple of years before becoming the first master of St John's.[38] Further evidence that Fisher had a flexible view on non-residence in parish livings is provided by the fact that he acquired the patronage of livings specifically to reward his administrators. In 1531, he completed negotiations to take over the patronage of Ipstock, Leicestershire – thus giving his episcopal colleague at Lincoln all the potential problems of non-residence.[39] He was, however, diligent in examining other patrons' candidates for livings. In November 1508, he refused a living to Hugh Yardeley as he was unsuitable and unlearned and told him to go to a grammar school for a year. Refusals to admit to livings, or conditional admissions, are recorded from a number of dioceses and, as the evidence is not always based on registers, it seems reasonable to assume that they were more frequent than would at first appear. It is worth pointing out that even clergy admitted by Fisher could, in later years, fall foul of the authorities. One parish priest instituted by Fisher was later cited for non-residence by Bishop Holbeach. Fisher could also be malleable. In 1523 he appointed one of Princess Mary's chaplains to Reddersfield at the king's request, also granting the advowson for a turn. By 1532, with royal divorce proceedings well under way, the bishop was perhaps less well disposed towards the king, and he refused to appoint one Christopher Nelson to West Greenwich, in the king's patronage. Nelson had been expelled from Winchester diocese in 1528 by Bishop Fox for making indecent advances to a widow. Although, therefore, Fisher's refusal to appoint him would seem soundly based, within a few weeks Nelson had found a Rochester living, illustrating how broader political interests could overshadow pastoral needs and moral standards.[40]

Fisher was particularly careful to examine new appointees to the mastership of Strood hospital, and on each occasion the registrar recorded the appointment in particular detail. He was, as far as the records show, unique in the attention he paid to the personnel of his own cathedral priory, probably because he lived so close to it. In November 1508 he chose his own cathedral prior, William Fressell, a monk of St Albans, *per devolutionem*, as the chapter could not agree on a candidate. Fisher had gone out of his way to choose somebody suitable. Perhaps Fressell had come to his attention the previous year whilst passing through Hertfordshire.[41] In any case the move paid off as the two worked well together on heresy examinations, elections, institutions and, perhaps, ordination examination.[42] Fisher also demonstrated more than the usual concern, and control, over the election of the other monastic officers: he took their professions in person, as he did all regulars and hermits in the diocese.[43] In one case we have an indication of how closely a resident bishop could monitor his priory. In October 1522 Laurence Merworth, 'lately cellarer, through our suggestion freed from office' was readmitted after 'certain considerations' – ill health had perhaps disabled Merworth for a time. Merworth gave good service which even Fisher's reforming successor, Hilsey, acknowledged. By then he had resigned his ultimate office of prior but Hilsey wrote to Cromwell saying he would like him back as there was chaos in the priory.[44]

Fisher clearly favoured the regular clergy, more so than one would expect from a secular bishop. When Lesnes Abbey was dissolved in August 1525 to endow Wolsey's Cardinal College, it was done with Fisher's consent, and he then appointed the last abbot, William Tisehurst, to several livings and made him his chaplain.[45] One further point emphasises the conventionality of Fisher's approach in his use of patronage. He was quite happy to issue dispensations to hold plural livings or dispensations to receive orders below the canonical minimum age (the latter not surprising in view of his own career).[46] In one case, George Cromer, archbishop of Armagh, was allowed to hold four livings including the mastership of Cobham College. Fisher stressed that a resident must in turn be appointed by the archbishop, and it was common that such livings should provide revenue for non-resident pluralists in many dioceses. This makes the fact that Strood Hospital was never given to a non-resident all the more notable – Fisher's regular contact with the hospital perhaps made him less inclined to treat it in the same way other bishops treated prebendal livings.[47]

Turning now to examine Fisher's performance in the sphere of discipline, it is clear that he placed considerable emphasis on visitation of his diocese. According to the early *Life*, supervision and correction of both clergy and laity was a high priority for Fisher:

And first, because there is small hope of healthe in the membres of yt bodie where the head is sicke he began his visitacion at his head church of Rochester, calling before him the pryors [sic] and the mounkes, exhortinge them to obedience, chastitie and true observacion of their monasticall vows; and where any fault was tryed, he caused it to be amended. After that he carefully visited the rest of the parish churches within his diocesse in his owne person; and sequestring all such as he found unworthie to occupie that high function, he placed other fitter in their roomes . . .[48]

The register bears out much of this. Fisher certainly carried out all his triennial visitations in person up to that of 1523, and it is probable that this and those of 1529 and 1531 were also carried out by him and he heard some abjurations in person.[49] Little visitation material survives, but the significant point is that Fisher was personally involved, unlike many of his colleagues. In 1498 even the diligent Fitzjames had commissioned others to carry out visitations at Rochester – although he did carry out the 1502 visitation himself.[50] Indeed, of 144 bishops holding English and Welsh sees between 1500 and 1560 only thirty are definitely known to have conducted their own visitations *or* to have presided in their own consistory courts (there are, however, only thirteen dioceses from which we have any information, and chance survival of records must be taken into account here).[51] Fisher would have had little difficulty in conducting the visitation of Rochester in person – 123 parishes in four deaneries could be covered in perhaps three days or so, if the visitations under Bishop Cox of Ely in the 1560s are used as a guide.[52] Most of the follow-up to visitation was not conducted by Fisher himself but by his commissaries. This was the norm for most dioceses and in the sixteenth century, even in Elizabeth's reign, few bishops conducted consistory court work in person, although exceptional cases might merit a bishop's attention. For example in 1511, presiding in consistory, Fisher absolved a priest from contumacy and, notwithstanding, suspended him.[53]

Heresy cases nearly always attracted Fisher's personal attention, as was the case with many other bishops. There are ten abjurations in the register, eight before Fisher himself, as well as another two in consistory court records.[54] From Fisher's own writing and sermons it is clear why he was personally involved. Indeed, he felt that his episcopal colleagues could do more to suppress heretics, wolves 'intendygne corruption amonge a flocke of shepe'. In 1526, preaching at Saint Paul's Cross at the abjuration of Robert Barnes, Fisher declared:

> It shalbe moche rebukefull and moche worthy punishment / if we for our party shall nat gyve diligence for the defence of the true christen people / from these heretice / as these heretickes gyve for the corruption of the same.

Again, he rebuked the Church for 'so lytell dyligence', for 'heresy is a perillous wede / it is the sede of the devyll / the inspiration of the wicked spirites / the corruption of our hartes / the blynding of our sight . . .'. Rotten members of the body politic or of the Church could not be tolerated as they were a danger to others.[55] Reconciliation was, nevertheless, always his principal aim. Most of the heresy Fisher encountered was of the traditional Lollard type, although one man possessed Lutheran books and was clearly much more of a concern than the norm. Just how effective the Church courts were in suppressing heresy is open to question – it was often difficult to detect and difficult to prevent relapses – but perhaps the most surprising fact from our point of view is the relative lack of heretics in Rochester diocese under Fisher, when, one assumes, the detection machinery, for all its faults, was at its best. In 1511 there was a concerted drive against heresy under Warham's leadership. Fitzjames of London, Oldham of Exeter, Blythe of Coventry and Lichfield, Fox of Winchester all participated but there are no records of Rochester heretics that year.[56]

The majority of consistory business was carried out by commissaries perfectly adequately and in a small diocese accustomed to seeing the bishop regularly perhaps the lack of episcopal presence at every session was not so serious a fault as it might appear. All bishops had to delegate, and, given good appointments, this seems to have been a perfectly workable system. Fisher probably made use of rural deans to ensure repairs deemed necessary at visitation were carried out. Certificates of such repairs, as well as monitions to rural deans to ensure they were carried out, survive from Norwich, Hereford and Worcester dioceses.[57] But, if everyday administration could be delegated, there were occasions when the weight of episcopal presence was necessary or could prove an inspiration to the unsure or unsteady. The Rochester diocesan synod met twice under Fisher, in 1518 and 1527, and concubinage and other issues arising from legatine decrees were discussed.[58] Fisher preached to the assembled clergy himself but whether the synod was as regular as it was in Ely and Norwich dioceses is impossible to say. It could be that the Rochester synods, and that of Hereford in 1519, were 'one off' affairs, prompted by national rather than diocesan considerations.[59]

The most important of the bishop's sacramental duties was to offer the sacrifice, a function which he shared with all other priests. Evidence for the daily or regular celebration of mass by bishops is rare – most references are to masses, christenings or weddings at court.[60] Fisher's early biographer indicates that he celebrated mass frequently at Rochester cathedral or in his manor chapels – usually with a human skull on the altar to remind him of death, a further indication of how much Fisher was a man of his time.[61] Certainly other bishops, Fox of Winchester for example, regularly visited their cathedrals to say mass, and a number of others were usually in or near their cathedral cities at major feasts and so were likely to do so. Of the other specifically episcopal duties, only ordination has left an appreciable mark on the records. Surprisingly, considering the importance of the sacrament, few bishops carried out their own ordinations. William de Melton, chancellor of York, published a sermon on the importance of ordination in 1510,[62] and Fisher could have been inspired by his old tutor's attitudes as he was particularly diligent in this respect, carrying out thirty-nine out of forty-two ceremonies in the period 1505–35 (this is set in context in Appendix 3). It must be said that an ordination at Rochester was not so protracted and burdensome a duty for the bishop as it was at York or Lincoln at the same time. Only forty-four priests were ordained at Rochester between 1505 and 1534, an average of one per ordination, and most were regulars. Given Fisher's interest, it seems likely that each of these candidates for ordination would be examined with at least as much rigour as elsewhere. At York, Melton implied that, with forty to fifty priests per ordination on average, examination was not always what it might have been, but at least it was carried out. The only bishop known to have examined ordination candidates in person in this period was Fitzjames of London,[63] and examinations are not even mentioned at Rochester. Canon law was not specific as to who should conduct examinations and it is possible that most bishops, including those who were otherwise very diligent such as Atwater or Oldham, felt that contact between themselves and ordinands was so brief that the whole process could be delegated to, and satisfactorily carried out by, suffragans and commissaries.

Where the other purely episcopal sacraments and duties are concerned there is very little evidence of other diocesans participating in person. Confirmation, consecration and reconciliation of consecrated ground polluted by bloodshed were usually delegated. Fisher confirmed children during visitations, according to the early Life[64] – the only evidence for this canonically recommended practice, to be found in a register for the period 1500–60, refers to Sherburne of Chichester in 1521.[65] Fisher did carry out duties which his fellow bishops normally delegated, however. In 1510 he consecrated a rebuilt chapel at Gravesend and reconciled Woldingham cemetery and that of Strood. Occasionaly he delegated the duty and, in 1518, Richard Young, Fitzjames' suffragan, reconciled Sutton cemetery.[66] By way of contrast, a predecessor of Fisher, Savage, after his promotion to York, always delegated these duties, though again that diocese posed particular problems where travel is concerned.[67]

When dealing with Fisher's charitable works we have to resort largely, though not entirely, to statements made by Harpsfield or the anonymous biographer. We can imagine that there was little in the way of extravagance in his household. The inventory of his palace goods at Rochester and Halling made after his imprisonment in 1534 shows sparse establishments[68] – but probably not untypical of middling to poor episcopal houses – and in 1521 his entire household expenditure was only £128 – in 1532 it was £6 less.[69] Harpsfield said that the household was not sumptuous but 'mean and yet honest'[70] and the anonymous *Life* recounts how he never 'dyned before the poore people were served and rewarded with a penny a pece or more as he saw necessyty'. In 1532–3 he expended £230 on alms, gifts and taxes, although we do not know how much he spent on each.[71] The early *Life* also mentions the bishop visiting the sick and poor: 'Many times it was his chaunce to come to such poore howses as for wante of chymneys were verie smokie and therby so noysome, that scant any man could abide in them.' Fisher was, however, happy to stay, climb ladders where 'stayres were wantinge' and leave alms for the sick and needy.[72] It is impossible to verify this but, whilst it is typical martyrologist's material, it would not be out of character for Fisher. Would Savage, Audley or Ruthal have done so? The bishop's household was a focus for learning, though not on the scale of Morton's or Langton's, and Fisher set an example with his own devotion, doubtless in one of the well-equipped manor chapels, often also leaving his guests 'at ther pastymes' to retire to his library, which contributed to his ill-health according to the hypochondriac Erasmus.[73] Fisher's learning and patronage of learning is amply treated elsewhere in this volume, but it is worthy of note here that he spent so much money on it while holding the poorest English diocese and, unlike Fox and Oldham, two of the greatest patrons of learning of the time, never held lucrative secular office.

Finally, of Fisher's preaching we have ample evidence. Surtz and others have dealt with his sermons and writings in great depth and the fact that so many were printed, or commissioned specially, is sufficient testimony to contemporary opinion. One further, very significant, point might serve to highlight Fisher's preaching. The majority of the surviving sermons were intended for the court or special public hearings at St Paul's Cross, but we know that as well as preaching specifically to the clergy he also preached in parish churches to ordinary people. Indeed the difficulties he had at St Paul's once (allowing for the unusual conditions of that church) might indicate he was more used to the parish church than elsewhere.[74]

How then, can Fisher's long association with Rochester be assessed? He does not emerge from the evidence as a notable diocesan reformer. The records show none of the financial and procedural changes of Sherburne's Chichester, none of the consistory court activity of Atwater or Hooper, none of the preaching marathons of Toby Matthew. But all of these men were exceptions by any standards. Given normal considerations of time and energy most bishops, often hampered by illness or the advance of years which usually accompanied senior office, had to compromise when attempting to fulfil their duties.

Inevitably the manner in which St Paul's recommendations were to be followed elicited a great number of individual interpretations. The significance of Fisher was that he was consistently active in virtually all aspects of his office, whether in parliament or Convocation, as controversialist and preacher, whether in feeding the poor, being diligent and conscientious even in the more onerous duties. Moreover, he was extraordinarily active as writer, preacher and educational patron, none of which was apparently detrimental to the diocese. Until 1534 and his imprisonment, the Rochester registers were comprehensive and systematically kept, more so than in any other diocese at the time save Hereford. It is a measure of Fisher's influence that this order vanishes after his removal, declining to the post-medieval bare lists of institutions (often incomplete) under Hilsey, Heath and Holbeach. It was to be some time before the diocese again enjoyed the care of one so dedicated for so long.

Notes

1 Quoted in T. E. Bridgett, *Life of Blessed John Fisher, Bishop of Rochester* (London, 1888), p. 53.
2 Quoted in E. Surtz, *The Works and Days of John Fisher* (Cambridge, Mass., 1967), pp. 385–6.
3 Surtz, *Fisher*, p. 386.
4 I Timothy 3:1–7.
5 For example in *Sacri Sacerdotii Defensio contra Lutherum* (Cologne, 1525), Prologue. There are only two other English bishops who have left their thoughts on the pastoral role of the clergy from this time: J. Alcock, *Gallicantus Johannis Alcock (Episcopi Eliensis ad Confratres Suos Curatos in Sinodo apud Bernwell)* (London, 1498), fo. 3; J. Longland (bishop of Lincoln), *Tres Conciones* (London, 1527), Second Sermon, fo. 29.
6 Surtz, *Fisher*, pp. 54ff.
7 *EW*, p. 124.
8 J. Fisher, *Confutatio Assertionis Lutheranae* (Cologne, 1526), cited in Surtz, *Fisher*, p. 310.
9 Surtz, *Fisher*, pp. 43–4, 52; *EW*, p. 123; J. Fisher, *The Defence of the Priesthood*, ed. and trans. P. Mallett (London, 1935), pp. 32, 108.
10 A. H. Thompson, *The English Clergy and their Organisation in the Later Middle Ages* (Oxford, 1947), pp. 6, 7, 40.
11 Maidstone, Kent County Archives Office, Diocesan Records c/R7 ('Register of John Fisher') (hereafter KCA, DR c/R7), fo. 40; J. Le Neve, *Fasti Ecclesiae Anglicanae*, 12 vols., I, 39.
12 For example, Savage of York refused to be enthroned in person though present at Cawood only seven miles up river, much to the indignation of the chapter. Hilsey was enthroned in person; KCA, DR c/R7, fo. 184v.
13 Nicholas Harpsfield, *The Life and Death of Sir Thomas More*, ed. E. V. Hitchcock

(Early English Texts Society, original series, 186 (1932)), p. 249; Bridgett, *Life of Fisher*, p. 24.

14 *Life*, X, 212.

15 *The Letters of Richard Fox, 1486–1527*, ed. P. S. and H. M. Allen (Oxford, 1928), pp. 53–4.

16 *Valor Ecclesiasticus temp. Henrici VIII*, ed. J. Caley and J. Hunter (London, 1810–34), *passim*. For a full discussion of episcopal incomes, see Felicity Heal, *Of Prelates and Princes* (Cambridge, 1980), esp. ch. 3.

17 P. Hughes, *The Reformation in England* (London, 1954), I, 33–4, 35.

18 J. F. Davis, *Heresy in South East England 1520–1559* (Oxford, 1981).

19 Heal, *Prelates*, pp. 76–8, 85, 120–1.

20 This section is based on entries under individual bishops in Le Neve, *Fasti*; *DNB*; Emden, *Oxford*; Emden, *Oxford, 1501–40*; and Venn.

21 *Life*, X, 214.

22 Mayor, *Statutes*, pp. 238, 342; Bridgett, *Fisher*, p. 25.

23 W. Lyndwood, *Provinciale Seu Constitutiones Anglie* (London, 1534), p. 34; *LP*, III (2), no. 2795.

24 T. Gascoigne, *Loci e Libro Veritatum*, ed. J. E. Thorold Rogers (Oxford, 1881), pp. 23–36. See also S. Thompson, 'The Pastoral Work of the English and Welsh Bishops, 1500–1558', unpublished Oxford D.Phil. thesis, 1984, pp. 9ff.

25 Mayor, *Statutes*, ch. 3. See also *Early Statutes of Christ's College*, ed. H. Rackham (Cambridge, 1927), pp. 46–7.

26 *EW*, pp. 76–7. If he was preaching in one place, Fisher maintained, somewhere else was suffering because of his absence, *A Sermon Had at Paul's* (London, 1526), sig. Aiii.

27 *Life*, X, 217.

28 Thompson, 'English and Welsh Bishops', p. 230.

29 For a full treatment of Rochester's episcopal palaces, A. J. Pearman, G. A. Tait and H. Percy Thompson, 'Residences of the Bishops of Rochester', *Archaeologia Cantiana*, 33 (1918), 131–51.

30 *Life*, X, 149, 220, 223.

31 KCA, DR c/R7, fo. 55v. Fisher's episcopate also saw the completion of the Lady Chapel at Rochester: N. Pevsner and P. Metcalfe, *The Cathedrals of England, Southern England* (London and New York, 1985), p. 243.

32 *Life*, XII, 168–9.

33 Thompson, 'English and Welsh Bishops', pp. 9–10.

34 *LP*, II, nos. 1153, 1248; III (1), nos. 702, 703, 734; III (2), 2288.

35 For Fisher's attitude to the distraction of state affairs, see Lewis, *Fisher*, I, 73–4, also *Life, passim*.

36 KCA, DR c/R7, fo. 49v.

37 Thompson, 'English and Welsh Bishops', pp. 9–17.

38 KCA, DR c/R7, fo. 75v. Metcalf was an active diocesan administrator, ibid., e.g. fos. 41v, 42v, 44, 48, 51, 54v.

39 Ibid., fo. 161.

40 Ibid., fo. 51; KCA, DR c/R7, fo. 16v; Thompson, 'English and Welsh Bishops', pp. 34–8; KCA, DR c/R7, fos. 110, 165; *LP*, IV (2), no. 5095.

41 KCA, DR c/R7., e.g. fos. 76–76v, 53.

42 Ibid., fos. 53, 60, 76, 103v.

43 Ibid., e.g. fos. 51, 53v, 54, 56v, 72, 72v, 74, 108, 138v, 179v; cf. Robert Sherburne, bishop of Chichester, 1508–36.

44 Ibid., fo. 108v; *LP*, XIII (1), no. 1391.

45 KCA, DR c/R7, fos. 129v, 132.

46 Ibid., fo. 160.

47 Ibid., fo. 149v.

48 *Life*, X, pp. 216–17.

49 KCA, DR c/R7, fos. 42, 49v, 56, 71, 74v, 102, 127v, 133v, 145v, 158, 163, 167.

50 Ibid., fos. 23, 32.

51 Thompson, 'English and Welsh Bishops', p. 78.

52 Cambridge UL, Ely Recs., B/2/3 *passim*.

53 For visitation in general , see Thompson, 'English and Welsh Bishops', chs. 4 and 5, especially p. 119 for Elizabethan bishops in consistory.

54 KCA, DR c/R7, fos. 42, 47v, 62, 74, 127v, 133, 158v, 163, 167; KCA, DR/P/8, fos. 53–4.

55 J. Fisher, *A Sermon Had at Paul's* (London, 1526), sig. A iv[v], A ii, A iii[v]; *EW*, p. 340; Surtz, *Fisher*, p. 94.

56 Surtz, *Fisher*, p. 48; Thompson, 'English and Welsh Bishops', pp. 121ff.

57 Norfolk and Norwich Record Office, Bishop's Register, vol. 14, fos. 6v, 54v; *Registrum Caroli Bothe*, ed. A. T. Bannister (Canterbury and York Society, 28 (1921)), pp. 244, 265. Hereford and Worcester Record Office, BA2648, 8i, p. 217; 8ii, fos. 5, 33.

58 KCA, DR c/R7, fos. 77v, 138v.

59 For Ely and Norwich, Cambridge UL, Ely Recs, B/2/1, fos. 28, 40, 52; D. Wilkins, *Concilia Magnae Brittäniae* (Oxford, 1761 edn), III, 712; Bodleian Library, Oxford, MS film 1385, fo. 8v, *Reg. Bothe*, p. 66.

60 Thompson, 'English and Welsh Bishops', pp. 175ff.

61 *Life*, X, 220.

62 W. Melton, *Sermo Exhortatorius Cancellarii Eboracensis . . . (Sermo ad Iuvenes)* (1510).

63 London, Guildhall, MS 9531/8, fos. 20vff.

64 *Life*, X, 217.

65 West Sussex Record Office, Ep. Reg. 1/1/4, fo. 77.

66 KCA, DR c/R7, e.g. fos. 54, 54v. For commission, fo. 77.

67 Borthwick Institute, Reg. Savage, fos. 3v, 89v, 96. Reg. Bainbridge, fo. 2.

68 Bridgett, *Life of Fisher*, pp. 62ff.

69 Heal, *Prelates*, p. 84.

70 Harpsfield, *Life and Death of Sir Thomas More*, p. 250.

71 *Life*, X, 149. Heal, *Prelates*, p. 97.

72 *Life*, X, 221.

73 Ibid., X, 222–3; Harpsfield, *Life and Death of Sir Thomas More*, p. 251. Heal, *Prelates*, p. 79. Thompson, 'English and Welsh Bishops', p. 211. Bridgett, *Life of Fisher*, p. 62.

74 E. E. Reynolds, *St John Fisher*, 2nd edn (Wheathampstead, 1972), pp. 35ff. Fisher, *A Sermon Had at Paul's*, sig. A4.

Fisher and Erasmus

H. C. PORTER

Erasmus probably first met Fisher in 1505, during his second visit to England. Erasmus's base was the house of Thomas More in the City of London. Erasmus and More were collaborating on translations into Latin from the Greek of Lucian; and one of Erasmus's concerns was to meet Greek scholars, such as William Latimer. Fisher knew no Greek. But one of Erasmus's surviving letters from London at the end of 1505 is 'from the bishop's palace'.[1] That might have been the residence, near Lambeth Palace, of the new bishop of Rochester (consecrated November 1504). Fisher was also (October 1504) chancellor of Cambridge University. The University *Grace Book* for the academic year 1505–6 has an entry allowing Erasmus to proceed to the doctorate of Theology (presumably at the 1506 July commencement).[2] In fact he left England early in June, and took his doctorate in Turin in September 1506. A tradition within Queens' College in the later sixteenth century was that Erasmus lodged there at some time in the second half of 1505 or the first half of 1506 (when Fisher was president of the college).[3] John Caius added the information that this was at a time when Henry VII visited the University.[4] On the (scanty) evidence of his surviving correspondence, it seems that Erasmus was out of London in April and early May 1506. On 23 April the Grand Feast of the Order of the Garter – the 'great solemnity' annually celebrated on St George's Day – was held not at Windsor but in King's College Chapel.[5] Henry VII, on his pilgrim's way to Walsingham, arrived in Cambridge on the 22nd, and stayed for two nights in Queens'. Fisher led the religious observances in King's Chapel on the eve, the feastday, and the morrow. It is possible that Erasmus was with the royal party, or joined it when it lodged in Queens'. What is certain is that, when Eramus settled into his extensive suite in Queens' in August 1511, he owed the invitation to Fisher, as chancellor, to whose 'acts of great kindness and generosity to me' he paid tribute at the time.[6] The first actual reference to Fisher in Erasmus's surviving correspondence is in a Cambridge letter of September 1511.[7]

Erasmus was slightly older than Fisher: the most authoritative assumptions are that Erasmus was born in 1467, Fisher in 1469. Their lives had been very different. Fisher was a Yorkshireman, the eldest of four children of a fairly affluent man of business. John's brother Robert, trained as a lawyer, became MP for Rochester and also steward of the episcopal household. He eventually provided some comforts for the imprisoned bishop, and brought to the Tower news of proceedings in the House of Commons. He died four months before John Fisher's execution.[8] They had a half-sister, Elizabeth – their mother had remarried after their father's death – who became a nun, and for whom Fisher wrote *A Spirituall Consolation* when he was imprisoned in the Tower. The family was evidently close-knit and rather 'establishment' in both Church and state. Erasmus was born in Rotterdam, in the Burgundian Netherlands.[9] He was illegitimate: his mother, it seems, was a widowed housekeeper, mistress for some years of a cleric, or ordinand. The father went away, and both father and mother died in about 1483. At that point Erasmus, aged fifteen or so, came under the care of guardians. He had been educated first at a church school in Gouda, and then, after a time as a chorister at Utrecht, at a school in Deventer run by a pupil of the Italianate Frisian humanist, Rudolph Agricola (1433–98). Erasmus may have learned some Greek here. He once met Agricola; and regarded himself, by way of the headmaster, as a grandson in the family of scholarship.[10]

Fisher was to write to Erasmus in 1515, full of enthusiasm for a new purchase, Agricola's book of logic *De Inventione Dialectica*:[11] 'I never read anything, so far as that art is concerned, more enjoyable or better informed: he seems to have put every point so clearly. How I wish I had had him for a teacher! I had rather that – and I am speaking the truth – than be made an archbishop.' The sentiment, even after allowances have been made for rhetorical convention, suggests that Fisher was aware that his own education had been rather restricted. He probably went to the school attached to the collegiate church of St John the Evangelist (the Minster) in his home town, Beverley. 'I heard as a boy that heretics must be avoided . . . other heretics arise from their ashes'.[12] Then, in 1483, the eight-day journey south to Cambridge. At that time nearly 80 per cent of Cambridge students lived in hostels or lodgings.[13] Fisher went to one of the twelve colleges, Michaelhouse. The colleges were essentially pious seminaries, Michaelhouse more so than some others. Fisher became Bachelor of Arts in 1488, and was ordained priest, as a fellow of Michaelhouse, in 1491. By 1488 Erasmus had spent four years at a school at 's-Hertogenbosch connected with the forward-looking Brethren of the Common Life. Then his guardians placed him in a monastery of Augustinian canons at Steyn, one mile from Gouda. He studied there, fruitfully enough, until about 1492, when he was ordained priest. He then became secretary to the bishop of Cambrai, a senior ecclesiastic at the Burgundian court. Disliking his native province of Holland, Erasmus thought of central Burgundy as his *patria*, at any rate until 1514, when his Rhine journey to Basle convinced him that he was a German.[14] In 1495 –

the year in which Fisher, now Cambridge senior proctor, first met the Lady Margaret Beaufort – Erasmus was sent to Paris to study theology. His sojourn in a college proving disastrous, he moved into lodgings. Erasmus took pupils in Paris. One was the young Lord Mountjoy, William Blount (born in 1478), who had studied at Queens'. It was Blount who invited Erasmus to England in 1499. Another was Robert Fisher, a kinsman of John (not the brother). In 1498, when Robert was leaving for Italy, Erasmus gave him some notes in manuscript on 'the method of writing letters' – a hasty first draft on a theme with which Erasmus continued to toy (at Cambridge in 1511, for example).[15] Erasmus was greatly annoyed when, in October 1521, the 1498 manuscript was printed, without permission, in Cambridge by the German printer John Siberch, who had arrived in the town in 1520. Aware of his 'boldness', and in an attempt to protect himself, Siberch printed with the text of *De Conscribendis Epistolis* a letter of dedication to Fisher as chancellor.[16] The book was 'dedicated a long time ago to one of your kinsmen'; Siberch intended to serve Erasmus, Fisher and 'all students of good learning'. He begged Fisher, 'all powerful with Erasmus', to be 'my protector with him, that he may not bear me ill-will for having published it without his consent'. Fisher's reaction is unrecorded. Erasmus, confirmed in his feeling that printers and publishers have no shame, set to work again on the material, and published an authoritative text at Basle in 1522. The introduction referred to the late Robert Fisher as 'a friend of dubious loyalty' ['amicus parum sincerus'].[17] (Erasmus was always alert to 'deceit and perfidy' in friendship.)[18] What he thought of John Fisher's association with the Cambridge version, involuntary though it apparently was, is not known.

When Erasmus came to England in 1499, he was an obscure Dutch monk of lowly and dubious origin. Fisher was a rising academic politician, with royal connections. But, comparatively, Fisher's education and experience had been provincial. Erasmus had realised that Greek was the key to the new learning and gave priority to perfecting his knowledge of the language. During the visit to England, of five or six months, the friends Erasmus mentioned (apart from Colet at Oxford) were based in London, and had an eye to the Greek: William Grocyn, Thomas Linacre, Thomas More. There is no mention of Fisher in the surviving documentation for this visit.

Erasmus was based in Cambridge from August 1511 to January 1514, though he was away for longish periods.[19] Any meetings with Fisher would probably have been in London; Fisher, when chancellor, did not often visit Cambridge. Early in 1512, after Erasmus's first term in Cambridge, Fisher was named as a delegate to the Fifth Lateran Council, due to start in April, and he invited Erasmus to accompany him to Rome. Erasmus said he heard of the offer 'too late to have time to set my affairs in order'[20] – or, in another version, that he had made preparations for the journey when the English delegates found that their participation had been postponed.[21]

Erasmus at this time professed himself to be 'almost entirely transformed into an Englishman'.[22] The comment was rueful. He had visited Rome in 1509, and, in a letter of 1512 to a cardinal there,[23] he lamented the cancelled expedition, as he was 'racked with longing' for Rome: 'the climate, the green places, the libraries, the colonnades, and the honeyed talks with scholars' – all those 'prospects that I put from me so readily' (by leaving Rome for England after the death of Henry VII in 1509). As it was, Erasmus did not leave England until July 1514.

His next visit to England was brief, in May 1515, when he was working on his edition of the letters of Jerome. He stayed in London; saw a great deal of Thomas More and Cuthbert Tunstall, chancellor to Archbishop Warham; and wrote of the high ecclesiastics who were especially kind to him[24] – Bishop Thomas Ruthall of Durham, Wolsey (the new archbishop of York), Fisher, and especially Warham, always Erasmus's favourite prelatical patron in England. Whether he visited Fisher, in London or Rochester, is not known. The Dover–London route was via Canterbury, Rochester, Gravesend, then by boat to Billingsgate. An overnight stop was advisable, but not necessary, as the journey could be done in one day.

Erasmus had originally intended to dedicate to Fisher his edition of the New Testament, published in Basle in February 1516: Greek and Latin texts in parallel columns, with prefatory material, and copious annotations at the end. In the event, it was dedicated to Leo X. Erasmus explained his change of mind in a letter to Fisher, now missing. But surely, he wrote to Fisher in June 1516, you will approve of the papal dedication: 'with your habitual generosity ['humanitas'], not to say wisdom'.[25] That letter was written in St Omer, before Erasmus again crossed the Channel. The two men did meet in 1516; but the encounter was not entirely happy. In July Fisher was in Cambridge for the opening of St John's College.[26] Erasmus, in London, was on the point of riding to Cambridge when he heard that Fisher was expected in London. He waited for several days, but Fisher did not appear.[27] Finally, in the middle of August, when Erasmus was on his way to Dover, Fisher persuaded him to stay for ten days in Rochester. 'I was stuck in Rochester'[28] – helping Fisher with rudimentary Greek – Erasmus wrote from Rochester to his young Italian friend in London, Andrea Ammonio; the promise to stay for ten days was regretted 'more than ten times over . . . I am to turn him from a Latin into a Greek – that is the metamorphosis I have undertaken.'[29] He managed to get away to Dover by the 24th. Later in the year the idea was put forward, partly by More, that William Latimer should stay at Rochester 'for a month or two' to continue the Greek tuition.[30] Latimer refused, pleading that an adequate Greek course could take up to seven years.[31] There was provision for the teaching of Greek in Fisher's 1516 statutes for St John's college.[32] And Fisher gave Erasmus details of the renewed Cambridge of 1516, compared with the University he had known in the 1480s. Erasmus was often to use this information, particularly in praising Fisher's chancellorship.[33] Because of Fisher, he wrote in 1519, Greek is taught in Cambridge 'without disturbance'[34] – a reference to disputes at Oxford in spring 1518.

Erasmus made a brief business trip to London in April 1517, and may have called on Fisher at Rochester. In the summer Fisher sent Erasmus his considered comments on the 1516 New Testament.[35] He took pride in being able to point out printer's errors and omissions in the Greek text. Also, 'up to a point I can make conjectures in places where the Greek and Latin do not exactly correspond'. This he owed to Erasmus: what a pity he'd been unable to stay longer in Rochester in 1516! Erasmus sent Fisher a copy of his Latin version of the Greek grammar of the Byzantine Theodore Gaza.[36] And in an essay published in 1526 Erasmus commended Fisher for taking up Greek (and Hebrew) 'with uncommon enthusiasm on the verge of old age'.[37]

The 1517 visit to England was, as things turned out, Erasmus's last. He had hoped to cross the Channel again in spring 1518. He wrote to Fisher from Louvain, in pessimistic mood: 'I shall therefore turn entirely to you, as to a people on the edge of the world ['velut extra orbem'], and perhaps the least infected province of Christianity' – least infected by rapacious rulers, overbearing ecclesiastics, and disturbances among the people. But his health was especially bad, and he must go south – could Fisher send him 'a suitable horse not afraid of hard work'?[38]

Erasmus was at Louvain in June 1520 when Fisher and More were with the royal party at the 'summit conference' with Francis I, held near Calais: the Field of the Cloth of Gold. Ill health was the excuse for Erasmus's not attending the ceremonies. He met More in July at Calais. There is no evidence for a meeting with Fisher. The last surviving letter from Erasmus to Fisher was in September 1524. There were later ones. It seems, for instance, that Erasmus wrote to Fisher from Freiberg in spring 1534 – a letter received by Fisher in the Tower, where he was imprisoned on 16 April. Robert Fisher cleared the letter with Thomas Cromwell before passing it on to his brother.[39] Erasmus later said that he wrote no more letters to Fisher after news of the imprisonment had reached him.[40] In the September 1524 letter, written from Basle, Erasmus had been concerned about Fisher's health.[41] He attributed Fisher's illnesses in part to the unwholesome situation of Rochester, on the Medway, and partly to the brick and lime of the episcopal palace. The library, 'which for you is paradise', Erasmus would not care to occupy for three hours. Healthy rooms have wooden floors and panelling. They do not have glass windows, the panes of which are always badly fitted, letting in germs. Presumably Erasmus preferred a cover of transparent cloth.

The 'Rochester library' letter was printed in 1529. That brought to seven the number of letters from Erasmus to Fisher printed in their lifetimes. Allen added six: five first printed in 1703, in the Leiden *Opera Omnia* of Erasmus, and one, a British Library manuscript, printed in the 1750s. That is meagre enough. Fisher's letters fared even worse. Allen has only five letters from Fisher to Erasmus, the first in November 1511, the last in June 1517. Moreover, four of the five were not printed until the 1703 edition of Erasmus's correspondence. The fifth was printed in 1516, but indirectly – Erasmus quoted it in a letter to Reuchlin. Yet Erasmus said in 1517 that Fisher wrote to him 'quite often'.[42] He acknowledged an enjoyable letter from Rochester in 1519: 'You increased my delight by not only writing, but writing a long letter; for kind your letters always are.'[43] Fisher was hurt by the lack of references to himself (and, perhaps, the absence of letters from himself) in the collections of letters published by Erasmus in April 1517 and August 1518. 'If you are seldom mentioned in my letters', Erasmus replied, 'the reason is only my respect for your high position.'[44] He offered as consolation the fact that a letter written by him to Fisher from Cambridge in September 1511 had been printed in July 1518, as the preface to Erasmus's Latin translation of an essay by St Basil. Soon things turned sourer. Erasmus, early in 1520: 'In three letters now you allude to I know not what.'[45] The three letters do not survive. The tensions of 1519–20 will be discussed later.

The essay by St Basil of Caesarea (d. 379) published in 1518 was the only fruit of a project which tantalised Erasmus in 1511. He brought with him to Cambridge that summer a Greek manuscript of about 200,000 words, borrowed from William Grocyn: Basil's commentary on Isaiah – 'the most eloquent of theologians', Erasmus wrote to Fisher, 'on the most eloquent of prophets'.[46] During his first weeks in Cambridge Erasmus continued to work at his Latin translation. Why not publish it under Fisher's auspices, as a work 'from his own university'?[47] In the event, Erasmus abandoned work on the commentary, doubting its authenticity. It was not to be included in the Greek edition of Basil published at Basle by Froben, and overseen by Erasmus. It seems that it may have been a text based on notes, not definitively edited by Basil.[48]

However, in September 1511 Erasmus was still working on the translation. He wrote to Colet: 'I shall give a sample of it ['gustus'] to the Bishop of Rochester and find out whether he is willing to give me a little something by way of emolument.'[49] (Erasmus's income in his Cambridge years never matched his expenditure.) The 'gustus' was sent to Fisher late in September: a Latin version of Basil's preface, no more than 3,000 words, eventually to appear in 1518 in a volume of assorted Erasmus works. Professor Screech has compared Erasmus's Latin with the Greek text; and urges the importance of this essay (concerned with inspiration and revelation) for the interpretation of *Praise of Folly*.[50] Fisher 'seemed rather unenthusiastic' about the sample. So wrote Erasmus to Colet, in a letter he published in 1519. When he published it again in 1529, Erasmus gave a fuller text:[51] 'as I have learned from a friend, he suspects I am polishing up a previous version, and not translating from the Greek. What won't men think of?' Allen suggested that this remark indicated a cooling in the 1520s of Erasmus's feelings for Fisher.[52]

It also seems that Erasmus was under a misapprehension about the goods and monies given to Fisher by the Lady Margaret Beaufort before her death in 1509, and the bequests in her will. Malcolm Underwood discusses the problems arising from the will, so far as the founding of St John's was concerned. In November 1511 Fisher wrote of the *depositum* which Erasmus appeared to think was at the disposal of Fisher: 'yonder larger-than-average trust fund'.[53] In fact, 'whatever people may say, there is no money lodged with me which could be dispensed as I solely chose. The bestowal of the money you refer to is prescribed for me so strictly that I cannot alter it, however much I may wish to do so.' (If the reference to the money was in a letter, the letter has not survived.) After Fisher's death Erasmus mentioned the 'huge sum of money' received by Fisher from the Lady Margaret, to subsidise those 'she had found fit to instruct the people in the wisdom of the Gospels'. Fisher organised this money 'either in promoting churchmen or in helping those in need'. He also added to it 'out of his own resources'.[54] In 1511 Fisher stressed his own 'slender resources', and sent Erasmus a 'small present ['munusculum']'. He promised to help when he could, and to encourage potential patrons: 'I can see how indispensable you are to our own university.'[55] When Erasmus left England in July 1514 he received (in 1986 equivalents) £1,125 from Bishop Ruthall of Durham, and £225 from Fisher.[56]

In September 1511 Erasmus sent to Colet from Cambridge, among other manuscripts, his Latin translation of the Mass of St John Chrysostom; not published until 1536, but meant from the start as an offering to Fisher.[57] In October 1513 Erasmus, still based in Cambridge, feared the loss of his *Mathaeus*. This was probably a series of notes on St Matthew's Gospel, rather than a new Latin translation. Erasmus always maintained that his intention after leaving England in 1514 was to publish a Greek text of the New Testament, with notes; that he thereafter thought of printing the Vulgate Latin alongside the Greek; and that only in 1515 was he persuaded to undertake a corrected Vulgate. Thus, he said, his work on the February 1516 New Testament developed. Andrew J. Brown, in an article published in 1984,[58] accepted Erasmus's account, and argued that a new Erasmus Latin translation (such as was to appear in the New Testament editions of 1519 and 1522) was never part of the original intention. Therefore it could not have been among Erasmus's Cambridge concerns. However this may be, the 'Matthew' had been borrowed. Earlier in 1513 Erasmus had lent Fisher various items at different times. He wrote to Colet: 'If my Matthew is not in your possession, it must be in the Bishop of Rochester's. This is what I rather guessed anyway.'[59] Fisher had returned some things, but not the 'Matthew', lent separately and remaining separated. 'If it is lost', Erasmus continued, 'I shall blame myself, and shall punish myself by the tedium of work done over again' – as a penalty for 'facilitas': willingness to oblige. Further stages in this check to Erasmus's affability are unknown.

Fisher, after a year's study of the 1516 New Testament, wrote that it 'can offend no one of any sense'.[60] He seems to be referring to the Latin text – still basically traditional. According to More, Fisher in fact found the 1516 Latin editing too 'scrupulous': in its retention of linguistic relics from 'the history and ritual of the Jews'.[61] Fisher, said More, 'does not admit a single word that was unfamiliar to a Roman's ear'. No doubt More was being partly playful. But at that time Erasmus was working on his *Paraphrase on Romans*, to be published at Louvain in November 1517, and was much concerned by the fact that Paul's Greek had an 'admixture everywhere of Hebrew idiom'. Erasmus's aim in the Pauline paraphrases (to be distinguished from a translation) was 'giving Hebrew turns of speech a Roman dress',[62] presenting Paul 'speaking like a Roman to the Romans' – in a Latin in which the reader 'would not recognise the Hebrew speaking, but would recognise the Apostle'.[63] So far as the Latin of the New Testament edition was concerned, More asked Fisher to send to Erasmus a list of suggested changes. And Erasmus wrote to Fisher in 1518 asking to see any 'corrections' for the 'fuller and more accurate' edition he was preparing.[64] On at least one occasion Fisher preferred Erasmus's Latin to 'the old translation'. This was in *Sacri Sacerdotii Defensio* (1525), at a point where Erasmus's rendering of a Pauline phrase seemed to Fisher satisfactorily sound on the theme of the sacrificing priest.[65] In general, however, Fisher by the late 1520s came increasingly to insist on the authority of the Vulgate. Linguistic disputes would confuse the simple laity. Biblical texts were much bandied about in the debates concerning Henry VIII's 'divorce' – though these were as much from the Old Testament as the New. Fisher would have approved of the decision of the Council of Trent in 1546 to retain the Vulgate as the authentic translation.

So far as Erasmus's annotations in the 1516 New Testament are concerned, Fisher's initial reaction (at least as expressed to Erasmus) was friendly:[66] with the help of the 'fresh commentary' the New Testament 'can now be read and enjoyed by anybody with much more pleasure and satisfaction than before'. In 1519 Erasmus asked Fisher 'to write down for me the notes which you think to be of some account'.[67] Fisher made a marginal note here in his copy of the 1529 edition of Erasmus's correspondence:[68] 'vehemens obtestatio', an ardent supplication. Erasmus claimed in the mid 1520s that Fisher approved of the annotations.[69] This may have been an attempt to invoke a respectable witness – Erasmus was writing to the conservative Faculty of Theology in Paris.

Before leaving England in 1514 Erasmus received a letter from Johann Reuchlin, scholar of Hebrew language and literature, advocate of the sanctity of Hebrew.[70] In reply, Erasmus told him that there were two eminent Reuchlin admirers in England: Colet and Fisher ('a man of singularly high character, and a most accomplished theologian').[71] Fisher had a copy of Reuchlin's grammar and Hebrew/Latin dictionary *De Rudimentis Hebraicis* (1506). In 1515 Fisher wrote to Erasmus about Reuchlin; this is the letter known only because Erasmus quoted it in a letter of his own to Reuchlin.[72] 'I find his type of scholarship very congenial', said Fisher: 'I know no one who comes closer to Giovanni Pico.' Pico della Mirandola was a pioneer of Christian use of Cabbala, the Jewish tradition of mystical interpretation of the Old Testament. Reuchlin was influenced by Pico, and developed his own cabbalistic interests in such works as his dialogue *De Verbo Mirifico* (On the Wonder-Working Word), published in 1494, the year of Pico's death. Fisher presumably had a copy of this. Pico, wrote Lewis Spitz, 'saw the possibilities in the Cabbala for the Christian thinker, the authority of antiquity in Hebrew, the value of an oral tradition, the fascination of esoteric symbolism, and the utility of a source outside revelation for supporting Christian dogma'.[73] So did Reuchlin, and the theme fascinated Fisher. In another letter to Erasmus,[74] Fisher wrote that, in knowledge of the *arcana*, secret mysteries involving both theology and philosophy, Reuchlin 'seems to me, in comparison with everyone else whose works I have read so far, to be the best man alive today'. That was in 1516. In March 1517 Reuchlin published *De Arte Cabalistica*, and sent a copy to Fisher by way of Erasmus. (In June Fisher had still not received it, as it had gone to More, who lent it to Colet. Please forgive, wrote Erasmus, 'I know your *humanitas*'.)[75] Fisher appealed to the Cabbala in his May 1521 English sermon against Luther: 'secret eruditions not written in the Bible', 'derived from man to man by mouth only and not by writing'.[76] The unwritten teaching of the Old Testament prophets is 'of as great authority, as that that was written'. Thus the Cabbala could support Fisher's insistence on 'other testimony, than only what is written in the Bible'. He translated St Paul (II Thessalonians 2:15) on keeping *traditiones* which 'ye have learned of us, either by mouth or else by writing'. Fisher's rendering of *traditiones* (Authorised Version: 'traditions') was 'instructions and eruditions'. It has been suggested that Fisher's concern with what Colet called Reuchlin's 'Cabbalistic philosophy'[77] was one factor in the typically impolitic interest he took in the 'prophecies' of Elizabeth Barton, the 'nun of Kent', executed in 1534.

Reuchlin died in June 1522, and shortly afterwards Erasmus published the Colloquy 'The Apotheosis of that Incomparable Worthy John Reuchlin'. Erasmus admired Reuchlin for his linguistic pioneering.[78] But he thought Hebrew far less important than Greek ('if only the Church of Christians did not attach such importance to the Old Testament').[79] And he 'never felt the attraction of Cabbala'.[80] In 1518 he had dismissed the Cabbala as 'words, words, words'. 'I would rather have Christ mixed up with Scotus than with that rubbish of theirs.'[81]

In 1517 Jacques Lefèvre of Étaples published in Paris a book on 'Mary called Magdalene'. In the tradition of the Greek Church, a distinction was drawn between Mary Magdalene, Mary sister of Martha and Lazarus, and Mary the forgiven sinner. Modern scholarship supports that distinction. Dom David Knowles wrote that 'the separation of the three individuals seems to be established beyond reasonable doubt'.[82] But the Latin middle ages preferred Mary Magdalene, sister of Lazarus, penitent sinner, follower of Christ. Rosalind and Christopher Brooke have described the strength of the cult of the Madeleine in France from the eleventh century.[83] Lefèvre drew on the Greek tradition of multiple Marys. 'I liked his book', wrote Erasmus.[84] Fisher published a reply to Lefèvre in Paris, February 1519: De Unica Magdalena. He appealed especially to the 'general consensus of the whole church':[85]

I immediately thought of how many difficulties would confront the whole church if Lefèvre's opinion were ever to be accepted. How many authors would have to be rejected, how many books would have to be changed, how many sermons formerly preached to the people would now have to be revoked! And then, how much uneasiness would arise among the faithful, how many occasions for loss of faith. They will soon doubt other books and narratives, and finally the mother of us all, the Church, who for so many centuries has sung and taught the same thing.

A month or so after publication Erasmus wrote to Fisher saying he had 'only dipped into' De Unica Magdalena.[86] But he warned Fisher that some of its readers 'are sorry to see you sometimes treating rather harshly (as they think) an old man and a good man like Lefèvre . . . One's pen may sometimes get out of hand unintentionally.' In a later letter to Fisher he said the book was too sharp and stinging ('aculeatus').[87]

This was a sensitive point to Erasmus, because of his own Apologia against Lefèvre (August 1517). The French humanist had criticised the 1516 New Testament annotations, and Erasmus chose to take this as 'a bitter and insidious attack on a personal friend'.[88] Lefèvre 'treated the affair in a spirit so unpleasant that it was not open to me to say nothing'.[89] But, he told Fisher, 'I held my righteous anger on a tight rein.'[90] There were no references to Lefèvre in the 1519 New Testament: in 1516 he had been quoted approvingly.[91]

So Fisher's 'unflagging pungency'[92] against Lefèvre touched a raw nerve in Erasmus. Erasmus's unease about De Unica Magdalena was fed by the fact that some people took him to be the author − though 'the style is so entirely unlike mine' (and 'I fall so far short of that gifted prelate as a scholar').[93] In September 1519 Fisher published a second book against Lefèvre. Erasmus, spying an escape route, wrote to Fisher saying that he had been on the point of sending the notes he had made on *De Unica Magdalena*, but that would be pointless now that he had the second book – which he intended to read soon.[94] But what a pity Fisher had not been satisfied with his first onslaught. 'He does not readily give up the struggle, once he has warmed up.'[95]

In his books on Mary Magdalene, Fisher sought support from a succession of scholastic theologians, ranging from Anselm (d. 1109) to Nicholas of Cusa (d. 1464). Fr Edward Surtz SJ published material on Fisher and the scholastics.[96] In *De Veritate Corporis et Sanguinis Christi in Eucharistia* (1527) the chronological range was narrower, from Alexander of Hales (d. 1245) to Gregory of Rimini (d. 1348). Surtz argued that Fisher was not influenced by late-medieval scholasticism: post 1350. Fisher praised Peter Lombard (d. 1160); for Erasmus, the 'Master of the Sentences' raised impious questions and superfluous difficulties. Duns Scotus (d. 1308) was to Fisher a theologian of 'perspicacious and vigorous intellect'.[97] Erasmus's Duns was, in spite of some talent, the mandarin of complications. In Fisher's 1524 statutes for St John's College, Duns and his pupil, Francis of Meyronnes (Mayronius: d. 1328), were among the set authors for the theology course.[98] Duns appeared again in the 1530 statutes:[99] which also provided for the possible replacement of a lectureship in Hebrew by instruction based on Duns, 'if he can be turned into better Latin'.[100] Fisher's gifts to the college library included works by Albertus Magnus (d. 1280) and Alexander of Hales. Erasmus respected those two theologians, but warned of the danger of confusing their work with the word of God in Christ.[101] For Erasmus, the scholastics – even those most in touch with scripture and the Fathers – were men of their specific time, useful in their period. Fisher was much more addicted: however lacking in true eloquence, they had spoken with both skill and universal authority. Robert Barnes, Cambridge Augustinian friar of the 1520s, branded the University chancellor as among 'Master Duns' men'.[102]

Surtz, and, earlier, Elizabeth Nugent, argued for the importance of Fisher as a Thomist.[103] Sometimes Fisher quoted Erasmus as an admirer of Thomas Aquinas.[104] In the New Testament annotations, certainly, Erasmus praised him as 'a man whose greatness has stood the test of time': unrivalled for carefulness, sane wisdom, wide learning, sanctity – and the skilful use of the resources available to him in his day.[105] But in 1519 Erasmus criticised those who placed Aquinas 'almost above the Gospels', and commended Luther, who dared 'to show little esteem for the doctrine of St Thomas'.[106] Erasmus said that he had 'begun a more careful study' of Aquinas after two discussions with Colet. This must have been before 1514, and may have been as early as 1499. A remark of Erasmus that Aquinas had 'studied both scriptures and the early Fathers' provoked an outburst from Colet against 'that writer' who 'tainted the whole doctrine of Christ with his profane philosophy'. Erasmus's subsequent 'careful study' of Aquinas (he was writing in 1521) meant that 'my estimate of him was undoubtedly diminished'.[107] Respect for the scholastics, he insisted in 1523,[108] should not encourage us to 'clamour against good literature, springing up again everywhere'.

Fisher's books about Mary Magdalene prompted one strong objection from Erasmus: he wished 'that your pains had been devoted to some other subject'. What about the manuscript he had shown to Erasmus in England, on the *series* and *sensus* of the Gospels? This, if printed, 'would in my judgement have added something more worth having to your reputation'.[109] Also, and crucially, Erasmus was offended by 'your endeavours to turn the matter into a problem of faith ['causa fidei']'.[110] Four months earlier, discussing Luther's critics, he had made the same point: 'it is not necessary to turn everything into a question of faith ['questio fidei']'.[111] Invocations of 'the Church', 'the articles of the faith', 'the truth' were inappropriate in considering points of divinity about which 'I think it would be wiser to make rather less fuss'.[112] The Church was not strengthened by 'headstrong dogmatism'.[113] Yet in general it seemed (1521) that what had been 'probable opinion', suitable for debate, was increasingly hardening into Articles of Faith.[114] The remedy: to 'define as few matters as possible and leave each individual's judgement free on many questions'.[115] Gaspar, in the 1522 Colloquy 'The Whole Duty of Youth', told what he had learned as a boy in Colet's household: 'What I read in sacred scripture and the creed called the Apostles' I believe with complete confidence, nor do I search further. The rest I leave to theologians to dispute and define if they wish'.[116]

In 1519 things did not go well between Fisher and Erasmus. They had not met since August 1516, or possibly April 1517, and they never met again. It was early in 1519 that Fisher commented on the lack of references to himself in Erasmus's published correspondence. It became obvious that Erasmus disapproved of Fisher's campaign against Lefèvre, launched in February. In April Erasmus wrote to Fisher that 'evil tongues' have 'tried to persuade you that Erasmus does not approve of you': 'Erasmus tibi non favere'.[117]

The haters of 'heresy' seemed to be gaining too much ground. 'All error is not heresy', Erasmus wrote, in another letter of April 1519, 'nor does something become heretical if this man or that disapproves of it. They do not always advance the cause of the faith who attach grand labels of this kind.'[118] In May 1521 Erasmus reflected on the state of affairs in 'our Germany'.[119] Harsh bombast, 'violent reproaches', characterise the times. Both Erasmus and Luther have their 'wrangling critics'. Where is 'Christian moderation', the 'courtesy and gentleness' of the 'evangelical spirit of Christ'? (Certainly not in Luther, whose 'manner and method', as distinct from his opinions, offend.) In that same month of May 1521 Fisher preached his Paul's Cross sermon 'against the pernicious doctrine of Martin Luther', the introduction to a burning of books.[120] Erasmus would doubtless read the Latin version, by Richard Pace, published in 1522 by Siberch at Cambridge. The theme was the 'black cloud of heresy'; the villains were those, from Arius onwards, who follow 'their own brain and fantasy, led by the spirit of error and ignorance' – evil men, murderers of souls, worse than tyrants or Jews.

In March 1523 Erasmus wrote to the pope (Adrian VI from Utrecht) complaining that in the Low Countries he had been talked of, both privately and publicly, as a heretic.[121] The hurt could be hidden, Erasmian style, in humour. The youth visiting a brothel in the Colloquy 'The Young Man and the Harlot' (August 1523) says that on a visit to Rome, hoping, unlike most such visitors, to improve himself, he took a copy of Erasmus's New Testament.[122] 'Erasmus?', replies the harlot: 'He's half a heretic, they say.' 'You don't mean that man's reputation has reached even this place?' 'No name is better known to us.'

The last surviving letter from Erasmus to Fisher was in September 1524.[123] Erasmus complained that he was under attack from all sides. Concerning Luther's doctrines: many he didn't understand; many he was doubtful about; and many 'I would not dare to profess for reasons of conscience ['propter conscientiam']' – even if it were safe'. Earlier in the year his book against Luther had been published: *De Libero Arbitrio*. Erasmus was dismissive about it in the letter to Fisher – not really 'in my province ['arena']'. So 'I have resolved henceforth to keep aloof from theological controversy, and spend my leisure translating Greek, or profane yet morally fruitful writings.'

Fisher, on the other hand, in the words of Richard Rex elsewhere in this book, was a 'tenacious controversialist'. And in February 1526 he preached another English sermon at St Paul's against those 'holding the heresies of Martin Luther'.[124] The preface to the published text advocates the 'full extirpation of heresy': 'heresy is a perilous weed, it is the seed of the devil, the inspiration of the wicked spirits, the corruption of our hearts, the blinding of our sight, the quenching of our faith, the destruction of all good fruit, and finally the murder of men's souls'.[125] The invective is shriller than in the 1521 sermon. Fisher's 1530 statutes for St John's presented the college as a fortress against the 'perilous plague' of heresy:[126] the virus carriers were the followers of Wyclif, Huss, Luther and Oecolampadius.

Fisher's book against the Eucharistic theology of Oecolampadius was published early in 1527: *De Veritate Corporis et Sanguinis Christi in Eucharistia*. At that time Erasmus's own thinking about the Eucharist may have been closer to Oecolampadius than to Fisher. And when, by June 1529, he had accepted 'orthodoxy' on the Real Presence, he relied on the consensus of the Church, not on the New Testament.[127] This seemed to Fisher, on that particular point, perverse.[128] When Erasmus published a work on the Real Presence, in 1530 at Freiberg, he side-stepped the personalities of the 1520s. The book was an edition of a text written about 1110 by the Netherlands theologian Alger of Liège, who had taken an 'orthodox' line in the Eucharistic disputes of the eleventh and early twelfth centuries.

Among Fisher's points in the 1526 St Paul's sermon was that heretics 'be singular, and have opinions by themself'. Further, they 'would have every man left to their liberty'. ('If every man should have liberty to say what he would, we should have a marvellous world.') Duty towards such is clear: to 'reduce them unto the ways of the Church'. And 'many must be compelled, according as the gospel saith'. The allusion is to the story told by Christ in Luke's Gospel (ch. 14) of the man who invited guests to a feast, only to have empty places when some of the invited did not appear: 'Go out into the highways and hedges and compel them to come in that my house may be filled.' To Fisher, in 'matters concerning our faith', a person 'must be compelled to conform him to the wholesome doctrine of the church'.[129]

'Compellite eos intrare': compel them to come in. It is difficult to imagine any directive more alien to the mind of Erasmus. He wrote in 1523: 'We force men by intimidation to believe what they do not believe, to love what they do not love, and to understand what they do not understand. Compulsion is incompatible with sincerity, and nothing is pleasing to Christ unless it is voluntary' ('Non potest esse syncerum quod coactum est, nec Christo gratum est nisi quod voluntarium').[130] It is true that in October 1527 Erasmus expressed regret that the 'spiritual freedom' supported in his earlier writings might degenerate into 'unbridled carnal license'.[131] In his copy of the 1529 Opus Epistolarum, Fisher marginally commented that this regret came rather late in the day.[132] But Reedijk has convincingly argued that such moods in Erasmus were fleeting.[133] Two days later he was refusing to go back on anything he had ever written.[134] Among Erasmus's favourite biblical passages was a section of Isaiah quoted by Matthew. Isaiah 42:3 characterised a servant of God: 'He will not break a bruised reed nor snuff out a smouldering wick.' Matthew repeated the passage (12:20), telling how Christ fulfilled the prophecy. Erasmus commented: 'He who alone of all men was wholly free from error did not break the bruised reed nor quench the smoking flax.' How 'display a character worthy of a Christian'? By 'charity in correction, mildness in finding fault'; and 'no haste in coming to a decision'.[135]

On 20 May 1535 the imprisoned Fisher was named as a cardinal. He was executed on 22 June. Nine weeks later Erasmus wrote from Basle, 'There is a persistent rumour here, probably true, that when the king discovered that the bishop of Rochester had been appointed to the College of Cardinals by Pope Paul III, he speedily had him led out of prison and beheaded. In this way did the king bestow upon him the red hat' ('sic ille dedit rubrum galerum').[136] By the end of August, reports of the deaths of Fisher and More had been confirmed. The 'holiest and best pair of men England ever had' – though Erasmus sounded a personal note for More only: 'I feel as if I had died myself; there was but one soul between us.'[137] Early in September Erasmus published his book on preaching, *Ecclesiastes Sive de Ratione Concionandi*, which he had intended to dedicate to Fisher. In the new preface Erasmus noted the deaths of Fisher and More, describing Fisher, with whom he had 'an old and close friendship', as 'a man of unexampled piety and learning'.[138] But it was the death of More which attracted attention. In October 1535 an account of the trial and execution of More was published in Basle, with some brief material on Fisher. Erasmus was involved with the publication, and at least one editorial remark has an Erasmian ring: 'I would have liked the King to show less severity, and the victims not to defy the storm openly.'[139] (Fisher had been more open than More.) As E. E. Reynolds has commented, 'the interest taken in the trial and fate of Bishop John Fisher was meagre'.[140]

In his will of January 1527, 'Erasmus of Rotterdam, Doctor of Theology, and priest of the diocese of Lower Utrecht' had given instructions to his executors about the publication of 'all my writings', preferably by Froben of Basle, within three years of his death.[141] There were to be twenty presentation sets, six of them for England: to Cambridge, 'for deposit at Queens' College in the public library of that college'; to More; to Warham; and to Bishops Fisher, John Longland of Lincoln and Cuthbert Tunstall of London.

But Tunstall was beginning to be worried about the effect of Erasmus's writings. In 1528 there came before him one Thomas Topley, Augustinian canon (Erasmus's order), who had come under the influence of Miles Coverdale, Cambridge Augustinian friar (Luther's order). Topley, of Suffolk, and Coverdale 'did commune together of Erasmus's works'.[142] Topley borrowed the *Colloquies*: and 'my mind was almost withdrawn from devotion to saints'. Topley's recantation included this: 'All Christian men beware of consenting to Erasmus's fables, for by consenting to them, they have caused me to shrink in my faith.' In a letter to Erasmus in 1529 Tunstall was very reserved about the *Colloquies*, especially 'A Fish Diet' (1526).[143] Surely many simple folk ('non eruditi') would be offended and confused by the material on Church rules and ceremonies, pilgrimages, and prayers to saints. The concern for loss of faith among the people echoed Fisher's objection to Lefèvre in 1519.

Erasmus died at Basle in July 1536, having returned to that protestant city from orthodox Freiberg in May 1535. In his wills of 1533 and 1536 a posthumous collected edition was not mentioned. In the will of February 1536 some of the monies left at the disposal of the executors were to be devoted to the maintenance of poor students at the University – a 'contribution towards the resurrection of learning in the Protestant city of Basel'.[144] A posthumous edition did in fact appear: the nine-volume *Opera Omnia*

H. C. PORTER

published by Froben, 1538–40. The set now in Queens' College, Cambridge, was probably presented by Sir Thomas Smith, fellow of Queens'. In 1543, copies of the edition were publicly burnt in Milan, together with works of Luther, with the approval of the local representative of the Emperor Charles V.[145] A short biography of Erasmus was included in the *Opera Omnia*.[146] The author was Beatus Rhenanus (Beat Bild of Rheinau) who, as the editor of his works for Froben at Basle, had known Erasmus well for twenty years. Beatus listed Erasmus's English friends: Lord Mountjoy, Warham, More, Colet, Tunstall, Grocyn, Linacre, Pace, William Latimer. There was no mention of Fisher.

Notes

Erasmus's surviving correspondence is printed in *Opus Epistolarum Des. Erasmi Roterodami*, ed. P. S. Allen, completed by H. M. Allen and H. W. Garrod, 11 vols. (Oxford, 1906–47). Volume XII, 'Indices', came in 1958. References to the edition are given here as 'Allen', letter number followed, in brackets, by volume number: Allen, 237 (I). Where a page reference is given, it is cited as follows: Allen, I, 590–3. A complete English translation of the eleven volumes will be part of *Collected Works of Erasmus* (*CWE*), in the course of publication by the University of Toronto Press. At the time of writing, six volumes of letters have appeared (1974–82), down to Allen, 992 (June 1519). The translators are Sir Roger Mynors and D. F. S. Thomson. These volumes are referred to here as *CWE*, volume number, page number: *CWE*, VI, 288 (the letter numbers are as in Allen). In 1968 Fr Jean Rouschausse of the Catholic University of Angers published *Erasmus and Fisher: Their Correspondence 1511–1524* (Librairie Vrin, Paris). This has the Latin text of the letters, a dutiful English translation, and very helpful introduction and notes (all in English, although the book is vol. XVI in the series 'De Pétrarque à Descartes'). References here appear thus: Rouschausse, p. 50.

1 Allen, 186 (I); *CWE*, II, 100.
2 P. S. Allen, 'Erasmus at Cambridge in 1506', in Allen, I, 590–3 (appendix VI).
3 Cambridge UL, Queens' College Muniments, Bk 79, fo. 135. Erasmus 'fuit pensionarius 21° Henrici Sept.'.
4 John Caius, *Historiae Cantabrigiensis*, in *Works*, ed. E. S. Roberts (Cambridge, 1912), pp. 102–3. (Caius entered Cambridge in 1529).
5 Elias Ashmole, *The Institution, Laws and Ceremonies of the Most Noble Order of the Garter* (London, 1672), pp. 487, 558.
6 Erasmus to Fisher, Cambridge, September 1511. Allen, 229 (I); *CWE*, II, 173.
7 Erasmus to Colet, Cambridge, 13 September 1511. Allen, 227 (I); *CWE*, II, 171.
8 Brief biography of Robert Fisher (with incorrect birth date) by Helen Miller, in S. T. Bindoff (ed.), *The House of Commons 1509–1558* (London, 1982), p. 136. For John, see Emden, *Cambridge*, pp. 229–30.
9 P. S. Allen, 'Erasmus' Early Life', in Allen, I, 578–84 (appendix II). The *Compendium Vitae* (1524) by, or attributed to, Erasmus, is in Allen, I, 46–52; *CWE*, IV, 430–10 (with notes by J. K. McConica, pp. 400–3). I rely heavily on N. H.

96

Minnich and W. W. Meissner, 'The Character of Erasmus', *American Historical Review*, 83 (1978), 598–624.

10 Margaret Mann Phillips, *The 'Adages' of Erasmus* (Cambridge, 1964), p. 49.

11 Fisher to Erasmus, Halling, May 1515. Allen, 336 (II); *CWE*, III, 110.

12 Quoted from *Confutatio* (1523) by T. E. Bridgett, *Life of Blessed John Fisher* (London, 1888), p. 13.

13 T. H. Aston *et al.*, 'The Medieval Alumni of the University of Cambridge', *Past and Present*, 86 (1980), 14–19.

14 James D. Tracy, 'Erasmus Becomes a German', *Renaissance Quarterly*, 21 (1968), 281–8.

15 Erasmus to Roger Wentford, Cambridge, November 1511. Allen, 241 (II); *CWE*, II, 196. Erasmus's 1498 covering letter to Robert Fisher is Allen, 71 (I) and *CWE*, I. 147, with editorial notes in both cases.

16 Translated in E. P. Goldschmidt, *The First Cambridge Press in its European Setting* (Cambridge, 1955), pp. 7–8.

17 Allen, 1284 (V). Translation by Charles Fantazzi in Toronto edition of 1522 text: *CWE*, XXV, *Literary and Educational Writings 3*, ed. J. K. Sowards (Toronto, 1985). Fantazzi's introduction (pp. 2–9) does not supersede Goldschmidt (see above, note 16), pp. 5–9.

18 For example, Erasmus to Jacob Voogd, Torneheim, July 1501. Allen, 157 (I); *CWE*, II, 44.

19 D. F. S. Thomson and H. C. Porter (eds.), *Erasmus and Cambridge* (Toronto, 1963).

20 Erasmus to Antoon van Bergen, London, 6 February 1512. Allen, 252 (I); *CWE*, II, 213.

21 Erasmus to Domenico Grimani, London, 15 May 1515. Allen, 334 (II); *CWE*, III, 96.

22 Allen, 252 (see above, note 20).

23 Erasmus to Robert Guibé, London, 8 February 1512. Allen, 253 (I); *CWE*, II, 214.

24 Erasmus to Raffaello Riario, London, 15 May 1515. Allen, 333 (II); *CWE*, III, 86–7.

25 Erasmus to Fisher, St Omer, 5 June 1516. Allen, 414 (II); *CWE*, III, 293.

26 Fisher to Erasmus, Rochester, 30 June 1516. Allen, 432 (II); *CWE*, III, 324.

27 Erasmus to John Watson, Brussels, 13 January 1517. Allen, 512 (II); *CWE*, IV, 182.

28 Erasmus to Ammonio, Rochester, 22 August 1516. Allen, 455 (II); *CWE*, IV, 43.

29 Erasmus to Ammonio, Rochester, 17 August 1516. Allen, 452 (II); *CWE*, IV, 39.

30 More to Erasmus, London, 31 October 1516. Allen, 481 (II); *CWE*, IV, 114.

31 Latimer to Erasmus, Oxford, 30 January 1517. Allen, 520 (II); *CWE*, IV, 202.

32 Mayor, *Statutes*, p. 375.

33 To Henry Bullock, August 1516: Allen, 456 (II); *CWE*, IV, 456. To Mountjoy, May 1519: Allen, 965 (III); *CWE*, VI, 362–3. To Vives, June 1520: Allen, 1111 (IV). To Alfonso of Fonseca, May 1529: Allen, 2157 (VIII). Preface to *Ecclesiastes*, August 1535: Allen, 3036 (XI). See Thomson and Porter, *Erasmus and Cambridge*, pp. 188–205.

34 Erasmus to Peter Mosellanus, Louvain, 22 April 1519. Allen, 948 (III); *CWE*, VI, 316.

35 Fisher to Erasmus, Rochester, June 1517. Allen, 592 (II); *CWE*, IV, 397–8.
36 Erasmus to Fisher, Antwerp, 8 September 1517. Allen, 653 (III); *CWE*, V, 105–6.
37 Phillips, *'Adages'*, p. 379.
38 Erasmus to Fisher, Louvain, 5 March 1518. Allen, 784 (III); *CWE*, V, 325.
39 *LP*, VIII, no. 858, p. 332 (notes on a 12 June 1535 interrogation of Fisher).
40 Erasmus to Schets, Freiberg, 21 February 1535. Allen, 2997 (XI), line 65 (I owe this reference to Richard Rex).
41 Erasmus to Fisher, Basle, 4 September 1524. Allen, 1489 (V); Rouschausse, p. 83.
42 Erasmus to Reuchlin, Calais, 27 August 1517. Allen, 457 (II); *CWE*, IV, 55.
43 Erasmus to Fisher, Antwerp, 2 April 1519. Allen, 936 (III); *CWE*, VI, 288.
44 Allen, 936 (III); *CWE*, VI, 291.
45 Erasmus to Fisher, Louvain, 21 February 1520. Allen, 1068 (IV); Rouschausse, p. 75.
46 Erasmus to Fisher, Cambridge, late September 1511. Allen, 229 (I); *CWE*, II, 173.
47 Erasmus to Colet, Cambridge, 29 October 1511. Allen, 237 (I); *CWE*, II, 183.
48 R. Devreesse, review in *Revue Biblique*, 42 (1933), 145–6.
49 Erasmus to Colet, Cambridge, 13 September 1511. Allen, 227 (I); *CWE*, II, 171.
50 M. A. Screech, *Ecstasy and the Praise of Folly* (London, 1980), pp. 206–10.
51 Erasmus to Colet, Cambridge, 29 October 1511. Allen, 237 (I); *CWE*, II, 183.
52 Allen, I, 469, 477 n. The Toronto editors repeat the comment (*CWE*, II, 183 n.).
53 Fisher to Erasmus, London, 18 November 1511. Allen, 242 (I). Trans. Thomson and Porter, *Erasmus and Cambridge*, p. 130. *CWE*, II, 196, has 'that fund over and above my modest means'.
54 Preface to *Ecclesiastes*, August 1535. Allen, 3036 (IX). Trans. Thomson and Porter, *Erasmus and Cambridge*, p. 188.
55 Allen, 242 (see above, note 53).
56 Erasmus to Ammonio, Hammes, 8 July 1514. Allen, 295 (I); *CWE*, II, 293. I have multiplied by 450.
57 Erasmus to Colet, Cambridge, 13 September 1511. Allen, 227 (I), with note p. 467; *CWE*, II, 170, with note.
58 Andrew J. Brown, 'The date of Erasmus' Latin translation of the New Testament', *Transactions of the Cambridge Bibliographical Society*, 8 (1984), 351–80.
59 Erasmus to Colet, Landbeach, 31 October 1513. Allen, 278 (I); *CWE*, II, 260.
60 Fisher to Erasmus, Rochester, June 1517. Allen, 592 (II); *CWE*, IV, 397.
61 More to Erasmus, London, 31 October 1516. Allen, 481 (II); *CWE*, IV, 115.
62 *CWE*, XLII: *Paraphrases on Romans and Galatians*, ed. Robert D. Sider (Toronto, 1984), p. 2.
63 Ibid., p. 14.
64 Erasmus to Fisher, Louvain, 5 March 1518. Allen, 784 (II); *CWE*, V, 323.
65 *Defence of the Priesthood*, trans. Philip E. Hallett (London, 1935), p. 105.
66 Fisher to Erasmus, Rochester, June 1517. Allen, 592 (II); *CWE*, IV, 397.
67 Erasmus to Fisher, Louvain, 17 October 1519. Allen, 1030 (IV); Rouschausse, p. 73.
68 The copy bought by Fisher of the 1529 *Opus Epistolarum* is in the Houghton Library, Harvard. Fr Germain Marc'hadour has studied Fisher's marginal notes,

etc., and used them in a lecture given at Tours in 1969 (G. Marc'hadour, 'Erasme et John Fisher', in Jean-Claude Margolin (ed.), *Colloquia Erasmiana Turonensia* (Toronto, 1972), II, 771–80). The 'supplication' remark is on p. 775.

69 Erasmus to Noel Bédier, Basle, 28 April 1525 (Allen, 1571 (VI)); 15 June 1525 (Allen, 1581 (VI)); Edward Surtz, *The Works and Days of John Fisher* (Cambridge, Mass., 1967), pp. 136–7.

70 Reuchlin to Erasmus, Frankfurt, April 1514. Allen, 290 (I); *CWE*, III, 7.

71 Erasmus to Reuchlin, Basle, August 1514. Allen, 300 (II); *CWE*, III, 7.

72 Erasmus to Reuchlin, Basle, 1 March 1515. Allen, 324 (II); *CWE*, III, 62–3.

73 Lewis W. Spitz, *The Religious Renaissance of the German Humanists* (Cambridge, Mass., 1963), p. 79.

74 Fisher to Erasmus, Rochester, 30 June 1516. Allen, 432 (II); *CWE*, III, 325.

75 Erasmus to Fisher, September 1517. Allen, 653 (III); *CWE*, V, 105 ('kind heart').

76 *EW*, pp. 331–6.

77 Colet to Erasmus, London, June 1517. Allen, 593 (II); *CWE*, IV, 398.

78 *The Colloquies of Erasmus*, trans. Craig R. Thompson (Chicago, 1965), p. 86.

79 Erasmus to Wolfgang Capito, Louvain, 13 March 1518. Allen, 798 (III); *CWE*, V, 347.

80 Erasmus to Wolsey, Antwerp, May 1519. Allen, 967 (III); *CWE*, VI, 368.

81 As above, note 79.

82 *The Tablet*, 22 July 1972.

83 R. and C. Brooke, *Popular Religion in the Middle Ages* (London, 1984), pp. 39, 92–3.

84 Erasmus to Henry Glareanus, Louvain, 18 January 1518. Allen, 776 (III); *CWE*, V, 283.

85 Translated from *De Unica Magdalena* by Anselm Hufstader, 'Lefèvre d'Etaples and the Magdalen', *Studies in the Renaissance*, 16 (1969), 44.

86 Erasmus to Fisher, Antwerp, 2 April 1519. Allen, 936 (III); *CWE*, VI, 288–9.

87 Erasmus to Fisher, Louvain, 21 February 1520. Allen, 1068 (IV).

88 Erasmus to Fisher, Louvain, March 1518. Allen, 784 (III); *CWE*, V, 324.

89 Erasmus to Peter Barbier, Louvain, 7 September 1517. Allen, 652 (III); *CWE*, V, 104.

90 Allen, 784 (III).

91 Albert Rabil, Jr, *Erasmus and the New Testament: The Mind of a Christian Humanist* (San Antonio, Texas, 1972), p. 116.

92 Allen, 1068 (IV); Rouschausse, p. 75.

93 Erasmus to Wolsey, Antwerp, 18 May 1519. Allen, 967 (III); *CWE*, VI, 371.

94 Erasmus to Fisher, Louvain, 17 October 1519. Allen, 1030 (IV); Rouschausse, p. 71.

95 Erasmus to Stephen Poncher, Louvain, 21 October 1519. Allen, 1016 (IV); Rouschausse, pp. 101–2.

96 Edward Surtz, 'Fisher and the Scholastics', *Studies in Philology*, 55 (1958), 136–53; Surtz, *Works and Days*, ch. 9.

97 Quoted in Surtz, *Works and Days*, p. 164.

98 Mayor, *Statutes*, p. 313. Cf. Underwood, 'John Fisher and the promotion of learning', above, pp. 25–46.

99 Mayor, *Statutes*, pp. 110, 122.

100 Ibid., p. 252.
101 1516 'Paraclesis' (preface to New Testament), in *Christian Humanism and the Reformation: Desiderius Erasmus, Selected Writings*, ed. and trans. John C. Olin (New York, 1965), pp. 103–4.
102 Quoted in Surtz, *Works and Days*, pp. 229–30.
103 *The Thought and Culture of the English Renaissance: An Anthology of Tudor Prose 1481–1555*, ed. Elizabeth M. Nugent (Cambridge, 1956), p. 398.
104 Surtz, *Works and Days*, p. 142.
105 Rabil, *Erasmus and New Testament*, p. 107.
106 Erasmus to Albert of Brandenburg, Louvain, 19 October 1519. Allen, 1033 (IV). *Erasmus and his Age: Selected Letters of Desiderius Erasmus*, ed. Hans J. Hillerbrand (New York, 1970), p. 148 (the translations in this volume are by Marcus A. Haworth).
107 From Erasmus's biographical sketch of Colet, June 1521. Allen, 1211 (IV). Olin, *Christian Humanism*, p. 183. In general, Jean-Pierre Massaut, 'Erasme et St Thomas', *Colloquia Turonensia*, II, 581–611.
108 Preface to edition of Hilary of Poitiers. Allen, 1334 (V). Trans. in John C. Olin, 'Erasmus and his Edition of Hilary', *Erasmus in English* (annual newsletter from University of Toronto Press), 9 (1978), p. 11.
109 Erasmus to Fisher, Antwerp, 2 April 1519. Allen, 936 (III); *CWE*, VI, 292.
110 Erasmus to Fisher, Louvain, 21 February 1520. Allen, 1068 (IV); Rouschausse, p. 75.
111 Erasmus to Albert of Brandenburg, Louvain, 19 October 1519. Allen, 1033 (IV). Olin, *Christian Humanism*, p. 144.
112 Erasmus to Henry Glareanus, Louvain, 18 January 1518. Allen, 766 (III); *CWE*, V, 284.
113 Erasmus to Herman of Wied, Basle, 19 March 1528. Allen, 1976 (VII). Trans. in an essay on which I have much relied: C. Reedijk, 'Erasmus' Final Modesty', in C. Reedijk (ed.), *Actes du Congrès Érasme* (Amsterdam, 1971), pp. 174–92 at p. 177. The Conference was in Rotterdam in 1969.
114 Erasmus to Justus Jonas, Louvain, 10 May 1521. Allen, 1202 (IV). Olin, *Christian Humanism*, p. 161.
115 Preface to Hilary (as above, note 108).
116 Thompson, *Colloquies*, p. 41.
117 Erasmus to Fisher, Antwerp, 2 April 1519. Allen, 936 (III); *CWE*, VI, 291.
118 Erasmus to Frederick of Saxony, Antwerp, 14 April 1519. Allen, 939 (III); *CWE*, VI, 298.
119 Erasmus to Justus Jonas, Louvain, 10 May 1521. Allen, 1202 (IV). Olin, *Christian Humanism*, p. 161. Subsequent quotations (in order): pp. 155, 163, 157, 153, 152.
120 *EW*, pp. 312, 345, 341, 340 (in order of quotation).
121 Erasmus to Adrian VI, Basle, 22 March 1523. Allen, 1352 (V). Hillerbrand, *Erasmus and his Age*, p. 171.
122 Thompson, *Colloquies*, p. 156.
123 Erasmus to Fisher, Basle, 4 September 1524. Allen, 1489 (V); Rouschausse, pp. 83–5.
124 The 1526 sermon was not included in *EW*, but was added to the 1935 reprint, pp. 429–76.

125 *EW* (1935 edn), p. 434.
126 Mayor, *Statutes*, p. 212. Cf. Underwood, 'John Fisher and the promotion of learning', above pp. 25–46.
127 Erasmus to Justus Decius, Freiberg, 8 June 1529. Allen, 2175 (VIII), lines 21–6.
128 For Fisher's comment on the published letter, see Marc'hadour, 'Erasme et John Fisher', *Colloquia Turonensia*, ii, 776.
129 *EW* (1935 edn), pp. 440–2.
130 Preface to Hilary (as above, note 108).
131 Erasmus to a monk, Basle, October 1527. Allen, 1887 (VII). Trans. in Reedijk, 'Erasmus' Final Modesty', p. 182.
132 Marc'hadour, 'Erasme et John Fisher', *Colloquia Turonensia*, ii, 775.
133 Reedijk, 'Erasmus' Final Modesty' (n. 113), especially p. 182.
134 Erasmus to John Gacy, Basle, 17 October 1527. Allen, 1891 (VII).
135 Erasmus to Frederick of Saxony, Antwerp, 14 April 1519. Allen, 939 (III); *CWE*, VI, 299. Passage previously used in 1515: 'War is sweet to those who don't know it', Phillips, *Adages*, p. 346. Subsequently used in October 1519 (Allen, 1033 (IV); trans. Olin, *Christian Humanism*, p. 138) and 1523 (Allen, 1334 (V), lines 618–21).
136 Erasmus to Bartholomew Latomus, Basle, 24 August 1535. Allen, 3048 (XI). Hillerbrand, *Erasmus and his Age*, p. 286.
137 Erasmus to Peter Tomiczki, Basle, 31 August 1535. Allen, 3049 (XI). Hillerbrand, *Erasmus and his Age*, p. 288.
138 Allen, 3036 (XI). Trans. in Thomson and Porter, *Erasmus and Cambridge*, p. 188.
139 Ernest E. Reynolds, *The Trial of St Thomas More* (London, 1964), p. 5.
140 Ibid., p. 2.
141 Allen, VI, 503–6 (appendix XIX) (trans. D. F. S. Thomson).
142 John Foxe, *Acts and Monuments*, ed. S. R. Cattley (London, 1848), V, 40.
143 Tunstall to Erasmus, London, 24 October 1529. Allen, 2226 (VIII), lines 56–62.
144 Reedijk, 'Erasmus' Final Modesty', p. 189. 1536 will, Allen, XI, 362–5 (appendix XXV).
145 Reedijk, 'Erasmus' Final Modesty', pp. 191–2.
146 Allen, I, 56–71. Olin, *Christian Humanism*, pp. 32–54.

Fisher and More: a note

GERMAIN MARC'HADOUR

To make it clear at once that the portraits in my diptych are not of spiritual twins, let me begin with an impression of clash between More the apologist and Fisher the preacher. You remember that a nameless 'Messenger' is More's guest and interlocutor in *A Dialogue Concerning Heresies*. In a long passage added to the second edition (1531), the young man exploits 'a proper boke & a very contemplatyue . . . entytled yᵉ image of loue'. The 'good holy man' who wrote it is nostalgic, he says, for the good 'olde tyme' when 'they had trene chalyces and golden prestes / and nowe haue we golden chalyces and trene prestes'. More takes issue with the 'feruent vndyscrete' of *The Image of Love*, and specifically with that 'proper', that is clever, comparison between golden and wooden, antiquity and today: 'I thynk he sayth not trouth / that the chalyces were made of trene when the prestes were made of golde.'[1] The Yale editors remind us that the comparison was not new, as More must have known. It is found in Savonarola's best-seller *De Simplicitate Christianae vitae* and in Gratian's *Decretum* – a handbook of More's in his legal training; it was even ascribed to the eighth-century West Saxon missionary St Boniface.[2]

A nearer precedent was Fisher. He uses another version of the antithesis in a sermon which many of More's readers must have read, since *The Fruitful Sayings of David* had gone through at least eight editions over the previous two decades.[3] More startles us by waiving the comparison as untrue, as we have every reason to believe that he read – and, with his exceptional memory, remembered – the sermons of the bishop who was considered England's best preacher and to whom, for that reason, their common friend Erasmus planned to dedicate his treatise on pulpit oratory. Did More know that he might have given the impression of being in disagreement with his best, nay his only, ally in the current controversy against heresy? If he did, he only showed his independence of mind. In the *Dialogue*, the layman repeatedly deplores the views and practices of bishops who deny their flock the pleasure and profit of reading God's word in the English tongue, or who admit to ordination a rabble of unworthy clerics where they should 'take vnto presthed better ley men and fewer'.[4] And what was innocent in a 1508 sermon may no longer be so twenty years – and a religious revolution – later. In 1532, to deprecate the notion that he must approve everything in *The Praise of Folly* for the simple reason that the book was written in his own house by 'Erasmus his darling', More points out that merry jests and clever paradoxes, which were bandied innocuously about in days of peace and church unity, have become odious and dangerous in times when people infected with heresy turn even honey into poison.

Just as More never used *ipse dixit* as a final argument when he enlisted Erasmus's philological authority, even in 1523 when the scholar's prestige was still almost undimmed, just so he would not follow uncritically the bishop he considered matchless 'in wisdome, learning and long approved virtue together'. The autonomy he had asserted in the field of doctrinal exposition he also claims in the matters of conscience. No utterance perhaps characterises More better than what he writes from prison to explain why the news that Fisher had finally agreed to swear to the supremacy could not shatter his own resolve: 'Verely, Daughter, I neuer entend (God being my good lorde) to pynne my soule at a nother mans backe, not euen the best man that I know this day liuing; for I knowe not whither he may happe to cary it. Ther is no man liuing of whom while he liueth, I may make myself sure.'[5]

Nevertheless, as spiritual guides, Fisher and More belong together. The author of *Utopia* and the drafter of College statutes avoid divorcing grace from nature, man's free will from God's Holy Spirit. The wise Hebrew agrees with the pagan sages that 'in virtue is pleasure and in sin is pain',[6] and with those who, having experienced both paths, 'have ben more glad inwardly in the penytent lyfe' than in 'the laborous way of iniquity'.[7] The hunt is Fisher's protracted parable of a strenuous life being also exciting and rewarding and therefore most appealing. Hence, of course, the two saints' use of hairshirt and whipping cord; hence the unremitting exercise by which they grew fit for the tough encounters. Of course, the wisdom of the stoics and of the Old Testament tallies with the wise folly of the loyal knights who will follow their master (or captain, or king: More uses all three terms of Christ) into the 'spiritual battle', for which More listed twelve rules and twelve weapons in stanzas of his youth.

Fisher is less wary than More in accepting traditions which we now view as apocryphal embroidery. There is no harm where, in his sermons, he says that Martha was Lady of the Castle of Bethany, that the risen Lazarus never laughed, that their sister Mary 'took upon her great penance'.[8] Lack of caution is more perilous when he accepts and publicly echoes rumours such as that concerning Luther's child born within weeks of marriage.[9]

Fisher is also more attracted to the arcane. He follows Reuchlin in linking the name of Jesus, that *verbum mirificum*, to YHWH, with the letter *shin* in *Yeshuah* humanising the Sinaitic tetragram, making it, as it were, pronounceable. More is chary of such esoteric lore: 'I can no scyll of the Iewys Talmud', he retorts to Tyndale.[10]

Balance is no doubt the main common feature of the two saints' Christian wisdom. Using different metaphors – the two millstones, or the two spurs of a rider – they temper dread with love and hope. They never lose sight of God's initiative and the priority of grace when they stress man's responsibility and assert the freedom of his will, Fisher rather more insistently than either Erasmus or More. They proclaim the starkness of self-renunciation, but always link 'the sweetness of hope' with present tribulation. They have inherited medieval devotion to the wounds bored in the Saviour's flesh by our sins and His love, and all their exhortations lead to a requital of that love. The fullest expression of their spirituality is perhaps Fisher's prayer to the Father begging an infusion of the Spirit of Love. Not too surprisingly, it was first ascribed to More – by A. G. Dickens – before Fisher's handwriting was identified. Three French translations of it have appeared. Its final lines provide the best image of the souls of the prisoners awaiting death in the Tower:

I beseech thee to shed upon my heart thy most holy spirit by whose gracious presence I may be warmed, heated and kindled with the spiritual fire of charity and with the sweetly burning love of all godly affections, that I may fastly set my heart, soul and mind upon thee and assuredly trust that thou art my very loving father, and according to the same trust I may love thee with all my heart, with all my soul, with all my mind and all my power. Amen.[11]

Hardly less typical is the very last line of More's last and most quoted prayer: 'The things, good Lord, that I pray for, give me the grace to labour for.'[12]

More has been accused of cruelty, not merely because several heretics were burnt at the stake during his chancellorship, but also for the virulence of the words he flings at them in his polemical works, and the *haereticis molestus* of his epitaph. By contrast, some historians find John Fisher gentle and courteous, though the bishop too approved of the death penalty for the crime of heresy. And he set the tone for Catholic denunciations of Luther's wedding: 'A frere and a nounne together, can this be any good marriage? . . . A very mad man, he to marry, & yet to affirme that this sacrament hath no vertue in it . . . The couplyng of hym and his mate to gydere is a veray brothelry & a detestable sacrilege' (February 1526 sermon).[13] He also preceded More in imputing to Luther the chief responsibility for the 'murdre of men . . . aboue an C thousande'[14] resulting from the Peasants' War. He uses very strong epithets of Oecolampadius too in the *De Veritate* of 1527, his last theological treatise, after which his attention was wholly absorbed by the 'King's Great Matter'.

Yet both he and More, capable of wrestling with vigour and of hitting hard against heresy, evince an equal capacity for tender love, which asserted itself especially after the crucible of persecution had purified their humours, and incarceration had demobilised them from battle on the front lines. Surtz sees only one strong human affection in Fisher's life, his near filial bond to the Lady Margaret. Isn't there also fraternal love in the bishop's dedication of two prison treatises to his own half-sister Elizabeth? This somewhat parallels More's choice, as dedicatee of his first English book, of a 'Poor Clare', 'his ryght enteyerly beloued syster in Chryst, Joyeuce Leygh'.[15]

Their devotion to Mary Magdalen was, I think, more fervent than that of their contemporaries, which is saying a lot. At the start of his second book against Lefèvre, Fisher says that Book I has amply vindicated the traditional identity of the saint as being at the same time a sinner, the sister of Martha and Lazarus, the breaker of the pot of nard over Jesus and the messenger of his resurrection. Yet, he adds, I want to continue in the field because for many years I have been a devoted client of the Magdalene – 'cuius tutelae me jam annos multos deuoui'.[16] His triple book may have confirmed More's own attachment to a saint he enlists to serve a variety of arguments, especially in the roles 'canonised' by Christ himself: as the contemplative, 'whose ydle sitting at her ease & herkening he accounted and declared for better busines then the busy styrring & walking aboute of his good hostesse Martha', and as the extravagant lover whose foil in St John's Gospel is Judas 'the jolly merchant'.[17] Though the protestants, like their master Judas, loathe her for wasting both good time and good money, she shall be remembered down the ages, that is praised in the liturgy, and emulated by the faithful.

For Fisher and More the Eucharist, which Catholic piety has later associated too exclusively with the refreshment of the individual soul and the intimacy of Christ's presence, was primarily the builder of Church unity. This explains why they devoted more pages to it than to any other single issue; why they immediately held the Swiss Sacramentarians to be far worse than the Lutherans; why More kept a vigilant eye on the Zwinglian Simon Grynaeus during his visit to the libraries of England; why he ordered a public 'striping' of the young boy who in his household spread 'his vngracyouse heresye agaynst the blessed sacrament'.[18]

This emphasis was not merely a reaction against the deniers of the Real Presence. As early as 1509, Fisher praised both Henry VII and the Lady Margaret for their devotion to the Blessed Sacrament. A similar reverence before the *viaticum* was also shown by Francis I of France and Michel de Montaigne, to name two Catholics one does not readily associate with pietism. Richard Fox, bishop of Winchester, gave the name of *Corpus Christi* to the college he erected at Oxford; it was inaugurated in 1516, and ten years later Fisher chose Fox, for that reason, as the dedicatee of his Latin volume, asserting 'the truth of the body and blood of Christ in the Eucharist'. More wrote no such massive treatise, but the bulk of his production on the Blessed

Sacrament is none the less impressive. Leaving aside the many pages in the *Responsio adversus Lutherum*, where the battleground has been mapped for him by Luther and Henry VIII, and several chapters which his English polemics of 1529–32 devote to the mass as sacrifice and the priest as its minister, we find the Eucharist as sole or main topic of no fewer than four works: *The Letter Answering Frith* (1532), the *Answer to the Poisoned Book* (1533), the unfinished *Treatise upon the Passion* (1534), which actually does not go beyond the Last Supper, and the short *Treatise to Receive the Blessed Body* (1534). The influence of Fisher's *De Veritate* is clearest in two works of More's: the commentary on the sixth chapter of St John's Gospel – Christ's discourse on the Bread of Life – which occupies the preface to Fisher's Book V fills four out of the five books of More's *Answer*, while Fisher's learned essay on the names of the Eucharist in Book II provides the substance of More's 'second lecture' in the *Treatise upon the Passion*[19]

The deaths of Fisher and More have been more examined than their lives, and they themselves would have it so. As Fisher wrote when his own death was getting near, 'to dye well' is man's 'chiefe and princypall buziness',[20] and death looms even larger in More's works, from the poems of his youth, through the meditation on *The Four Last Things* which he put on the loom in the prime of his life, to his resolve to bestow all his time at the Tower on pondering 'Christ's passion and mine own passage out of this world'.

'Dost thou not marke that this is our wedding daie?'[21] said the bishop to his man on the morning of Tuesday 22 June 1535. More had used the nuptial metaphor six weeks earlier, as he watched five priests being dragged to Tyburn gallows; with rueful humour he had hinted that the stark equation of death with marriage was hardly suitable for a man like him, enmeshed, for better and for worse, in the web of wedlock. His wife and family were the main source of both his comfort and tribulation; they were his best friends and his worst enemies; they kept him continual company by their affectionate prayer and, whenever they could, visited him in the flesh; they wished him heaven, yet laboured hard to make him change his mind. Fisher was spared these subtle temptations while he also lacked these sweet comforts. His cell was seldom graced with friendly faces, and his headless body claimed by no pious mourner: his bridal attire being booty for the hangman, his carcass lay naked on the scaffold until it was dumped into the nearest burial pit. It was on 6 July, as Heaven would have it, when Fisher's head was replaced by More's on London Bridge, that his body also was carried, along with More's, back into the Tower, where their mortal remains lie presumably side by side underneath the pavement of St Peter in Chains. Margaret Roper was allowed to wrap her father's body in a shroud, and it was then, presumably, that she kept a cervical vertebra struck loose by the axe, and now revered as a relic. She also secured More's head, which otherwise, after a fortnight's exposure, would have been dropped into the Thames.

When Leo XII on 29 December 1886 beatified a group of fifty-four English martyrs, eighteen of them Carthusian monks, the first name on the list was John Fisher, the second was Thomas More. Sometimes it may seem that the Church was discriminating against the small fry by putting these two grandees at the head of the procession, but the order of glorification actually followed that of vilification. Fisher and More were arrested before anyone else, and most of the other martyrs drew resolution from their example.

Notes

1 Thomas More, *A Dialogue Concerning Heresies*, ed. T. M. C. Lawler *et al.*, *The Complete Works of St Thomas More*, VI (1) (New Haven and London, 1981), 41.

2 Ibid., VI (2), 608, 758.

3 *EW*, p. 180.

4 More, *Dialogue* VI (1), 295, 341.

5 *The Correspondence of Sir Thomas More*, ed. Elizabeth F. Rogers (Princeton, 1947), no. 206, at p. 521.

6 *The Workes of Sir Thomas More Knyght . . . Wrytten by Him in the Englysh Tonge*, ed. William Rastell (London, 1557), p. 98.

7 *EW*, pp. 43, 263.

8 Ibid., pp. 114, 290, 306.

9 Ibid., p. 473.

10 Thomas More, *The Confutation of Tyndale's Answer*, ed. L. A. Schuster *et al.*, *The Complete Works of St Thomas More*, VIII (1) (New Haven and London, 1973), 73.

11 Reproduced in E. E. Reynolds, *Saint John Fisher* (Wheathampstead, Herts., 1955), pp. 319–21 (appendix C).

12 *The Complete Works of St Thomas More*, XIII, ed. Garry E. Haupt (New Haven and London, 1976), p. 231.

13 *EW*, p. 472f.

14 Ibid., p. 475.

15 *The Correspondence of More*, p. 9.

16 *Opera*, col. 1425.

17 *The Workes of Sir Thomas More . . . in Englysh*, p. 304. See other references to the 'blessed Mary Maudlin' under Luke 10:38 in G. Marc'hadour, *The Bible in the Works of St Thomas More*, part 2 (Nieuwkoop, 1969), p. 110.

18 Thomas More, *The Apology*, ed. J. B. Trapp (New Haven and London, 1979), p. 117.

19 *The Complete Works of More*, ed. Haupt, pp. 152–7.

20 *EW*, p. 362.

21 *Life*, XII, 191.

The polemical theologian

RICHARD REX

John Fisher's career as a polemical theologian did not begin until 1519, his fiftieth year, and, since his previous publications had all been of a devotional or pastoral nature, there was nothing in his background – except perhaps his Yorkshire birth – to suggest that he would become such a tenacious controversialist. This clearly sets him apart from such humanist or scholastic contemporaries as Cajetan, Clichtove, Eck and More, whose argumentative dispositions became apparent far earlier in their careers. Yet, despite his lack of experience, his works against Lefèvre d'Étaples, Luther and Oecolampadius earned him a reputation as a theologian of considerable weight. Indeed, Lord Acton was to write, 'Of all the works written against Luther in the beginning of the Reformation, his [Fisher's] were the most important.'[1] Although it might be argued that this was a dubious accolade, Acton's judgement is confirmed by the esteem in which Fisher and his work were held even before his martyrdom, by the success of his books, and by the use made of his work in later Catholic polemics and at the Council of Trent. But, before considering the motives which led Fisher to engage in theological controversy, and the qualities which made his works, at least in Catholic circles, among the most influential of their time, it is worth setting the scene by sketching the course of his polemical career. This can be conveniently divided into two phases, separated by the watershed of the condemnation of Luther in 1520.

In the earlier period, Fisher was embroiled in an often acrimonious debate over the identity of Mary Magdalene. In late 1517 or early 1518 the French humanist, Jacques Lefèvre d'Étaples, published his *De Maria Magdalena*, a book in which he argued that the figure at the heart of the popular devotion to 'Mary Magdalene' was in fact a conflation of three separate women – Mary the sister of Martha and Lazarus, the Mary from whom Christ had expelled seven demons, and the notorious sinner of Luke 7:36–50. His explanation that the confusion had arisen because certainly the first two women, and perhaps the third also, were called 'Mary Magdalene' in the gospels fatally weakened what was otherwise a very strong case. Fisher's reply to this, the *De Unica Magdalena Libri Tres*, was published at Paris on

22 February 1519. Assuming without argument that, as Lefèvre agreed, at least some of the scriptural references to 'Mary Magdalene' referred to the sister of Martha, Fisher went on to demonstrate that these references all refer to one person (which most critics would accept), and that therefore Mary Magdalene (i.e. the demoniac) and the sister of Martha were one and the same (which most critics would not accept).

Shortly after Fisher's book appeared, Lefèvre's long-time friend and collaborator, Josse Clichtove, published his *Disceptationis de Magdalena Defensio*. This was a defence of Lefèvre's thesis against an earlier reply from Marc de Grandval, the *Apologia Seu Defensorium*. Although Clichtove did not mention, and presumably had not seen, Fisher's book, Fisher set to work on a refutation, the *Eversio Munitionis*, which was published some time in the summer. But, while Fisher was engaged in refuting Clichtove, Lefèvre himself was rethinking his position in the light of Fisher's criticisms. In his *Secunda Disceptatio*, also published some time in the summer, Lefèvre abandoned the view that there were two or three women all called 'Mary Magdalene', and moved to a more defensible position by distinguishing clearly between the demoniac Mary Magdalene, and the sister of Martha. Fisher was not satisfied with this reformulation. His *Confutatio Secundae Disceptationis* of September 1519 acknowledged that Lefèvre now agreed there was only one Magdalene, but continued in effect to accuse him of heresy for his rejection of the traditional identification of her with Martha's sister. In a recent survey of this pamphlet war, Fisher's three contributions to the tally of some twenty publications were described as 'certainly the most interesting of the conservative tracts'.[2] Curiously enough, his interest in the Magdalene question may have contributed to his involvement with the Holy Maid of Kent, Elizabeth Barton. For, when she claimed to be receiving revelations from, among others, Mary Magdalene, Fisher sent his chaplain to her with a list of questions intended to test her authenticity. One of these questions concerned the identity of the Magdalene,[3] and, since Fisher continued to credit the Maid, one assumes she gave the right answer.

The second phase of Fisher's polemical career began in 1521, and saw him occupied in rebutting the doctrines of the reformers. On Sunday 12 May he preached a sermon at what was the public commencement of the English government's campaign against Lutheranism – the burning of Luther's books in St Paul's churchyard. The sermon was published within a year, both in the original English, and in a Latin translation by Richard Pace. Though intended for popular rather than academic consumption, the sermon is not without merit as a work of theology, and shows that right from the start Fisher penetrated to the heart of Luther's position. He picked out for attack the doctrine of justification by faith alone, the appeal to scripture alone, and the rejection of papal authority. The analysis and critique that he adumbrated here foreshadowed the more solid defences that he was later to erect against Lutheranism.

Fisher's next work was published in November 1522. The *Convulsio Calumniarum* was a defence of the tradition concerning St Peter's ministry and martyrdom at Rome. This had been denied in the *Libellus* printed in 1520 over the name of Ulrich Velenus, who has been identified by the recent research of A. J. Lamping as a minor Bohemian humanist and printer. According to Lamping, Velenus saw his work as completing the overthrow of papal claims begun by Lorenzo Valla's exposure of the Donation of Constantine, and continued by Luther's re-interpretation of the Petrine texts.[4] Fisher was not slow to appreciate the implications of this for Catholic ecclesiology, and broke off from work on a larger-scale refutation of Luther in order to deal with what he regarded as a further example of Lutheran arrogance. His reply to Velenus, founded on the unanimity and antiquity of the tradition, is a capable and economical presentation of all the evidence then available – and, unlike his position on the Magdalene question, has been vindicated by the consensus of modern scholarship. In Lamping's view, it 'marked a culminating point in the polemics which was not attained again in the later history of the controversy',[5] although he has also suggested that Fisher's reply probably gave the original denial far wider circulation than it would otherwise have achieved.[6]

The larger-scale work, which appeared shortly afterwards, in January 1523, was the *Assertionis Lutheranae Confutatio*, a 200,000-word reply to the *Assertio Omnium Articulorum* published by Luther in December 1520. Luther's work was a justification of the forty-one propositions condemned in the Bull *Exsurge Domine* of June 1520. They covered a wide field, and Luther's defence of them extended the debate still further, so that Fisher's huge refutation, even broader in scope, became, if not a comprehensive summary and refutation of Lutheranism, then certainly the nearest thing to one available at that time. And it seems to have served as just that. Until it was overhauled by John Eck's *Enchiridion* in the later 1520s, it was, along with Henry's *Assertio*, the best-selling (or at least the most frequently reprinted) scholarly attack on Luther's doctrines.[7]

The next task Fisher undertook was a defence of Henry VIII's *Assertio Septem Sacramentorum* (which he had allegedly helped compose) against Luther's vitriolic reply. But the *Defensio Regiae Assertionis*, a work of some 70,000 words, is as much a new attack on Luther as a defence of Henry. In the first two chapters Fisher adopts Henry's tone and method, scoring debating points, and trying to show that Luther is inconsistent. Chapters 10 and 11 deal with scripture and authority, and the twelfth and last chapter with holy orders and matrimony. The bulk of the work, however, chapters 3 to 9, forms a comprehensive attack on Luther's Eucharistic doctrine, defending against him both the sacrifice of the mass, and transubstantiation. The *Defensio Regiae* was written and published in parallel with the *Sacri Sacerdotii Defensio* (the texts refer to each other, and both were issued by Peter Quentell, the Cologne printer, in June 1525). This latter work was a reply to Luther's *De Abroganda Missa Privata* of 1522, in which Luther had set out in detail his contention that the priesthood of the New Testament was common to all believers and that therefore the special priesthood of the Catholic Church, together with its sacrifice, the mass, was a blasphemous abomination. Since Fisher dealt at length with the mass in the *Defensio Regiae*, he confined himself in the *Sacri Sacerdotii* to a defence of the special priesthood. With the exception of a second sermon preached early in 1526 at the recantation of Robert Barnes and printed at an unknown date, these works were the last Fisher published against Luther.

Fisher's last published work of purely theological controversy – this essay does not propose to cover his tracts about Henry VIII's marriage – was the *De Veritate Corporis et Sanguinis Christi in Eucharistia*, written in 1526 and printed in January 1527. His longest work, at some 220,000 words, it is a thorough defence of the Real Presence against the figurative interpretation of the Eucharist expounded by John Oecolampadius in his *De Genuina Verborum Dei . . . Expositione* of September 1525. The *De Veritate* was reckoned by T. E. Bridgett, Fisher's first modern biographer, to be his masterpiece.[8] It is divided into five books that provide a line-by-line refutation of Oecolampadius's text. Each book has its own preface, and these prefaces, which amount to about a sixth of the work, form in effect self-contained treatises on various aspects of Eucharistic theology. The first is a general introduction to the whole work. The second explores the rich significance of the Eucharist by recounting the many different titles applied to it by the Fathers of the Church. The third preface proposes fourteen arguments in corroboration of the Real Presence, while the fourth presents an expanded version of one of them – an argument from the unanimous consent of the Fathers. The final preface sets out to demonstrate against Oecolampadius that the famous sixth chapter of John's Gospel does indeed refer to the Eucharist. The prefaces are not restricted by the exigencies of detailed refutation, and are therefore more coherent and readable than the books they precede – which probably explains why Cochlaeus issued them without the accompanying text in a German translation (*Funff Vorredde*, Leipzig, 1528).

Why then did Fisher take to controversy so late? That excellent civil servant, Richard Morison, found his motives easy to explain in *Apomaxis Calumniarum*, the cynical libel with which he attempted to vindicate the justice of the bishop's execution. He contended that Fisher wrote only out of a desire for worldly glory – 'he spent his whole life wrangling with Luther and Oecolampadius, more eager for glory than zealous for the flock entrusted to him' – and that he went to the block only out of false pride – 'It was easier for him to die in the hope of immortal fame than to contradict the constant testimony he had borne in so many works'[9] (even a Morison, it seems, could not deny Fisher's consistency, although he did snipe at More's). The charge of ambition is hard to reconcile with what is known of Fisher's character. His writings reveal none of the humanist desire for literary glory that appears so clearly in the works of his contemporary and co-religionist John Eck. Moreover, by 1529 he had decided to retire from the polemical field. Cochlaeus records a letter from him to this effect,[10] and the early *Life* notes that Fisher once told a Carthusian monk who had praised his writings against Luther that his time would have been more usefully and meritoriously spent in prayer[11] – hardly the comment of a man addicted to controversy or worldly glory.

In fact, most of Fisher's works, whether devotional or polemical, seem to have been written or published at the request of others. He may have been, as Erasmus remarked, a man who did not cool down easily once he had warmed up,[12] but he also seems to have been a man who needed a spark from someone else to set him ablaze. Even among his earlier works, the sermons on the Penitential Psalms and the funeral sermon for Henry VII were preached and printed at the request of the Lady Margaret Beaufort.[13] And his involvement in the Magdalene controversy was certainly occasioned by the influence of others. In the preface to the *Confutatio Secundae Disceptationis* he tells how Cardinal Campeggio had asked him 'some time ago' what he felt about this question. What is interesting is that Fisher replied that he was inclined to Lefèvre's opinion.[14] It was not until another visiting diplomat brought the matter once more to his attention that he changed his mind – and even then only after some hesitation. Stephen Poncher, bishop of Paris, who came to England in late August 1518 at the head of a French embassy,[15] found time from his official duties to send Fisher the second (and expanded) edition of Lefèvre's book, along with Grandval's reply. He asked for an opinion. When he received much the same reply as Campeggio, Poncher wrote again, more insistently, pointing out the damage that a dispute of this kind could do to the piety of the simple faithful, and asking Fisher to step in and settle the question definitively. Only then did Fisher examine the arguments more closely, and conclude that they required refutation.[16]

Several of Fisher's writings against Luther were also produced at the instigation of others. The sermon of 1521 was preached at the command of Wolsey, and that of 1526 at the command of Henry VIII.[17] The *Convulsio Calumniarum* seems to have been suggested by Tunstall, who sent Fisher a copy of Velenus's *Libellus* early in 1522.[18] The *Defensio Regiae* can be presumed to have been written on at least an unofficial commission from the king. As for the *Confutatio* itself, Fisher began writing it in 1521 when Henry issued a general order to English scholars to attack Luther, and the first edition appeared with a warrant under the Privy Seal praising the book and giving it the royal privilege for three years.[19] Moreover, all the editions of Fisher's works printed by Quentell – all three major works against Luther as well as the *De Veritate* – carried the royal coat of arms on the title page. This may have been merely a decorative foible of Quentell's, but it may indicate that Fisher wrote in some official capacity. There is no evidence that the *De Veritate* was inspired by any request, but Fisher did keep John Cochlaeus in touch with progress on the work throughout 1526;[20] and in 1528 Cochlaeus told Erasmus that he was asking Fisher to write against the Anabaptists[21] – a request to which the response was perhaps news of Fisher's retirement from controversy.

The role of Fisher's friends and colleagues was not restricted to suggesting works for him to undertake. It was a commonplace for Fisher that an unaided individual (such as Lefèvre or Luther) was far more likely to err than was a group, and acting on this principle he circulated drafts of his writings among his acquaintances for educated comment. The dedication to Nicholas West of the *Defensio Regiae* tells us that West had approved an earlier draft two years before publication.[22] And the dedication to Tunstall of the *Sacri Sacerdotii* reveals not only that Tunstall had offered comments on that work, but that he had performed the same service for the *Confutatio*, and to great effect.[23] A letter from Richard Sharpe to Nicholas Metcalfe records that 'learned men' were impressed by early versions of Fisher's articles on indulgences and the papacy from the *Confutatio*, while other letters among the muniments of St John's College suggest that friends from his student days at Cambridge, William Melton and John Constable (respectively chancellor of York and dean of Lincoln), may also have been among those consulted.[24] Finally, the recent editor of Eck's *Enchiridion* has concluded that Eck must have read the *Defensio Regiae* before its printing in 1525.[25]

If Morison was clearly wide of the mark in charging Fisher with ambition, he was equally mistaken in assuming that the polemical concerns of the author were a distraction from the pastoral duties of the bishop. Fisher's high sense of episcopal responsibility incuded the duty to protect the souls of his flock, and those of the Church at large, by securing the spiritual foundations of sound doctrine and sound devotion against the attacks of heresy. It was towards this, and not the conversion of his opponents, that his polemical efforts were directed – as he himself repeatedly affirmed. In support of his attitude he cited St Paul's comment that, after false teachers have been admonished twice and have still not recanted, they are to be avoided.[26] Rather, he says,

I intend to confirm the faith of the weaker brethren, whose faith has for too long now been poised on the knife-edge between heresy and orthodoxy . . . It was for their sake that the order to which I belong was everlastingly established . . . if this flock should perish through our negligence, the blood shall be upon our heads.[27]

To turn now to the writings themselves, we can first notice a few points of style. Fisher's polemics combine two main approaches to argument. In one, he grapples with his opponents' views in line-by-line refutation – a method popular, or at least common, at that time, but not to the modern taste. In this vein his work is uneven, because there is much tedious repetition, and he is obliged to treat the trivial and the significant with equal seriousness. If the discipline of this approach prevents him from digressing, it sometimes causes him to miss the wood for the trees. Fortunately, his polemics are saved by his use of another method, which is to establish his own theological positions in short and self-contained treatises. These generally form the prefaces to his works, or to new stages of argument within the works, and are of two kinds. One is a chain of argument that proceeds from premiss to conclusion by a series of links which he believes no reasonable man can deny. This is first seen in his *Eversio Munitionis*, where he employs '8 Truths' to finish off the book and Clichtove. But examples occur in most of his works, the most effective being the preface to the *Confutatio*, where he enumerates '10 Truths' in support of ecclesiastical tradition and authority in interpreting scripture, and the '14 Corroborations' of the Real Presence in Preface 3 of the *De Veritate*. Since he first uses this method in his reply to Clichtove, he may have been inspired by the '8 Suppositions' on which his opponent had founded his defence of Lefèvre.[28] The other type of treatise defends a position with an orderly collection of scriptural citations backed up by an impressive range of patristic interpretation. The best example of this is the preface to article 25 of the *Confutatio*, a defence of Peter's primacy among the apostles.

The language of Fisher's polemic, at least in comparison with that of Luther, Henry, or More, is refreshingly free from coarseness – although the delicate taste of Erasmus found the tone of the *De Unica Magdalena* 'too bitter' and 'too sharp'.[29] But Fisher's prose is so free from obscenities that it is hard to understand a later comment of Erasmus to Luther that 'the attacks of Roffensis' are 'so full of insults'[30] – unless perhaps 'Roffensis' has been confused with 'Rossaeus' (i.e. More). Fisher explained his policy in the introduction to the *Confutatio*, saying 'Do not be surprised, dear reader, if I make no response to these insults of Luther's.' His opponent's coarse language was in his view nothing more than an index of moral and intellectual bankruptcy. And, when Luther tried to justify his style by an appeal to Paul's facing up to Peter at Antioch, Fisher preferred to upbraid him with Paul's deference to the High Priest at Jerusalem, citing the Deuteronomical admonition, 'Curse not the prince of the people.' He declared that Luther's jibes did not harm the pope, but, in a rare allusion to bodily functions, observed mildly that 'Luther is like one who spits at heaven, as they say, and finds that what he has spat falls back upon his own head.'[31]

More important than the style of Fisher's polemical works is their content.

While the range of subjects on which he wrote precludes a complete treatment in an essay of this length, it is possible to provide a cursory analysis picking out the major points and the recurring themes. There is in particular one common thread running through all his works, whether against Lefèvre, Luther, or Oecolampadius. This is his concept of the teaching and the teaching office of the Church, comprising his views on the relationship between scripture and tradition, and on the role of authority in the Church. It is important to realise that his position on this complex of ideas was established in its essentials in the controversy with Lefèvre, even before he had been faced with the question of Lutheranism. Lefèvre seemed to Fisher to be proposing scripture alone as the rule of faith. So Fisher's first argument in the first paragraph of his *De Unica Magdalena* takes issue with this.

Are the scriptures really so clear that we have no need of commentators or interpreters to help us understand them? If so, then whence arise such varied interpretations? If not, then whom should Christians trust the most in this field? In my judgement they should trust first of all the popes, then the orthodox fathers and writers, and finally the popular preachers . . . and if but one falsehood should be taught with the consent of all of these, then I do not see why anyone should ever trust any of their teaching.[32]

With this clear assertion of the importance of tradition, and of the infallibility of the Church in matters of faith, Fisher stepped fully armed into the arena of controversy.

It is hardly surprising that Fisher, and other Catholic polemicists, defended tradition against Luther's appeal to scripture alone. But it has been suggested that their reaction was often so extreme as to make tradition superior to scripture as a source of revealed truth. In Fisher's case, one commentator has alleged that his position was tantamount to a belief in a continuing post-apostolic revelation.[33] Careful examination of his writings does not bear out either of these hypotheses, although it does explain how such misapprehensions could have arisen. The theory that he was willing to accept new revelation rests on his undeniable interest in Christian Cabbalism, and on his frequent use of what are now called private revelations – two characteristics which perhaps show a predilection for the arcane. Christian Cabbalism was a peripheral phenomenon of the contemporary intellectual milieu which attracted such different men as Pico della Mirandola, Reuchlin, and Eck, and repelled such men as Colet, Erasmus, and Hoogstraten. Its foundation was the idea that among the Jews the transmission of scripture had been accompanied by an oral tradition, which also derived from Moses, and which was later preserved in the Talmudic writings. Its attraction for some Christians lay in the prospects they thought it offered of proving Christian doctrines from Judaic sources, and of obtaining through it a quasi-magical control over nature. But there is no evidence that either of these attracted Fisher. In his polemics he uses Reuchlin's cabbalistic derivation of the word 'missa'[34] and cites some rabbinical exegesis of the sacrifice and priesthood of Melchisedek in defence of the sacrifice of the mass.[35] And in his sermon of 1521 he explicitly presents the Cabbala as the prefigurement in the Old Law of apostolic tradition in the New Law.[36] But all this would be quite compatible with an interest in the Cabbala as nothing more than an extra tool of scriptural interpretation.

The appeal to the testimony of private revelations was a consistent feature of Fisher's polemic. As much in his first work, against Lefèvre, as in his last, against Oecolampadius, he was prepared to draw on the writings of Mechtild, Hildegard of Bingen, Elizabeth of Schöngau, and Bridget of Sweden. Yet he never attributed to them anything like the authority he attributed to scripture, or even to the writings of popes, councils, or fathers. For example, in his discussion of the development of the doctrine of purgatory, he certainly gave private revelations a role.[37] But he emphasised that purgatory was neither a new nor an extra-scriptural doctrine, saying 'because sacred scripture is a sort of treasure chest holding all things that it is necessary for a Christian to know, there can be no doubt that it contains the doctrine of purgatory'.[38] And as he said of the Apocalypse in a letter to Cochlaeus of 1526, 'It has always seemed to me almost impossible that anybody, without a new revelation, should ever adequately explain the mysteries that are presented there beneath such various and obscure metaphors.'[39] Revelations were for him just one of the Church's tools for the interpretation of scripture.

Once this is understood, the elements of Fisher's thought on scripture and tradition fall into place. To extend Fisher's metaphor, he regarded tradition as the key to the treasure chest of scripture, and of course the Church (and pre-eminently the successor of St Peter) held that key. The task of the Church was to clarify, define, and convey existing truth. Revelation could not be added to. He stressed that neither popes nor councils could make something part of the faith if it was not already so. All they could do was make explicit what was already implicitly part of the faith.[40] However, there remained an unreconciled conflict in his work between the assertion that scripture contained all that it was necessary to believe, and the equally clear assertion that Christians accepted many things that were not clearly expressed in scripture. He seems to have oscillated between seeing tradition as an independent vehicle of revealed truth, and as an authoritative interpretation of the revealed truth contained in scripture. In his defence of tradition against its detractors he inclines to the former view, but in his polemical practice he tends towards the latter. The fullest treatment that Fisher gave to the question is to be found in the introduction to the *Confutatio*, where he paraded the '10 Truths' as the weapons with which he proposed to overthrow Luther. He maintained that those who had tried to argue from scripture alone had often gone far astray; that disputes, especially about scripture, could be settled only by the authority of the Church; that the indefectibility of the Church was guaranteed by Christ's promise of the guidance of the Holy Spirit; that the Holy Spirit worked through the orthodox Fathers, legitimate councils, apostolic traditions and ecclesiastical customs; and that therefore none of these was to be scorned with impunity.

At the deepest level, the difference between Fisher and Luther over scripture was that, whereas the latter saw it as essentially self-explanatory and accessible, Fisher saw it as frequently obscure and indeed counter-intuitive. His principal demonstration of this was the case of the fourth-century heretic Elvidius. Relying on the literal sense of the Gospels, Elvidius had denied the perpetual virginity of Mary. Fisher conceded that the strict letter of scripture if anything supported his thesis, but sided against him with Jerome (who had adduced the consensus of the Church in favour of the dogma), insisting that scripture could be read only according to the Church's interpretation. This argument, which first appeared in the *Eversio Munitionis*, found a place in Henry VIII's *Assertio*, was expanded in the *Confutatio*, and went on to become a commonplace for the continental polemicists – even Erasmus appealed to it.[41] The difficulty Fisher saw in correctly understanding scripture explains his lifelong commitment to providing learned preachers to explain it to the people, and to securing the educational reforms that were a prerequisite of such provision. But, while he welcomed the assistance humanist methods could give, correct interpretation of scripture remained for Fisher a magisterial rather than a philological process. The Church remained the custodian of the correct interpretation of scripture, as well as of the scriptures themselves.

Since Fisher's ecclesiology is being considered more fully elsewhere in this volume, it calls for only brief treatment here. Again, the first thing to emphasise is that Fisher's ecclesiology, like his views on scripture and tradition, was at least sketched out in the Magdalene controversy, before he was forced to meet the challenge of Luther. The second thing to stress is that Fisher's ecclesiology was highly papalist. Even though Lefèvre had not attacked the papacy, Fisher could not resist extolling it in the *De Unica Magdalena*, where he affirmed, 'There is nothing on earth more powerful than the Supreme Pontiff, to whom Christians should have recourse in all controversies, and whose decrees they should obey, especially in those matters that concern the faith of the Gospels.'[42]

While he dealt incidentally with papal primacy in most of his works, and even devoted a whole book to Peter's residence at Rome, it was in article 25 of the *Confutatio* that he presented his fullest defence of the papal prerogatives. Before getting to grips with Luther's text, he set out his own views in a short treatise. Basing his case on twenty passages from the New Testament, adding to this a wealth of Greek and Latin patristic material, and finishing with the decree of reunion passed by the Council of Florence (1439), he produced a strong argument for Peter's primacy among the apostles, and for papal succession to this primacy.[43] This article was immediately recognised as a classic of its kind – Thomas More referred the readers of his *Responsio ad Lutherum* to it rather than deal himself with a matter which was not perfectly clear in his mind.[44] However, Fisher has left it tantalisingly unclear just how high his papalism was. If he was capable of writing 'Before which judge shall we go, if not the see of Peter, which will never lack divine assistance in handing down to us the certain truth in doubtful matters, especially those relating to the faith?',[45] he was also capable of sidestepping the issue when Luther charged Catholics with believing that 'the Church – that is, the Pope – cannot err'.[46] He did not face the question of how to reconcile his exalted view of the papacy with his firm and often expressed conviction that it was possible for any individual, as such, to err.

Since Luther rejected not only popes but also councils where he reckoned they contradicted scripture, Fisher was concerned to defend conciliar as much as papal authority. This has left it unclear as to how Fisher felt about the relative powers of the two. He expressed doubt about decisions where 'Pope dissents from council, or council from Pope',[47] but did not expand on this. The prevailing tendency of his language in the *Confutatio* is to present the relationship between pope and council as one of co-operation rather than of conflict (e.g. 'Innocentius cum concilio', 'pontifex in concilio').[48] This suggests an interesting parallel with the Tudor constitutional theory of king-in-parliament – which would have been seriously embarrassed by a question about possible disagreement between the two. As with the issue of papal infallibility, one suspects that Fisher's failure to grapple with this question occurred less by accident than by design.

Although the same ecclesiological and exegetical foundations underpinned all of Fisher's polemical writings, the writings themselves clearly varied with the opponents he faced. But even at this level there remains a common factor, namely Fisher's concern for the pastoral implications of doctrine. In controversy with Lefèvre and Clichtove the point at issue was simple, whether there were three women called Mary Magdalene, or merely one. Yet the composite personality of the Magdalene was a potent figure in medieval spirituality,[49] and an attack on her, however harmlessly intended, was bound to raise a storm – albeit in modern eyes a storm in a teacup. What was at stake for Fisher was not merely a question of scriptural exegesis, however important this undoubtedly was to him. The conflict was one of rival spiritualities. The three stages of the Magdalene's career – repentance, active ministry to Christ, and contemplation – were traditionally seen as the model for the Christian life, as respectively the beginning, growth, and consummation of sanctity. For Fisher and the tradition in which he wrote, the whole point of identifying the three stages in one person was to emphasise that no matter how sinful people might be, the love and mercy of God could always raise them up even to the peak of sanctity.[50] As Fisher explained, he wrote 'so that wretched sinners should not despair, but rather be encouraged by her example to acknowledge their sins and to lament them with tears and bitter penitence, and thus hope to regain their lost grace',[51] and he urged that the devotees of the Magdalene should not be deterred from their prayers by the specious doubts of his opponents.[52]

In fact Lefèvre did not deny the sanctity of any of the three women, but he does seem to have regarded them as essentially models of three separate vocations. And both he and Clichtove seem to have felt it incongruous and even dishonourable to imagine that Martha's sister, whom Christ loved so much, should be supposed to have been a public sinner.[53] Fisher saw this as pharasaical distaste for the sordid reality of sin. But one suspects that Lefèvre and Clichtove wanted to encourage people to avoid sin, and felt that to present Martha's sister as a sinner would be counter-productive;[54] while Fisher wanted people to acknowledge and to repent sin, and felt that to present such a woman as Martha's sister as a repentant sinner would be a great encouragement to them to do so. It might even be suggested that this was a difference between a medieval and ascetic piety imbued with an Augustinian distrust of the natural capacities of man, and a Renaissance or humanist piety with a neo-platonic confidence in those capacities. Fisher's position could perhaps be located between the humanist faith in man's natural powers and what was soon to emerge as the Lutherans' lack of faith in them. But in any case the themes of repentance and conversion were certainly potent in Fisher's psyche. They appear as strongly in his earlier works, such as the sermons on the Penitential Psalms, and the Funeral Sermon for Henry VII, as in his polemics – where Mary Magdalene was one of his favourite examples. Nor should we overlook Fisher's personal commitments in this controversy. In the course of it he confessed to a deep devotion to the saint,[55] and a statue of her was among the personal effects he made over to St John's College by deed of gift in 1525.[56]

Against Luther, Fisher's position was inevitably far more complex. He was obliged to attack not only Luther's doctrine of *sola fide*, but also his rejection of free will and his novel views of the sacraments, notably baptism, penance, the priesthood and above all the Eucharist – not to mention the many subsidiary issues. In the first article of his *Confutatio*, as in his 1521 sermon, Fisher identified the doctrine of justification by faith alone as the root of Luther's errors.[57] Moreover, he reckoned that Luther's doctrine of faith was highly and designedly equivocal. When Luther said that there could be no faith without a 'magna concussio animae', he made faith seem so difficult as to be impossible. Yet when he described faith as belief in God's words and promises, he made it seem so easy that not even a nominal Christian could be thought to lack it.[58] Luther's doctrine seemed to him to lead not to balanced devotion, but either to presumption or despair. Fisher resolved what he saw as this contradiction in Luther's teaching by applying the scholastic distinction between 'fides informis' and 'fides formata', between dead and living faith. Obviously he agreed with Luther that faith was indispensable. But while he defended Scotus from the charge that his view of the sacraments dispensed with the need for faith, he clearly saw Luther's idea of faith as dispensing with the need for the sacraments.[59] In later works Fisher was to take his analysis further. Where Luther maintained that those who had faith were absolutely certain of it, he replied that men could not be certain of the quality of their faith.[60] In his view, the sacraments were instituted so that people who frequented them properly and devoutly could obtain a reasonable certainty about their state,[61] and thus be saved from the despair that might otherwise engulf them because of the coolness of their faith and charity.

Luther's doctrine of faith entailed a radically new approach to the questions of sin, free will, and grace, and in the course of the *Confutatio* Fisher elaborated a system of ideas in opposition to it. At the root of the disagreement between the two lay Luther's concept of imputed justification, with its corollary that even after baptism the just man remains sinful, and indeed sins in every good work. The sinfulness of the just man was identified by Luther with the 'concupiscence of the flesh' which was generally acknowledged to remain even after baptism, and which he regarded as culpable in itself. To Fisher, as to all Catholic theologians since Augustine, it represented not sin as such, but a weakness or proneness to sin. While the scholastics had proliferated subtle distinctions on this question, Fisher argued, it was better to go beyond them back to Augustine, and to rely on his original distinction between the 'actus' and the 'reatus' (guilt) of sin.[62] Baptism cleansed away the 'reatus' not the 'actus', but the guilt, the sin as such, consisted in the 'reatus' alone. The crux was that actual sin required the consent of the will; and that concupiscence, which resided in the flesh, not the will, could not be sin as such. As for Luther's theory that sin and grace co-existed in the just ('simul iustus et peccator'), this was simply anathema to Fisher, for whom grace wiped away sin, and subsequent sin lost grace. When in his zeal against Pelagianism Luther not only denied the power of free will without grace to do anything except sin, but denied free will altogether, Fisher was aghast. His concern here was as much with the practical as with the theoretical consequences of the doctrine. 'It is horrible to contemplate', he wrote, 'the abyss of despair into which sinners might be plunged if they believed these words.'[63] He thought that Luther's teaching made God the direct author of sin − an error worse than that of the Manichees, who at least avoided this conclusion by postulating two opposing principles in creation.[64] His article in defence of free will, article 36, was the longest in the *Confutatio*, and it included a mass of patristic material on the subject, relying especially on Augustine.

In view of the allegations of Pelagianism and Semipelagianism that historians, following Luther, have freely levelled against late medieval and Renaissance Catholic theologians, it is worth noting that Fisher at least can be absolved of both. His teaching on grace is to be found throughout the *Confutatio*, but nowhere more than in article 36. He states firmly that salvation is available by grace alone.[65] And, if he seems to tend towards Semipelagianism in his insistence that good works can be performed before justification as a preparation for grace, he maintains that these works can only be done by virtue of an 'auxilium divinum'.[66] Nor is this identified in his thought, as it is by some late medieval theologians, with the 'generalis influentia dei' by which all actions are performed. It is distinguished from the 'generalis influentia' by the epithets 'speciale auxilium', 'auxilium divinae gratiae', and even 'gratia preveniens'.[67] And it is noteworthy that in article 36 the only scholastic that Fisher cites is the notoriously anti-Pelagian, Gregory of Rimini, and that it is precisely Gregory's tripartite analysis of God's influence in the world into 'generalis influentia', 'gratia gratis data' and 'gratia gratum faciens' that he cites.[68] And Fisher dissociates himself from the late scholastic theory that grace can be merited 'ex congruo', although he adds that this error of the scholastics, if indeed it is such, in no way justifies Luther's contrary and more pernicious error.[69]

It is not possible in an essay of this length to do full justice to Fisher's case against Luther. On the sacrament of penance, he upheld the doctrines of contrition, confession and satisfaction with a mass of scriptural and patristic argument.[70] Indulgences he justified primarily by appeal to the papal power of the keys. But he accounted for their late appearance in the Church in a way that shows not only his continuing concern with the pastoral aspects of doctrine, but also a relatively sophisticated level of historical explanation. He suggested that, in the primitive Church, charity had burned so ardently that there had been no pastoral need for indulgences. But, as Christians had become more tepid, the doctrines of indulgences and purgatory had become necessary to obviate despair.[71] His explanation for the origin of the two doctrines was that 'the belief grew gradually, partly from revelations and partly from scripture, until at last it was generally received by the orthodox Church'.[72] In defence of the special priesthood, Fisher also argued from history, tracing the description of Christian ministers as 'priests' back to the sub-apostolic era, and challenging Luther to find an apostolic church without priests.[73] Where Luther argued that the New Testament used the word 'priest' for all Christians rather than just for their ministers, Fisher replied that the Jewish people had also been called a 'royal priesthood', but that this had not stopped them having a special priesthood. He further suggested that the apostles had avoided calling their ministry a priesthood in order to prevent confusion with the Levitical priesthood then still officiating in the Temple.[74]

In his final controversy, with Oecolampadius, Fisher was once more dealing with but a single issue, whether the body and blood of Christ were really present in the Eucharist, or were merely signified by it. He was eager to emphasise how Oecolampadius differed from Luther as well as from the Church over the Eucharist, because this vindicated his position on the difficulty of finding the correct interpretation of scripture without the guidance of the Church. So, in the first preface to the *De Veritate*, he explained that behind the increasing disagreements between the reformers he saw the avenging hand of God[75] – a view that was to become common coin among the Catholic polemicists, and which was to find its classic expression in Bossuet's *Variations of Protestantism*.

From the Catholic point of view, the interaction of doctrine and devotion could never be more intimate than in the theology of the Eucharist. Fisher believed that both Luther and Oecolampadius missed the true point of the sacrament, and in each case, unsound doctrine led to unsound devotion. Luther saw it as a sacrament for the forgiveness of sins, and Fisher disapproved of the indifference to the danger of unworthy reception that he thought must arise from this view.[76] Oecolampadius seemed to empty the Eucharist of its essence. If Christ was not present, then as far as Fisher was concerned the mass was of no more use as a memorial of Christ than any other meal of bread and wine.[77] Besides which, denial of the Real Presence precluded worship of the Blessed Sacrament. Since late medieval and pre-Tridentine Catholic theology has been criticised for putting attendance at mass above communion, it is worth noting that the basis of Fisher's Eucharistic theology was that the sacrament was ordained for communion with God, and was therefore both the instrument and the consummation of the unity of the Church;[78] and that one of his main objections to Oecolampadius's 'nuda memoria' was that merely looking on at the mass would be as good a memorial as receiving communion.[79] The Church could be Christ's body only if there was some real physical bond between the head and the members. And he could not see this bond of body with body anywhere except in this sacrament, in which Christians, by eating Christ's body, were assimilated to it.[80] This strongly incarnational aspect of his Eucharistic devotion emerged clearly in the ninth corroboration of the third preface, where he explained that those who piously receive communion grow in all virtues, claiming in evidence that fluctuations in the level of the moral and spiritual life of the Church could be correlated with the ebb and flow of Eucharistic devotion.[81]

The thorough and impassioned treatment of the Real Presence in the *De Veritate* shows that the work meant more to its author than the mere defence of a thesis. His considerable devotion to the sacrament emerges clearly in the preface to Book II, where he explored the various titles applied to the

Eucharist by the Fathers. He emphasised that, while all the names drew attention to some particular aspect of it, none provided an exhaustive definition of the great mystery;[82] and elsewhere he observed that, while theology could say something about the Eucharist, it was not possible for the human mind to grasp its full significance[83] – an attitude more reminiscent of the *devotio moderna* than of the excessive curiosity often attributed to late scholasticism. It is clear that Fisher took the body of Christ very seriously, whether as the sacrament or as the Church, and that this was as true of his inner as of his public life. The passage of the early *Life* which describes how he was often reduced to tears when celebrating mass need not be mere hagiographical convention.[84] And it was in 1504, when his influence over the Lady Margaret Beaufort was probably at its peak, that his patroness published her translation of the fourth book of the *Imitatio Christi*,[85] about the Eucharist. Finally, in some surviving manuscript fragments of a lost devotional treatise on the Eucharist, the description of the benefits to be derived 'ex cotidiano huius sacramenti usu' reveal Fisher in an interesting light, as an early exponent of daily communion.[86]

The caricature of Luther's Catholic opponents that has long prevailed is of a group of blinkered and backward dogmatists whose lamentable ignorance of scripture forced them to depend on canon law and scholastic theology in their vain resistance to the tide of reform. This picture, originally sketched by the humanists as a portrayal of the 'theologi', the enemies of Erasmus and Reuchlin, was applied by Luther to the Catholics, and from there passed into history. Recent work has done much to correct this view, which is certainly not an adequate account of Fisher. Of course, like most of the Catholic writers, he rejected the appeal to scripture alone. But he drew on scripture at least as heavily and widely as Luther. On the other hand he made remarkably little use of canon law, nor did he often appeal to the scholastics. Of some 300 works cited by author and title in the course of his publications, barely a dozen are the works of scholastic authors. And those dozen are hardly mentioned more than two or three times each. Within this tiny sample it is possible to detect a preference for the 'via antiqua' over the 'via moderna', in that references to Thomas and Scotus easily predominate over all others. However, Fisher always retained a healthy respect for the scholastics, even if he deplored their barbarous latinity.[87] His attitude is well expressed in his provision at St John's for a lecture on Scotus to replace the Hebrew lecture under certain circumstances – 'if he can be turned into better Latin'.[88]

It was on the Fathers, not the scholastics, that Fisher really founded his arguments. And of all the Fathers it was Augustine that he cited most frequently – especially against Luther. But the Greeks as well as the Latins were grist to his mill. Origen, Cyril of Alexandria, Cyril of Jerusalem, Gregory of Nyssa, Gregory Nazianzen, Cyprian, Chrysostom, Dionysius (the pseudo-Areopagite), and John Damascene figure as prominently as Tertullian, Jerome, Ambrose, Hilary of Poitiers, Cassian, and Gregory the Great among the forty or so authors of some 200 patristic texts named in his works. This statistic lends some credence to the claim of the early *Life* that his library was the greatest of any bishop in Europe.[89] A comparison between Fisher's library (as reconstructed from his writings) and some late fifteenth-century Cambridge libraries reveals that his intellectual horizons were considerably broader than those of his predecessors. Of those earlier libraries it has been remarked that Ambrose, Gregory the Great, Jerome and Augustine were partially represented, but that no other major Latin fathers, and scarcely a single Greek, were to be found.[90] And even in the 1520s there were still those at Cambridge to whom acquaintance with the works of the notorious heretic Origen was itself tantamount to heresy.[91] It is easy to see in Fisher's reliance on the Fathers, and especially in his penchant for Origen, the influence of Erasmus. But, as Malcolm Underwood argues elsewhere in this volume, Fisher's formation must also have owed something to his tutor William Melton, whose library (of which an inventory survives) also included a wealth of patristics, and in fact showed a very similar composition to his pupil's.[92]

A common view of Fisher's career holds that, like Thomas More, he blossomed into Christian humanism under the beneficent influence of Erasmus, only to wither, beneath the heat of the Reformation, into a reactionary and scholastic conservatism. But this interpretation, though tempting in its simplicity, is no more true of Fisher than of More. The career of John Fisher manifests far greater consistency and unity than it allows for. He was neither as progressive before the Reformation nor as reactionary afterwards as it suggests. Fortunately his polemical career spans the watershed of 1520, and it is therefore possible to reach a more balanced assessment. Certainly there is substantial evidence of Fisher's humanist inclinations. His admiration for Pico, his correspondence and friendship with Reuchlin and Erasmus, his enthusiasm for 'bonae literae' and his leadership by example in renewing the study of Greek and Hebrew, as well as his commitment to clerical and educational reform, mark him out as a worthy citizen of the humanists' Christian Republic. Yet this is not the whole story. Fisher's writings show almost no acquaintance with the secular authors of classical antiquity. And his polemical début, made against one of the leading humanist scholars of the age, Lefèvre d'Étaples, found him in the company of die-hard scholastics like Marc de Grandval and Noel Beda (later a persecutor of Erasmus). His stance in this controversy was decidedly anti-humanist. Lefèvre and Clichtove were upholding the application of the critical method even to doctrinal authority itself, irrespective of the consequences. But, while Fisher did not repudiate humanist techniques (for he was able to argue with his opponents as an equal over the interpretation of Greek and Latin texts), he adopted a position for dogmatic authority against critical method that was fundamentally irreconcilable with the humanist ideology. On the other hand, Fisher's later polemical works continue to show humanist tendencies. It was in the *Confutatio* that Fisher remarked that he was wholly in favour of promoting 'bonae literae'.[93] And, as we have seen, the whole burden of his argument is patristic rather than scholastic in nature. His use of Origen is a particularly Erasmian touch, and he shows no signs in his polemics of losing faith in Erasmus, although perhaps his references to him show more an awareness of the weight his name could carry than a deep commitment to his principles. For Fisher, 'no author is so bad that one can find nothing good in him'[94] – a principle he extended even to the scholastics, perhaps in emulation of Pico della Mirandola, from whose example he may have derived his eclecticism.

Throughout his polemical career, Fisher blended humanism with scholasticism, often using humanist techniques to defend scholastic positions. But it would be wrong to see him as nothing more than a transitional figure. For it is arguable that the intellectual position Fisher developed was to become an independent tradition of theological scholarship, on both sides of the Channel, and on both sides of the denominational divide. In England we can perhaps put him with Cranmer at the start of a tradition of massive patristic learning which was to include Whitgift among the Anglicans, and Stapleton among the Catholics. On the continent he stands at the beginning of a tradition which blended the 'via antiqua' with the 'tres linguae', and was to flourish especially among the Jesuits, in such figures as Suárez. And if in Fisher the humanist cannot be separated from the scholastic, neither can the polemicist be separated from the pastor, nor indeed from the person. Fisher's holy life and heroic death gave his polemical works a seal of moral authority that was to make them especially influential at the Council of Trent. And it is his integration of the bishop's concern for his flock with the theologian's concern for truth, encapsulated by his willingness not just to live, but to die, for his beliefs and his Church, that explains the attraction he held for such diverse figures as the Cardinals Borromeo and Bellarmine, the archetypal pastor and polemicist of the Counter-Reformation.

Notes

The following abbreviations have been used in citing Fisher's polemical works. For convenience, references are given where possible to the *Opera Omnia* (1597) as well as to the original editions. The Klaiber (Kr) numbers refer to the useful bibliography of sixteenth-century Catholic polemical theology, W. Klaiber's *Katholische Kontroverstheologen und Reformer des 16. Jahrhunderts* (Münster 1978 – see note 7).

ALC   *Assertionis Lutheranae Confutatio* (Antwerp: M. Hillenius, January 1523), folio (Kr 1185)

CC   *Convulsio Calumniarum* (Antwerp: G. Vorstermann, November 1522), quarto
      (Kr 1184)
CSD   *Confutatio Secundae Disceptationis* (Paris: Josse Bade, September 1519), quar-
      to (Kr 1182)
DRA   *Defensio Regiae Assertionis* (Cologne: Peter Quentell, June 1525), quarto (Kr
      1186)
DUM   *De Unica Magdalena Libri Tres* (Paris: Josse Bade, February 1519), quarto (Kr
      1180)
DVC   *De Veritate Corporis et Sanguinis Christi in Eucharistia* (Cologne: Peter
      Quentell, January 1527), folio (Kr 1189)
EM   *Eversio Munitionis* (Louvain: Thierry Maartens, 1519), quarto (Kr 1181)
SSD   *Sacri Sacerdotii Defensio* (Cologne: Peter Quentell, June 1525), quarto (Kr
      1187)

1 *Quarterly Review*, 143 (1877), 14–15. Acton's comment was made in the course
  of a review of *LP*, IV. See Edward Surtz, *The Works and Days of John Fisher*
  (Cambridge, Mass., 1967), p. 416 for the attribution to Lord Acton.
2 A. Hufstader, 'Lefèvre d'Étaples and the Magdalen', *Studies in the Renaissance*,
  16 (1969), 31–60, especially p. 36.
3 Thomas Cromwell to John Fisher, 20 February 1534, *The Life and Letters of
  Thomas Cromwell*, ed. R. B. Merriman (Oxford, 1902), II, no. 68 at p. 375.
4 A. J. Lamping, *Ulrich Velenus and his Treatise against the Papacy* (Leiden, 1976),
  p. 2.
5 Ibid., p. 157.
6 Ibid., p. 161.
7 W. Klaiber, *Katholische Kontroverstheologen und Reformer des 16. Jahrhunderts,
  Reformationsgeschichtliche Studien und Texte*, CXVI (Münster, 1978), pp. 109–11
  (Fisher), and 135–6 (Henry VIII). This volume does not include Eck or Cochlaeus,
  for whose bibliographies see M. Spahn, *Johannes Cochläus* (Berlin, 1898), and *Tres
  Orationes Funebres*, ed. J. Metzler, *Corpus Catholicorum*, 16 (Münster, 1930).
8 T. E. Bridgett, *Life of Blessed John Fisher*, 4th edn (London, 1922), p. 123.
9 Richard Morison, *Apomaxis Calumniarum* (London: Berthelet, 1537) (*STC*,
  18109), fos. 77v, 83v.
10 Johannes Cochlaeus, *Fasciculus Calumniarum* (Leipzig, 1529), dedication to
  Fisher, sig. Ai v. It may merely have been, however, that Fisher was forced to
  abandon theological polemics in order to devote his efforts to the king's Great
  Matter, in which he was involved from June 1527. As late as 1533, a *motu proprio*
  of Clement VII, allowing Fisher to replace his recitation of the canonical hours
  with prayers of his own composition, gave as reasons his age and his preoccupation
  with the study of scripture and the refutation of recent heresies (24 October 1533).
  See *Römische Dokumente zur Geschichte der Ehescheidung Heinrichs VIII von
  England*, ed. S. Ehses (Paderborn, 1893), no. 132.
11 *Life*, X, p. 220. But see also Thomas More's comment that his readers would spend
  their time better by reading devotional works such as the *Imitatio Christi* than by
  dabbling with books of theological controversy. *The Confutation of Tyndale's
  Answer*, ed. L. A. Schuster et al., *The Complete Works of St Thomas More*, VIII (1)
  (New Haven and London, 1973), 37. I owe this reference to Dr Eamon Duffy.

12 Erasmus to Poncher, 2 October 1519, *Opus Epistolarum Des. Erasmi Roterodami*, ed. P. S. Allen (Oxford, 1906–47), III, no. 1016, pp. 73–4.

13 *Sermons on the Seven Penitential Psalms* (Kr 1177), *EW*, p.i; *Funeral Sermon of Henry VII* (Kr 1178), *EW*, p. 268.

14 *CSD*, fo. II r.

15 Poncher to Wolsey, 28 August 1518, *LP*, II (2), no. 4401.

16 *DUM*, Bk 1, fo. IIIr, (*Opera*, col. 1395). *EM*, sig. Aii r–v. *CSD*, fo. II r–v.

17 *Sermon against Luther* (London: Wynkyn de Worde, 1521) (Kr 1183), title page, *EW*, p. 311. Longland to Wolsey, 5 January 1526, *LP*, IV (1), no. 995.

18 *CC*, sig. Aii r.

19 *ALC*, title page, verso.

20 Cochlaeus to Pirckheimer, 15 September 1526, quoted in Surtz, *Works and Days*, p. 337, from *Documenta Literaria Varii Argumenti*, ed. J. Heumann von Teutschbrunn (Altdorf, 1758), p. 53.

21 Cochlaeus to Erasmus, 8 January 1528, *Erasmi Epistolae*, VII (Oxford, 1928), no. 1928, p. 228.

22 *DRA*, Dedication, sixth leaf recto (*Opera*, col. 101).

23 *SSD*, Dedication, sig. a 4r (not included in *Opera*).

24 Richard Sharpe to Nicholas Metcalfe, 4 July 1522, St John's College Muniments, D.105.43. Transcribed in 'Letters of Bishop Fisher', ed. G. J. Gray, *The Library*, 3rd series, 4 (1913), 133–45, on p. 142. John Constable to Fisher, 12 November (1521 ?), St John's College Muniments (SJC) D.56.18.

25 John Eck, *Enchiridion Locorum Communum*, ed. P. Fraenkel, *Corpus Catholicorum* 34 (Münster, 1979), p. 24*.

26 *ALC*, Dedication to the Reader, fo. 1r (*Opera*, col. 272).

27 *ALC*, Dedication to the Reader, fo. 2r (*Opera*, col. 273).

28 J. Clichtove, *Disceptationis de Magdalena Defensio* (Paris: Henri Estienne, 1519) (Kr 707), fos. 95v–96r.

29 Erasmus to Fisher, 2 April 1519 and 21 February 1520, *Erasmi Epistolae*, III (Oxford, 1913), no. 936, at p. 522; and IV (Oxford, 1922), no. 1068, at p. 192.

30 Erasmus to Luther, 11 April 1526, *Erasmi Epistolae*, VII (Oxford, 1926), no. 1688, p. 306.

31 *ALC*, fos. 4v–5r (*Opera*, cols. 277–8).

32 *DUM*, Bk 1, fo. IIIIr–v (*Opera*, cols. 1396–7).

33 G. H. Tavard, *Holy Writ and Holy Church* (London, 1959), p. 171.

34 *DRA*, ch. 8, fo. 86r (*Opera*, col. 204), citing J. Reuchlin, *De Rudimentis Hebraicis* (Pforzheim, 1506), fo. 289v.

35 *SSD*, Axiom 10, fo. XXIIv–XXIIIr (*Opera*, cols. 1266–7). Fisher, without acknowledgement, cited various rabbis, from the *De Arcanis Catholicae Fidei*, 1516, of Petrus Galatinus, an Italian Hebraist and Cabbalist. See F. Secret, *Les Kabbalistes chrétiens de la Renaissance* (Paris, 1964), pp. 228–9.

36 *Sermon against Luther*, sig. C iiii r. *EW*, p. 332.

37 *ALC*, Article 18, fo. 111v (*Opera*, col. 497), 'partim ex revelationibus, partim ex scripturis fuisse creditum'.

38 *ALC*, Article 37, fo. 222v (*Opera*, col. 718).

39 Rupert of Deutz, *Commentariorum in Apocalypsim* (Cologne, 1526), Cochlaeus's dedication to Henry VIII, title page verso.

40 *ALC*, Article 28, fo. 159v (*Opera*, col. 593).
41 *EM*, sig. B 2v–B 3r. Henry VIII, *Assertio Septem Sacramentorum* (London: Pynson, 1521) (Kr 1461), sig. m 4r (*Opera*, col. 50). *ALC*, Fourth Truth, fo. 8v (*Opera*, col. 285). *Hyperaspistes Des. Erasmi, Opera Omnia Erasmi*, X (Leiden, 1705), col. 1305. Thomas More, *Responsio ad Lutherum*, ed. J. M. Headley (*The Complete Works of St Thomas More*, V (1) (New Haven and London, 1969), 88–91, 100–1 and 396–7.
42 *DUM*, Bk 3, fo. XLVII v (*Opera*, col. 1453).
43 *ALC*, Article 25, fos. 127v–134v (*Opera*, cols. 530–44).
44 *Responsio ad Lutherum*, ed. Headley, pp. 138–41.
45 *ALC*, Fourth Truth, fo. 9r (*Opera*, col. 286).
46 *ALC*, Proem, fo. 15r (*Opera*, col. 298).
47 *ALC*, Article 29, fos. 161v–162r (*Opera*, col. 598).
48 *ALC*, Articles 27, 28, and 29 *passim*, fos. 154v–164r (*Opera*, cols. 583–602).
49 Hufstader, 'Lefèvre d'Étaples', pp. 32–4.
50 Ibid., p. 55.
51 *DUM*, Bk 2, fos. XXVI v–XXVII r (*Opera*, col. 1425).
52 *EM*, Dedication to the Reader, title page verso.
53 *CSD*, fo. XXXIIv, quotes Lefèvre's *De Tribus et Unica Magdalena Disceptatio Secunda* (Paris: Henri Estienne, 1519), fo. 17r, 'far be it from us to imagine that such a dear friend of Christ had at some time been a sordid and disreputable sinner'.
54 Hufstader, 'Lefèvre d'Étaples', pp. 55–9.
55 *DUM*, Bk 2, fos. XXVIv–XXVIIr (*Opera*, col. 1425).
56 Indenture between Fisher and St John's, 27 November 1525, printed in R. F. Scott, 'Notes from the College Records', *The Eagle*, 35 (1914), 2–35, on p. 26.
57 *ALC*, Article 1, fo. 22v (*Opera*, col. 314).
58 *ALC*, Article 1, fo. 22v–23r (*Opera*, col. 314).
59 *ALC*, Article 1, fos. 34v and 36r (*Opera*, cols. 337–8 and 341).
60 *DRA*, ch. 2, fo. XIIr–v (*Opera*, cols. 119–20).
61 *DVC*, Bk 1, ch. 6, fo. VIr (*Opera*, col. 769).
62 *ALC*, Article 3, fo. 54v (*Opera*, col. 378), 'Quanquam de peccato originali variae sunt apud scholasticos opiniones, ego tamen libenter Augustinum sequor . . .'
63 *ALC*, Article 36, fo. 198r–v (*Opera*, col. 670).
64 *ALC*, Article 36, fo. 216v (*Opera*, col. 707).
65 *ALC*, Article 1, fo. 26v (*Opera*, col. 321).
66 *ALC*, Article 36, fo. 196r (*Opera*, col. 665).
67 *ALC*, Article 36, *passim*. For 'gratia preveniens', see fo. 219r (*Opera*, col. 712).
68 *ALC*, Article 36, fo. 199r (*Opera*, col. 672).
69 *ALC*, Article 36, fo. 215r (*Opera*, col. 704).
70 *ALC*, Article 5, fos. 57v–64v (*Opera*, cols. 385–99).
71 *ALC*, Article 17, fos. 105v and 107r–v (*Opera*, cols. 485 and 488).
72 *ALC*, Article 18, fos. 111r–v (*Opera*, cols. 496–7).
73 *SSD*, fo. IIr (*Opera*, col. 1233), 'Ostendat Lutherus, si potest, in toto orbe ecclesiam aliquam . . . quae ritum istum non sequitur.'
74 *SSD*, Congressus Tertius, fo. XXX (*Opera*, cols. 1278–9).
75 *DVC*, Proem to Bk 1, sig. BB 4v (*Opera*, p. 749), 'Quis hic non manifeste videt ulciscentem Dei manum?'

76 *ALC*, Article 15 *passim*, fos. 92v–99r (*Opera*, cols. 457–71).
77 *DVC*, Bk 2, ch. 24, fo. XLVIIr (*Opera*, col. 889).
78 *DRA*, ch. 3, sect. 18, fo. XXIXr (*Opera*, col. 145).
79 *DVC*, Bk 5, ch 18, fo. CLIIIr (*Opera*, col. 1180).
80 *DVC*, Preface 5, fo. CXXXIIIr–v (*Opera*, cols. 1127–8).
81 *DVC* Preface 3, fo. LXIr (*Opera*, p. 924).
82 *DVC*, fo. XXIXv (*Opera*, p. 839).
83 *DVC*, Bk 1, ch. 4, fo. IVv, 'quis non videt, quantum istud omnes humani ingenii vires transcendat?' (*Opera*, col. 764).
84 *Life*, X, p. 220.
85 *The Forthe Boke of the Folowynge of Cryst*, trans. the Lady Margaret Beaufort (London: R. Pynson, 1504) (*STC*, 23955). Also ed. J. K. Ingram, *Early English Text Society*, extra series 63 (London, 1893).
86 PRO SP6/9, fos. 159–64. Fragments in Fisher's hand, clearly from a devotional treatise on the Eucharist, fit the description in Arundel MS 152 fo. 279 (transcribed in *Life*, X, p. 141): 'Scripsit decem considerationes de fide, de spe, et de charitate ad exhortandas hominum mentes ad eucharistiam maiori cum devotione suscipiendam. Cum prologo, quem vidi, sed non integre.'
87 *DUM*, fo. XLIr (*Opera*, col. 1444), where he speaks of the 'sermo incultior' of medieval authors.
88 *Statutes*, p. 252.
89 *Life*, X, p. 244.
90 J. B. Mullinger, *The University of Cambridge*, I (Cambridge, 1873), pp. 326–7.
91 Ibid., p. 598.
92 *Testamenta Eboracensia*, V (*Surtees Society*, 79 (1884)) 251–63.
93 *ALC*, Article 36, fo. 221r (*Opera*, col. 716).
94 *ALC*, Proem, fo. 15r (*Opera*, col. 300).

Fisher's view of the Church

BRIAN GOGAN

It could be argued that John Fisher's treatise *Assertionis Lutheranae Confutatio*, published in Antwerp in January 1523, is one of the most distinguished pieces of theological writing to come from England in the six-teenth century.[1] Certainly, few works were greeted with such acclaim in the author's lifetime and few continued to exercise the influence this treatise did in subsequent decades. The *Confutatio* was reprinted in Paris in the same year, 1523, then subsequently in Cologne, Venice, Augsburg and Louvain. Twenty editions of the book were published between 1523 and 1564. It also went into translation: the greater part of Article 15 was translated into German by Cochlaeus and published as early as 1523. Further articles were published subsequently and the entire book appeared in German in Dresden in 1525 and Leipzig in 1526. Throughout the rest of the century Fisher's *Confutatio* was a recognised resource for Catholic apologists in their controversial writings and speeches. One evident reason for this was the framework of the book, which corresponded quite directly with both the content of the papal Bull excommunicating Luther as well as with one of Luther's earliest replies to this detailed condemnation. Hence the *Confutatio* provided a convenient compendium of Catholic theology relating directly to the main points of divergence, according to Rome, between Martin Luther and Roman Catholic orthodoxy. However, it was not merely the framework which appealed. The thoroughness with which Fisher dealt with the issues involved, most notably, of course, his treatment of the Roman primacy in Article 25 and those which followed, drew the plaudits of contemporary Catholic apologists.

The work covered most of the main themes which Roman theologians controverted in the Lutheran position. It did not deal *ex professo* with ecclesiology, though it did develop significant themes notably concerning the papacy and the general council. In this essay I shall give first an outline of the historical and theological context of the *Confutatio*. Secondly, I shall examine the theology of Roman primacy and general council which it contains.

The task of examining the orthodoxy of Martin Luther's writings had been given to a commission of theologians presided over by Cardinals Cajetan and Accolti in 1518. Their work culminated in the publication of the Bull *Exsurge Domine* in 1520, which enumerated forty-one condemned propositions culled from seven of Luther's works.[2] In November 1520 Luther replied to the Roman sentence with a pamphlet published in Wittenberg, *Adversus Execrabilem Antichristi Bullam*. Shortly afterwards, at the request of Frederick of Saxony, he published a more considered response to the papal excommunication. This tract was published by Melchior Lotther of Wittenberg at the beginning of January 1521 under the title *Assertio Omnium Articulorum D. Martini Lutheri per Bullam Leonis X . . . Novissimam Damnatorum*. A German edition was published at the same time and further editions appeared in Worms and Basel in the weeks that followed. In this work Luther protested against the Roman theologians who had condemned his 'articles' without any proofs taken from scripture. He wished to clarify his position and to free Christian people from the Roman tyranny by giving them the necessary weapons with which to know, confess and defend the most profound truths of the faith. He therefore undertook to deal with each of the forty-one propositions condemned and to give a background to each of them. The tone of the book was far from that of detached theology. Rather was it a furious polemic reflecting the time and mood in which it was written. The propositions rebutted dealt with familiar Lutheran themes concerning the sacraments, sin and concupiscence, sin and forgiveness, Eucharist, indulgences, excommunication, as well as matters concerning the institutional Church which were now coming into clearer focus – the questions of the pope's primacy, of his authority and that of the general council, liberty of the will, and the doctrine of purgatory.

Luther's approach to the theology of the Church is of some significance to this essay.[3] The essential core of Luther's theories on the Church reached maturity in the years between 1518 and 1521 but the main lines were already laid down in the *Psalm Commentaries* of 1513. According to Wilhelm Maurer, the starting point of Luther's ecclesiology was his Christology. Christ and his body, the Church, are two in one flesh. This view leads easily to an eschatological perspective on the Church seen in its final historical consummation, not as sinful but as the 'mystical Israel', 'the faithful people.' This viewpoint sets in relief inward values of holiness and purity. The true Church is made up of those who both *numero et merito* belong to the Church – not those who *numero* merely are members. The true Church in this world is identified with those who, believing in Christ, will finally achieve salvation. As the debate evolved, Luther's position led him inexorably to reject openly both the authority of the bishop of Rome and of the general councils. While in the heat of controversy Luther had originally appealed from the papal legate, Cardinal Cajetan, to the pope and then subsequently to the general council, in the course of disputation it became clear that he was not going to receive support from either the Roman see itself or from the bishops of Christendom. This led him to reject even the council's supreme authority. These viewpoints find their echo in the *Assertio Omnium Articulorum*, in his criticism of the sacramental system, his attack on indulgences, and his repudiation of both pope and Council as final arbiters in disputed matters of faith and discipline. The pope, to whom a few months earlier he had appealed for justice, had become for Luther a pagan idol, 'adversarium Christo et Euangelio' (*WA*, 7, 131/3). Councils are to be ignored when they teach doctrines contrary to scripture, 'potius hominum conciliabula quam Ecclesiae concilia dicere possis' (*WA*, 7, 134/18–19). Even still, Luther held on to one strand of the complex web of medieval theology by appealing in justification of his position to the Sicilian canonist Nicholas de Tudeschis Panormitanus. Years earlier in the conciliar debate, applying the Ockhamist principle that true faith might be kept alive in only one believer, Panormitanus had claimed that, in certain situations, a simple believer rather than pope or bishops might possess the authentic message of Christ: 'plus esse credendum uni privato fideli quam toti Concilio aut Papae, si meliorem autoritatem vel rationem habeat' (*WA*, 7, 134/30). Luther assumed that he himself was such a faithful individual upholding authentic Christian faith against a multitude of renegades. Together with the Holy See and many Catholic theologians and apologists, the bishop of Rochester did not agree.

The response to Luther published by John Fisher in 1521, the *Confutatio*, does not contain a complete ecclesiology. The list of contents of his book in fact depends on Luther's own *Assertio Omnium Articulorum*. Hence his main concern is with those aspects of the Church which had been dealt with by the Wittenberg reformer. The book itself begins with an introduction in which Fisher says his aim is not to convert someone who has already chosen ('airesis') his doctrines according to his own wishes. Fisher rather wants to protect his sheep from the attacks of the one he terms this 'wild wolf'. He follows this with a preface, in the course of which he lays down ten basic principles of Catholic theology according to which he will reply to Luther. The rest of the volume is taken up with a point-by-point confrontation with Luther based on the forty-one Articles of the original Bull of condemnation which formed the framework of Luther's own *Assertio Omnium Articulorum*. In the course of dealing with each of these Articles in turn Fisher allows himself to write at times small theological treatises in respect of each in a manner common in sixteenth-century controversial theology. For those interested in detailed examination and, where possible, refutation of an opponent's views, the method is thorough and exact. This explains the approval of Fisher's work by controversialists and its frequent republication. However, in terms of popular interest or propaganda it is less than successful. Still less does it make exciting reading at a distance of four hundred years. None the less, a study of Fisher's work is revealing of his own personal faith and his understanding of the mysteries in which it was engaged. The main ecclesiological content of the work occurs in Articles 25 to 30 which deal with the papacy and its powers as well as with the authority of the general council.

On the basis of the *Confutatio* and other sources, it is evident that John Fisher's view of the Church was fundamentally spiritual in character.[4] He saw it as the Body of Christ, inspired by the Holy Spirit, who brings all its members into unity, guides their individual and collective activity and leads them into truth and holiness of life. The Pauline concept of the Body of Christ enabled him to link spiritual and empirical aspects of the Church. Though primarily spiritual in nature because of the presence of the Divine Spirit, the Church of Christ can be identified as a social and moral body, an empirical community whose divine origin is recognisable through certain visible manifestations. While each member of the Body receives the grace and guidance of the Spirit, the role of the individual believer outside the circle of personal and family life tends to be rather passive. Active care and administration of the Church is the province of bishops and their co-operators, the clergy, in accordance with Christ's institution. These duties are carried out under the guidance and direction of the bishop of Rome who draws his authority from Christ. The clergy's role is to govern the Church, administer the sacraments and actively guide their flocks into the knowledge of divine truth. This revealed message is transmitted in the Church, according to Fisher, through the scriptures on the one hand and on the other by tradition, which he saw as a channel of revelation distinct from scripture, holding out even for a secret, oral tradition in the cabbalistic mode. In this he clearly distinguished himself from Martin Luther for whom the scriptures understood in their literal sense were the determining source of divine revelation.

For Fisher, the Church has a role to play in relation to revelation — to authenticate it, accept it, but also under the guidance of the Spirit to interpret and clarify it. The contemporary Church does not add to the body of revelation but makes clear what revelation actually contains. This is done through the *concordia* or *consensus* of all believers, as well as through the mouth of Peter and of conciliar assemblies. In the *Confutatio* he dealt at length with these institutions, so crucial to the rest of his case against Luther.

Although Article 25 of the *Confutatio* takes one of Luther's assertions as its starting point and spends a good deal of time in argument with Luther, it stands in its own right as a minor treatise on the Roman pontiff. Fisher's aim was to establish that the Roman pontiff is the supreme head of the whole Church, 'summus pontifex sit totius ecclesiae caput'. He sought to establish this position by copious use of scripture, as well as by drawing on the testimony of the Fathers and the councils. He gave ten arguments from the gospels, described ten situations in the Acts of the Apostles where Peter's primacy is evident, went on to deal with the Fathers, drawing on a lengthy list of Latin writers as well as a full complement of Greek theologians, and concluded with a final argument, for him the clinching one, the evidence of the Council of Florence (1439). He then proceeded to examine various objections put forward by Luther, including those based on a study of the Petrine text, Matthew 16:18–19. This treatment was complemented by Article 26, which deals with the papal authority 'to bind and loose', and Article 27, which argues for the pope's prerogative in determining questions of faith and morals. His exposition of Roman primacy concluded with Article 28, which insists on the pope's authority in matters both of doctrine and government.

It was the renaming of Simon as Peter which Fisher selected as the fundamental evidence for his pre-eminence in the apostolic college. Such an alteration of title was, he urged, a matter of great significance in the biblical world (Mark 3:16; Mark 10:2–4; Luke 6:14–16).[5] The changing of the names of Abraham, Sarah and Israel had been occasions of great mystery. Similarly in the case of Peter, the conferring of a new title gave to him a special authority over his brethren and the first place among them. This pre-eminence of Peter was recognised on other occasions. The evangelists themselves always placed Peter first when listing the apostles. Christ told Peter that he had prayed for him lest his faith fail, and commissioned him to confirm his brethren (Luke 22:32). When Christ had risen from the dead, the angel at the tomb commanded the women, who had come to honour the dead body of their master, to go to Peter and the other disciples (Mark 16:7; John 20:2). Here Peter was specifically named and the others grouped collectively, again suggesting a position of honour, even command, for Peter. This testimony, Fisher suggested, was corroborated by the incident which occurred after the resurrection when Peter and John reached the empty tomb. John arrived first but held back to allow Peter to be the first to enter (John 20:5–6). John implied by this action, Fisher claimed, Peter's unique dignity. Fisher supported this interpretation by appealing to a range of other texts. First among them was Peter's confession of Christ's divine mission and the subsequent commission to Peter by his Lord: 'Thou art Peter and upon this rock' etc. (Matthew 16:17–19). This promise, Fisher contended, was made to Peter alone and not to the rest of the apostles. The donation of the keys of the kingdom was correspondingly limited. The other apostles received the power of binding and loosing 'sed in caelo singulariter', as it were in a mansion of heaven corresponding to each one's proper earthly jurisdiction. Peter, however, was given the keys not of one heaven but of all the heavens ('caelorum') at the one time. By this usage, Fisher urged, the evangelists indicated the difference in power between the two. While the apostles received jurisdiction over a limited portion of the city of God, the whole divine municipality had been assigned to Peter. This argument, however, since it

135

depends on post-apostolic developments in Church organisation and administration, is not greatly convincing. Similarly based is Fisher's use of the incident recorded in John's Gospel which took place some time after the resurrection. Christ, having tested Peter's love for him, committed to him in turn the care of 'his lambs' and of 'his sheep'. Fisher's comment is 'these words show Peter to have been appointed head of the Church'. He concluded the exposition of this portion of his case with the note 'after these things Christ said to him "follow me". These words clearly imply that Peter was to be pre-eminent in the following of Christ' (John 21:15–17). Fisher had little doubt concerning the conclusions which must be drawn from these texts:

> Whoever reflects on these ten prerogatives and puts them together as if joining one line to another, will be obliged by conscience to confess that Christ willed Peter to have greater authority than the others, that he appointed him his vicar on earth, and at the same time placed in his charge the administration of the whole Church. Otherwise, why should he have given him a special name? Why should he be placed first in order? Why should he have promised to found his Church first upon him? . . . Why indeed should Christ have given so many honours to Peter unless he was to be his vicar and head of the whole Church?[6]

Fisher, apparently, considered the doctrine of Peter's primacy to be adequately attested by the gospel narrative itself. However, he went on to offer further evidence for his thesis from the Acts of the Apostles, citing incidents which he claimed revealed Peter's position of primacy in operation.[7] Among them we may notice his presidency over the council held to fill the vacancy left by the defection of Judas from the apostolic office (Acts 1:18–26). Again, after the descent of the Holy Spirit, it was Peter who went out and addressed the multitudes (Acts 2:14), just as it was he who dealt with the deceit of Ananias and Sapphira (Acts 5:1–11). Of Peter alone was it said that people were cured when his shadow fell upon them (Acts 5:15). Furthermore, it was through Peter's dream that the Lord made it known that in the new dispensation Christians could eat flesh meat (Acts 11:1–18) – a most important development which was to have serious implications for the evangelisation of the Gentiles. Finally, Fisher referred to one of Paul's epistles, Galatians, in which, he points out, Paul made it clear that he regarded himself as subordinate to Peter (Galatians 1:18; 2:1–14). If Paul – to subsequent generations Peter's only possible rival as head of the Church – denied to himself this privilege, even though he stood up to Peter at times, it must indeed belong to the latter.

Fisher's argument for Roman primacy drawn from tradition consisted in a catena of patristic references, more heavily weighted, as one might expect, on the Latin than on the Greek side. All the evidence, Fisher held, pointed to the fact that Peter was divinely appointed head of the apostolic Church, Christ's vicar on earth and foundation stone as well as head of the whole

Church: 'Per Fidem Utiq; Christiani super Christum fundantur. At haec Fides haudquaquam in ipso Christo est, sed in ipsis Christianorum pectoribus. Quam quia Petrus primum confessus fuerat et ipse primus post Christum lapis vivus in huius aedifici structura repositibus fuit.'[8]

In his employment of the conciliar argument, Fisher referred to the decrees of a number of early ecumenical councils. However, the principal witness he summoned in support of his thesis was the decree of the Council of Florence on papal primacy.[9] This is contained, though he does not mention its title, in the Bull of Unity, *Laetentur Caeli*, issued on 6 July 1439. Fisher's extract runs as follows:

We decree that the holy Apostolic See and Roman Pontiff hold the primacy throughout the whole world, and that the same Roman Pontiff is successor of Blessed Peter, Prince of the Apostles, true vicar of Christ, head of the whole Church, father and teacher of all Christians. Blessed Peter was given by Our Lord Jesus Christ full power of teaching, ruling and governing the universal Church, according to the Acts of the Ecumenical Council and the Sacred Canons.

We must pause to examine Fisher's use of this text. In his mind this conciliar definition clinched the argument and placed the divine origin of the Roman see and its primacy in the Church beyond the boundaries of reasonable doubt. On the other hand, he ignored conciliar decrees favouring conciliar supremacy: the decrees of Constance (1414–18), *Haec Sancta* and *Frequens*, whose tendency was in favour of the council, as well as those of Basel (1431–49), one of whose decrees explicitly proclaimed the proposition 'The General Council is above the pope' as a dogma of the Catholic faith.[10] Fisher gave no definite reasons for ignoring both Constance and Basel, but two may be suggested on the basis of his own declarations. One which we shall see at greater length at a later stage was his scepticism regarding the definitions of any council where pope and council were at variance. The other was the unique importance he attached to the Council of Florence.

The Council of Ferrara–Florence was an off-shoot of the Council of Basel. For the first time in almost five hundred years representatives of the Latin, Greek, Armenian and lesser oriental churches sat down together in council.[11] This remarkable event was largely due to political pressure from the emperor under threat from Islam. The representatives of Eastern Christendom were able to reach an unusual degree of agreement on doctrinal matters with their brethren from the West, the most welcome fruit of the meeting being the Bull of Unity, *Laetentur Caeli*, the key passage of which has already been quoted. Though Fisher does not tell us how much he knew of the process underlying the Council of Ferrara–Florence, he regarded approval by both Greeks and Latins of the definition of Roman primacy at that council as of critical importance. He took pains to emphasise that in his view this was not a mere political stratagem on the part of an over-powerful theocratic ruler, but rather a genuine doctrinal rapprochement between East and West.[12]

Having established to his own satisfaction the origins of the Petrine office, Fisher went on to examine its role. He saw an organic relationship existing between the authority of the pope and that of other members of the Christian hierarchy. Peter and his successors are seen in a dynamic relationship to the rest of the Church. Drawing on a variety of metaphors, Fisher affirms that Peter is the very foundation stone on which the main structure of the Church is built, the deepest root from which it grows.

Christ said to Peter 'Thou art Peter etc. . . .'. In this context you hear of stone, of building, of church. The stone spoken of is a rational being. And these same stones are to be built into a spiritual church. This can be none other than the Church and if the living stones with which it is built are men, what more suitable foundation than Peter? Christ strictly speaking is the rock on which the church was founded but he allows Peter to share in the name.[13]

Elsewhere Fisher expressed this idea by means of other metaphors. He drew, for example, an analogy between the role of the pope in the Church and the root of a tree. As a multiplicity of branches springs from one true root, so the multitude which is the Church is united into one living body by its attachment to this see of Rome. The papacy, therefore, is one essential principle on which the Church is founded and is thereby constituted source of unity for the whole edifice, visible source of nourishment for the living body.[14]

Fisher goes on to argue by analogy from other polities, celestial and terrestrial, that Petrine primacy is an appropriate form of government for the Church. The synagogue, which foreshadowed the Church, was ruled over by one man; the Church triumphant, exemplar of the Church militant, is ruled over by God himself, the bees by one queen, the flocks by one shepherd, a team of oxen, by one driver. Even in political societies the administration of the whole is conferred on one person. 'From all this we may conclude', says Fisher, 'the Church never to have been governed rightly except when all its orders were subordinate to one head.'[15]

Fisher, therefore saw the pope as the stone on which the Church was founded, the principle of unity in the whole edifice from which the living body draws nourishment and even divine life itself. He expressed this conviction in rather far-reaching terms when he said: 'have we not observed that Christians are born of priests, priests of bishops and that bishops are generated by the sovereign pontiff (as often as it be necessary)?'[16] This innocent-sounding statement suggests a fundamental confusion regarding the nature of sacramental grace and its link with the pastoral authority or jurisdiction of Church leaders as it was termed by the canonists. From the standpoint of sacramental theology one can accept that there is analogically a new birth at baptism, a quasi-birth of a new ministry of the Church at ordination, but to say that the gift of diocesan jurisdiction to a bishop is a form of new birth strains the analogy. It puts two things into one class which belong to separate categories, namely, the giving of sacramental grace and the conferring of specific jurisdiction on one who has received the grace of episcopal orders. Fisher here seems to reflect the confusion which appeared most significantly in Catholic theology in the thirteenth century when jurisdiction and sacramental grace at ordination were not merely distinguished, but their origin, reception and exercise carefully separated out. At the theoretical level the concept of jurisdiction was immensely expanded by the use of concepts drawn from both Roman juristic tradition and Hellenistic philosophy. Ironically, the separation of pastoral government from sacramental order provided Henry VIII with one of the excuses he needed to claim juridical authority over the Church in England, and also clouded the minds of the bishops who assented to it. In Convocation and outside it, Fisher opposed Henry's invasion of the ecclesiastical realm, but he may well have suffered himself from similar misconceptions concerning the significance of pastoral authority, its relation to the sacramental grace of episcopal ordination and the extent to which it owed its origin to papal initiative.

Not surprisingly, therefore, John Fisher had a profound respect for papal authority and power and affirmed it unambiguously. The primacy of Peter extends not merely to

all those churches connected with the Catholic Church as members . . . not only for these is the Roman Pontiff responsible . . . but for all others, even Turks and Jews although they do not wish to admit it . . . indeed over all men, even rebels, the Sovereign Pontiff's power extends. For Christ said 'Other sheep I have who are not of this fold'.

This means that the successor of Peter has the duty of leading all men to the unity of the true fold. The rebellion of some groups in no way diminishes this power.[17] Underlying this position is the doctrine of the plenitude of papal power, the 'plena potestas Romani pontificis' beloved of medieval canonists. Fisher did not expand upon the nature of this power, its spiritual ramifications, or whether it extends into the temporal sphere or not. What is striking, however, is the universality of authority he ascribes to Rome. The fact that the pope exercises no power over some of those under his care in no way diminishes his fundamental authority. As Christ did not exercise all the power given to him in heaven and earth, neither does his vicar.[18]

In his treatment of the teaching power of the Church, Fisher recognised a twofold office: one to deal with ordinary matters as part of the maintenance of routine discipline – the papacy; the other, fortified by divine promises of inerrancy, to pronounce on weightier matters – the council. To take the first of these, Fisher was apparently direct in his statements concerning papal teaching, though in fact somewhat equivocal. He did affirm a real authority in the papacy to determine doctrinal issues of everyday importance. Underlying this may have been some impatience with the uncertainties of the conciliar epoch. Certainly Fisher felt the need for such authority. Within his own experience as bishop of Rochester he had had some contact with Lollardy and its contemporary residues. Evidently he was aware of the tumult developing in the German principalities on the heels of Luther's revolt. Whatever the explanation, Fisher was both emphatic and explicit on this point. Whenever dissension arises as to what is true doctrine, the deciding voice is that of the pope. In all such matters he is supreme judge. If the faithful wish to ensure the doctrinal orthodoxy of their beliefs, they can take no surer path than conformity to the Roman pattern. He wrote:

> Is it believable that Christ after his Ascension, should have left the Church without a leader, so that no decision could be given in doctrinal matters, law suits or controversies, in suppressing unlawful innovations or revolts, in settling other disturbances, without recourse to a council, even for matters of little moment? Hence whatever he should approve who is head of the whole Church and to whom the care of the entire world is given by Christ's decree, together with leading men of the Church, ought to be acceptable by all others, unless really serious arguments can be brought forward to the contrary.[19]

Thus it is clear that Fisher saw the bishop of Rome as the one who was given by God the responsibility for settling disputes in the ordinary course of the Church's existence. It is worth noting that he did put in some qualifications on the role of Rome in this regard. He notes that the pope's decision is valid when it is in agreement with that of 'the leading men (*proceres*) of the Church'. Secondly, it 'ought to be acceptable by all others, unless really serious arguments can be brought forward to the contrary'. This leaves two loopholes in his assessment of papal authority. First, who are the leading men of the Church? Are they the cardinals, the bishops, the leading theologians, or the university faculties? This question can be answered from another section of the *Confutatio* in which he refers to the 'proceres' of the Greek Church – 'hoc est, ij qui probitate simul et eruditione praestabant' – men outstanding in learning and virtue.[20] Note the double qualification – virtue and learning. In today's language this would refer to theologians in good standing with the Church. Consequently it must be said that Fisher did not believe the papal office should be exercised from a height over the Church, as it were, but rather in a dynamic relationship to the community and its traditional wisdom as reflected in the views of its loyal and skilled exponents. Elsewhere he stresses even more obviously the ecclesial pole to this dualism when he writes 'the authority of the Sovereign Pontiff is great, but it is still greater if the custom of the Roman See is added to it, and it is greatest if the consent of the whole Church accrues to it'. Thus the authority of the papal teaching office is qualified by that of the community evidenced through Roman custom ('consuetudo'), the universal consensus of the faithful and the opinions of theologians in good standing. All of this provides a context for the second rider he adds to his exposition of papal teaching authority: if 'really serious arguments can be brought forward to the contrary', then one might be justified in dissenting from the Roman judgement.

On both these counts Luther would have been able to claim the right of dissent from papal condemnation – support from eminent theologians coupled with his own argumentation. Even if the first count were not admitted, he would certainly have satisfied the second condition, namely that he had a serious theological argument against the Roman decision. Fisher made no attempt to nullify this escape clause in his exposition of papal authority. Nor does he seem to have taken full account of the implications of this for the position of the unorthodox except when he discussed the excommunication of someone who, in good faith, dissents from judgement. He was quite willing to hold in that instance that the person in question might still be in good standing in the eyes of God. This did not, of course, prevent Bishop Fisher from handing over for judgement to the civil authorities those he judged guilty of heresy. Be that as it may, Fisher saw the Petrine office as essentially evangelical in character. Christ, he says, was Peter's voice when he prayed to the Father that Peter's faith should not fail. Correspondingly, Christ told Peter to confirm his brethren. 'Was he who was to confirm the others in faith not thereby the voice of Christ? And was this not one of the main reasons why Christ came into this world?' As Fisher expressed it in another work, since Peter is the voice of Christ in the world, he is truly his vicar.[21]

Though Fisher attributed a role of utmost importance to the pope in the pastoral care of the Church, he none the less recognised the general council as the supreme ecclesiastical authority in both matters of doctrine and discipline – that is, the council in conjunction with its president, the bishop of Rome. His perception of the role of the council sprang from an underlying theology of the Church to which we have already adverted. The Holy Spirit is given to the Church to animate it, to guide it, to direct it and lead it into all truth. The Holy Spirit resides in the Church, 'sacrum in Ecclesia residere Spiritum'.[22] The Holy Spirit is with the Church to guide it in its decisions, as, for example, when it shifted ground on such matters as the Immaculate Conception, the Assumption of Mary, the veneration of images, as well as on practical issues such as the manner of celebrating the Eucharist – altering the words of institution, mingling water with the wine, and the use of unleavened bread in the mass ritual.[23]

The Holy Spirit is given to the entire Church; consequently, these qualities of inerrancy in faith apply to the Church. Fisher uses the term 'concordia veritatis' to describe this harmony of belief which is the result of the working of the Spirit: 'spiritus ille non sit schismatis auctor, sed unitatis, neque repugnantia doceat, sed concordia'.[24] Linked with this notion of concordia, and virtually synonymous with it, is the concept of consensus. This he uses, for example, referring to the power of binding and loosing given to the Church, but denied by Luther when he says, 'nec ignoras totius ecclesiae consensum'.[25] In the *Confutatio*, and indeed in his other writings, Fisher sees the institutional instrument by means of which explicit consensus is achieved as the general council of the Church. For example, he points out that, when debate arises concerning the interpretation of scripture, there is need for some means of resolving disputes other than depending on the opinions of individual believers or scholars. There is no other way of finally deciding these matters except by the consent and decree of the whole Church, 'totius ecclesiae consensus & decretum'. This consent cannot be arrived at, explicitly, at least, other than by gathering together the Christian people of the entire world in one place.[26] However, since it is impossible to bring this about, it is fitting that the task of resolving disputes among Christians should be undertaken by the bishops: 'Episcopi de quaque natione Christianitatis statim conuenirent, litis eius dirimendae gratia'.[27] This gathering of bishops of the world is guaranteed the assistance of the Holy Spirit who will lead it into all truth. The faithful are expected to accept the decrees of such a gathering since they reflect the concord of the Church.[28] What is of interest here is Fisher's theology which, consciously or not, reflects a representative view of the council. Ideally speaking, Fisher says, the whole Christian world should assemble in one place and there together determine matters of faith. However, since this is not possible, the bishops of the world must meet. He does not speak of them explicitly as representatives of the whole gathering, but that is the conclusion to be drawn. Presumably the bishops come in their own right both as Christians and as ordained ministers of the Church with a special mission to teach, guide, and minister to the faithful. Once there, the Christian faithful being unable to attend, the bishops become their representatives.

When speaking of the power of the council once it has met, Fisher uses explicitly the language of representation to describe its role and authority. He says the Church cannot err in those things which pertain to the substance of the faith, and goes on: 'simul & credo, scripturas id omnino velle, maxime cum probatissimo pontifici concilium generale consentit. Nam pontificem una cum concilio non est dubium Ecclesiam universalem repraesentare.'[29] Here, without developing the thought, Fisher unambiguously declares that the pope and general council together represent the universal Church. They do so not, presumably, as elected representatives, but as representatives chosen for this office by divine call and sacramental ordination, just as in certain medieval political theories the king was held to represent the whole body of the nation even though not elected. Fisher did not adopt the populist democratic stance of the Ockhamite school on the relation of council to Church. None the less his position was at a safe distance from the extremes of curial hegemony and, indeed, more moderate than that of papal monarchists in the Thomist tradition. Both pope and council function as co-ordinate powers by crystallising in dogmatic definition the underlying concordia or consensus of the universal Church. In this context, where the linkage between pope, council and Church is explicitly maintained, it is worth noting that in principle Fisher recognised the right of the Christian people to be present at such gatherings. The council, in his view, comprehends all orders of the Church, each one present by divine right. The general council represents, therefore, for Fisher the entire Church. Its membership consists of the bishops of the world who have been summoned by the Roman pontiff. Its decisions bear the full weight of divine authority when its decrees have been approved by the apostolic see.[30] In this regard Fisher makes the telling statement, 'I always view as suspect those decisions where the Pope differs from the Council or where the Council differs from the Pope, unless this happens through the palpable fault of the Pope.' Essentially he is saying here that normally the approval of both council and pope are needed to give authority to conciliar decisions. He goes on to say, 'where both agree and meet in charity, no doubt can exist that what they have decreed concerning the faith is to be firmly and solidly held by all'.[31] This reinforces what he had said earlier concerning plenary councils which have been convened by the Roman pontiff and to which they have given full assent in the Holy Spirit. Fisher was aware of the recent history of councils acting independently of the Holy See and seeking authority, indeed, over the Roman pontiff. Referring perhaps to Basel and/or Pisa, he said in his *Sermon agayn Luther*, 'And the councelles also thoughe some one of the last councelles whiche perauenture was not gadred in that mekenes & charyte that was expedient, thoughe one of them (whiche thyng I wyl not afferme) in some artycle were permysed to goo amysse.'[32] His awareness in this regard undoubtedly reinforced his conviction that agreement between pope and council was the surest guide to truth in disputed matters of faith.

Fisher quotes Scotus to the effect that 'the Church cannot establish whatever it pleases to be true or not'.[33] Concerning this he remarks that 'although the sovereign pontiff together with the Council, that is, the Church Catholic, cannot make anything either true or false, nor create new articles of faith as such, nevertheless, whatever they propose to our assent as an article of faith, all true Christians ought to accept as nothing less than an article of faith'.[34] Here Fisher was explaining the role of the Church in relation to divine truth. The Church does not reveal a particular formula as divine truth but rather it points out what it believes to be already of the substance of revelation. A defined proposition does not derive veracity from the authority of the Church but is true in its own right as the Word of God. The formula which the council adopts should be regarded by the believer as an accurate formulation of what revelation contains. Because of this one is obliged to accept the teachings of the council: 'If he refuses to hear the Church, let him be to thee as the heathen and the publican' (Matthew 18:17). 'But when are we to hear the Church more than when the Council agrees with the Pope and the Pope with the Council? For these (beyond all controversy) represent the Catholic Church.'[35] Hence, in relation to questions of doctrine, Fisher attaches utmost importance to the statements of the Church. He is careful not to put the Church 'over' God's word in defending his position against Luther's accusation that the Church, through its ministers and councils, places itself 'over' the scriptures rather than submitting to them. Rather it exercises a ministerial interpretative role. Divine revelation is its own authority.

So far we have been discussing conciliar authority with respect to doctrine. The council's authority over moral action is no less weighty or worthy of respect.

Similarly in regard to laws concerning morals and good works, who would doubt but that when both pope and council should see fit to condemn certain customs as contrary to the Christian faith, every Christian is bound to avoid them as dangerous to his soul. Otherwise Paul would have spoken in vain: 'Obey your leaders' (Hebrews 13:17), and Christ also: 'Who despises you, despises me' (Luke 10:16). And again, 'He who will not hear the Church let him be to thee as the heathen and the publican (Matthew 18:17).[36]

Interestingly enough, even in administrative and moral issues, Fisher associates pope and council. He stresses that when pope and council are in agreement on any issue of Christian practice, their judgement must be accepted as that of the Church. This holds therefore for moral as well as doctrinal issues.

Does this mean that every general council receives the full support of John Fisher? In his vernacular *Sermon agayn Luther* he made it clear that this was not so, for he recognised that certain councils had acted in an irresponsible fashion. Having admitted that some of the Fathers of Christian antiquity had incorporated false teaching in their writings, he added the qualification cited earlier concerning conciliar errors, 'And the councelles also thoughe some one of the last councelles whiche perauenture was not gadred in that mekenes & charyte that was expedient, thoughe one of them (whiche thyng I wyl not afferme) in some artycle were permysed to goo amysse.'[37] The erroneous teaching in question may have been the decree of Basel proclaiming the authority and superiority of the council over the pope. Fisher, however, gave no hint as to what was in his mind. None the less, he did reveal his views as to the conditions which make for the validity of conciliar decrees and set up a criterion by which the authenticity of any particular council may be determined. These conditions include insistence on associating both pope and council in decisions. He wrote, 'we speak of plenary councils which have been convened by pontiffs, and to which they have given full consent in the

Holy Spirit', thus affirming the absolute necessity for papal authority to approve the convention of the council and its decisions.[38] However, he was also on his guard against councils which consisted exclusively of papal cronies. He held only those conciliar decrees to be genuine 'when all those have been invited [to the council] whose business it is to be present. Such a council I believe cannot err in matters of faith'.[39] Moreover, he was cognizant of the theological tradition which upheld the right of the Church to correct and reprove a pope who has been seriously at fault and, indeed, to depose him if recalcitrant: 'I suspect those councils in which the pontiff disagrees with the council, or the council with the pope, unless the pope has been most clearly shown to have been at fault.'[40] This was a long-standing principle of both theology and canon law and was used extensively by theologians of the conciliar epoch to justify the calling of councils to reform the Church and the papacy, and in some cases to set aside those claiming the papal office. This power, when used at Constance, provided for the deposition of Pope John XXIII and the election of a new pope. Presumably, then, Fisher regarded such actions justified whenever the pope is guilty of heresy or serious wrongdoing detrimental to the well-being of the Church, and when all other recourse has been exhausted.

Finally, it is worth noting that, while Fisher attached importance to papal authority in administering the Church and in deciding ordinary matters of doctrine where the pope's judgement should normally be respected, he left major decision-making in the Church, especially in doctrinal matters, to the general council. One of the authorities he quoted on church teaching was the Franciscan doctor Duns Scotus. It was in the Franciscan tradition that the doctrine of papal infallibility had emerged with greatest clarity in the fourteenth century.[41] It was formulated 'by Franciscan propagandists eager to defend the inviolability of Nicholas III's Bull *Exiit qui seminat* (1279), which endorsed the Franciscan doctrine of apostolic poverty as a matter of revealed truth'.[42] While upholding an exalted view of papal authority, Scotus, whom Fisher had cited in this context, did not teach the inerrancy of papal teaching. It is no surprise, therefore, that any affirmation of papal infallibility was missing from Fisher's treatment of the papacy. He accepted the judgement of the pope in ordinary matters, but for final decision on questions of faith he referred back to the general council, as did Duns Scotus. In these deliberations, of course, the pope, he believed, had a special position.

At this point it may be helpful to try to see how Fisher's theories of the Church relate to views current in his time. I intend to draw brief comparisons between Fisher's ecclesiological views and those of his fellow English apologists, Henry VIII and Thomas More, as well as those of Thomas de Vio Cajetan, leading papal spokesman against Luther, and John Major, the Scottish theologian-in-exile in Paris who wrote on conciliar issues before the outbreak of reform in Wittenberg.

Compared with Henry VIII Fisher, not unexpectedly, laid greater stress on the supernatural character of the Church, on its guidance by the Spirit of Christ dwelling within it. This indeed was a common theme in late medieval ecclesiology, though the spiritual dimension tended to be stressed in less coherent treatises such as psalm commentaries (Luther himself had written on the Church in this context)[43] or in other areas of theology such as Christology. However, in Fisher's own lifetime John Colet, notably in his work *The Celestial Hierarchies*, had expounded a predominantly spiritual view of the Church based on neo-platonic models.[44] This, perhaps, influenced Thomas More, who was closer to Colet than Fisher, for his ecclesiology is more profoundly Spirit-centred and spiritual in character.[45] This spiritual view of the Church, of course, underlay what Cajetan wrote but was less to the fore perhaps than in the humanist writers who drew more directly on the patristic traditions.[46] John Major, whose writings considered here were occasional rather than systematic, is the one least overtly concerned with the spiritual aspects of ecclesiology.[47]

All five writers recognised the hierarchical nature of the Church as a body of people with its own specific organisation and objectives, and its own leaders endowed with spiritual authority. Fisher noted that one of the principal aims of the Church was the administration of the sacraments and, as might be expected, in this he was in tune with his fellow writers. This had fundamental implications for Church structure since the sacraments laid the foundation for the division within the faithful between priest and layman as between priest and bishop.[48] All saw this hierarchical structure underpinned by the presiding role of the bishop of Rome. Fisher agreed with Cajetan, Major, Thomas More and Henry VIII in pronouncing the papacy to be of divine foundation.[49] Furthermore, in attributing to the pope a certain ordinary power of managing the daily affairs of the Church, Fisher was thinking on the same lines as Cajetan, Major, More and Henry VIII.[50] However, Fisher, like Major and More, circumscribed this power of the pope more than did Cajetan. He insisted that the pope's decisions should be respected only when they were in accord with those of the 'proceres' of the Church. In practice, though he may not have realised it, such a proviso could virtually destroy Roman prerogative since any theologian with solid backing from some of the major schools could claim the right to stand out against papal authority. This indeed is what Luther, at least in his early stages, felt he was doing. Such, of course, was not Fisher's intention and perhaps common sense would suggest that this limitation would apply only to decisions of major significance. It would be contrary to the practice of his own day to require the consent of leading churchmen to the ordinary administrative decisions of the pope. None the less, by insisting that papal decisions carry greater weight when reinforced by those of 'leading men in the Church' – or, as he put it somewhat differently elsewhere, 'if the custom of the Roman see is added to it . . . and the consent of the whole Church accrues to it' – he placed himself firmly in the broad 'constitutional' tradition of ecclesiology. The Roman primacy does not exist at the apex of a platonic hierarchy of power, as Cajetan and other papal monarchists tended to view it. Rather the Petrine office exists and acts in a constant dynamic relationship to the congregation it serves. It does not exercise its function independently of the community or its tradition, but rather echoes what is most authentic in each of these. These views strike a common chord both with Major's theology of the council as supreme authority in the Church and in More's doctrine on consensus. They are mirrored most evidently in Fisher's friend and correspondent Erasmus.[51] Not surprisingly, perhaps, of the writers in question Cajetan was the only one explicitly to uphold papal infallibility.[52]

As regards the constitution of the Church, John Fisher with More and John Major adopted a pluralistic view – one in which each rank in society received its own particular standing directly from God by means of sacramental baptism or ordination.[53] Fisher did attribute some special authority to the pope in this regard in a rather obscure statement referred to earlier where he speaks of bishops being born of the pope. He would seem to refer here to the conferring of jurisdiction on a bishop by the Roman see. He would still have viewed episcopal ordination as the moment in which the candidate received full sacramental authority. Cajetan also saw the role of sacramental consecration as of importance but he maintained that all ecclesiastical power belongs immediately to the pope and that other members of the Church derive their standing in this respect from Christ through the mediation of Peter's successor.[54] Papal powers, he insisted, are greater than those of the rest of the Church taken singly or in combination, thereby reflecting a predominantly juridical view of ecclesial society. In keeping with this, Cajetan adopted a high view of the plenitude of papal power. Oddly enough, Henry VIII, who recognised fully the importance of ordination, at least in the case of priests – he did not expand on the significance of episcopal consecration – also took a rather strong view of the power of the papacy. Perhaps, as later history suggests, he was fascinated by the power of jurisdiction. He specifically mentions that the priest's capacity to judge in the sacrament of penance derives from the bishop. He spoke less explicitly of Roman authority but his awareness is evident in the fact that he sees some sins as pardonable only 'by the hands of the pope himself'.[55]

Concerning the general council of the Church, John Fisher, John Major and Thomas More adopted similar positions in that they saw the council of the Church as representative of the whole body of the faithful with each order of the Church represented in its ranks: the laity through the bishops who attend, while bishops are present in their own right.[56] Henry VIII had little to say about the council except to recognise its ability to make laws for the Church.[57] Cajetan, on the other hand, played down conciliar authority in a manner consistent with his view of the papacy. For him all power and authority in the Church reside in the pope. The council by itself adds nothing to this. The only authority it has is drawn from the pope and is exercised in co-operation with him. Hence the vigour of its decisions is strictly speaking an emanation of the power of the pope.[58] If the pope wishes, he may both define dogma and make law without the council. Putting it crudely, the council in Cajetan's view is very much a creature of the papacy. When it came to a discussion of the authority of the Council, Fisher, like John Major and Cajetan, recognised the role of the council together with the pope in determining matters of faith, morals and church administration.[59] On this score there is no real difference. Fisher, like More, took pains to declare that he accepted only those councils which were duly convened. He went beyond More in explaining what he meant by due convocation. For Fisher the pope should convene the council and approve its decrees. More remains vague on this issue, perhaps deliberately so. The papal role in administrative activity is all the more evident in Cajetan, who attributes little independent influence to the council. John Major, on the other hand, while recognising the distinct role of the papacy and its divine origin, stresses the council's autonomy. For Major, supreme authority resides in the council. In the case of a dispute between pope and council, the council's decisions can override those of the pope so that even definitions of faith can be published in its name. Supreme authority rests with it and it cannot err in matters of faith or morals.[60]

While Fisher and More recognised the authority of the council to correct an erring pope, John Major made great play with this particular point. Writing as he did in the conciliar tradition and from a Parisian standpoint, he used this common position in Catholic theology to argue for conciliar superiority.[61] This did not lead him to propose a *plena potestas* theory of council but rather to affirm the superiority of conciliar power to that of the papacy, each organ possessing its own divine rights. Cajetan on the other hand, while he accepted the traditional position concerning the right of the Church to correct an erring pope, did not see it as a superior power but rather as a ministerial and temporary function of the council not exercised directly in relation to the Roman pontiff himself; he makes thus a rather subtle distinction regarding the link between pope and Church.[62] In this way he upheld papal supremacy over all other organs of the Church. On all of these issues Henry VIII remained silent. Concerning the link between papacy and council, Fisher was adamant that the only councils he recognised were those which were convened by the pope or with his approval and whose final decisions had the stamp of Roman approbation. Less affirmatively More spoke of 'lawful assembly' without defining it. He also took pains to declare that he had never considered the pope 'above the council'. Hence he was clearly not a papal monarchist. This left open the question of conciliar superiority or equality in a co-ordinate relationship as envisaged by Fisher.[63] John Major on the other hand, while recognising the right of the pope to participate and preside over the council, could envisage situations where it might be necessary for the council to proceed alone and exercise its authority independently of 'an erring pope', without determining the conditions on which a pope might be judged by a council to be erring.[64] Obviously here he was leaving room for manoeuvre by the council *vis-à-vis* the pope. Cajetan of course adopted a maximalist view of Roman authority, holding for the totally independent and complete power of the papacy within the Church. The council as such is convened by the pope; it is there to assist him, its decisions must have his approval and it has absolutely no authority independent of him – except in the case already noted of a pope who falls into heresy or similar fault.

In relation to other contemporary trends in ecclesiology, where did Fisher stand? In the later middle ages, there were at least five different models of the constitution of the Church in circulation, each with its own variants: the populist-democratic view proposed by William of Ockham; the constitutional or pluralist view expounded by Gelnhausen, Zabarella and John Major, among others; the episcopalist view put forward by Jean Gerson and others of his school; the hierocratic/curialist view proposed by Ferrer and Flandrin; the monarchist view supported by Thomists such as Torquemada and Cajetan.[65] Within this frame of reference, Fisher can be seen as supporting a constitutional, pluralist theology which understood the institutional Church to consist of a multiplicity of powers or corporations. Within this body, pope and bishops possess supreme authority by divine institution, though total sovereignty resides in the whole not in any one corporate body nor in any one office. This puts Fisher in the same school of thought as that of moderate conciliarists of the time such as John Major, his Scottish, Parisian contemporary, as well as earlier scholars such as Zabarella and Gelnhausen. On the other hand, he is more 'episcopalist' than Thomas More, who laid stress on the common corps of Christendom, 'the great unwashed masses' of believers endowed nevertheless, he believed, with the Holy Spirit.

In Fisher's view, despite the failings of its members, the Church was essentially spiritual in character. Its visible constitution he envisaged in pluralistic terms. This places Fisher's ecclesiology to the 'left' as it were of both the curialist and the papal monarchist view of the Church upheld by Luther's official adversary, Thomas de Vio Cajetan. It locates him in the broad stream of medieval constitutionalism upheld by moderate conciliarists such as Jean Gerson, Francesco Zabarella and John Major, though he is markedly less concerned with the common people than his fellow controversialist Thomas More. There is little doubt that Fisher, had he lived 150 odd years earlier, could have been one of the leading lights of the conciliar reform movement. He would have found himself quite at home at the Council of Constance. Sadly, he came later on the scene and found himself in conflict with an even more radical renewal movement whose inner inspiration he never really grasped, as well as falling victim to the pseudo-reform of Henry VIII, whose purposes he recognised, feared and finally opposed, and under whose axe he ultimately perished.

Notes

For citations of Luther's works, vol. and page nos. refer to *Weimarer Ausgabe, D. Martin Luthers Werke*, 90 vols. (Weimar, 1883), abbreviated to *WA*.

1 On Fisher's life and writings see Edward Surtz, *The Works and Days of John Fisher* (Cambridge, Mass., 1967); Michael Macklem, *God Have Mercy. The Life of John Fisher of Rochester* (Ottawa, 1967); Jean Rouschausse, *John Fisher, Vie et oeuvre* (Angers and Nieuwkoop, 1972). Studies of Fisher's theology can be found in Surtz, *Works and Days*, and in Rouschausse, *Vie et oeuvre*. For studies of the *Confutatio* see Rouschausse, *Vie et oeuvre*, 161–82 and Rouschausse, 'Polémique antiluthérienne de John Fisher: Réfutation de l'Assertio de Luther', unpublished thesis, Tours, 1968.

2 R. E. McNally, 'The Roman Process of Martin Luther', in J. Coriden (ed.), *The Once and Future Church* (New York, 1971), pp. 111–28; Remigius Bäumer, 'Der Lutherprozess', in R. Bäumer (ed.), *Lutherprozess und Lutherbann* (Münster, 1972), pp. 18–48; D. Olivier, *The Trial of Luther* (London, 1979).

3 Jaroslav Pelikan, *Spirit versus Structure, Luther and the Institutions of the Church* (New York, 1968) is still a useful introductory study; further references in my essay 'The Ecclesiology of Martin Luther', in *Ecclesiological Themes in the Writings of Sir Thomas More*, a thesis presented in the National University of Ireland, 1978, II, 648–86.

4 For studies of Fisher's ecclesiology, see the early work by G. Duggan, 'The Church in the Writings of St John Fisher', Dissertation presented for the Doctorate in Theology in the Angelicum, Rome, 1937; Surtz, *Works and Days*, pp. 31–9; my 'The Ecclesiology of St John Fisher', pp. 589–613.

5 *Assertionis Lutheranae Confutatio, Opera*, cols. 530–4. Subsequent citations are drawn from this edition. I have added the biblical references from the RSV edition of the Bible.

6 *Confutatio*, col. 533.

7 *Confutatio*, cols. 534–39.

8 *Confutatio*, col. 585: 'Certainly, through faith Christians are founded on Christ. But this faith is scarcely in Christ himself but in the very hearts of Christians. Since, therefore, Peter first confessed so he was the first of the living stones after Christ on which lay the structure of the edifice.'

9 *Confutatio*, cols. 543–4. Critical text in *Enchiridion Symbolorum Definitionum et Declarationum de Rebus Fidei et Morum*, ed. H. Denzinger, revised H. Schönmetzer (Herder, Barcelona etc. 1963), p. 332, par. 1307.

10 Mansi, *Sacrorum Conciliorum Nova et Amplissima Collectio*, XXVII, 590 and 1159; commentary and English translation in Sidney Z. Ehler and John B. Morrall (eds.), *Church and State through the Centuries. A Collection of Historic Documents with Commentaries* (London, 1954), pp. 104–6.

11 Joseph Gill, *The Council of Florence* (Cambridge, 1959), pp. 270–304.
12 *Confutatio*, cols. 543–5.
13 *Confutatio*, cols. 560–1.
14 *Confutatio*, col. 550.
15 *Confutatio*, cols. 550–1.
16 *Confutatio*, col. 555. On the medieval background to this understanding of episcopate, see Yves Congar, *L'Église de Saint Augustin à l'Époque Moderne* (Paris, 1970), pp. 169–74.
17 *Confutatio*, col. 545. Cf. 'Christus haud dubie primatum hunc ei plenissime contulit, super omnes omnium hominum congregationes', ibid., col. 547.
18 *Confutatio*, col. 547.
19 'Quando igitur is, qui primus est, & totius Ecclesiae princeps, cuique totius orbis cura, Christi decreto commissa fuit, hunc vel illum sensum vna cum caeteris Ecclesiae proceribus approbauerit, istis nimirum alios (qui reliqui sunt) nisi rationem efficacissimam in contrarium attulerint, se conformare decebit', in *Confutatio*, col. 591.
20 *Confutatio*, col. 480. There is here, it seems, an echo of the 'magistère des docteurs' described by Congar, *L'Église*, pp. 241–4.
21 John Fisher, *Euersio Munitionis Quam Iodocus Clichtoueus Erigere Moliebatur Aduersus Unicam Magdalenam* (Louvain, 1519), sigg. Y4–a6, cited Surtz, *Works and Days*, p. 71.
22 *Confutatio*, col. 309.
23 *Confutatio*, col. 480.
24 *Confutatio*, col. 302. See also ibid., col. 299, where Fisher speaks of St Augustine as a dependable interpreter of scripture: He would not be so useful 'si . . . proprio spiritui fuisset innixus, & non magis concordi totius Ecclesiae spiritui'; ibid., col. 608.
25 *Confutatio*, col. 581. Here I differ somewhat from John M. Headley in the introduction to his masterly edition of Thomas More's *Responsio ad Lutherum*, in *The Complete Works of St Thomas More*, V (2) (New Haven and London, 1969), 744–5, where he claims that for Fisher concordia refers to common agreement about the faith begotten by the Holy Spirit, while consensus has overtones which are 'human and legal'. This does not always seem to be the case since in certain passages these terms are used almost interchangeably, as in *Confutatio*, cols. 457–6.
26 *Confutatio*, col. 475. This same imagery is found in Thomas More, *Responsio*, p. 626/21–7, tr. p. 627/24–33, and More, *The Confutation of Tyndale's Answer*, ed. Louis A. Schuster, Richard C. Marius, James P. Lusardi and Richard J. Schoeck, *Complete Works*, VIII (2) (New Haven and London, 1974), pp. 938/14–23, 924/9–34. It is possible that More was dependent on Fisher for this concept, though he may simply have drawn on a common source.
27 *Confutatio*, col. 475.
28 *Confutatio*, cols. 475–6: 'quicquid ab hoc venerando patrum coetu communi concordia fuerit decretum, id caeteris omnibus ratum & firmum haberi merito debet.'
29 *Confutatio*, cols. 592, 593.
30 *Confutatio*, cols. 595–8.
31 *Confutatio*, col. 598.

32 John Fisher, *Sermon Made agayn the Pernicyous Doctryn of Martin Luther* (1521), in *EW*, p. 338.

33 *Confutatio*, cols. 583–4. Fisher's reference is to *Sent.* IV, dist. 11, q.3., to be found in John Duns Scotus, *Scriptum Primum Oxoniense Subtilissimi Theologi Ioannis Duns Scoti Ord. Minor Super Quarto Sententiarum* (Venice: Octaviani Scoti, 1522), col. 46v.

34 *Confutatio*, col. 583.

35 *Confutatio*, col. 584.

36 *Confutatio*, col. 584.

37 Fisher, *Sermon agayn Luther*, *EW*, p. 338.

38 *Confutatio*, col. 598.

39 *Confutatio*, col. 597. 'Neque ego penitus cuiuscunque concilij decreta probanda censeo, sed eius quodcumque fuerit in Spiritu sancto pontificis auctoritate cunctisque praemonitis, quorum interest adesse conuocatum.'

40 *Confutatio*, col. 598.

41 Francis Oakley, *The Western Church in the Later Middle Ages* (Ithaca and London, 1979), pp. 167–9, indicates the literature.

42 Ibid., p. 168. See also Brian Tierney, *Origins of Papal Infallibility 1150–1350* (Leiden, 1972), pp. 140–6, where he unravels the development of this doctrine through the medieval period, discussing Duns Scotus's position.

43 See, for example, the excellent study by Scott H. Hendrix, *Ecclesia in Via. Ecclesiological Developments in the Medieval Psalm Exegesis and the 'Dictata super Psalterium' (1513–1515) of Martin Luther* (Leiden, 1974).

44 John Colet, *In Ecclesiasticam Divi Dionisii Hierarchiam*, in *Ioannes Coletus super Opera Dionysii, Two Treatises on the Hierarchies of Dionysius by John Colet, D.D.*, ed. J. H. Lupton (London, 1869). See my essay, 'The Ecclesiology of Dean John Colet', in *Ecclesiological Themes*, II, 559–88.

45 Brian Gogan, *The Common Corps of Christendom, Ecclesiological Themes in the Writings of Sir Thomas More* (Leiden, 1982), pp. 279–81, 322–6 and *passim*.

46 See, for example, Cajetan (Thomas de Vio), *Tractatus de Fide et Operibus adversus Lutheranos, ad Clementem VII. Pont. Max. in Duodecim Capita Diuisus*, in *Opuscula Omnia* (Venice, 1588), cap. 9, pp. 290–1, which contains a brief exposition of his teaching on the Church as Christ's body. On Cajetan's ecclesiology see Charles Journet, 'L'Âme créée de l'Église selon Cajétan', *Revue Thomiste*, new series, 17 (1934–5), 246–65; O. de la Brosse, 'Le Pape et le concile. La Comparaison de leurs pouvoirs à la veille de la Réforme', *Unam Santam*, 58 (Paris, 1965), 147–81, 185–335; Ulrich Horst, 'Die Lehre von der Kirche in den Kommentaren des 16. Jahrhunderts zur theologischen Summe des Hl. Thomas von Aquin', in R. Bäumer (ed.), *Lehramt und Theologie im 16. Jahrhundert* (Münster, 1976), p. 65, who gives further indications to the literature.

47 On Major's thought see Francis Oakley, *Natural Law, Conciliarism and Consent in the Late Middle Ages, Studies in Ecclesiastical and Intellectual History* (London, 1984), pp. 681–90, 786–806.

48 Henry VIII, *Assertio Septem Sacramentorum adversus Mart. Lutherum, Henrico VIII. Angliae Rege Autore* (Parisiis, Apud Sebastianum Niuellium sub Ciconiis, via Jacob, 1562), fos. 76r–89r; John Major, *Disputatio, Excerpta ad Verbum ex Eiusdem Commentariis in Librum Quartum Sententiarum Distinct. XXIV. fol. CCXIII* in

E. Du Pin (ed.), *Ioannis Gersonii Doctoris et Cancellarii Parisiensis Opera* (Paris, 1606), cols. 681–2. Major speaks here of the separate ordination of the apostles by Christ. See, for example, Thomas More, *The Confutation of Tyndale's Answer*, pp. 190/29–191/21, 305/31–4, 911/3–32.

49 Henry VIII, *Assertio*, fos. 9r–11r; Cajetan, *De Comparatione Authoritatis Papae et Concilij, in Uigintiocto Capita Diuisus*, cap. 1–2, in *Opuscula Omnia*, pp. 5–6; Thomas More, *Responsio ad Lutherum*, p. 272/25–9, tr. p. 273/32–36, p. 328/25–30, tr. p. 329/26–32, p. 196/14–21, tr. p. 197/19–25; John Major, *In Librum Quartum Sententiarum*, col. 676.

50 Cajetan, *De Comparatione Authoritatis*, cap. 7, 8, *Opuscula omnia*, pp. 10–12; John Major, *In Librum Quartum Sententiarum*, cols. 676–8. This idea is implicit in Major's treatment of the Church as a monarchical society ruled by the pope. The same assertion can be found in Henry VIII's *Assertio* by reading between the lines, for example, when he refers to the pope as 'supreme pontiff' ('summi pontificis'), 'chief priest' and 'supreme judge upon earth' ('sacerdoti omnium summo . . . supremo in terris iudici'). Each of these titles implies pastoral and administrative authority; see Henry VIII, *Assertio*, fo. 10v. More's position can be most clearly seen perhaps in *Responsio*, p.196/4–20, tr. p. 197/5–25, in his discussion of John 21:16, 'feed my lambs' and his focus on the word *poimainein*, ascribing to Peter a function in the Church analogous to that of a shepherd with his flock.

51 See, for example, Erasmus's remarks about consensus, in particular his comment on conciliar decisions: 'Idem arbitror de Conciliorum decretis, praesertim si consensus populi Christum profitentis accesserit', in Erasmus, *Lingua, Opera Omnia*, IV (Leiden, 1703–6), 170, 703 E.

52 Cajetan, *De Comparata Authoritate Papae & Concilij. Apologiae*, part 2, cap. 13, in *Opuscula Omnia*, pp. 40–1.

53 John Major, *In Librum Quartum Sententiarum*, cols. 675–82. This is the point of Major's arguments for the institution of the Roman primacy and the separate ordination of the other apostles, to whom bishops succeed by ordination. For a brief exposition of More's views, see Gogan, *Common Corps of Christendom*, pp. 283–4.

54 Cajetan, *De Comparatione Authoritatis*, cap. 9, *Opuscula Omnia*, pp. 12–14; 'potestas Papae est tota potestas Ecclesiae universalis, & aliae potestates sunt participationes ipsius . . .'.

55 Henry VIII, *Assertio*, fo. 5r; arguing for the authenticity of papal office, he speaks of 'its vast power' ('tantam ac tam late fusam potestatem'), *Assertio*, fo. 9r.

56 'A council lawfully convened and representing the universal Church is above the sovereign pontiff' (note the words 'representing the universal Church'), in John Major, *Excerpta ex Eiusdem Commentariis in Matthaeum, Cap XIIX*, in *Gersonii Opera*, col. 878; More, *The Confutation of Tyndale's Answer*, pp. 940/33–941/8.

57 Henry VIII, *Assertio*, fo. 59r: 'as if many of the laws, which he [Luther] calls murdering laws, were not ordained in former times by the Holy Fathers and public consent of all Christians in synods and general councils'.

58 Cajetan, *De Comparatione Authoritatis*, cap. 9, *Opuscula Omnia*, p. 13 *passim*: 'non plus potest papa & Ecclesia quam papa solus'.

59 Cajetan, *De Comparatione Authoritatis*, cap. 8, *Opuscula Omnia*, pp. 11–12; In a letter to Cromwell, More observed that the teaching of a general council should be believed provided that it be 'assembled lawfully'; in a conversation with his

daughter Margaret he spoke of 'a well assembled generall counsaile', *The Correspondence of Sir Thomas More*, ed. E. F. Rogers (Princeton, 1947), pp. 499/239–40, 526/448. He did not specify what he meant by lawful assembly; his thoughts can only be surmised from constitutional analogies: see my *Common Corps of Christendom*, pp. 262–5.

60 Major, in *Gersonii Opere*, cols. 878 (*In Matthaeum*), 884–5 (*Disputatio*).

61 Major, in *Gersonii Opere*, cols. 880–1 and *passim* (*In Matthaeum* and *Disputatio*).

62 Cajetan, *De Comparatione Authoritatis*, cap. 17–21, *Opuscula Omnia*, pp. 19–23.

63 I have argued elsewhere that, based on parliamentary analogies, it is more likely that More favoured a position similar to that of Fisher – with pope and council viewed as complementary and co-ordinate constitutional entities. See Gogan, *Common Corps of Christendom*, pp. 292–3.

64 Major, in *Gersonii Opere*, cols. 884–5 (*In Matthaeum* and *Disputatio*).

65 This is my own schematisation. See Gogan, *Common Corps of Christendom*, pp. 60–3. On the background to this, see among others Francis Oakley, in *The Western Church in the Later Middle Ages* (Ithaca and London, 1979), pp. 157–74; Yves Congar, *L'Église de Saint Augustin à l'Époque Moderne* (Paris, 1970), pp. 215–352.

Fisher, Henry VIII and the Reformation crisis

J. J. SCARISBRICK

A few facts taken almost at random from the curriculum vitae of John Fisher will be enough to demonstrate what a remarkable life his was. After an exemplary early academic career, he became vice-chancellor of his University when he was a mere 32 years old. In 1504, then aged 35, he was elected chancellor. He was re-elected chancellor annually thereafter until 1514, when the electors decided to face facts and chose him for life. He was ordained a priest at the age of 22, four years below the canonical minimum and thanks to a papal license.[1] He became a bishop when he was 35 and was thus one of the youngest men ever to have been raised to the Bench. It was Henry VII who procured the promotion – unprompted, for once, by anyone. As he explained to his mother, the Lady Margaret, whose friend and confessor Fisher already was, there was no better way of beginning to make amends for the unworthy promotions for which he had been responsible than by nominating to Rome someone of Fisher's qualities of mind and life.[2] Fisher is the first English bishop ever to have been put on trial for treason, found guilty and executed. He is the only English Catholic bishop to have suffered that fate. He was the first chancellor of Cambridge to be so treated, but not the last. He is the only cardinal ever to have been martyred.

He had at least four separate, though overlapping, careers. First, there was Fisher at Cambridge. Then, there was Fisher of Rochester – the zealous pastor who refused to exchange what was the smallest and poorest see in England for something plumper, and gave it thirty-one years of careful oversight. Next, there is Fisher the religious controversialist: the fierce opponent of Luther and Oecolampadius, among others. He was the Reformation's most formidable enemy in England and probably the first Catholic writer anywhere to undertake a comprehensive review of and reply to early protestant theology. There is nothing before his *Assertionis Lutheranae Confutatio* of 1523 which attempts a full-scale response to Wittenberg; and by 1525 he had turned his guns against Swiss Eucharistic theology. It is a measure of his self-assurance and energy that he should have taken on so much so swiftly; and a measure of the quality of those works, stentorian and unwieldy though they may seem to us today, that they should immediately have won

155

a European reputation. Furthermore, they were esteemed not only among the later English recusants; 'Roffensis' was an authority to whom Bellarmine as well as Stapleton deferred.[3] Finally, of course, there is Fisher the opponent of Henry VIII, playing the major role in defying the king's matrimonial plans and chief architect of Catherine's defence, and thereafter defender of the Church against an increasingly predatory Defender of the Faith.

For any one of these roles Fisher would probably have merited a respectful mention in the more respectable history books. But for achieving so widely and variously he begins to stand apart from fellow countrymen. And perhaps there was a fifth role. Perhaps we should separate out from the story of Fisher at Cambridge an appreciation of him as patron and practitioner of early-sixteenth-century humanism. One thinks not just of his evidently sincere devotion to Erasmus but of his delight in Rudolf Agricola, his interest in Reuchlin and the like. His library was exceptionally well stocked. He himself began serious study of Greek under Erasmus's tuition when he was 47 years old. He embarked on Hebrew three years later and had acquired sufficient competence therein to use it occasionally, and to good effect, in his polemical writing.

There was almost a sixth career. Thrice (apparently) Fisher planned to go to Rome. On two of these occasions he was nominated to the English delegation to the Fifth Lateran Council.[4] For reasons that are far from clear, he never got there (and seems to have been out of England only once – to the Field of the Cloth of Gold, i.e. just beyond Calais). We can only speculate on what impact the forceful, devout English bishop might have had on that ineffectual assembly and wonder what else Christendom might have owed to him if he had found himself in alliance with the few other zealots, like the general of the Augustinians, who were there and saw the need for radical reform as keenly as he did.

He was no ordinary man, therefore. His confrontation with the king underlines this fact. Instead of following the familiar story of his defence of the independence of the Church in England and of papal authority against the monarch, however, let us turn at once to what was surely the climax of his opposition to royal policies and perhaps the most extraordinary moment in an extraordinary life.

In September 1533 Fisher called upon the Emperor Charles V to invade England and help depose its king. John Fisher, mere bishop of Rochester, a man not given to ill-considered words or vain gestures, a hitherto loyal supporter of the Tudor dynasty to which he owed much and an ecclesiastic who had always had a clear view of the need for Church and state to respect each other's prerogatives, was calling upon the most powerful monarch (in theory) whom Christendom had perhaps ever seen to use violence against his anointed king. We are not told exactly what Fisher envisaged, but we may presume that he looked for an imperial invasion force (perhaps sailing into the Thames) to be the signal for a rebellion at home that would topple Henry. Perhaps he also looked for a marriage between Mary, Henry VIII's daughter, and Henry Courtenay, marquis of Exeter, or even the exiled Reginald Pole, each of whom had enough royal blood in his veins to make a convincing consort to the princess, who would then ascend the throne.

We know about this because Fisher communicated secretly with the emperor via the imperial ambassador in England, Eustace Chapuys. The latter's despatches show that Fisher had been dealing with him, sometimes using a secret messenger, since 1531.[5] However much one may doubt Chapuy's judgement of men and situations, there can be no doubting the substance of this story. Chapuys reported in two separate letters to the emperor that Fisher had sent secret word to him, calling upon Charles to take in hand promptly action which, the bishop declared, would be as pleasing to God as war upon the Turk.[6] Never before or since has a bishop (an English bishop, at any rate) taken so extreme a step. The Rubicon had been crossed. Yes, in the eyes of his prince, Fisher had committed treason. But, as one who subscribed to the traditional medieval view of the hierarchy of laws and the right, eventually the duty, of resistance to injustice, Fisher would have known that his action was righteous in the eyes of God. What would we think now of him if Henry had discovered his treason and exacted revenge? What would we think of him if Charles had responded?

It must be quickly added that Fisher was not alone in wanting this action. According to Chapuys, innumerable people from many ranks of society were 'deafening' him with similar calls. They insisted, he said, that a small force would suffice. A mere embargo on trade was not enough. The emperor must send ships and men – which would be the signal for an uprising at home.[7] But Chapuys was so vague about who those 'innumerable' others were that we may suspect exaggeration on his part. Fisher was the first one whom he named. For the moment Fisher was the only one he named. In subsequent months Chapuys identified a number of others. But there was never another cleric among them.

For Fisher this drastic step was the climax of six years of almost unremitting opposition to the king. Since 1527, when Henry had first made public his desire to be shed of Catherine of Aragon, Fisher had been the queen's most constant champion and played a leading role in presenting her defence at the legatine court in 1529 and thereafter. He spoke up for her in parliament. He wrote so much in defence of her marriage that, at the end, he could not remember exactly how many treatises had come from his pen.[8] Almost incredibly, as late as mid 1532 he was still thundering from the pulpit against Henry's plan to marry Anne Boleyn and in support of the queen.

Since 1529 Fisher had been no less active in mobilising clerical resistance to the royal attack on the Church and papal authority in England, and no less outspoken. He had reacted vigorously to anti-clerical legislation which came up to the House of Lords from the Lower House in the first session of the Reformation parliament. He and the archbishop of Canterbury, William Warham, had held their brethren steady in early 1531, when the first direct royal attack was launched against the English Church, culminating in the so-called Pardon of the Clergy. It was Fisher who proposed the famous saving clause in response to the royal demand for recognition of overlordship, namely, that this would go no further than 'the law of Christ allows' (that is, not very far at all).

According to the early *Life* of Fisher, about this time it was urgently proposed to Convocation that the clergy should agree to the surrender to the crown of a number of religious houses, allegedly in recompense for the expenses incurred by the king in seeking his divorce.[9] There is no mention elsewhere of this proposed *beau geste* by the clergy and, indeed, no suggestion elsewhere that as early as 1530–1 there were any royal plans to pilfer monastic wealth. But that *Life* is usually reliable and contains so much material gathered from people who had been eyewitnesses of the events it reports that we must give some credence to the story. And once more, we are told, Fisher was to the fore and rallied Convocation by telling them the fable of the axe that lacked a handle and persuaded a forest to yield up a sapling with which to supply its need; whereupon the axe proceeded to fell the whole forest. The king was refused.

Fisher's intransigence had not been acquired suddenly. In 1523 he and his friend Richard Fox, bishop of Winchester, had opposed the grant of a clerical subsidy to the king who desired it in order to prosecute war against the ancient enemy, the French.[10] If Fisher opposed the grant for the same reason as did Fox, he was probably motivated by conscientious objection to vainglorious warmaking and not solely clerical parsimony. So four years before Henry encountered this episcopal opposition to his matrimonial plans, he had encountered similar resistance to his militarism. And that was not the first example of what must eventually have seemed like habitual obstructiveness. There is extant among the papers that were presumably seized when Fisher was eventually arrested an intriguing manuscript which could well be the text of a speech delivered to Convocation or the Lords several years previously in defence of ecclesiastical liberties (benefit of clergy, sanctuary, etc).[11] It may date back to the famous furore of 1514–15 when Church and state came into noisy conflict and many sparks flew. Or it may belong to an earlier date – perhaps the parliament of 1512, which produced an act curtailing clerical immunity from the criminal law. That act was hesitant and curiously muted.[12] If Fisher's speech was delivered then, perhaps that fact owes something to his opposition. His words were uncompromising. Ecclesiastical liberties, rights of Church courts and of sanctuary, etc, were *de iure divino*. The king could not despoil them without violating his coronation oath; the bishops could not surrender them without imperilling their immortal souls and flouting scripture, the Fathers, the common consent of Christendom, and so on. It was therefore no shy, inexperienced prelate who entered the fray in 1527. Fisher was a seasoned adversary.

As has been said, he was prominent in opposition to royal policies from 1529 onwards in the upper houses of Southern Convocation and parliament. His influence did not stop there. It is striking that on the one occasion when we get a glimpse of the attitude of the lower house of Southern Convocation – this is a lengthy protest against royal actions belonging to early 1531 – Rochester's clergy are conspicuous among the signatories.[13] Furthermore, the president of that lower house, one Peter Ligham, a thorn in Henry's side, was a good friend of Fisher.[14]

Unfortunately, there is little information about how members of the lower house of the Reformation parliament thought and voted. But a list probably recording members who were opposed to the act in restraint of appeals of 1533 – a major piece, of course, of the Reformation programme – includes the two representatives of the city of Rochester, one of whom was the bishop's brother Robert.[15] Yet more revealing is the story of Sir George Throckmorton, member for Warwickshire and a leading figure in a parliamentary group which used to meet in the Queen's Head in Fleet Street and there discuss parliamentary matters.[16] Throckmorton and his friends were undoubtedly opponents of the Henrician Reformation to varying degrees; and they were dangerous opponents because weighty knights of their shires. Fisher was in direct and regular contact with Throckmorton. The latter sought advice on how to conduct himself in parliament. Fisher gave him a book he had written about the papal primacy (to which we shall return shortly).[17] Fisher was also in touch with other clerical opponents of the regime, like Friar Peto and the Bridgettine Richard Reynolds.

Care must be taken not to overstate the case. It is likely that Fisher had a direct hand in stiffening the conservative opposition in the lower house of Southern Convocation as he had done in the upper house; it is likely that the conservatism of Rochester's parliamentary representatives was not accidental. To that extent the bishop may have directly instigated others' resistance to Henry's policies. But the evidence will not allow us to see him at the centre of a web of dissidence that he had organised or was co-ordinating. His relations with Throckmorton illustrate the point. Throckmorton consulted Fisher frequently and more than anyone else. But he consulted several others as well, including Thomas More. Fisher doubtless encouraged him heartily. But Fisher also restrained him, assuring him that he was not required to speak out in parliament against the king's measures if there was no chance of halting them. Throckmorton did not have to court martyrdom. Furthermore, Throckmorton apparently came for advice *after* he had begun to protest.

Fisher was more active in opposition – and in fostering it in others – than anyone else and had wider contacts than any other opponent of the king. He was the only bishop to be so involved. So it was that by September 1533 he came to that final step of calling for armed intervention by the emperor. Why he had come to that awesome decision is obvious enough: all other attempts to halt the king had failed. Henry had defiantly married Anne, she had been crowned queen, parliament had passed the momentous act in restraint of appeals which largely severed England's allegiance to Rome. But we can still ask why Fisher did what he did precisely when he did it.

A number of reasons suggest themselves. First, Rome was apparently about to excommunicate the king. The decision had been taken and a document prepared several months before, but not promulgated. By the late summer of 1533 execution was expected any day. A papal anathema accompanied by deposition would be a clear signal for military action and a necessary preliminary to it. As Fisher explained to Chapuys, against people as obstinate as these, the pope's weapons would be ineffectual unless the emperor took the matter in hand himself.[18] The time for strong action had arrived. Moreover, there was the prophecy of the nun Elizabeth Barton, the 'Holy Maid of Kent', who had been causing a considerable stir by reason of her claims to have received visions of Our Lady and many mystical favours from heaven, and because since 1530 she had become publicly involved in the royal divorce issue. She had told Henry to his face that if he repudiated Catherine and married Anne he would cease to be king within seven months. Fisher had seen a good deal of her and been so impressed that, we are told, he wept when he heard her words.[19] By September 1533 the seven months were nearly spent. The excommunication would authenticate her prophecy, and vice versa. Both would legitimise invocation of the temporal arm against the king.

Finally, there was the royal birth on 8 September 1533. To the confusion of physicians, astrologers and cunning men who had predicted that it would be a boy, and to the bitter disappointment of the king, who had planned splendid pageants and tournaments to celebrate the birth of the longed-for heir, Anne was delivered of a girl.[20] Years of pleading, pushing and bullying had come to naught. Henry had been publicly mocked – and perhaps, in Fisher's view, judged. With the king's dynastic plans in disarray, and the succession and hence the kingdom less secure than ever, the bishop could well have had a final reason for regarding this as the propitious moment for direct action.

In the event, of course, Rome lost its nerve and did not release its thunderbolt. Emperor Charles, as we know, had more pressing concerns than English ecclesiastical affairs. At that particular moment he was preparing an expedition to North Africa to check the Moslem threat to his Spanish kingdom – a fact which perhaps explains the inwardness of Fisher's remark that to send an imperial task force to England would have been a work as agreeable to God as fighting the Turks. With hindsight some may also doubt whether a small imperial expedition would have ignited a sufficiently large rebellion within England.

So we may ask, were Fisher and the others being absurdly unrealistic? There is some evidence that they were not. In trying to uncover conspiracy and covert disaffection, however, particularly if they came to nothing, we are inevitably dealing with hints and fragments, faint footmarks and noises off-stage. There is always a temptation to overwork such evidence. On the other hand, since, of its nature, conspiracy which would have earned immediate death if discovered and which, in the event, did not erupt into action cannot be expected to leave many traces in state archives, the smallest clue deserves close attention.

There is no doubt that Lords Darcy and Hussey were seriously disaffected. Darcy would claim that 600 'great gentlemen' of the North were ready to rise and promised to put 8,000 of his own men into the field.[21] The earl of Derby was also suspect.[22] Then there was the Pole family, Lady Margaret, Lord Montague, Sir Geoffrey – of direct White Rose (Yorkist) descent – as well as Henry Courtenay, grandson of Edward IV and head of a family with a considerable clientele. There was George Lord Abergavenny or Burgavenny, head of the Neville dynasty and son-in-law of the duke of Buckingham executed in 1521. George himself had had a taste of the Tower. His wife was a friend of Princess Mary. In September 1533 Chapuys reported that George and he had met at court. Burgavenny had made his feelings dangerously clear to the ambassador and assured him that no gentleman in England was more disposed to serve the emperor than he – this in the full view of Thomas Cromwell.[23] Fisher would have known Darcy, Hussey and the others through the House of Lords. He knew Burgavenny more than slightly: they had exchanged gifts; George had even invited him to go hunting.[24]

Fisher also knew Lord Sandys, lord chamberlain and deputy of Calais. He, too, was in contact with Chapuys (using his physician as a messenger) and, it seems, eventually feigned illness in order to avoid the court and its policies. He withdrew to his lair, The Vine, near Basingstoke.[25]

The list is a long one. Rather than peruse a lengthy catalogue of discontent, let us focus on two particularly interesting examples. Both concern peers who had tell-tale connections and were in trouble. First, there was Edmund Lord Bray, who in March 1535 was suddenly accused of 'multiplying', that is, alchemy. Why this had made him guilty of a felony we are not told. Since alchemy in itself was hardly a crime, suspicions are aroused at once. They are heightened by the fact that an unnamed friar and a doctor who seem to have been involved in Bray's misdeeds were in secret contact with Chapuys, and indicated that Bray was also involved in prophecy. They told that the intended mutation of base metal into gold was a portent of political mutation, that is, the overthrow of the government of the realm.[26] The story is obscure. We are probably dealing here with the semi-lunatic edge of discontents. But sixteenth-century England took such things seriously; and it could have taken all sorts of people to make the new world for which Fisher and the others looked. Bray had important contacts: his sister was married to Lord Sandys; his wife was in Catherine of Aragon's household. He himself had been engaged in some land deals with that George Throckmorton, the parliamentary representative for Warwickshire already mentioned.[27]

Secondly, there was Lord Dacre of the North. Like his namesake of the South, he was involved in interesting legal tangles at this time. Warden of the West Marches, a chieftain in the borderlands between Scotland and England, head of a large dynasty and notable landowner in Cumberland especially, he was in deep trouble in late 1533, having been accused of treasonous dealings with the Scots. The details do not matter here. There is no evidence that he was the victim of government malice, though one may be suspicious. At his trial by his peers in July 1534, however, the trenchant, articulate Dacre delivered a seven-hour speech in his defence and was acquitted, an achievement almost unique among sixteenth-century set-piece political trials; whereupon new charges were brought against him and a large fine, secured by a recognisance of 10,000 marks, imposed.[28] Dacre was reportedly a staunch supporter of Catherine and Mary. Darcy claimed him as an ally. And in attacking a peer of Dacre's importance the crown could have acquired a dangerous new enemy.

The imperial ambassador was, of course, a key figure in building up this network of malcontents. Doubtless Fisher would in part have learnt about them from him – as well, perhaps, as providing him with some details. But Chapuys was not the only, or necessarily the most important, intermediary. As has been said, Fisher had direct contact with fellow peers in the House of Lords and, via his brother and George Throckmorton, with the Commons. George Throckmorton's brother was in Reginald Pole's entourage and in touch with the Pole/Courtenay circle in England; and so on. There were two other important focal points of opposition and places where information could be exchanged. The first was the Bridgettine house at Syon – not far from Westminster. It was much frequented by distinguished visitors, especially of the more devout, conservative sort. Many of its inmates were themselves well connected – the prioress was a de la Pole, for instance – and Richard Reynolds was a man with a wide circle of friends, including George Throckmorton and John Fisher. Then there was Mary's household. The chance survival of accounts for 1533 enables us to see what interesting visitors she had: Lady Burgavenny, Lord Sandys, Lord Montague, Sir Geoffrey Pole, Lady Kingston (whose husband, governor of the Tower of

London, was also reported to be disaffected), the countess of Derby, the earl and countess of Essex, the earl and countess of Oxford among them.[29] We cannot presume that they were all committed friends. But to visit Mary and to stay with her (as some did for several days) was not the best way to show goodwill towards the king; and it is difficult to imagine that only small talk passed between the princess and all her guests. Once again, several of Mary's visitors were Fisher's friends or contacts whose names are already familiar to us.

It is wrong to assume that Fisher's appraisal of the situation was wildly unrealistic simply because the invasion and rising did not take place. The number of peers and gentlemen thought to be ready to rebel was larger than the faction led by Richard duke of York and his son in 1460–1 which toppled Henry VI. Henry Tudor had a smaller following when he faced Richard III at Bosworth. In late 1533 the political situation in Ireland was fraught, with the Kildare rebellion only a few months away. Unfortunately it is impossible to know how much Fisher and Chapuys knew of the Irish scene or took it into account in their calculations. But any explosion in England would surely have had repercussions in Ireland and equally surely the revolt of the Fitzgeralds of Kildare, perhaps brought forward a few months, would have made upheavals at home much more dangerous. Had the king of Scotland decided to take advantage of the situation and had Burgavenny stirred his manred in Wales, how would the king of England have fared? We must always remember how fragile power then was, how uncertain the fortunes of dynasties and kings. When also sanctioned by the pope and actively abetted by the emperor, deacon of the Church and temporal leader and guardian of Christendom, would not a *coup d'état* of the kind envisaged have been more than a possibility?

If Henry had known about it, Fisher's treason would have been immediately punished. There are hints later on that the government had begun to sniff out the truth. After their deaths there was talk about how Fisher and More had planned insurrection and conspired against their liege lord.[30] The case against Fisher is much stronger than that against More. But, at the time, neither was under suspicion, unless the attempt to implicate both in the treason charges brought against Elizabeth Barton in early 1534 is evidence to the contrary. But Fisher's name was probably added because of his known opposition to the crown and his known association with the nun – which he never tried to hide.

Fisher had fought the king in Convocation, in parliament and from the pulpit. He had entertained treasonous conspiracy and the use of force. There was one more thing that he could and did do. He could take up the pen again. Probably not long after he had completed the last of his treatises against the divorce he began the first of two tracts in defence of the old Church against Henry's ecclesiastical revolution.[31]

It was probably written in connection with the celebrated Submission of the Clergy in May 1532. Fisher fell seriously ill shortly before and did not take a direct part in that affair (though a delegation of frightened fellow clergy came to his sick-bed for advice). The treatise we are now considering, a defence of the Church's legislative independence, was presumably compiled as the crisis was brewing (and before his illness) or in its aftermath, when he was sufficiently recovered.[32]

The second work was apparently a defence of the papal primacy and may have been completed in 1533. For obvious reasons, neither it nor the earlier piece was ever printed. The reason for believing that it ever existed is chiefly that George Throckmorton said categorically later on that Fisher had once given him a copy of a book of his own devising 'on the authority which Our Lord gave to Saint Peter'.[33] Shortly before, a West Country priest had been pursued for possessing a book in defence of the Roman primacy by the former bishop of Rochester.[34] It is a reasonable guess that this was the same work. It cannot have been that first treatise on ecclesiastical independence because there is no mention therein of the authority of Rome. Nor is it likely to have been a copy of a Latin work, written years before, defending the traditional belief that St Peter died in Rome against the early protestant claim that he had never reached that city. But perhaps it was Fisher's anti-Lutheran sermon of 1521 defending papal authority or taken from a later anti-Lutheran tract – and so not new. We cannot know. And it may have been this work which, during the Pilgrimage of Grace in 1536, Robert Aske held up before the rebels, saying that if they lacked books to help them shape their demands, here was one of the bishop of Rochester's making which would aid them.[35]

As for the earlier work, a Hildebrandine defence of the clerical estate, two fragments exist which were presumably discovered when the palace at Rochester was ransacked after Fisher's arrest in April 1534.[36] One is an early draft of about a quarter of the book in Fisher's own abominable hand. The other is part of a fair copy of the whole – indeed, so fair that one may presume it was intended for circulation. Happily, this second fragment includes a synopsis of the complete work listing the twelve 'maner of ways' in which the treatise would show that bishops have immediate authority under Christ to make 'suche lawes as they shall thynke expedyent for the weale of men sowles', three of which twelve are spelled out in the other fragment.

This last surviving polemical work from Fisher's pen is of unusual interest. First, it is written in English and in a very direct, pithy style designed for a wide readership. It bases its case for the legislative independence of the Church on scripture, the history of the early Church, the 'customable usage of generall counsailles', and the witness of saints. It points to the punishment meted out to those guilty of 'mysentreatyng' or 'contemnyng' their priests, pagan or Jewish, and the punishment by God of emperors and kings who have contemned the priests of Christ. It ends by lauding the 'great prosperitie that was gyven to suche christen princys for the obeying unto suche priests'. To us this may seem naive special pleading. But when it was written it would have been difficult to brush aside quickly. It was all the more effective because Fisher chose an extraordinarily modern base for his argument. He opens his case thus: in every society that we know about, whether Jewish, infidel or Christian, which has had 'eny pretence to godly frame or godly ordre', there has always been a 'convenyent portion of men' deputed to oversee its religious worship. And these have also been accorded a special place in society and been shown special honour. 'Were they never so moche paynums and heathen' and whether they worshipped one or more gods, all nations have had a revered and endowed clergy to offer prayer and 'other sacrifices'. We find this in Ethiopia, in India (namely, brahmins, men 'of highe lernying and of syngler vertue'), in ancient Rome, in pre-Christian Europe and England, as well as among the Jews. If pagans do this and honour clergy 'wiche were but mynisters unto the idols and fals gods', how much more should Christian kings and princes and 'the trew christen people . . . have in honor and reverence the veray priestes and mynsters' of Christ's Church? How favourably should they 'entreate there rightes, privileges and liberties'? How ready should they be 'to obey there holsom counsailles and ordynaunces'? And if pagans were punished for spurning their priests, how much more shall Christians be?[37]

In other words, Fisher has tackled the cause from an unexpected direction, treating religion as a basically anthropological phenomenon, and calling upon evidence from Strabo, Josephus, Cicero and the like to build his picture of non- or pre-Christian societies. In the process he carries a good deal of learning lightly and elegantly. To repeat: this may not impress a twentieth-century reader, but the sixteenth-century had not heard it before. This tract could well have been one of the most interesting and original of the polemical works produced in the English Reformation. Would that we possessed the complete text.

It is the courage and integrity of the man that impress, of course. So, too, does his intellectual and physical energy: the energy that enables a sick man in his early sixties to embark on so original an essay as the treatise just analysed, or made it possible for a busy bishop to take up Hebrew in his fiftieth year. To dogged courage and abundant energy we must add extraordinary self-assurance, decisiveness and clear sight. He struck out swiftly and with complete confidence against Luther − as against Henry's divorce plans. He quickly grasped what was at stake in the king's struggle with Rome and his confrontation with the Church in England, and refused to be deceived by soft words, deflected by threats or undermined by dwindling support. At the end he was almost alone but still defiant, having warded off two charges of misprision of treason, several verbal threats to his life and a period of confinement at the time of Anne's coronation.[38] He had been told to stay away from parliament but had attended none the less, avoiding the king by slipping out early from the high mass which marked the opening of the new session.[39] There had been an attempt to poison him in 1531 – which may have been government inspired. According to the early *Life*, not long afterwards a gunshot pierced the roof of his residence in Lambeth: it came from across the river exactly where the Boleyn's house stood.[40] We can make of that story what we will.

He was an austere, formidable man. There was no surplus flesh or fat on him. His seriousness, deep sense of sin and of the vanities of this world may make a forbidding picture, but this should be tempered by the moving account in the early *Life* of the lord bishop of Rochester visiting the humblest poor in their homes and being with them at their deathbeds.[41] Similarly, the uncompromising conservatism of the man and his unhistorical view of the Church's teaching and discipline must be set against an openness of mind that enabled him to welcome Erasmus, revel in the modernity of Agricola and the new world revealed by Reuchlin.

Doubtless he and Henry VIII had never liked one another. Fisher's true friend among the Tudors was the Lady Margaret; his *pietas* and *gravitas* would not have been to her grandson's taste. Possibly Fisher, for his part, had spotted early on the clear signs of the dangerous self-centredness of a clever, spoilt child in that grandson. Henry probably never expected to be able to break him and had failed to silence him. By early 1534 he had become an intolerable nuisance. Once lodged in the Tower – for the third time charged with misprision of treason (for which the punishment was imprisonment during the king's pleasure) – there was every hope that his failing body would succumb to the cold, loneliness and damp. But again Fisher defied the king and refused to die a convenient natural death.

We know what happened next, so there is no need to repeat the story here. It suffices to let Fisher have the last word with two typical, haunting remarks: the first, the terrible rebuke to his brother bishops that 'the fort has been betrayed, even of them that should have defended it'; the second, the unanswerable declaration to Thomas Cromwell – 'not that I condemn other men's conscience; their conscience may save them and mine must save me'.[42]

Notes

1 For the dispensation (dated 14 June 1491), see *Calendar of Papal Letters Relating to Great Britain and Ireland*, XV, ed. M. J. Haren (Dublin, 1978), no. 739.

2 *Life*, X, 211–12. In the dedication of his *De Veritate Corporis et Sanguinis Praesentia, etc.* (1525) Fisher says that Richard Fox of Winchester commended him to

Henry. Maybe; but Henry's letter to his mother virtually asking permission to promote her confessor confirms what the *Life* says.

3 And one would like to know the circumstances in which his *Opera Omnia* was published at Würzburg in 1597. It is a tribute to Fisher's reputation in Counter-Reformation Europe. As an example of the survival of his works among English recusants, in 1583 a book described as John Fisher 'contra Lutherum' was among a large haul of Catholic writings and vestments found in recusants' cells in Winchester gaol (PRO, SP 12/158, no. 9).

4 *LP*, I, nos. 1048, 1067, 1083, 3495; II, pp. 1454, 1466.

5 *LP*, V, no. 62, 112, 707.

6 *LP*, VI, nos. 1164, 1249; *Calendar of State Papers, Spanish*, ed. G. A. Bergenroth, P. de Gayangos and M. A. S. Hume, 20 vols. (London, 1862–1954), IV (2), nos. 1130, 1133. In the first of these two letters to Charles (dated 27 September), Chapuys said Fisher had spoken to him 'some time ago' – which could mean, say, a fortnight previously; in the second (dated 10 October) that Fisher had made his remarks 'not many days ago', i.e. perhaps a week before?

7 *LP*, VI, no. 1249; *Calendar of State Papers, Spanish*, IV (2), no. 1133.

8 *LP*, VIII, no. 859 (p. 336).

9 *Life*, X, 342–4.

10 Polydore Vergil, *The Anglica Historia*, ed. D. Hay, Camden Society, 74 (1950), 306–7.

11 BL, Add. MS 4274, fos. 212–13. It is in Latin and extensively corrected. At one point it refers to 'vestras dominationes', whom I take to be fellow members of Convocation – or possibly of the House of Lords. The only clue to its date is a reference to the coronation oath which the king had recently ('nuper') sworn. It can thus hardly be dated later than 1515.

12 The Act (4 Henry VIII, *c*. ii) did not touch benefit of *ordained* clergy and was 'to endure to the nexte parliament' only.

13 See my *Henry VIII* (London, 1968), pp. 277–8, for the story.

14 Thus in October 1532 Ligham wrote a chatty letter to Fisher thanking him for some venison and asking for news of 'our good gracious queen' (*LP*, V, no. 1411).

15 S. T. Bindoff (ed.), *The History of Parliament. The House of Commons 1509–1558*, I, 10–11.

16 *LP*, VII (2), no. 952.

17 See below, p. 164.

18 *LP*, VI, no. 1164.

19 *LP*, VI, no. 1468 (5). He gave her three interviews and stoutly defended her thereafter. Others apparently believed that the nun had said Henry would be punished within one month of marrying Anne. Fisher said seven months (*LP*, VII, nos. 239–40).

20 *Calendar of State Papers, Spanish*, IV (2), nos. 1123–4.

21 *LP*, VII, no. 1206 (*Calendar of State Papers, Spanish*, IV (2), no. 611). *LP* renders 'sez C' as 1600. I prefer the more modest '600' in *Spanish Calendar*.

22 Ibid.

23 *LP*, VI, 487.

24 M. Macklem, *God Have Mercy. The Life of John Fisher of Rochester* (Ottawa, 1967), p. 215.

25 *LP*, VIII, 15. Cf. *LP*, VI, nos. 1307, 1556.

26 *LP*, VIII, 131, 346. This incident, of course, occurred 18 months after Fisher's appeal to the emperor; but it seems likely that Bray had been a dissident for some time before he came under royal attack.

27 *LP*, IX, nos. 488, 838.

28 *LP*, VII, nos. 962, 1013, 1270. He had been fined £10,000, of which 7,000 marks were paid. The bond was security for the rest – and for good behaviour.

29 *LP*, VI, no. 1540.

30 *LP*, IX, nos. 213, 240; X, no. 235.

31 PRO, SP 6/11, fos. 38–40v and fos. 215–23.

32 Macklem, *God Have Mercy*, p. 238, suggests that the treatise was produced during 'the struggle between King and clergy during May of 1532'; but if Fisher was ill then, it was more probably written well before or after. Since it cannot have been put together quickly to meet a particular crisis, perhaps it was compiled after the event. Macklem is wrong to suppose that BL, Add. MS 4274, fos. 212–13 (see note 11 above) also belongs to 1532.

33 *LP*, XII (2), no. 952.

34 *LP*, XI, no. 1041.

35 *LP*, XII (1), no. 1021. It is incorrect to say, as some have, that PRO, SP 6/5, fos. 46–83, another Fisher MS, is the missing treatise on the papal primacy. It is a history of the Septuagint, as *LP* says. But what is now its flyleaf (fo. 45) has the intriguing heading: 'Argumentes from the olde and newe testament for the prufe of the popes Aucthorytie'. This is in a sixteenth-century hand. It is further evidence that Fisher did indeed compose such a work, which has now completely disappeared.

36 PRO, SP 6/11, fos. 38–40v and fos. 215–23.

37 Ibid., esp. fos. 38–40v.

38 *LP*, VI, nos. 324, 653. He was in the charge of the bishop of Winchester, Stephen Gardiner.

39 *LP*, V, no. 737. Chapuys says that Anne Boleyn had previously tried to have him dissuaded from attending – on health grounds. So *LP*, V, no. 120.

40 *Life*, X, 346–7. Allegedly he and others who stood firm in 1531 were threatened with being thrown in the Thames (*LP*, V, no. 112). For the poisoning episode, see *Life*, X, 344–6, and *LP*, V, no. 120. Later, Chapuys tells how Fisher has adapted to the troublous times: they communicate secretly via a third party; Fisher has told the ambassador to take no notice of him when they meet. So *LP*, V, no. 707 (11 January 1532).

41 *Life*, X, 221–2.

42 *LP*, VII, no. 136.

Royal ecclesiastical supremacy

HENRY CHADWICK

In the draft bull excommunicating King Henry VIII, of the year 1535, three themes are linked together as providing overwhelming grounds for the condemnation: the divorce of Catherine of Aragon, the claim to be supreme head of the Church of England, and the judicial murder of John Fisher.[1] The saintly and renowned humanist Fisher, the man Henry VIII himself had been heard by Pole to describe as the most learned man he knew, is a symbolic figure by his unyielding opposition to the divorce and to the king's consequent expulsion of papal authority from his realm in response to the humiliation of Pope Clement's rejection. None of the three acts was well regarded in Europe at large, and together they looked like the tyranny of a Night of the Long Knives. Reginald Pole's *Defence of the Unity of the Church* must have been telling Henry what the king already knew when the writer observed that Henry's actions had brought political danger — whether from Charles V or from the French — a severing of a branch from the root of God's tree by rejecting the universality and unity embodied by Peter's see, and a threat of civil insurrection and future conflict about the succession to the throne once Mary had been declared illegitimate. That seemed a lot of trouble to buy. As for the title 'head of the Church', Pole acidly remarked that this head was chiefly noted for plundering the Church. It seemed absurd that one claiming such a title could not minister the sacraments, and yet could constitute himself as the judge of controversies in matters of faith. Flatterers might tell him that royal supremacy over the Church was enjoined by the Bible, in St Peter's exhortation to 'honour the king', and try to set scripture up against tradition and Catholic consensus; but Pole mercilessly demolished such flimsy arguments. Everyone knew that the title of supreme head of the Church had been conceded most reluctantly after intimidation. It was an act of power lacking moral authority. As for the loot Henry had taken from the Church, Pole tersely reminded him that tyrants usually fall for lack of friends, not for lack of money. The whole story of the moral disintegration of a man who had once been enthusiastically acclaimed as a paragon among English kings is seen by Pole as almost an instance of *ate*, an insanity depriving the king of his wits and impelling him into storms for which he had no one but himself to blame.

My purpose in this essay is to try to set Fisher's protest and martyrdom in a broader context than the particularities of Henry VIII and his quarrel with the papacy, broader even than the now commonplace observation that well before 1534 there was growing tension between canon and common lawyers in England. It was not new for conciliar minds to seek some limitation and restriction upon the apparently total autocracy claimed for the papal monarchy by recalling that the authority of emperors and kings was also, according to scripture, God-given. Therefore, in insisting that the Church's canons should not be enforced where they passed into realms governed by the statutes of the king in parliament, they were not necessarily setting aside the law of God. Moreover, canonists such as Gascoigne were aware that even the pope can make no enactment or dispensation contrary to God's word, or indeed to natural law. *Plenitudo potestatis* was not unlimited in practice, and there was to be some bias in the protestant contention that the pope claimed to 'add, alter, and diminish, nay also to dispense with the words that Christ himself spake, as well as the writing of the Apostles'. At least, that opinion was taking sides in a canonists' dispute, and the 'Protestant' barb (which I have cited from Archbishop Matthew Parker)[2] would have had plenty of critics among some medieval canonists of repute. The general opinion was that the pope could interpret, but not dispense from, the word of God.

Accordingly, whatever might be the precise extent of authority contained in the power of the keys entrusted to Peter (Matthew 16:18–19), these powers had to be balanced by the truth that the powers controlling the secular order were also no less ordained by God. Could one not affirm both the king's supremacy and the pope's, recognising them to have different spheres of responsibility? In his second book Reginald Pole insists, 'I shall not diminish the authority of the king if I preserve his authority and Peter's side by side.'[3] Indeed, as the English Reformation advanced under Henry's son, Edward VI, it became alarmingly clear that the religious and social upheaval of the age could put the monarchy itself at risk. Many pages of the fiercely protestant John Hooper[4] are devoted to the assertion of royal supremacy not against the claims of the papacy, though Hooper did not forget that theme, but against the sedition of Anabaptists. He wanted the clergy in his diocese of Gloucester to read Romans 13 to the people every Saturday and Sunday: to have shown the pope the door did not mean that there could be room for corrupt Englishmen with minds full of 'contempt, hatred, grudge, and malice against their king, magistrates, laws, orders, and policies'.[5] The king's determination to be master in his own realm (as none of his predecessors had been) did not mean that all Englishmen admired his break with the catholicity represented by Rome. Evidently some Englishmen were just as hostile to royal absolutism as to papal. To remove papal authority could entail moral and social collapse.

Contemplation of the relations between the Church and civil government through the long course of Christian history suggests that Romans 13 has usually been more influential than the Apocalypse of John.[6] By one of the more paradoxical twists of exegesis, the Apocalypse's warnings against the Babylonian harlot of the Roman government have been ingeniously read-dressed in the post office to apply to the bishops of Rome, the list of whom has its fair share of martyrs. The more tough-minded English reformers regarded it as self-evident, something every schoolboy knew, that as long as there are seven hills beside the Tiber, it is certain that the pope is the very whore of Babylon and Antichrist.[7] Admittedly this opinion was to be much dented by Grotius's exposition of the Book of Daniel,[8] and in the middle of the seventeenth century Archbishop John Bramhall associated the antipapal exegesis with 'Protestants out of their wits'.[9] But a century earlier this ex-egesis of the Apocalypse was general, and had had notable medieval ex-ponents from the Waldensians to Frederick II (Hohenstaufen). Cranmer himself followed Wycliffe in holding that in accordance with Revelation 20:2 Satan had been released from his prison after precisely a thousand years.[10] There might be disagreements about the exact date on which his millennium of imprisonment had started, and therefore some hesitation about the point at which evidence of his release should be located; but at least by the six-teenth century one could be confident that Satan was well and truly released and active in subtle infiltration of the Church.[11] Surely he had taken posses-sion of the Roman see, sitting where he ought not in the very sanctuary of the Lord, the 'man of sin'? So Romans 13 and the Apocalypse were har-monised, idealising the prince and rubbishing the pope. Admittedly, some medieval popes, and especially at the beginning of the sixteenth century, had discredited themselves and damaged the office.

The persisting strength of English Lollardy is shown by the enthusiasm with which leading reformers took up the Antichrist theme. Moreover, Wycliffe had proclaimed that the civil power's duty was to reform the Church, with a moral right to remove and redistribute its endowments.[12] In *Piers Plowman* even Langland (who, with Chaucer, could easily be regarded as a fellow traveller by Lollards) had a famous prophecy of the coming king who was to cleanse God's temple of impurities.[13] Both Langland and Wycliffe took a low view of the Donation of Constantine. It must be a source of surprise that the dissident Lollards allowed their hostility to the Church, to priests both as a caste and as a male preserve, to tithes, to all sacramental actions for which laity are dependent on clergy, to take them so far as to lead them to put trust in princes. Was not that to trust in the arm of the flesh indeed? Moreover, Lollards (as their Conclusions of 1395 declared)[14] were pacifists who rejected killing whether in war or justice, and soon found that the secular authorities were as unsympathetic as the ecclesiastical. But con-fronted by a body as powerful as the medieval clergy, with financial resources in land topped up by fees for requiems which Lollards especially abominated,[15] they could turn to no source of power other than the king and the nobles. There was plenty to make Henry VIII's revolution look like the fulfilment of a dream among humble farmers and 'white-collar workers' in Kent, Sussex and East Anglia, where Wycliffite translations, especially of the Apocalypse and of the epistle of James (with its denunciations of opulent Christians), were studied at clandestine meetings in barns. Admittedly Lollards suffered under Henry; but some of his programme was in line with much they had been saying. For example, Wycliffe and his followers objected to the quantity of money exported from the country either to the papacy or to international religious orders. (Cranmer himself felt that the papal fee for his consecration and pallium was excessive.)[16] Lay power was to be the instrument and weapon to liberate Englishmen in soul and body from the burdens imposed by an opulent and essentially foreign hierarchy, an alien multinational corporation. One cannot say that all Englishmen of the sixteenth century manifested xenophobia, since a number of documents speak of their hospitable welcome to foreigners. But Wycliffe anticipated some of the nationalist feeling apparent in the declaration, astonishingly found in the gentle, rational, and learned Matthew Parker, that 'Almighty God is so much English'.[17]

When one reads in John Hooper that bishops have no duty other than to preach God's word whereas it is the duty of the prince to judge whether or not their preaching and teaching are correct,[18] it is difficult not to feel that the Reformation let loose some strange notions about Church and state. Yet the doctrine of the theological responsibility of the prince had a long history going back far beyond Wycliffe, and beyond the medieval struggles about investiture. Educated men of the sixteenth century read Justinian. Lectures on the civil law were part of the standard syllabus at Oxford and Cambridge.[19] In Justinian's *Code*, and in the *Novels* supplementing it, it is axiomatic that the emperor's authority extends beyond matters merely temporal and secular. He has a duty to protect orthodoxy and to harass heresy. So Justinian legislated to safeguard and enforce the true faith against heresies such as the Monophysite alternative to Chalcedon. He legislated to ensure the clergy did their duty. He issued formal edicts regulating the number of clergy on the establishment at Hagia Sophia. He provided controls for orphanages and hospitals which were ecclesiastical foundations. His enactments were intended to ensure that endowments were used as intended by the pious benefactors, and not bent to profane purposes or private gain.

As in the sixteenth century, so also in the sixth, the imperial responsibility to legislate against heresy was no private matter; the unity of the Church in truth profoundly affected the social and political cohesion of the empire. Dogmatic disputes shared with excessive interest rates the largest responsibility for causing urban riots. Justinian's subjects were deeply divided on the issue of Christology, above all whether one should say *in* (two natures) or *of*. But he could not be neutral. He could not gain political control of Italy and the West unless he made Chalcedonian orthodoxy, and the preposition *in*, a foundation for his ecclesiastical policy, so that his personal convictions were reinforced by political necessity. The great emperor Anastasius, his predecessor but one, creator of the conditions necessary for the greatness of his own *imperium*, had run into endless trouble with Italy and the West because he was not sound on Chalcedon. He upheld the reunion formula or 'Henoticon' of Zeno with its very cool reference censuring heresies 'even if held by bishops at Chalcedon or elsewhere'. In 518–19 papal pressure to gain recognition for Chalcedon was to entail riots with large loss of life in some Eastern cities. Justinian's Monophysite subjects in Syria and the Nile valley, with a few advance outposts in the monasteries of Constantinople itself, looked for support to his wife Theodora. In her highly unregenerate youth she had once been spiritually assisted by an anti-Chalcedonian priest in Alexandria, and never forgot her debt. She hid numerous Monophysite bishops in her large palace, and even provided for them the noble church of St Sergius and St Bacchus, still standing today, to give them a place of liturgical assembly.

The Monophysites deeply objected to Theodore of Mopsuestia, Ibas of Edessa, and Theodoret of Kyrrhos – all long dead, but masterful expositors of 'two-nature' Christology and stern critics of the doctrine of one nature. In 543 Justinian issued a decree condemning their doctrines as expressed in selected excerpts or 'chapters', and included in his censure speculations ascribed to Origen by monks of the New Lavra in Palestine. But the imperial edict was not the end of dissension. Did it not need an ecumenical council to ratify the emperor's condemnations? Was the emperor, even if possessed of immense theological learning, the judge of fidelity to the word of God? An ecumenical council naturally had an aura about it, and for Justinian it could have the attraction that he would be seen to be doing for the Church in his time what the great Constantine had once done at Nicaea. But an ecumenical council needed Roman concurrence, and indeed that of all the patriarchs and a great body of the metropolitans, unless it could be satisfactorily shown that a patriarch himself had lapsed into grave heresy. The West suspected, with some reason, that a condemnation of the 'Three Chapters' was intended to swamp the Scotch of the Chalcedonian definition with a flood of Monophysite soda. In Italy Pope Vigilius might be safe from interference. His predecessors before 518 (when communion between Rome and Byzantium was restored after more than three decades of schism) had enjoyed freedom from imperial interference. Paradoxically, the Byzantine decision to give the popes everything they asked for meant that the kiss of peace in 518 was to turn into a lethal squeeze, once Justinian had reabsorbed Italy into his empire and again made the pope his subject. Vigilius could not decline the summons to travel to Constantinople. Justinian's general council of 553 was an assembly with papal consent for its assembling.

173

Predictably, the Council ratified the emperor's censures on Origen and on the Three Chapters. But could Vigilius be brought to agree? Though residing in or close to the city and the Council, he had declined to attend the conciliar debates, wishing to preserve his independence of decision on the question of ratification. In his estimate the Council had only an advisory role, giving a demonstration of the general opinion, after which he would announce the final verdict. The Greek bishops gathered in Council regarded this as extraordinary arrogance. They threatened Vigilius with ex-communication, and used the remarkable formula, later to enjoy Gallican echoes, that even if they withdrew their communion from Vigilius, they maintained it with the *sedes*; only not with the *sedens*.[20] To the ancient Church, authority resides in the throne rather than in the person who may happen to be sitting on it. After several changes of mind and rough treatment at the hands of Justinian's minions, Vigilius finally surrendered to the emperor's will and assented. It was a manifestation of imperial supremacy, and everyone knew it. Yet the outward form of ecumenical conciliarity was preserved, and subsequent tradition knew how to deal with awkwardnesses in some of the language used at the council by means of the rigorous critical process of 'Reception'.

In the Greek Orthodox tradition this process of Reception went so far that, because of one or two moments of embarrassment for readers (especially when Vigilius strenuously asserted the rights of his see and indiscreetly spoke of one *operatio* or *energeia* in Christ),[21] the Acts were left uncopied. The Greek Church remembered the canons and formal decrees, but not the actual Acts, which survive as a whole only through the Latin tradition.

Justinian's imperial supremacy did not shut out the pope. It subjected him to torture and splendid banquets as alternating methods of extracting agreement. In the emperor's political theory there was no element of secular nationalism. Nevertheless it is possible to find in antiquity at least a regional patriotism as joining forces with antipapal feeling. Dissident bodies snubbed by the emperor, such as the North African Donatists, spoke of the empire as an agent of Antichrist with whom the Catholic Church was on altogether too cosy terms. Even Donatists were not above appealing to the magistrate whenever it seemed in their interest to do so.[22] But they had a highly in-dependent estimate of Church authority, with a clericalised ecclesiology defined by rigorously preserved apostolic succession and a high sacramental doctrine of episcopal power.[23] Their doctrine of legitimacy did not include either the *cathedra Petri* or the emperor. 'What has the emperor to do with the Church?' asked Donatus.[24] Donatus would much have liked the Roman see to recognise his party; as it had not done so, it had *ipso facto* discredited itself. By associating with the wrong group, it had acquired the pollution of communion with apostates.

In reply, Augustine's anti-Donatist writings do not work with a strong dualism of Church and state. More than once he criticises the Donatists for being out of communion, not merely with the *Catholica* represented by Rome or Jerusalem or 'the apostolic sees' (usually, not always, plural), but also with the communion acknowledged by the emperor.[25]

In one passage of the third book of his *Contra Rufinum* (III, 18) Jerome confidently avers that an imperial rescript can legitimately overthrow a synodical decision. Western Christians imagine such ideas to be rather more at home in Byzantium than in the West. Yet it is in Greek canon law, not Latin, that one finds the first prohibition on bishops appealing to the court for review of a synodical censure: in the twelfth canon of the Council of Antioch, *c*. 330.[26]

Distance between the emperor and the Church was naturally desirable from the point of view of the imperial government. Successive emperors, from Constantine the Great onwards, found that a close involvement brought them down into the sandy arena of gladiatorial combat between the different factions of party strife with which Christian history has been plagued. The ruler was faced with the great problem that to enjoy the wholly loyal support of his Christian subjects, he had to be orthodox in their eyes. In the conflicts between Chalcedonian and Monophysite there were no doubt some who regarded the christological intricacies as quite beyond their powers of discernment, and who were therefore content to say that what was good enough for the emperor and the patriarch was good enough for them.[27] But to a Monophysite in the Nile valley, his own patriarch at Alexandria was the man who counted, and anything emanating from Constantinople was suspect from the start. Once Pope Leo I had decisively sided with Chalcedon's two-nature christology, the authority of Rome counted for nothing too. For Copts, Ethiopians, Syrian 'Jacobites', and Armenians, the papacy was thereby involved in irremediable heresy and its authority reduced to zero. The same held good for the Byzantine emperors.

The close involvement of the secular ruler in the party strife had a further disadvantage, namely that dissent from the position supported by the emperor was more than a religious disagreement: it amounted to disaffection in political terms, and was on the way to becoming treason. In the seventh century the Egyptian and Palestinian opponents of Chalcedon did not invite the Arabs to invade. But, once the Arabs had conquered, they found themselves able to enjoy far greater religious freedom (qualified as that might be) than they had done under the Byzantine emperors. During the bitter iconoclastic controversy, John of Damascus could compose fulminous denunciations of the heresies of the iconoclast emperors and enjoy serene impunity because he was an Arab living outside the territories where the emperor's writ still ran.

The authority and power of the Roman see in the Western Churches evolved in large measure because in situations of sharp controversy a final court of appeal was required. Popes found themselves being appealed to for decisions substantially before anyone thought of developing a theory or an exegesis of Petrine texts to provide a ground for this exercise of jurisdiction. Appeals to Rome over the head of local regional authority, however, could be feared and unpopular in both Church and state. English kings of the medieval period disliked such appeals as much as the North African bishops of St Augustine's time. Disputes were frequent about episcopal appointments. The Germanic races had an instinctive sense that rights over people go with ownership of land, and that the lord of the land has special rights in relation to the priests appointed to serve the churches which the landlord has himself built.[28] The lord was the *patronus* of the *beneficium*.[29] Accordingly, kings expected to exercise rights of patronage. On the other hand, the *ecclesia catholica* was not a national body; and the cathedral chapters expected to nominate as well as to elect. When kings nominated one candidate and chapters nominated another, the dispute might be taken to Rome, and the popes could produce a third.[30]

Norman kings of England were self-willed men who wanted their own way with the Church. William Rufus declared that Anselm of Canterbury had no business to vow obedience in homage both to the king and to the apostolic see: two allegiances were mutually incompatible, and, if the archbishop recognised Urban as his lord *in spiritualibus*, that was disloyalty to the crown. When Anselm wished to go to Rome for his pallium, the king would not allow the act, as an acknowledgement of foreign authority. Eadmer says that sycophantic bishops told the king that, if Anselm in any way acknowledged the pope's jurisdiction, he was breaking the faith he owed to the king.[31] Anselm eventually defied the king and was received at Rome by Urban's successor Paschal. William then forbade Anselm to return to England unless he renounced obedience to the pope, and he insisted on his own right of investiture. Eventually Anselm was readmitted by Henry I. In August 1107 the king held a council in London to decide on nominations to the numerous vacant sees, and granted Anselm the decisive voice in the choice of candidates and the right of investiture by the giving of the pastoral staff. But the king insisted on homage by bishops and abbots after their election and before the archbishop went forward with the consecration. After all, the Church had owed its place in society to the patronage of kings and nobles in the barbarian kingdoms; one tenth-century pope could rebuke the archbishop of Cologne (in a row over a nomination to Liège in 921) for ignoring the custom that only the king could confer the episcopate.[32] After Gregory VII such language was unimaginable.

Papal power was enforced through 'provisions' or nominations to bishoprics and benefices and through the power of dispensation. In the letters of St Augustine it is taken for granted that, when appeals go up to Rome, the pope's prime duty is to see that conciliar canon law is observed.

He is the principal executive officer to enforce the rules of procedure laid down by Church councils. Nevertheless, situations may arise where the strict adherence to canon law will produce riots in the city or other disadvantages. In such cases Augustine assumes that the bishop of Rome in conference with the local primate of Carthage has the power to dispense from strict canonical procedure.[33] Dispensing power later became of the greatest practical importance because of the Church rules about forbidden degrees of affinity in matrimonial cases. Questions of marriage and divorce were of special concern if people were to remain in good standing in the eyes of the Church. Papal power to dispense from rigid rules became a major source of authority. Unfortunately the system involved the Roman curia in all the costs and pettifoggery attaching to complex litigation. To Henry VIII and his lawyers it was a source of offence as well as of much lay irritation when matrimonial and other cases had to be taken to a foreign court for decision. But Henry was not a total innovator in demanding that the appointment of bishops and matrimonial causes depend on his royal authority. What was new and revolutionary in Henry was his shattering of the universal assumption that the English Church was without question part of a universal Church, or at least a Western Church,[34] of which the bishop of Rome was the executive head. Not even Wycliffe could have entertained a notion as radical as that. Marsilius and Ockham could write incendiary pages attacking papal power as currently operating, but could hardly have envisaged Christendom as a congeries of independent national churches established on the principle *cuius regio eius religio*. Nevertheless, once one set aside the ecclesiology of the Isidorian decretals, it was an easy move to thinking of the Church as organised territorially, with the metropolitan of the province exercising real jurisdiction in relation to his suffragans, with the life of the Church of the province ruled by scripture, by the canons of Church councils received by the universal Church and especially in the province in question, but not by the personal decisions of the bishop of Rome. There was truth in the contention that the primarily territorial structure was predominant in the ancient and early-medieval Church.

Henry VIII's apologists could defend his actions on the ground that it was his 'private' Church of England of which he claimed to be the head.[35] The defence presumably assumed the old Germanic notion of the landownership entailing religious control. But Henry's ideas of supremacy were certainly fuelled by his reading in Justinian. His address to the Convocation of York in 1533 makes an express appeal to Justinian's ecclesiastical legislation to prove that he is not claiming new powers.[36] There indeed was a great emperor, a master of the civil law, legislating with unquestioned sovereignty on matters which, in the medieval West, were ordered by canon in a pyramid of authority with the pope at the top, everything flowing down from the power of the keys entrusted to Peter. Protestant defenders of the thesis that the prince is judge of doctrine found Justinian an uncertain aid, because of the proposition in Justinian's Code (I.i.1) that the bishop of Rome is the acknowledged guardian of orthodox belief – a point which Philpot had to concede at his trial in October 1555.[37] But Jewel recalled hearing Peter Martyr lecturing at Strasbourg on Justinian's removal of two popes from office, Silverius and Vigilius, and felt encouraged enough to include the point in *The Defence of the Apology of the Church of England* (1570).[38] At least it was clear that Justinian did not derive *imperium* from the pope. His sovereignty as emperor was quite independent.

Awareness of the overlap and potential conflict between canon law and civil law first appears, to the best of my knowledge, in the fearful disputes about the legitimacy of Pope Symmachus at the time of the Laurentian schism at Rome at the beginning of the sixth century.[39] In England the issue arose sharply in Magna Carta (1215). English kings long before Henry had imposed penalties on clerics who appealed to Rome against the king, and had enacted such statutes as Praemunire, and the statutes of Provisors. With Henry VIII, what had been only brave words for Edward III was now being acted on.

In Henry's Inns of Court there were hard-headed anticlerical lawyers like Christopher St German (1460–1541) insisting that, where there is conflict between canon and statute law, canon law yields.[40] St German appears as a supporter of the king's unilateral 'reform' of the Church, and an opponent of canons and legatine constitutions encroaching on the proper rights of the temporal power. For him it is axiomatic that an opinion enforced with the threat of penalty for heresy must be supported by sufficient and unambiguous authority: can the bishops be said to have utterly clear authority for all that they enforce under the *ex officio* procedure? St German also thought that a secular ruler has the right to lay down judgements on history where that is done to provide a ground for political actions in the present. He was anxious to vindicate the thesis that Henry's Act of Supremacy of 1534 in no sense added new powers; the Act could not be understood to grant Henry the *potestas ordinis*. So St German justifies the assertion of the Act in Restraint of Appeals that this realm of England is shown from sundry ancient chronicles to be an empire. An 'Empire' here, as Walter Ullmann showed,[41] meant a sovereignty of jurisdiction in which the ruler was the source of all authority whatsoever, like Justinian an unquestioned master in his own house, and (to St German) because of his responsibility to defend truth in the Church, possessing the right to decide disputed points of biblical exegesis. The Act's historical assertion was of momentous consequence for the juridical conceptions underlying Henry's claims to ecclesiastical supremacy.

Did Henry need to do it? European monarchs and emperors had long used their powers to ensure that important sees were held by the men they wanted. Bishops were often well educated, frequently of aristocratic or even royal blood, and formed the nucleus of the king's council. (They are the oldest element in the English House of Lords.) Henry VIII was not the first, as also not the last, to use his powers to nominate figures politically congenial to him. That is not to say that political considerations were all-important even for him. Cranmer may have been timid and vacillating, but he was certainly learned; Cuthbert Tunstall was gentle and saintly; Stephen Gardiner a first-rate canonist as well as a fluent linguist in French and German and probably having some Italian. Even Henry wanted his bishops to be acknowledged for their godliness and good learning, not merely to have the right prejudices about his divorce and the iniquities of the pope. Moreover, Henry was far from being the only European monarch to expect to have a decisive voice in the choice of his principal bishops. The pope, Clement VII, did not object to the nomination of Cranmer to succeed Warham. Over episcopal appointments, then, Henry had not crossed swords with the Vatican. The Act of 1533, however, on the appointment of bishops – still on the English statute book today even if in practice other arrangements now prevail (as in the case of the Concordat with France in regard to episcopal appointments in Alsace and Lorraine) – is militant. It eliminates from the nomination process both the pope and any independence of mind on the part of cathedral chapters (though allowing them a nominal elective role). Yet did the Act make assertions about royal powers such as no one had heard in Europe before this time? Frankish kings of Merovingian and Carolingian times had exercised wide powers, which were in most cases taken for granted. Hincmar of Reims felt it necessary to admonish Louis III not to demand, please, that a candidate nominated by the crown be elected; he should keep the customary procedure by which the crown granted the neighbouring bishops leave to proceed to an election, authorised the entrusting of the temporalities to the new bishop, and permitted the metropolitan and provincial bishops to go ahead with the ordination. At the same time Hincmar carefully dissociated himself from the view (evidently held by some) that kings ought to confine themselves to temporal matters and to think Church affairs none of their concern.[42] The investiture struggle showed the Church trying to fend off established lay control, whereby the priest was no more than the landowner's chaplain and servant. Henry VIII's actions are evidently more than yet another act in the investiture controversy, but are nevertheless intelligible as a reassertion of lay power over the Church – and not only *de facto* but *de jure Angliae*. He claimed that he was not innovating but recovering ancient liberties – and that was the language of Gallicans, if not from the time of Philip the Fair, at least since the Council of Constance.[43]

Pope Paul III cannily suggested a Gallican liberty as a way of retaining England within Catholic unity.[44]. Why could not Henry take the French line, holding communion with the rest of the Western Church and Rome, yet strenuously keeping papal jurisdiction at a distance? Henry's father-in-law, Ferdinand the Catholic, ruled not only southern Spain but Sicily. He continued the secular independence of the Norman kings of Sicily, who had called councils on their own say-so, had forbidden appeals to the Curia, had refused entry to papal legates trying to visit the island, and had wholly controlled the nomination of bishops. The *Capitula* of the kingdom of Sicily include the text of a proclamation by Ferdinand dated 22 January 1514, which declares his devotion to the Roman Church, and then adds the proviso that in Sicily the king remains responsible for both spiritual and temporal affairs. The Curia is not to intrude.[45]

One wonders if Henry VIII might have followed his father-in-law's example, asserting both his royal supremacy and his devotion to Catholic doctrine, including the see of Peter if not the incumbent sitting on it. Henry's defenders liked to point to the deplorable corruption in holders of the Petrine office like Alexander VI – an argument to which Pole responded with the observation that the juridical rights of the English Crown were surely independent of the moral qualities of the kings wearing it. One could assert the honour of the office without having too much regard for the holder.

By an ironic paradox Henry's daughter Mary could restore papal supremacy over the Church of England only by invoking her royal prerogative, in face of the reluctance of many in parliament to see the Church restored to communion with Rome for fear that the pope and Pole would expect and require the restitution of confiscated Church lands, held by those whom even the strongly protestant John Foxe frankly described as 'cormorants'.[46] Pole suffered the humiliation of long delays before being allowed into the country with legatine authority. And in practice the example of Mary in voluntarily forgoing the confiscated Church properties was not followed by many.

Henry VIII's Act of Supremacy was not really thunder out of a clear sky. Philip the Fair of France had treated Boniface VIII in an analogous manner. In the pre-Reformation age the English people seem to have entertained mixed feelings towards the chair of Peter. Some certainly looked to it as a source of truth as well as a fount of canonical authority. But there were others who did not feel this way about it – who resented the manner in which Innocent III had dealt with King John. From the chronicle of Matthew Paris (1199–1259) one might easily gain the impression that English prosperity had been disastrously hindered by bribery and corruption at the Roman Curia.[47] Grosseteste thought the papal practice of stuffing foreigners into English bishoprics and benefices so disastrous that everyone ought to be stirred to resistance and protest. When Pope Innocent IV conferred a canonry at Lincoln on his own nephew, Grosseteste declared his simultaneous obedience to papal jurisdiction and his conviction that such an act could come only from Antichrist, on which ground he flatly declined to accept it: papal authority should be used for edification, not, as in this case, for destruction. Grosseteste wanted the spiritual and the temporal kept apart in distinct spheres, the secular arm concentrating on the defence of the realm, just administration of law, and upholding good conduct by example; the spiritual arm to minister the word and sacraments with holiness of life, vigils, fasts, and assiduous prayers. He wanted to keep the secular arm in England from intruding its power into the Church by patronage rights, and wished to maintain the independence of the Church courts. He expressed apprehension lest the coronation unction might give the monarch the illusion that he had received some sacerdotal powers together with this biblical sign of the seven gifts of the Spirit.[48]

Grosseteste was no doubt not the antipapal hero the Lollards made him out to be. Their feelings about the papacy were fairly unqualified. Wycliffe denied that the pope had any greater power of the keys than any other priests. He told King Richard II that royal sovereignty in England ought to have no rival, that the king was entitled to stop money flowing to Rome, and that the papacy as an institution was Antichrist. The temporal power had a moral right to take endowments from unworthy clergy. The canon law of the Decretalists should be set aside,[49] and the Church ordered in accordance with the Bible and the ancient Fathers.

The persisting influence of Lollardy into the England of Henry's age no doubt helps to explain why the influence of Luther on the English Reformation, while certainly substantial, was not always dominant. As early as the 1530s there were contacts with Bullinger and the Zwinglian polity of Zürich. Granted that many of the Thirty-Nine Articles owed much to the Augsburg and Württemberg confessions of 1530 and 1552, both striking for their conservative moderation and conciliatory tone; granted that in 1562–3 Bishop Edmund Guest, known for his Lutheran sympathies in Eucharistic theology, had drafted Article 28 of the Thirty-Nine Articles in terms which simultaneously denied Transubstantiation as eliminating the sign from the sacrament and (as Lingard saw) sought to protect the Presence of Christ – to the consternation of the Zwinglian faction; granted that the Thirty-Nine Articles actually recognised the bishop of Rome to be Catholic bishop of that city and denied only his jurisdiction in England and (what none could assert?) the permanent gift or habit of inerrancy in incumbents of that see: nevertheless, the puritan dissatisfaction with Cranmer's Prayer Book and Ordinal and Articles is naturally seen as a continuation of the underground dissidence of Lollardy. The agonies of the vestiarian controversy reflect Zwinglian influences, which regarded Luther and Brenz (and Bucer) as dangerous compromisers encouraging the English reformers to produce 'a mingled estate', 'a mixture of the gospel and popery'.[50]

One writer influenced more by Luther than by Lollardy provided a virtual blueprint for Henry VIII's revolution. In 1528 William Tyndale published *The Obedience of a Christian Man*, telling Henry that his duty was to reform the Church. The pope and bishops had gathered to themselves too much of the wealth of England. 'Monks devour the land.' Whatever goes into their treasury ceases to circulate; land bequeathed to them falls under the dead hand, mortmain. Clergy claim to owe no obedience to princes; their prime love is power; and they use auricular confession to extract personal and political secrets. Tyndale was one of the many who have imagined that because the pope has a priest in every parish, he must be wonderfully well informed. He was much offended when the clergy handed heretics over to the secular arm for 'just punishment mitigated by due mercy', a formula which everyone knew to mean burning. The bishops had made the king into the pope's hangman. Let Henry rid the land of the pope's usurped power. He should abolish Church courts through which bishops harass laymen, sometimes (as Foxe later complained) putting questions that simple artisans and yeoman farmers could hardly grasp. The king should subordinate to his own statute law the canon law by which laity are oppressed and to which they have given no consent. He should redeploy the resources of idle monks for educational purposes and the better instruction of a sadly ignorant clergy.

Tyndale's book was apparently put into Henry's hands by Anne Boleyn, whose family had at least anticlerical and perhaps protestant sympathies, and whose house was a place where imported Lutheran books might be found. But Tyndale's next book would not have been accepted there. He expressed vehement disapproval of the divorce, agreeing with Martin Luther, who declared that for Henry to divorce Catherine and marry Anne would be adultery, a considerable time before the vacillating pope came to give a verdict. Tyndale's condemnation was fatal to him. Living at Antwerp (where, despite the emperor's control over the port, it seems that protestant merchants and travellers could pass remarkably freely), he was eventually betrayed. As the flames rose round him he prayed, 'Lord open the king of England's eyes'.[51] In fact his book of 1528 may have done that already: for Tyndale there taught that kings, not popes are God's deputies on earth. Their subjects owe them an undivided allegiance. The king is answerable not to them but to God alone, and 'none may question whether his acts are right or wrong'. This was heady and intoxicating reading for a self-willed, egocentric monarch with the mind of a spoilt child.

Yet Henry's determination to be master in his own house went back to the very start of his reign. In his *Defence of the Unity of the Church* Pole tried to remind Henry of his coronation oath to uphold the liberties of the Church. He evidently did not know that at the time in 1509 Henry had attempted to add the qualifying proviso 'if not prejudicial to his jurisdiction and royal dignity'. As early as 1515 he had been claiming, 'We are by the sufferance of God king of England; and in times past the kings of England never had any superior but God; we will maintain the rights of the Crown like our progenitors.'[52]

The title 'supreme head, under God, of the Church of England and Ireland' cannot have looked anything but ridiculous and offensive to most of Henry's contemporaries. Tunstall's well-known remonstrance on the subject expressed what was surely a common feeling both to conservatives and to 'gospellers'.[53] 'Caput ecclesie' was a title protestants found no less irksome than Catholics. Both Luther and Calvin referred to the assertion, implying Henry to be pope in his own kingdom, with astonishment and scorn.[54] It is especially instructive to notice that at his trial in 1556 Cranmer was accused of having been personally responsible for seducing Henry into claiming the title, and that Cranmer, with eminent reasonableness, justly replied that the responsibility lay with his Catholic predecessor Warham, supported by the considered judgement of the universities of Oxford and Cambridge.[55] Royal supremacy was no protestant doctrine in the form in which Henry was to assert it, even though the German Reformation was to depend very much upon the decision of the princes.

A sensitivity to protestant feelings, more than any desire to placate her restive Catholic subjects, moved Elizabeth in 1559 to accept Lever's sugges-tion that she change 'head' to 'governor' (below p. 189).[56] It must be clear (though Henry himself had conceded the point) that the control of Church policy implied no claim to the *sacerdotium*. Even that and the explicit disavowal in Article 37 of the Thirty-Nine Articles were to be unacceptable to Cartwright and the puritans. During the 1560s the widening split between the Marian exiles entrusted with episcopal office and those who had not been so favoured reinforced the latter's conviction that a royal supremacy must be set aside. It was the queen's resolve which maintained the episcopal succes-sion, a 'popish pontifical' called the Ordinal, crucifixes, wafer bread, saints' days and surplices; and to puritans the authority which upheld such things was *ipso facto* discredited. Already in the 1570s Whitgift could foresee that an overthrow of the episcopal order could entail the destruction of the monarchy.[57] I suspect that John Foxe's surprising support for the queen and the episcopal order, despite his strong affinity with the puritan stance, explains why, when Cartwright accused Whitgift of gross insincerity in his laudatory words about Foxe, Whitgift was able to assert his cordial gratitude to the martyrologist.[58]

Professor Scarisbrick has given a brilliant elucidation of the gradualness of the evolution of Henry's notions of royal supremacy.[59] As late as 1530 the king could grant that in matters of heresy the pope ought to judge;[60] his jurisdiction was the point in dispute. But after the Act of Supremacy of 1534, Henry, with the undergirding of Cromwell, began to think himself responsi-ble for laying down norms of authentic doctrine in his private Church of England. Had not the Supremacy Act simply transferred to the king all the powers, ranging from dispensation up to dogmatic definition, ordinarily exercised by St Peter's successors? Could he not issue injunctions for his

Church *motu proprio*, without the least consultation with Convocation?[61] There was a more sensible, if in practice weaker, answer, namely that the dispensing powers had now passed to the archbishop of Canterbury, and that the responsibility for determining the doctrinal platform of the English Church fell to the college of bishops. The Ten Articles of 1536 bore only the king's name and title as their authority, but explicitly claimed to have had mature consideration by Convocation. Nothing is revealed of their extensive affinity with the Articles agreed at Wittenberg between an English delegation and the leading Lutheran divines;[62] but the 'protestantism' of the Ten Articles is of the most 'milk and water' kind apart from the emphasis on the non-fundamental character of images, saints' days, invocation of saints, holy water and candles and other ceremonies, and on the distinction between the accepted propriety of prayers for the departed and the abuses associated with purgatory. The statement on justification 'by contrition and faith joined with charity' anticipates Trent. Foxe thought the Ten Articles contained 'many and great imperfections and untruths not to be permitted in any true reformed Church'.[63]

The following year saw the appearance of the 'Bishops' Book', which for protestants was hardly more consoling;[64] and the revision of this in 1543 to produce the King's Book went so far in an unprotestant direction as to make everyone take for granted that Stephen Gardiner's hand was ubiquitous in it.[65] The King's Book includes a striking passage on the refusal of the Orientals and Grecians to accept the Council of Florence on Roman primacy, demonstrating lack of Catholic consent. The right of national churches to follow their own order is also asserted, with a duty to honour, after Christ the only head of the universal Church, 'Christian kings and princes which be the head governors under him in the particular churches'.[66]

To ensure royal control, Thomas Cromwell was nominated as the king's vicegerent to govern the bishops' proceedings, taking his seat in Convocation above the archbishops. A church historian might ask if he or Henry could have been aware of the presidency exercised at the fourth ecumenical council of Chalcedon in 451 by the long row of high-ranking lay officers of state nominated by Marcian and Pulcheria. The presidency of these lay officers of state could be deduced even from the jejune information, apart from a Latin translation of the Definition of Faith and the twenty-seven canons, provided in Merlin's *princeps* of the collected *Concilia*.[67] In 1536 and in 1538 Cromwell issued sets of ecclesiastical injunctions in the king's name, with a preamble making it explicit that they are grounded in the king's 'supreme authority ecclesiastical'. But this supremacy was enlarged by Cromwell to be held and exercised not by the king alone, but by the king in parliament. Henry's acts in relation to the Church were made parliamentary statutes, and it was only parliament which could make the denial of royal supremacy a crime. So the supremacy of the crown merged into parliamentary control.[68]

The lawyers were insistent that the Act of Supremacy was no innovation. A contemporary, George Wyatt, wrote that it was 'not done to give the king any new title or office, but to declare how that authority was always justly and rightfully due to the crown of the Realm, and that no foreign prince or potentate had anything to do in the same, as the bishops of Rome called Popes pretended and of long time usurped'.[69] To the common lawyers it was axiomatic that papal power had never been exercised in England except by the king's permission, and what the king could permit he could also disallow. Cromwell tied the autocratic omnipotence of the crown to that of parliament, and thereby began the long debate on what limitations there might be to the royal ecclesiastical supremacy.[70]

The flexibility of interpretation attaching to royal supremacy and the way in which it could be used by parliament to resist both king and bishops were brought out in a conversation between Bishop Stephen Gardiner and Lord Audley, Thomas More's successor as lord chancellor (1533–44). The conversation was reported by Gardiner in 1547 in a letter to the protector Somerset, in which Gardiner submitted to Somerset his difficulties about accepting Edward VI's injunctions for the Church.[71] Gardiner argued with some subtlety that these injunctions laid down prescriptions which were not authorised by Act of parliament. Could the royal prerogative override parliament in this way? He recalled how Wolsey had been caught, together with all the clergy of the Church of England, under the statute of Praemunire. Although it was at Henry VIII's express request to the pope that Wolsey was appointed as papal legate in England, nevertheless the lawyers held that his authority was contrary to parliamentary enactment even if he had been carrying out the king's wishes. The judges had appealed for precedent to the case of Lord Tiptoft, earl of Worcester, who fell from power in 1470 and was unable to avert execution by the defence that his savage cruelties on Edward IV's behalf had been carried out in the cause of his sovereign, and had been in accordance with the law he had learnt at Padua even if not with the enactments of parliament. Moreover, it was held against Wolsey that, in defiance of Magna Carta, he had issued injunctions which were against the common law. In 1545 Gardiner had been sent as ambassador to the emperor, in the course of which he had assured the emperor that the king of England was not above the order of the laws enacted in parliament. Only a year previously, under Henry, he had been concerned with members of the privy council about the dangers to the king in contravening an Act of parliament. His earlier conversation with Lord Audley had ended with Audley warning him off so delicate a subject. Audley observed that the Act of Supremacy confined the king to spiritual jurisdiction, and that another Act provided that no ecclesiastical law could stand against common law or parliamentary enactment. By this last proviso the laity were protected against king and bishops clubbing together to oppress them through canon law. Audley saw the uncertainties of interpretation of Praemunire as the principal source for lay liberty from ecclesiastical tyranny.

In his reply to Gardiner, Somerset seems not to have taken up the legal points raised, but rather to have confined himself to pressing Gardiner to accept the 1547 Book of Homilies. The royal injunctions for Winchester cathedral pointedly forbid anyone to call the doctrines of the Homilies heretical, or new, or any other such opprobrious epithet.[72] Gardiner's conscience was troubled by the possible antinomianism of Cranmer's homily on salvation, sufficiently at least to make him prefer to stay in prison.

Audley's interpretation of royal supremacy to mean lay power over the Church and even the crown prefigured the view that it was a basic 'principle of the Reformation' to deny to the Church any 'divine right', anything other than the right of a useful, merely human society within the sovereign state. Those who asserted that a bishop had jurisdiction inherent in the commission bestowed in ordination came increasingly to be regarded as Catholicising. In April 1628 the archdeacon of Durham, John Cosin, was accused of denying the king's power to excommunicate and the title 'head of the Church', and persuasively observed that, while the practical exercise of pastoral jurisdiction was made possible by the king, there was no sense in which the king could be said to be the source of episcopal authority. The source of that was clear from the rite of the Ordinal.[73] Nevertheless, the protestant thesis that divine authority lies exclusively in scripture implied a desacralisation of the Church and its ministers, which made it easier to interpret royal supremacy simply as expressing the view that authority in this Church lies with the secular power. It is deeply significant that the first sentence of Article 20 of the Thirty-Nine Articles ('The Church hath . . . authority in controversies of faith', echoing the Württemberg Confession, 1552) was so disliked by puritans that some printed editions of the Articles omitted it. Even King James I once imprudently suggested (in his *Apology for the Oath of Allegiance*, 1607) that the Bible being the sole source of divine truth, it was for each believer to judge of the dogmas of the faith – a proposition which removed all possible basis for the king's policy of coercion towards recusants and dissenters.

Even during Henry VIII's reign the doctrine of royal supremacy carried very different meanings to different people. During 1543 Stephen Gardiner was engaged in controversy with William Turner, alias Wraghton, author of *The Hunting and Finding out of the Romish Fox*.[74] Turner asked if the king's assertion of supremacy was a denial of the pope's name, or purse, or doctrine. To the majority it was hardly a denial of Catholic doctrine. For a short time Henry could look for friends among the Lutheran princes of Germany, and send divines to Wittenberg to reach agreed statements with the Lutherans which Luther and Melanchthon were to think insufficiently protestant except as a provisional measure. But in England the Latin mass remained intact, and the Six Articles Act strongly enforced transubstantiation and the necessity of priestly absolution in case of mortal sin. The bloody executions of 1540, especially that of Barnes, and the discarding of Anne of Cleves, were well understood to signify that the king was not by this time thinking of moving in a Lutheran direction.[75] Nevertheless, as the French ambassador shrewdly told Francis I in a letter of 6 August 1540,[76] it was no easy matter for Henry to keep a people in revolt against the Holy See and the authority of the Church, and yet free from the infection of heresy; nor on the other hand was it easy to keep those tenaciously attached to orthodoxy from looking with affection towards the papacy – an attachment which would increase as men like Cranmer showed mounting sympathy for Luther and then (from 1550) for Zwingli and Bullinger. Royal supremacy was tolerable on a temporary basis for the Erasmian Henrician bishops so long as they were not asked to accept heresy.

On the other side, the same was found to be true by the protestants. The extent of protestant disillusionment with Henry's policies for the Church of England is dramatically and bitterly set out in the well-known letter of Richard Hilles to Henry Bullinger, written from London in 1541. Hilles portrayed an arbitrary bloody tyranny by a king who had exchanged Romanising for womanising, and was now actively engaged in the persecution of godly men and women. The martyred Barnes (to whom no reason for his execution was given) had already told Luther that Henry's Church policy was wholly determined by political considerations, not in the least by religious conviction or the word of God.[77] The impression among both conservatives and radical reformers was that the royal supremacy was merely an act of naked power with no visible moral basis. William Turner initially refused to grant Henry the title of supreme head of the Church of England and Ireland, but dedicated his book of 1543 to Henry as 'supreme governor under God', explaining that this was to give him as much honour 'as is lawful to give unto any earthly man by the word of God'.[78] It had the further advantage of answering 'certain wanton persons where as I have been, call the king's highness pope of England'. Under pressure Turner was willing to concede that the king is 'supreme head of the Church of England and Ireland', with the proviso 'if ye understand by this word Church an outward gathering together of men and women in a politic order', and not the Church of which the New Testament speaks (!). 'Every vicious king is a member of the devil', and therefore not a member of that Church, still less head of it. On the other hand, Turner was firm that royal supremacy was grounded in scripture, not in Acts of parliament or the pope's canon law. To maintain all the pope's doctrines and ceremonies and to expel his authority seemed to Turner absurd nonsense. His book with its scathing attacks on the Henrician bishops strikingly anticipated the puritans of the 1560s and 1570s, for whom Elizabeth's claim to royal supremacy was intolerable when it meant the refusal to reshape the Church of England after the pattern of the best reformed churches such as that in Scotland. As Beza sharply put it, papal power had not been abolished, but merely transferred in its entirety to the queen.[79]

On the Catholic side, Stephen Gardiner, Bonner and Tunstall conceded the royal supremacy because the alternative was to follow More and Fisher to the scaffold,[80] because except for the authority of the pope no changes of any significance had been made in Catholic doctrine and little in ceremonies, and because to abandon their posts must be to hand the Church over to the wolves. William Turner lambasted them for imposing penalties on folk found eating meat on Fridays while keeping a thunderous silence about the king's sexual mores and 'four lords of England that put away their wives not for fornication but because they liked whores better', and likewise about the disgraceful plunder of the abbeys for which 'all the whole realm smarteth unto this day'.[81] But with Henry threatening to surrender to protestantism as a whip to bring them to heel, perhaps the bishops had less choice than Turner wanted to see. Who could tell how long the king would live? Protestantism might be quite strong in London and among Cambridge dons (Foxe sadly noted more than once Oxford's strong preference for the old religion),[82] but the main population of the land, especially in the North, was in no deep sense protestant in sympathy. Were they not a heartbeat away from restoring the status quo? It was not the last time that Catholic bishops would find themselves compromising with a hostile government for the sake of survival in hope of better days in future. But even Gardiner could not stand by his earlier defence of the royal supremacy when Edward VI was using it to introduce Swiss protestantism. Restored under Mary and elevated to be chancellor, Gardiner could pungently comment at long last that among the disadvantages of Henry VIII's assertion of his headship of the Church was the consideration that, if he had thereby taken the English Church out of communion with Catholic Christendom, he had no Church to be head of.[83] At his trial in 1556 Cranmer found himself in the bizarre position of being instructed by his sovereign, whose supremacy he asserted, to recognise that of the pope, which he felt bound to deny as incompatible with loyalty to the crown.[84]

Under Elizabeth the royal supremacy enforced the *via media* of 'golden mediocrity' as no other factor could do. In March 1560 Matthew Parker was writing to Nicholas Heath and the other deprived bishops regretting their request that the Church of England should again acknowledge the primacy of the Roman see. Like the ancient British Church before Gregory the Great, the Church of England was independent of Rome and of the papal claim to a universal jurisdiction; moreover to acknowledge the pope was treason.[85] But within a short time Parker was defending the royal supremacy against the puritans. Parker, admittedly, did not himself believe that the queen had powers as absolute as those claimed for the pope. When in 1566 he found her reluctant to give royal sanction to the Thirty-Nine Articles of 1563, he solemnly warned her that 'as governor and nurse of this Church' she would have to give account at the Last Judgement for her stewardship in this regard.[86] Certainly her prerogative was more than a papist would grant, but it was (he said) less than Burghley supposed.[87] Elizabeth found that Grindal preferred to resign rather than to acknowledge that the queen could exercise her supremacy so as to abolish prophesyings: 'Remember, Madam, that you are a mortal creature.'[88] Parker and Grindal both found that the queen and parliament were slow to grant that matters such as the Thirty-Nine Articles or 'prophesyings' were to be referred to the bishops and divines of the realm and unsuitable for lay decision.

Nevertheless, the royal supremacy prevented the Church of England from becoming presbyterian, and became increasingly hated by the puritans. The *Zurich Letters* printed an account of 'The State of the Church of England' by the vehement puritan Perceval Wiburn, bitterly complaining of the way in which very large numbers of clergy once ordained under the Latin pontifical were continuing in charge of parishes without any reordination as reformed ministers. (Not that he would have thought the English Ordinal anything but utterly popish.) Wiburn thought the royal supremacy the one and only doctrine one could be reasonably sure of being held by all the clergy of the Church of England. Hooker was explicit that royal supremacy could not mean unrestrained autocracy. The crown was limited by parliament, and parliament itself had acknowledged that the definition of orthodox doctrine must rest on scripture and 'the first four general councils or some other general council', and that if some future parliament were to declare something to be heresy it could only be 'with the assent of the clergy in the convocation'. Even parliament, therefore, allowed that dominion was limited. On the other hand, Hooker defended the right of the prince to nominate bishops and to maintain the order of the Church. He was able to reply to Counter-Reformation critics with the observation that Philip II of Spain had published the decrees of Trent in the Netherlands with an express proviso that there was no prejudice or diminution to his customary rights in nominating to benefices.[89]

At the Hampton Court conference of 1604 the puritan Reynolds hoped to ingratiate himself and the puritan cause with James I by a panegyric on the royal supremacy. James remembered that John Knox had similarly flattered Elizabeth by telling her to use her supreme power to suppress popish prelates. After the prelates had been suppressed, Knox and his friends had carried through a reformation of the Church of Scotland which in effect set aside the royal supremacy. Puritans, said the king, praise the royal supremacy to annoy the bishops. Once the bishops are out of the way and they have taken over the Church, the monarchy will fall also: 'No bishop, no king'. 'I notice', he added, 'that puritan preachers do not in the bidding prayer acknowledge me to be supreme governor in all causes.'[90]

To Henry VIII royal supremacy was the mark of breaking with Roman jurisdiction (not doctrine). Paradoxically, it became the bastion for maintaining Catholic episcopal order in England. But the Stuarts were to learn the hard way that, by defending the Anglican 'mingling of the gospel and popery', the monarchy itself would be brought down. Independents hated the contention that any ministerial structure in the Church belongs (as Whitgift was to claim for episcopacy) to an 'order placed by the Holy Spirit in the Church'.[91] When the Westminster assembly of divines wished to use the language of 'divine law' to suggest that the Church had some right to make its own decisions independent of the House of Commons, they were sharply instructed to think again and to revise their confession of faith.[92] A Victorian parliament and laity was disquieted when similar language began to come from the Tractarians.

Cardinal Allen in 1584 observed with a not unjustified bitterness that the royal supremacy over the Church, for refusal of which Catholic recusants were being brought to execution on the charge of treason (not heresy), was not actually believed by the protestants themselves; moreover, the doctrine of the supremacy treated national churches as if they were totally free to make all their own decisions in utter disregard of the Church universal, a proposition needing only to be stated for its inconveniences, not to say absurdity, to become evident.[93] Already by the reign of James I the fire of well-directed criticism was reducing the area defensible by loyal advocates.[94] None claimed that the monarch could minister the word and sacraments to the people of God, could absolve or excommunicate, and the only question at issue was whether it belonged to the king to call and preside at synods, sanction canons, hear ecclesiastical appeals, grant benefices, appoint and depose bishops. Moreover, the defenders of the supremacy had to assert that it was a moral right, not an act of mere power. They had to avoid shooting themselves in the foot by the argument that the powers claimed for the pope were so monstrous as to prove the papacy to be Antichrist whereas the same powers could be claimed by the secular ruler, as 'God's Vicar' in his own kingdom, without laying himself open to the same charge. The best defence lay in the godly prince of the Old Testament; but it was not evident that this commanded the consent of all sensible and educated men, or that the supremacy could be safely grounded either in natural law or canon law, and the brutal truth was that the New Testament offered no help at all. (One recalls Cranmer's bizarre observation in 1540 that the apostles did their best in appointing clergy because, *faute de mieux*, they had no Christian princes to whom to turn.)[95]

In 1988 belief among members of the Church of England in the reality and moral rightness of royal supremacy (very different from loyalty to the sovereign which can never have been stronger) must be described as tenuous to the vanishing point, and in actuality to mean no more than that the sovereign is the first lay person of a Church particularly characterised by the voice and honour traditionally accorded to the laity in its government. The notion that someone could die for refusing either to affirm it as did John Fisher, or to deny it as did Thomas Cranmer, has become incomprehensible except by a strong effort of historical imagination. It is a classic instance of how an idea intensely important and divisive in the sixteenth century has now faded into virtual insignificance. At the same time there remains a residual, perhaps atavistic anti-clericalism which can think of parliament as the means of voicing dislike of anything done by clergy or bishops or synods, and can appeal to the unquestioned power of the sovereign in parliament to order things as they will. There certainly continues an ill-defined feeling that the mystery of the monarchy is supported by the national character of the Church of England, so that to disestablish the Church could lead to an over-throw of the monarchy. Within the Church of England there is a sometimes sharp division between those who regard the Church as the English at prayer, with the freedom to do whatever the English wish, regardless of 'foreigners', and those who have never ceased to think of the Church of England as a parenthetically and sadly separated branch of the *Catholica*, which is not free to act on its own in handling fundamentals like creed or ministry.

A full history of the evolution which has led to this position would be a long and different story from that of the present essay. It would entail a study of the consequences of the suspension of Convocation early in the eighteenth century and of the constitutional revolution by the parliamentary reforms of 1828–32; a study of Wake, Gibson's *Codex*, Warburton's *Alliance*, Pusey's qualified and very Gallican defence of the supremacy at the crisis of the Gorham controversy, and an examination of the twentieth-century calls, first from high Anglicans but more recently and more vocally from Evangelical Anglicans, for disestablishment and the separation of Church and state. The contemporary attacks on the representativeness of the membership of the general synod of the Church of England mark a counter-move in the opposite direction. At least, by an informal concordat, the crown now, since 1977, nominates bishops by selecting one of two names, both being understood to be sufficient for the task of episcopacy, submitted by the ecclesiastical 'Crown Commission'; and this procedure is obviously a major and beneficial modification of Henry VIII's arrangements. Today most of the actuality of royal supremacy is the proposition that canon law may have no force in con-flict with common law or statute law – a proposition which belongs to the pre-Reformation debate and has nothing specifically protestant to it. In an age when the royal supremacy is in effect reduced to about the dimensions of the Cheshire Cat's grin, it is difficult to comprehend that Thomas

More and John Fisher suffered judicial murder rather than tolerate it. As the Scots showed James I, royal supremacy could be operated in such a way as to leave the Church independent in all essentials. And medieval Catholic kings could maintain sovereignty in their domains without taking their Church out of Catholic communion. In the sixteenth century, royal supremacy first took the Church of England out of communion with the *cathedra Petri* and then stopped (for a time) puritan forces from removing the episcopal succession and other Catholic elements in the Prayer Book and the Ordinal.

That was to require a redefinition of Catholicity closely akin to that of Gallicanism. The Greek refusal at the level of ordinary priests and laity to come to terms with the admission of Roman primacy by their representatives, except for Mark Eugenicus, at the Council of Florence made a deep impression in England, and especially on Henry VIII. As early as the King's Book of 1543, the authorship of which was generally attributed (despite his denials) to Stephen Gardiner, the root question is seen to be one of ecclesiology, defining Catholicity not in terms of Roman jurisdiction but in terms of the profession of the true faith in unity with other Catholic churches.

Such an ecumenical ecclesiology will have room for a focus of unity and universality in Roman primacy and need not exclude a salute of honour for royal supremacy, provided that such a secular assertion of power over the Church is (as the apostle said of apostolic authority) deployed for edification rather than destruction, for the support of the Church in its work in the world rather than as a formula for ensuring the permanence of Christian division.

Notes

1 David Wilkins, *Concilia Magnae Britanniae*, 4 vols. (London, 1737), III, 792–7. The text of the bull finally published in 1538 (ibid., 840–1) responded to the destruction of Thomas Becket's shrine at Canterbury in that year.
2 Matthew Parker, *Correspondence*, ed. John Bruce and Thomas Perowne (Parker Society, 1853), p. 110. In the 1560s Harding and Jewel had a sharp exchange about the degree of papal absolutism embraced by the great canonist Hostiensis: see John Jewel, *The Defence of the Apology*, in *Works*, ed. John Ayre, 4 vols. (Parker Society, 1848), IV, 830–2. For Jewel it was axiomatic that the more extravagant the claims made for the papacy, the more improbable to reason and ungrounded in scripture or tradition they appear. Harding's 'Gallicanism' was dangerously credible. The passage is an early instance of the protestant insisting that the authentic doctrine of papal authority is extreme Ultramontanism, the Catholic minimising.
3 Reginald Cardinal Pole, *Pro Ecclesiasticae Unitatis Defensione* (Strasbourg, 1555), II, 42: 'sed audi aliam conclusionem, quam ego ex ipsis tuis verbis, quae contra

Petri authoritatem proferes, inferam, primo ad confirmationem Petri authoritatis, deinde etiam regis: cuius quidem de authoritate nihil diminuam, cum Petro conservabo suam'. The Strasbourg edition was published in the protestant interest, with eight appended documents on papal authority, including pieces by Luther, Flacius Illyricus, Melancthon, Bucer, Calvin and Musculus. The first English translation of 1560, by F. Wythers (*STC* 20087), was similarly published as a 'seditious and blasphemous oration' intended to discredit the conservative case. There are modern translations in English, by J. G. Dwyer (Westminster, Md., 1965), and in French, by N. M. Égretier (Paris, 1967).

4 Hooper's writings, and especially his hostility to wearing 'Aaronic' episcopal vestments at his consecration, made him a hero to the puritans, but a source of embarrassment to Edmund Grindal. Grindal, however, was able to report that Peter Martyr and Henry Bullinger had regretted unguarded language in Hooper's work, *The Remains of Edmund Grindal*, ed. William Nicholson (Parker Society, 1843), p. 222 (Grindal to John Foxe, August 1556).

5 *The Later Writings of Bishop Hooper*, ed. Charles Nevinson (Parker Society, 1853), pp. 96, 79, 81. Many protestant texts of Edward VI's reign say alarming things about the moral disintegration of English society, a leap in the crime rate, and a slump in church attendance.

6 The major role played by apocalyptic in the Reformation age is well studied by Richard Bauckham, *Tudor Apocalypse* (Appleford, 1978), and K. R. Firth, *The Apocalyptic Tradition in Reformation Britain 1530–1645* (Oxford, 1979).

7 Hooper, *Later Writings*, p. 554: 'the see and chair of Rome . . . is indeed the very whore of Babylon that St John describeth in the Revelation of Jesus Christ, sitting upon a seven-headed beast, which St John himself interpreteth to be seven hills, and the children in the grammar school do know that Rome is called *civitas septem montium*, the city of seven hills'.

8 The assertion that the identity of the pope with Antichrist is no speculative conjecture but an article of faith was made by Gabriel Powel, *De Antichristo et Eius Ecclesia* (London, 1605), and was treated as a self-evident truth by Joseph Mede in the 1640s in works destined to exercise vast influence on Isaac Newton. Newton's editor, Horsley, dissented from the mathematician's axiom. In nineteenth-century England, scathing criticism of the papal Antichrist thesis came from the acid pen of the historian S. R. Gardiner. At the popular level the belief remains tenacious. Hugo Grotius's *Annotata ad Vetus Testamentum* (Paris, 1644) and *Annotationes in Novum Testamentum* (Amsterdam, 1641–50) caused consternation to protestants by denying that correct exegesis could identify the papacy with Antichrist or the whore of Babylon. He outraged many to whom (as to the authors of the Westminster Confession adopted in Scotland) the exegesis was an essential, load-bearing axiom in justifying separation from Rome while simultaneously treating Anabaptists as schismatics. Henry More, *A Modest Inquiry into the Mystery of Iniquity* (Cambridge, 1664) and *A Plain and Continued Exposition of . . . the Prophet Daniel* (London, 1681), sought to answer Grotius with equal erudition. He feared that Anglican enthusiasm for Grotius had alarmed many into thinking the Church of England soft on popery. More regarded the Apocalypse as vindicating the Crown and Church of England, especially royal supremacy: see the folio edition of his *Theological Works* (London, 1708), p. 713. Richard Baxter,

193

The Grotian Religion Discovered (London, 1658) warned that Grotius and some Anglican theologians such as John Bramhall were dismantling the defences against popery: G. F. Nuttall, 'Richard Baxter and *The Grotian Religion*', in D. Baker (ed.), *Reform and Reformation, Studies in Church History, Subsidia*, 2 (1979), 245–50.

9 Bramhall complained 'I am traduced as a factor for popery, because I am not a protestant out of my wits': John Bramhall, *Vindication of Grotius, The Complete Works of John Bramhall*, 2nd edn (Dublin, 1677), ch. 5 at p. 624. It merits notice that in 1986 the General Assembly of the Church of Scotland formally resolved that it does not today accept, or require any assent to, the Westminster Confession's censures on the pope and the mass.

10 Cranmer's answer to Smith (*Cranmer on the Lord's Supper*, ed. John Edmund Cox (Parker Society, 1854), p. 378): 'What wonder is it then that the open Church is now of late years fallen into many errors and corruption, and the holy Church of Christ is secret and unknown? seeing that Satan, these five hundred years, hath been let loose, and antichrist reigneth . . .'. For Wycliffe see John Foxe, *Acts and Monuments*, ed. J. Pratt, 8 vols. (London, 1853–70; repr. 1877), II, 800; Thomas Netter Waldensis, *Doctrinale Antiquitatum Fidei Catholicae*, ed. B. Blanciotti, 3 vols. (Venice, 1757–9; repr. Farnborough, 1967), II, col. 127f. A remarkably early identification of the actualities of the tenth-century papacy with Antichrist occurs in the speech of Arnulf of Reims, written by Gerbert (later Pope Sylvester II!), at the council of S. Basle de Verzy in 991 (*Acta* in *PL* 139, 287–338; *Monumenta Germaniae Historica, Scriptorum*, 3 (Hannover, 1839), 658–86).

11 Foxe, *Acts and Monuments*, I, 5, thought the first evidence of the devil's release from prison was found in Pope Gregory VII. He also surprisingly records a view that the millennium of incarceration began with Constantine and ended with Wycliffe (ibid., I, 291).

12 Hooker remarks on Wycliffe's 'palpable error' in denying the propriety of endowments in the Church: Richard Hooker, *Of The Laws of Ecclesiastical Polity*, ed. W. Speed Hill, 3 vols. (Cambridge, Mass., and London, 1981), III, 276 (VII.22.7). Tithes were for Wycliffe voluntary alms, not a compulsory tax: see Anne Hudson, *Selections from English Wycliffite Writings* (Cambridge, 1978), p. 147.

13 William Langland, *The Vision of William Concerning Piers the Plowman*, ed. W. W. Skeat (Oxford, 1886), I, 308, 127 (B X.317, C VI.169). In more modern editions such as Kane's the numbering of the lines is slightly different. The Kane–Donaldson edition of Langland is radically criticised by David C. Fowler, 'A New Edition of the B Text of *Piers Plowman*', *Yearbook of English Studies*, 7 (1977), 23–42.

14 Printed in *Fasciculi Zizaniorum*, ed. W. W. Shirley (Rolls Series, 1858), pp. 360ff. in Latin; the English text in Hudson, *Selections*, pp. 24–9, with commentary, pp. 150–5.

15 The anger of Thomas Cartwright on the subject shows that it cost less to die before the Reformation than after it. Instead of a sixpenny requiem, the clergy expected half-a-crown for a sermon: see John Whitgift, *The Defence of the Answer to the Admonition*, in *Works*, ed. John Ayre, 3 vols. (Parker Society, 1853), III, 378.

16 John Bramhall, *A Just Vindication of the Church of England from the Unjust Aspersion of Criminal Schism* (Dublin, 1677), II, 92, records 900 ducats – in a lengthy list of papal 'extortions', reinforced by a reference to Chaucer for the avarice in

his time. Foxe, *Acts and Monuments*, II, 109 asserts that in 1504 the archbishop of Mainz paid 27,000 florins for his pall.

17 Parker, *Correspondence*, p. 419, anticipated by Latimer in a letter to Cromwell of 1537 and followed by Aylmer, bishop of London. Ridley is found saying that truth is revealed to the English by God and the king (Foxe, *Acts and Monuments*, VI, 311). Haller's thesis that Foxe regarded the English as a uniquely elect nation is commonly dismissed today as an exaggeration. The thesis is, however, an exaggeration of an element certainly present in Foxe (e.g. *Acts and Monuments*, III, 142f), who was sure that national success and English protestantism were bound together in God's providence.

18 Hooper, *Later Writings*, p. 559. A similar doctrine is found in the *Decades* of Hooper's master, Bullinger.

19 See an account of the Oxford curriculum of 1552 in the letter from Conrad ab Ulmis to John Wolfius, printed in *Original Letters Relative to the English Reformation* (Parker Society, 1847), II, 459 (no. 219). He studied Aristotle's *Politics* in Greek, 6–7 a.m.; the *Digests*, 7–9; Peter Martyr on theology, 9–10; Melanchthon on logic at 10. After dinner, Cicero's *Offices*; Justinian's *Institutes*, 3–4 p.m., which were then memorised, 4–5; the evening spent in dialectical debates with other students. On the general background see John Barton, 'The Faculty of Law', in J. McConica (ed.), *The History of the University of Oxford*, III, *The Collegiate University* (Oxford, 1986), pp. 257–83.

20 *Acta Conciliorum Oecumenicorum*, ed. J. Straub (Berlin, 1971), IV.1, 202,12; the text is in *Sanctorum Conciliorum et Decretorum Collectio Nova*, ed. P. Labbe and N. Coleti, 23 vols., (Venice, 1728–33), VI, 197. For the role of the *sedes/sedens* distinction in Gallicanism, see A. G. Martimort, *Le Gallicanisme de Bossuet* (Paris, 1953), pp. 556–9.

21 *Acta Conciliorum Oecumenicorum*, IV.1, 187,22 and 188,8–21.

22 Augustine, *c. litt. Petiliani*, II.38.132.

23 Augustine (*c. ep. Parmeniani*, II.8.15) regarded the Donatist doctrine of the bishop as indispensable mediator of grace as being 'intolerable' to Catholic ears. He also (*Sermo*, 99.7–9) disliked the Donatist contention that the power of the keys in absolution and excommunication was wholly and without reserve delegated by God to the clergy. On succession, see *ep.* 53. Augustine did not, of course, regard succession as unimportant (e.g. *En. in Ps.* 44.32).

24 Optatus, III, 3.

25 'Sees': *De Doctrina Christiana*, II.12.25. 'See': *c. du. epp. Pelag*, II.3.5. *Ep. ad Catholicos de unit. ecclesiae*, 20.55 has 'reges nostrae communionis'. In *c. litt. Petiliani*, i.18.20, 'per regum communionem' is a synonym for 'per ecclesiam catholicam'.

26 This set of canons became ascribed to the Council of Antioch of 341. Text in *Die Kanones der wichtigsten altkirchlichen Concilien nebst den apostolischen Kanonen*, ed. F. Lauchert (Freiburg im Breisgau and Leipzig, 1896), p. 46.

27 This view, expressed by a member of one of the circus factions at Constantinople in the sixth century, is explicitly recorded, *Patrologia Orientalis*, ed. R. Graffin *et al.* (Paris, 1907–66; Turnhout, 1968–), VIII, 175.

28 The classic discussion by U. Stutz, *Geschichte des kirchlichen Benefizialwesens* (Berlin, 1895; repr. Aalen, 1961) and his lecture *Die Eigenkirche als Element des*

mittelalterlich-germanischen Kirchenrechts (Berlin, 1895; repr. Darmstadt, 1959, with bibliography to 1955); recent literature is noted in R. Schieffer, *Die Entstehung des päpstlichen Investiturverbots für den deutschen König* (Stuttgart, 1981), p. 16. Among the most interesting of early documents is the Tivoli Register (Louis Duchesne, *Le Liber Pontificalis* (Paris, 1886), I, cxlvi ff) recording the benefaction of a Catholic Goth, Valila, an army commander, who built a church on his estate with endowment to maintain the clergy, lights, and repairs, while retaining himself a life interest in other properties given to the Church. A number of sixth-century Gallic councils resist attempts by landowners to withdraw priests on their land from episcopal control. An eloquent statement of the evils of lay domination is in Agobard, *De Dispensatione Rerum Ecclesiasticarum* (*PL*, 104, 236). Hincmar, however, was not so unsympathetic: see W. Gundlach, 'Zwei Schriften des Erzbischofs Hinkmar von Reims I', *Zeitschrift für Kirchengeschichte*, 10 (1889), 92–145.

29 The earliest instance of *beneficium* in our modern sense of 'benefice' has lately come to light among the new letters of Augustine found by Johannes Divjak. It is instructive that in the context the opulent lady who owned the land evidently exercised a veto over the nomination of a bishop for her tenants, but did not at this stage actually nominate. I have discussed this in 'New Letters of St Augustine', *Journal of Theological Studies*, n.s., 34 (1983), 443. Pope Celestine's maxim states the general custom of antiquity: 'Nullus invitis detur episcopus' (*ep.*4, *PL*, 50, 434B). Leo I (*ep*. 167, *PL*, 54, 1203A) ruled none could be bishop without election by clergy, assent of *plebs*, and consecration by the provincial bishops, the metropolitan having a veto.

30 See, e.g., C. R. Cheney, *Pope Innocent III and England* (Stuttgart, 1976), pp. 121ff.

31 *Vita Sancti Anselmi*, ed. R. W. Southern (Oxford, 1972), p. 16.

32 Pope John X (*PL*, 132, 806).

33 *Sancti Aureli Augustini Epistolae*, ed. J. Divjak, *Corpus Scriptorum Ecclesiasticorum Latinorum*, 88 (Vienna, 1981), 22*. See Chadwick, above, no. 29, p. 446.

34 To the best of my knowledge the conscious distinction between 'ecclesia orientalis' and 'ecclesia occidentalis' is first explicit in Augustine, see Chadwick, above, n. 29, p. 428.

35 This formula was used by an English businessman at Bologna in February 1547 when his Italian hosts heard the news of Henry VIII's death and asked him for a defence of the English tyrant: see *The Pilgrim, a Dialogue on the Life and Actions of King Henry the Eighth by William Thomas*, ed. J. A. Froude (London, 1861), p. 32: the king, 'absolute patron of his private Christian dominion', acted as 'prince and apostle'.

36 Wilkins, *Concilia*, III, 764. There is trenchant matter on Justinian as model for Henry in F. W. Maitland, *Roman Canon Law in the Church of England* (London, 1898), pp. 93f.

37 Foxe, *Acts and Monuments*, VII, 618.

38 *Zurich Letters (i) 1558–79*, ed. Hastings Robinson (Parker Society, 1852), p. 19 (John Jewel to Peter Martyr, 28 April 1559); Jewel, *Defence*, in *Works*, IV, 1029ff. R. E. Rodes, *Lay Authority and the Reformation in the English Church, Edward I to the Civil War* (Notre Dame, Ind., 1982), writes perceptively on St German and the lay lawyers, Erastian and Utilitarian, who saw the Church not as a

sacrament of divine presence but as one of the institutions by which a Christian society could pursue its ends. To English pre-Reformation lawyers that was what it always had been.

39 I have tried to tell this story in my *Boethius* (Oxford, 1981), ch. 1.

40 St German's two *Dialogues* with his *New Additions* are edited by T. F. T. Plucknett and J. L. Barton, Selden Society, 91 (1974). There is also important matter in J. A. Guy, *Christopher St German on Chancery and Statute*, Selden Society Supplementary Series 6 (London, 1985), and in J. B. Trapp's Introduction in Thomas More, *The Apology*, ed. Trapp, *Complete Works*, IX (New Haven and London, 1979), xvi–xciii. See also G. R. Dunstan, 'Corporate Union and the Body Politic: Constitutional Aspects of Union between the Church of England and the Church of Rome', in Mark Santer (ed.), *Their Lord and Ours* (London, 1982), pp. 129–48.

41 Walter Ullmann, '"This Realm of England is an Empire"', *Journal of Ecclesiastical History*, 30 (1979), 175–203.

42 Hincmar, *ep.* 19 ad Ludovicum III regem Balbi filium (*PL*, 126, 110f.). Hincmar's ecclesiology gets a sympathetic study from Yves Congar in the journal of the Spanish Dominicans, *Communio* (Granada), 1 (1968), 5–18.

43 Victor Martin's well-known book, *Les Origines du Gallicanisme* (Paris, 1939) contains much matter illuminating for the mind of Henry VIII, even though Henry is far from Martin's field of study. His treatment of Marsilius makes it unnecessary for the present essay to consider the *Defensor Pacis* here, influential as the work was in England.

44 *LP*, X, 977.

45 F. Testa, *Capitula Regni Siciliae*, 2 vols. (Palermo, 1741–3), I, 576–7. The British Library and the Cambridge University Library possess this rare book (not the Bodleian). Foxe, *Acts and Monuments*, II, 465, pointedly noticed the powers of kings of Sicily to appoint bishops. .

46 Foxe, *Acts and Monuments*, VIII, 20.

47 Matthew Paris's portrait of Innocent III is one of limitless avarice and hunger for power. The anti-clerical resentment over King John is mentioned by many writers: Foxe, *Acts and Monuments*, II, 331–2 is representative, and Robert Barnes (himself author of a papal history intended to prove the papacy Antichrist) waxed eloquent on poor John's humiliations. In his *The Supplycacyon of Soulys* (London, 1529; *STC* 18092–3), p. 8, Thomas More denied that King John had power to surrender sovereignty over England to the pope, evidently hoping to ward off the anticlerical barb. But its tenacity is shown by its recurrence in, e.g., John Overall, *The Convocation Book of MDCVI*, Library of Anglo-Catholic Theology (Oxford, 1844), p. 250.

48 Medieval popes took seriously the exhortation of 1 Timothy 5:8 that there was a duty to provide for one's household. I have drawn together texts from *Roberti Grosseteste Episcopi Quondam Lincolniensis Epistolae*, 3ed. H. R. Luard (Rolls Series, 1861), epp. 72, 124, 128, 131. Grosseteste's critique of the curia receives a masterly discussion from R. W. Southern, *Robert Grosseteste, the Growth of an English Mind in Medieval Europe* (Oxford, 1986), pp. 272ff. For Wycliffe's appeal to his writings see ibid., pp. 298ff. The passage about the coronation unction (*Epistolae*, pp. 350–1) is reminiscent of Cranmer's very secular discourse at

Edward VI's coronation on 20 February 1547, explaining to the boy king how utterly insignificant this little ceremony is, reproduced in *Remains and Letters*, ed. J. E. Cox (Parker Society, 1846), pp. 126–7.

49 The effect on antipapal persons of the discovery that the Isidorian decretals were a forgery is never to be underestimated: see the stern words in, for example, Nicholas Ridley, *Works*, ed. Henry Christmas (Parker Society, 1841), p. 182; Foxe, *Acts and Monuments*, I, 279, 464.

50 Among many texts see, for example, Cartwright in Whitgift, *Works*, II, 441. Hooper regarded 'a mixed and mingled religion' as satanic, *Early Writings*, ed. Samuel Carr (Parker Society, 1843), p. 435 (1550). Bishop Richard Cox of Ely defended the prayer book and English ceremonial usages as modelled on St Paul's godly principle of being all things to all men, *Zurich Letters (i)*, p. 237 (Cox to R. Gualter 1571). In January 1559 Gualter had expressed to Queen Elizabeth his fears of 'an unhappy compound of popery and the gospel', *Zurich Letters (ii)*, *1558–1602*, ed. Hastings Robinson (Parker Society, 1844), p. 5 (Gualter to Queen Elizabeth). A similar letter from Gualter to Richard Masters (ibid., p. 11) fears that a religion of 'mixed, uncertain and doubtful character' may one day facilitate a 'return to papistical superstition'.

The proposition in Article 19 of the Thirty-Nine Articles that 'as the Church of Jerusalem, Alexandria and Antioch have erred; so also the Church of Rome hath erred . . .' is strikingly anticipated in Cummian's letter (*c.* AD 632) describing the position of the British churches in the paschal controversy: 'Roma errat, Hierosolyma errat, Antiochia errat, totus mundus errat; soli tantum Scoti et Britones rectum sapiunt' (*PL*, 87, 974 D).

51 Foxe, *Acts and Monuments*, V, 127. Tyndale's accusation that the confessional had been abused, principally by the seduction of foolish women and the betrayal of political secrets, is an angry anticlerical commonplace of the age. For sorrowful Catholic pages telling the same story, see the lawyer Conradus Brunus (1491–1563) in his memorandum to the Council of Trent, printed in *Conc. Trid.*, XII, 404ff. A warning that as a whole Tyndale is less absolutist about royal power than some sayings in his *Obedience* suggest is given by W. D. J. Cargill Thompson, 'The Two Regiments: The Continental Setting of William Tyndale's Political Thought', in D. Baker (ed.), *Reform and Reformation, Studies in Church History, Subsidia*, 2 (1979), 17–33.

52 See *LP*, II, no. 1313 (p. 353), and Ullmann, '"This Realm of England"', pp. 175–203. L. G. Wickham Legg, *English Coronation Records* (Westminster, 1901), pp. 240–1, with facsimile, does not think Henry could have had his wish.

53 Wilkins, *Concilia*, III, 745. Tunstall thought the qualifying clause whereby the bishops accepted Henry as head of the Church 'so far as the law of Christ allows' failed to make it explicit that the qualification meant death to the proposition.

54 Luther in 1531 rejected Henry's divorce out of hand (*Weimarer Ausgabe Briefwechsel* (Weimar, 1883ff), 6, 178–88, a letter to Robert Barnes), and his title 'head of the Church' in 1539 (WA Br. 8, 577–78, a letter to the elector John Frederick of 23 October 1539, concluding acidly 'Henry ought to be pope, as in fact he is in England'). The two letters are translated into English in Martin Luther, *Works*, ed. J. Pelikan *et al.* (St Louis, Mo., 1955–), 1 (1975), 196, 205. Calvin, *Readings on Amos*, VII, 13 (*Opera Omnia* (Amsterdam, 1667), V, 223)

tersely described Henry's claim as blasphemy, and goes on to express outrage at
having heard Stephen Gardiner argue not from scripture or from reason, but exclusively from the will of the king, to rule against clerical marriage or communion
in both kinds.

55 Foxe, *Acts and Monuments*, VIII, 53; also printed in Cranmer, *Remains and Letters*, pp. 214–15.

56 That Lever made the suggestion to the queen is stated by Sandys' letter to Parker,
30 April 1559, *Correspondence of Matthew Parker*, ed. John Bruce and T. T.
Perowne (Parker Society, 1853), pp. 65–6. For Elizabeth's assertion of supremacy,
see M. A. Simpson, *Defender of the Faith et cetera* (Edinburgh, 1978); N. L. Jones,
Faith by Statute, Royal Historical Society, Studies in History (London, 1982), p.
32. Much in the writings of Professor D. M. Loades also bears on this question.
If the application to the pope of the title supreme head was *ipso facto* to declare
him a forerunner of Antichrist, as John Bradford thought (Foxe, *Acts and
Monuments*, VII, 183), the same conclusion must also apply to the monarch.

57 Whitgift, *Works*, II, 239.

58 Whitgift, *Works*, II, 333–6. Foxe, as this Cartwright/Whitgift exchange shows, is
not easy to pigeon-hole in the variety of sixteenth-century English Church life.
Though evidently strongly reformed in religion, often 'Swiss' in sympathy, he
regarded the vestiarian controversy as a tragic squabble about trivialities (ibid., II,
750). Many passages uphold the right and duty of the sovereign to order the life
of clergy in his realm, and vehemently attack the infringements and usurpations
of papal power, especially by Gregory VII, Innocent III, and Boniface VIII. Yet
he also evidently longed for a reformed see of Rome focusing the unity of 'sister
churches' (ibid., II, 418), and was shocked at the spoliation of the Church of
England by Henry VIII. Erasmian influence may be seen in his desire that the
Apostles' Creed be the norm of orthodoxy (ibid., III, 103), his horror of elevating
school opinions to articles of faith (ibid., III, 729), and his stern criticism of capital
punishment for religious dissent (e.g. ibid., III, 99). Whitgift was not mistaken to
see an ally in him; Foxe would not have liked his treatment of John Penry. Foxe
disliked the title 'Book of Martyrs' already being ascribed to his work, and insisted
that he wrote *Acts and Monuments of Things Passed in the Church* (ibid., III,
392).

59 J. J. Scarisbrick, *Henry VIII* (London, 1968), pp. 375–86.

60 Ibid., p. 351.

61 See *Visitation Articles and Injunctions of the Period of the Reformation*, ed. W. H.
Frere and W. M. Kennedy (Alcuin Club Collections, 15), II, 2, 34. The Ten
Articles, however, were agreed by Convocation in July 1536.

62 The Wittenberg Articles were discovered in Weimar early this century and
published by their finder, Georg Mentz, *Die Wittenberger Artickel von 1536* (Leipzig, 1905). Luther regarded these Articles as representing something of a compromise between his own position and that of the English divines, but one he
could accept to help forward the Reformation (WA Br. 17, p. 383). An English
translation of the Wittenberg Articles is given by N. S. Tjernagel, *Henry VIII and
the Lutherans* (St Louis, Concordia, 1965), pp. 255–86.

63 Foxe, *Acts and Monuments*, V, 164. I am bound to think the protestantism of the
Ten Articles exaggerated by D. B. Knox, *The Doctrine of the Faith in the Reign*

of Henry VIII (London, 1961), and even by Professor Scarisbrick, *Henry VIII*, p. 438 ('blatantly heterodox'). What is no doubt true is that there was much left unsaid.

64 Foxe's verdict is again that in the Bishop's Book 'many things were slender and imperfect', *Acts and Monuments*, V, 87. He gives the names of the eight bishops responsible for its production (ibid., VIII, 11). Stokesley (London) and Gardiner (Winchester) could be relied upon to keep the protestantising sympathies of Latimer (Worcester) and Shaxton (Salisbury) in check. The preface signed by all the bishops in Convocation, headed by Cranmer, includes a declaration that 'without the power and licence of your majesty we acknowledge and confess that we have none authority either to assemble ourselves together for any pretence or purpose, or to publish any thing that might be by us agreed and compiled', *Formularies of Faith Put Forth by Authority during the Reign of Henry VIII*, ed. Charles Lloyd (Oxford, 1825, repr. 1856), p. 26. The declaration presupposes that the king is pope of the English Church, and the bishops are only advisory on dogmatic questions, deriving from him their spiritual jurisdiction. Hooker, *Laws*, VIII.2.16, is much more nuanced, but grants that the limitations of regal power over the Church (apart from the self-evident lack of power of order and jurisdiction) have 'not hitherto been agreed upon with so uniform consent and certainty as might be wished'.

65 Ridley in 1555 remarked that Stephen Gardiner was 'thought to be either the first father or chief gatherer' of the King's Book: Nicholas Ridley, *Works*, ed. H. Christmas (Parker Society, 1841), p. 135. Gardiner himself denied having had a hand in the book (Foxe, *Acts and Monuments*, VI, 61; cf. VI, 124, which shows that the denial was regarded with incredulity), and affirmed that the master hand was Henry himself. The king's annotations on the Bishops' Book, printed in Cranmer, *Remains and Letters*, pp. 83–114, suggest that Gardiner may have been correct.

66 *Formularies of Faith*, ed. Lloyd, pp. 285, 248. The Greek rejection of universal papal jurisdiction was a frequent theme in protestant argument that such a degree of centralised authority lacks Catholic consent, e.g. Foxe, *Acts and Monuments*, II, 608; III, 700; VI, 255.

67 Paris, 1524; 2nd edn, Cologne, 1530. Crabbe's edition did not appear until 1538, and the margins of Cranmer's copy of that were soon to be covered with his manuscript annotations.

68 John Rogers, on the protestant side, thought that the inconsistencies of parliament in consenting to the incompatible doctrines of Henry VIII, Edward VI, and then Mary totally discredited its authority as a judge of the interpretation of God's word: Foxe, *Acts and Monuments*, VI, 603. That under Edward VI the magisterium was vested either in the young king or in parliament, even to the actual exclusion of the clergy, is evident from the pathetic plea of the clergy to Edward VI (Wilkins, *Concilia*, IV, 15) asking if they could please be consulted, whether by being given an actual voice in any laws governing religion 'or that at least parliament enact no religious laws without consulting the clergy in convocation'. Sir Simonds D'Ewes's *Journal, The Journals of All the Parliaments during the Reign of Queen Elizabeth* (London, 1682), on 14 Eliz. (22 May 1572) records the queen's pleasure that no bills concerning religion be received in parliament unless first considered by the clergy.

69 *The Papers of George Wyatt*, ed. D. M. Loades, Camden Society, 4th series, 5 (1968), p. 153.

70 Cecil held that the power of the crown is limited by the advice of the privy council (Foxe, *Acts and Monuments*, VI, 68). The oration of the protestant layman John Hales, submitted to Elizabeth in 1558 (text in Foxe, *Acts and Monuments*, VIII, 673–9), in effect pleaded for the reinstatement of the royal supremacy: 'The title touched the commonwealth and realm of England more than the king . . . It was for the conservation of the liberty of the whole realm and so to exclude the usurped authority of the bishop of Rome.' In other words, royal supremacy meant in practice parliamentary control of the Church of England, or at least the negative proposition that the government of this Church could not make room for the pope.

71 *The Letters of Stephen Gardiner*, ed. J. A. Muller (Cambridge, 1933), p. 379 (no. 130). Foxe, *Acts and Monuments*, VI, 42–6, prints only about two-thirds of the text.

72 *Visitation Articles and Injunctions*, ed. Frere and Kennedy, II, 149.

73 See John Cosin, *Correspondence*, I, Surtees Society, 52 (1869), p. 147.

74 *The Huntyng and Fyndynge out of the Romische Fox* (Basel, 1543). *STC*, 24353 thinks it actually printed at Amsterdam by S. Mierdman. I have used the Bodleian copy (Tanner, 51).

75 How hostile was the English protestant reaction to Henry's dissolution of his 'pretended marriage' with Anne of Cleves may be seen in Richard Hilles's letter to Bullinger, Hastings Robinson (ed.), *Original Letters Relative to the English Reformation, 1531–58* (Parker Society, 1846–7), I, 205. Hilles is also eloquent on the execution of Barnes: ibid., I, 209f.

76 *LP*, XV, p. 484.

77 Luther (WA Br. 8, 577–8): 'Dr Antony [= Robert Barnes] several times declared: Our king has no respect for religion and the gospel.'

78 William Wraghton (pseud.), *The Rescuynge of the Romishe Fox Other Wyse Called the Examination of the Hunter Devised by Steven Gardiner* ('Winchester', 1545). *STC*, 24355, assigns it to L. Mylius of Bonn. Foxe, *Acts and Monuments*, VII, 602, identifies the author as Turner, dean of Wells. His defence of 'supreme governor' is at fo. Cii. In 1555 Turner wrote under his own name *The Huntyng of the Romysche Vuolfe* (*STC*, 24356), written after Latimer's death but before Gardiner's, i.e. in November 1555. This last work anticipates in content, verve and venom much that went into the puritan Admonitions to Parliament of 1571–2 and the Marprelate tracts.

79 Beza to Bullinger, 3 September (1566), *Zurich Letters (ii)*, 128, probably quoting the opinions of Perceval Wiburn: '. . . the papacy was never abolished in that country, but rather transferred to the sovereign . . . nothing else is now aimed at than the gradual restoration of what had been in any measure altered'.

80 In January 1555 Gardiner, Tunstal (Durham) and Nicholas Heath (Worcester) confessed expressly to John Rogers: in Henry VIII's time one could not say without pain of death that the king had no authority in spiritual matters such as forgiveness and authority to interpret God's word (Foxe, *Acts and Monuments*, VI, 593; cf. Bonner in ibid., VIII, 110). There is a parallel to the situation of the Henrician bishops in the Greek bishops who supported Chalcedon in the difficult times of the emperor Anastasius, 491–518. When the popes expressed the view that the Greeks had been guilty of grave compromise by holding communion with

the patriarchs of Constantinople who (though some were Chalcedonian) were not acknowledged by Rome because of the Acacian schism they replied that they had kept their faith intact, and that to have withdrawn communion from the patriarchs would have brought expulsion and the surrender of their flocks to the wolves: Pope Symmachus, *ep.* 12 (*Epistolae Romanorum Pontificum Genuinae*, ed. A. Thiel (Braunsberg, 1867–8), pp. 709–17; Henry Chadwick, *Boethius* (Oxford, 1981), pp. 181–3).

81 *The Huntyng of the Romysche Wolfe* (1555): 'When as Tunstal, Gardiner, Stokesay and the rest of the papists bare the swinge under king Henry the eighth, they suffered the kings and divers lords of the realm to put away and take as many wives as they list without any correction or admonition. If that they had done their duty, the virtuous lady Anne of Cleve had never been divorced and put away from the king her lawful husband . . . Henry with his covetous council took all the goods of the abbeys which belongeth for a great part as well unto Christ's church as the half of the goods of Ananias belongeth unto the Holy Ghost.' Turner omits to add that Bishop Latimer of Worcester, making the customary New Year's gift to Henry VIII, once gave him a New Testament wrapped in a napkin, inscribed 'Fornicatores et adulteros judicabit Dominus' (Foxe, *Acts and Monuments*, VII, 517). Turner was far from being the only protestant outraged by the deliberate ruthlessness with which Henry's dissolution of the monasteries enforced the annihilation of a major religious factor and a vast break with the past. See M. Aston, 'English Ruins and English History', *Journal of the Warburg and Courtauld Institutes*, 36 (1973), pp. 231–55, at pp. 234ff.

82 That Oxford, especially Magdalen College, had its protestants in Elizabeth's time is clarified by C. M. Dent, *Protestant Reformers in Elizabethan Oxford* (Oxford, 1983), following Professor Patrick Collinson.

83 Foxe, *Acts and Monuments*, VI, 577f.

84 Ibid., VIII, 51f.

85 Parker, *Correspondence*, pp. 109–13 (16 March 1560).

86 Ibid., pp. 292–4 (24 December 1566).

87 Ibid., p. 479 (11 April 1575). Perhaps Cecil agreed with Sir Francis Knollys that bishops derive all spiritual authority, including superiority to presbyters, wholly from delegation by the crown, not from God by the commission in ordination: C. Cross, *Royal Supremacy in the Elizabethan Church* (London, 1969), p. 177. Knollys's view is an ultra-Caesaropapism analogous to the Ultramontane stance of Archbishop Castagna of Rossano (later, for a few days in 1590, Urban VII) submitted to the Council of Trent on 20 October 1562. Castagna held that bishops are the pope's vicars and derive all authority from him, including superiority over presbyters, so that no further justification, such as 'divine right', is necessary, *Conc. Trid.*, IX, 59, 18.

88 *Zurich Letters (ii)*, p. 358.

89 Hooker, *Laws*, III, 401 (VIII.6.9); cf. E. T. Davies, *Episcopacy and Royal Supremacy in the Church of England in the XVI Century* (Oxford, 1950; repr. 1978), pp. 132ff.

90 Wilkins, *Concilia*, IV, 374, cf. 611 for the text of a censure by the University of Oxford, 21 July 1683, upon the presbyterian and puritan view that 'the king's supremacy in ecclesiastical affairs . . . is injurious to Christ'. On the Hampton

Court Conference see E. Cardwell, *Conferences Connected with the Revision of the Book of Common Prayer* (Oxford, 1840), pp. 202–3.

91 Whitgift, *Works*, II, 405; Hooker, *Laws*, VIII.5.10, 'the first institution of bishops was from heaven, was even of God, the Holy Ghost was the author of it'.

92 See the abrasive message from the House of Commons to the Westminster Assembly of Divines, 30 April 1646, printed in *Minutes of the Sessions of the Westminster Assembly*, ed. A. F. Mitchell and J. Struthers (Edinburgh and London, 1874), pp. 448–55, showing that the parliament hated papal and royal supremacy, but enthusiastically upheld its own in matters ecclesiastical. Any suggestion that authority in the Church might have a divine sanction was anathema to the men who had executed Laud and were soon to kill the king.

93 (W. Allen), *A True, Sincere and Modest Defence of English Catholics* (Rouen, 1584), answering Burghley's defence of the government's harassment of recusants. A modern reprint is edited by R. M. Kingdon (Ithaca, NY, 1965). An excerpt is in Cross, *Royal Ecclesiastical Supremacy* (London, 1969), pp. 154–5. There is a vehement attack on the idea that a national Church ought to wait for a general council before taking crucial independent decisions, in *The Decades of H. Bullinger*, ed. T. Harding, 4 vols. (Parker Society, 1849–52), IV, 116f.

94 Among the critics of James I's defence of the oath of allegiance, the learned and witty tracts of the Jesuit Martin Becan (in his collected *opuscula*, 5 vols. (Mainz, 1610–21)) are outstanding. James's best defender was Lancelot Andrewes.

95 Cranmer, *Remains and Letters*, 2 vols. (Oxford, 1833), I, 116.

The spirituality of John Fisher

EAMON DUFFY

St John Fisher's place in the history of English spirituality, like his place in the history of English humanism, is obscured by problems of definition. So austere a figure challenges expectations derived from the identification of the cause of the new learning (and the new piety) with Erasmus. Historians have therefore been tempted to describe his relation to the movements of the early sixteenth century in terms of contrast, rather than participation. Whether the polarities employed are those of 'medieval' as opposed to 'Renaissance', or 'unreformed' as opposed to 'reformed', the temptation is to opt for a single all-purpose descriptive category. C. S. Lewis, in what remains the most helpful brief account of Fisher as a religious writer, succumbs to temptation on both scores. Fisher, he claimed, 'is almost a purely medieval writer, though scraps of what may be classified as humanistic learning appear in his work', but 'he matters less as a literary figure than as a convenient representative of the religion in possession at the very beginning of the English Reformation. He was a bishop and died for his faith: in him we ought to find what men like Tyndale were attacking.'[1] For a mere historian to quarrel with Lewis about a matter of literature might seem as foolhardy as the attempt to anatomise the spirituality of a saint. Yet one may well feel that in Lewis's easy contrasts something has been omitted. It does not seem very useful to characterise any one figure as 'representative' of so complex a reality as late-medieval English religion. To do so in Fisher's case in particular is to risk missing what is distinctive about his use of the resources of the religious tradition he inherited. If it is true that he can be understood only in the context of late-medieval piety, he neither appropriated nor deployed with equal readiness every element in that background. His choice of genre and theme, and his distinctive range of imagery reveal a sensibility resolutely his own even when apparently at its most conventional. We must not be mesmerised into thinking that in Tudor England the devil had all the best tunes, that only the revolutionaries possessed individuality.

Nor should we willingly accept Lewis's stark contrast between 'medieval' and 'humanist'. It is certainly true that neither Fisher's preaching style, his choice of themes, nor his use of scripture show much overt sign of the new learning; every devotional piece he wrote can be paralleled in earlier writers. But both in theme and treatment many of them can be paralleled also among his younger contemporaries, and in many later writers too. Separating the 'medieval' from the 'Renaissance' elements in the works of Thomas More presents similar problems, and has become a sort of parlour-game for historians and literary critics, without greatly advancing our understanding of him. There is nothing in the religion of Fisher that could not be found in Colet or More: since any definition of English humanism that excluded them would be highly problematic, we should beware of excluding Fisher from the charmed circle on religious grounds, without closer scrutiny. Humanist and medieval religious ideals are not so readily or so starkly contrasted as has been assumed.[2] Moreover, much that seems most medieval in Fisher's work can be paralleled in the devotional literature, both Catholic and protestant, of Elizabethan and Jacobean England. If one concedes that, by and large, his attitudes and convictions found a more natural and congenial home in the Counter Reformation than within protestantism, that should not obscure the fact that Fisher's works look forward as well as back. It makes almost as much sense to read them in the light of the Baroque as of the Gothic imagination.

It is easy to see why Lewis opted for Fisher as a figure representative of late medieval Catholicism, which Lewis characterised primarily in terms of its world-denying and ascetical dimensions.[3] It is, certainly, as an ascetic that Fisher is most readily approached, whether in the gaunt and troubled Holbein sketch at Windsor, or the 'very mortified and meagre personage with a crucifix before him' in the portrait at St John's, or in contemporary accounts of 'his face hands and all his bodye, so bare of flesh as is almost incredible, which came the rather (as may be thought) by the great abstinance and pennance he used upon himself many yeres together, even from his youth'. When he was stripped for execution he seemed 'a verie ymage of death and as it were death in mans shape using a mans voice'.[4] Fisher himself cultivated the thought and the image of death: when he said mass 'he always accustomed to set upon one ende of the altar a dead man's scull, which was also set before him at his table as he dyned or supped'.[5] Mortification was the keynote of his devotional life. When the king's commissioners came to make an inventory of his goods at Rochester after his arrest in April 1534, they found in his private oratory a locked coffer, in which they assumed valuables were stored. On forcing it open, however, they found a 'a shirte of heare, and two or three whips, wherewith he used full often to punish himself'.[6] None of this is surprising, and represents the conventional stuff of early Tudor devotion. We are all familiar with Thomas More's similar austerities, with the help of which an elaborate hypothesis of sexual repression has been constructed. Lewis found the literary expression of this 'morbid' sensibility in Fisher's utterances on the body as 'stincking flesh', 'dirtie corruption', 'a sachell full of dunge', and in his undiscriminating disparagement of sex. Fisher believed that the 'flesshe that before hath ben polluted by the foule and fylthy pleasure of the body, feleth moch more unclene mocyons than dooth the fleshe which alwaye hathe ben clene and chaste'.[7] And perhaps most revealingly of all, Lewis argued, the essentially negative character of the religious tradition represented by Fisher appeared in the horrifyingly vivid evocations of purgatory scattered through his works, a purgatory conceived not as a place of hope and renewal, as in Dante, but as a torture-house designed to exact retribution from a sinful humanity. It is no wonder that given such a vision of mankind and its destiny the reformers 'felt that they were escaping from a prison', a theme taken up from Lewis by subsequent historians.[8]

All this, however, is to start at the wrong point, to isolate as distinctive of 'medieval' religion in general, and of Fisher's spirituality in particular, features which assume a false prominence because of their distance from twentieth-century sensibility. Fisher did have an almost wholly negative view of sexuality, a view he shared, for example, with Colet and probably most other early Tudor churchmen. In Colet's case, however, it is difficult to decide whether his repudiation of the body is part of a common medieval inheritance, derived from Augustine, or from his neo-platonic background, and part therefore of a widespread, though often ignored, tendency in Renaissance anthropology to devalue the physical.[9] Moreover, this loathing of the body and its functions is not peculiar either to Catholicism or to the middle ages. It is vigorously present among the reformers. John Bradford's immensely influential *Meditations*, a standard text among the godly well into the seventeenth century, denounced the body as

but a prison, wherein the soul is kept . . . foul and dark, disquiet, frail and filled up with much vermin and venemous vipers, (I mean it concerning our affections), standing in an air most unwholesome, and prospect most loathsome, if a man consider the excrements of it by the eyes, nose, mouth, ears, hands, feet, and all the other parts.

And so 'no Bocardo, no little-ease, no dungeon . . . no sink, no pit' is so evil a prison for the body 'as the body is for and of the soul'.[10] Bradford, as much as Fisher, believed that 'sensual gratification' left behind 'a certain loathsomeness and fulness', even when come by 'lawfully' within marriage.[11] If we are to consign Fisher to some pejorative 'medievalism' on the score of his views about sex and the body, we shall be obliged to send along with him a high proportion of religious writers on the subject before the twentieth century. In any case, if we wish properly to understand both the extent and the limits of Fisher's 'medievalism', we will do well not to isolate its more obviously negative aspects, but to consider his relation to the whole religious inheritance of early Tudor England.

The first thing to be said about Fisher's relation to his religious inheritance is that he was very much at home in it. The pattern of his piety was, in the very strictest sense of the term, conventional. Christ and his cross stand at the heart of Fisher's perception of God and the world, but they never beckon, as they do in Erasmus, away from external observance and the religion of the masses. In sacraments and sacramentals, for Fisher, we touch the reality of Calvary. It is by

theffusion of the moost precious blode of cryst Ihesu upon a crosse plenteously for all synners, wherby satysfaccyon was made to god the fader for the synnes of all people, whiche receyve the vertue of this precyous blode by the sacramentes of crystes churche & by it made ryghtwyse.

So in the sacrament of penance the sinner 'gooth awaye . . . ryghtwyse, not by his owne ryghtwysnes, but by the ryghtwysnes of cryst Ihesu'. The Church has nothing of its own to give, its ceremonies have no power in their own right, but 'there is a prevy & hyd vertue gyven unto them by the meryte of the passyon of Ihesu cryst & of his precyous blode'. So great is the merit of Christ in the sacraments that 'as ofte as ony creature shall use & receyve ony of them, so oft it is to be byleved they are sprencled with the droppes of the same moost holy blode, whose vertue perseth unto the soule, and maketh it clene from al synne'.[12] It is in the context of this absolute confidence in the sacramental efficacy of the work of Christ that Fisher's often formidable utterances on good works, his continual insistence on the need for penance, and his evocation of the horrors of purgatory should be seen. He says most about purgatory in the sermons on the Seven Penitential Psalms, which he preached as chaplain to the Lady Margaret Beaufort in 1504. These sermons represent an extended meditation on the sacrament of penance in its three parts – contrition, confession and satisfaction. It would be easy to compile from them a selection of passages to bear out the suggestion that Fisher's scheme of salvation was indeed a prison house for the spirit, that his God is one determined to exact from a guilty mankind the last measure of retribution: 'For truly over our hedes hangeth a swerde ever movynge & redy by the power of God, whose stroke whan it shall come shall be so moche more grevous that we so longe by our grete & manyfolde unkyndnes have caused almyghty god and provoked hym to more dyspleasure.'[13] But such a picture would be a parody of Fisher's teaching as a whole. The God of the Penitential Psalms is for Fisher above all a God of mercy and compassion, bearing with human failures, ever ready to respond to human repentance: 'The mercy and goodnes of almyghty god shewed upon synners is mervayllous grete whiche the more that they call unto theyr owne mynde and expresse theyr owne trespasses, so moch the more he forgeteth & putteth them out of his mynde . . .' For Fisher the sacrament of penance is not the expression of an essentially fearful and works-bound theology, but the form the divine graciousness takes in liberating us from the need to endure the consequences of our own sins: 'By the vertue of contrycyon our synnes be forgyven, by confessyon they be forgoten, but by sattisfaccyon they be so clene done away that no synne or token remayneth in any condycyon of them, but as clene as ever we were.'[14] Certainly he emphasises effort, and the need to do good works. Christ bought our salvation on the cross, 'but know this for a certayn, he nether bought this inherytaunce for the, ne made promyse thereof, but with condicyon . . .'. The condition is the performance of good works.[15] Yet good works are themselves the gift of God, the miraculous fruit of God's life-giving grace:

From the eyen of almyghty god whiche may be called his grace shyneth forth a mervaylous bryghtnes lyke as the beme that cometh forth from the sonne. And that lyght of grace stereth and setteth forwarde the soules to brynge forth the fruyte of good werkes. Even as the lyght of the sonne causeth herbes to growe & trees to brynge forth fruyte . . . O mervaylous mekeness of almyghty god shewed unto synners when they fle unto hym, whiche is so redy to comforte and graunte them helpe.

Every stage of the process of repentance is due solely to the grace of God: 'Thou arte sorry for thy synne, it is a gyfte of almyghte god. Thou makest knowledge of thy synne wepynge and wayling for it, it is a gyft of almyghte god. Thou are besy in good werkes to do satysffaccyon, which also is a gyfte of almyghte god.' If his vision of purgatory is indeed that of a prison, it is sin, not God, who is the gaoler – 'who that is in thraldome of synne is in full shrewd custody'. Yet in the last resort the escape route is not through human striving, but through a humbling of oneself to the mercy of God, as those prisoners do who 'sometyme undermyne the walles and crepe under them out at a strayte and narrow hole . . . and soo come unto the lyberte of grace'.[16] The grim evocations of purgatory are designed to stir an unspiritual people, content with lip-service to the notion of repentance, to avail themselves of this 'lyberte of grace', the divine mercy which would spare them the avoidable consequences of sin. 'Many there be that wayle & be contryte & also confesse theyr synnes, but scant one amonge a thousande can be found that dooth dewe satysfaccyon.' And, since satisfaction is the principal evidence of sincere and lasting repentance, it is 'to be drad leest any prevy gyle or decyte remayne in the soule, that is to saye it is not very contryte and truly confessed'.[17]

The effects of such penance in Fisher himself present at first sight a daunting picture of austerity and gloom. That, however, was not his own perception of the matter. Since true penitence and due satisfaction were gifts of God, they were a source of joy: 'the penytent hath more swete Ioye & gladnes inwardly in his soule than any other creature lyvynge may have in all the pleasures of the worlde'.[18] For in the Church we live under a 'newe lawe, not a lawe of fere & drede but a lawe of grace and mercy'. The Christian life was to be lived as a balance of 'hope with drede and drede with hope' so that we may neither 'truste in god without his fere, nor drede hym without

209

hope', neither 'lyfte up by presumpcyon nor caste downe by dyspayre'.[19] That balance is to be found even in unpromising places. Throughout his writings Fisher emphasises the value of penitential tears, real, salt and heart-rending, and he himself was accustomed to weep when he said mass. Here again he is wholly at one with his contemporaries, for the Sarum Missal, like the Roman Missal till recent times, contained a votive mass for the gift of penitential tears. However, for Fisher, such tears were a sign not of mankind's fearful moral activism, the attempt to placate an angry God, but evidence of the recreative work of the Spirit within us:

[T]he spiryte of god shall gyve so grete infusyon of grace to them that be penytent that the waters, that is to saye theyr wepynge teres shall flowe & be haboundaunte. Upon these waters the spyryte of almyghty god may flye and goo swyftely, which was fygured in the begynnynge of scripture, by the sayenge of Moyses, *Et Spiritus domini ferebatur super aquas*.[20]

With tears as the gift of the Spirit we are firmly in the popular devotional world of the late middle ages, the world of the Mater Dolorosa and St Mary Magdalene, of St Brigid of Sweden and of Margery Kempe. It was part of Fisher's confidence in the Church that he never questioned its devotional ethos, nor made any hard-and-fast distinction between official and unofficial piety. His first venture into theological controversy, *De Unica Magdalena*, was essentially an attempt to preserve popular devotion to the Magdalene from the corrosive scepticism of academic criticism. In defence of this traditional piety he invoked not merely the scriptures, fathers and popes, but the miracles of saints and the revelations of St Brigid.[21] His receptivity to the Nun of Kent was entirely of a piece with this ready acceptance of the thought-world of late-medieval popular Catholicism, an acceptance evident also in his frequent references to miracles and incidents from the lives of the saints culled from sources like the *Legenda Aurea*.[22] It was reflected more significantly and more deeply in his very choice of genres. The works on which an assessment of his spirituality must be principally based are traditional not only in content but in form. The sermons on the Penitential Psalms illustrate this admirably. These seven psalms were an invariable feature of the most popular devotional manuals for lay-folk, the Primers, and were probably the portions of scripture most familiar to lay people. The astonishing popularity of Fisher's sermons[23] reflects not only the quality of the works themselves, but the appeal of their subject matter: John Longland also preached a famous (and immense) series of sermons on these psalms, and some of Savonarola's sermons on them circulated in early Tudor England.[24] Fisher's virtuoso funeral oration for Henry VII reflects a similar instinct for and ease with popular and liturgical piety. Rhetorically the sermon is a *tour de force*. In it Fisher uses the opening psalm of the *Dirige*, again one of the most widely used of early Tudor devotions, for three distinct purposes: first to express his vision of the sinner's hopes; secondly to fulfil the classical pattern of mourning orations, in commendation of the departed, exhortation of the hearers to compassion and sorrow for the dead, and the provision of comfort; and thirdly to articulate the prayer of Henry himself *in extremis* to a merciful God. The virtuosity involved in sustaining all these objectives in a single, tightly structured sermon demonstrates with particular force the unselfconscious ease with which Fisher was able to appropriate the devotional forms of his own time. The skill with which Fisher places in Henry's mouth the words of the psalm also demonstrates what he had in mind when he says elsewhere that Christian people should use the psalms as 'lettres of supplycacyon and spedefull prayers'.[25]

The piety recommended in the funeral sermon for Henry VII is no less revealing, for it is the emotionally charged 'affective' and churchly piety of the world of Margery Kempe. In describing the last days of Henry VII, Fisher is most impressed by the king's extravagant devotion, the 'mervaylous compassyon & flowe of teres', weeping and sobbing, 'by the pace of thre quarters of an hour' with which Henry received the sacrament of penance. Two days before he died, the king desired the blessed sacrament to be brought to him and, though he was too weak to receive communion when the monstrance was brought to his bed,

he with such a reverence, with so many knockynges & betynges of his brest, with so quycke & lyfely a countenance, with so desyrous an herte made his humble obeyaunce therunto, & with soo grete humblenes & devocyon kyssed not the selfe place where the blessed body of our lorde was conteyned, but the lowest parte the fote of the monstraunt, that all that stode aboute hym scarcly myght conteyne them from teres & wepynge.

In all this Henry features as a type of the penitent sinner, whose assurance comes from the ministrations of Holy Church, the prayers of the saints, the mute eloquence of monstrance and image. After describing Henry's devotion to the crucifix on the day of his death, 'kyssynge it, & betynge ofte his brest', Fisher asks, 'Who may thynke that in this maner was not perfyte fayth, who may suppose that by this maner of delynge he faythfully beleved not that the eare of almyghty God was open unto hym & redy to here hym crye for mercy . . .'[26] There is no hint of irony here, despite the fact that the sermon operates at a variety of levels, and that the insistence on Henry's role as the penitent sinner is very deliberately used by Fisher to criticise the corruptions and sinfulness of his reign. For all Fisher's distrust of the pomp and the politics of the powerful, Henry's religion is here taken at face value, because it is Fisher's own religion that is being described.[27]

Similarly in the month's mind sermon for the Lady Margaret, it is her exemplary and entirely traditional piety that is commended. Fisher praises her devotion to the daily Office, her pious reading and translations, her zeal for special saints – Nicholas, Anthony, Mary Magdalene, Katherine – her daily hearing of 'four or fyve' masses, the 'stations' or visits she made to privileged and indulgenced altars and shrines, her recitation of the rosary, her devout confessions and houselling, her hair shirt and other mortifications, her generosity to Christ in the person of the poor, her readiness to go as a washerwoman for the troops on any future crusade. The educational foundations for which now she is chiefly remembered, and with which Fisher himself was so intimately and passionately involved, are produced primarily as evidence that she had true faith, for her Preachers were to 'publysshe the doctryne & fayth of cryste Ihesu' and her colleges 'to maytayn his fayth & doctryne'; they are mentioned in the same context as her chantry foundation in Westminster, where three priests were to 'praye for her perpetually'.[28]

The works addressed to Fisher's half-sister, Elizabeth White, an enclosed nun at Dartford, are equally traditional in form and content. The *Spirituall Consolation* is a dramatic monologue placed in the mouth of a sinner 'sodainly prevented by death', and is designed to act as a *memento mori* and an incentive to timely repentance. Not surprisingly, it contains some of Fisher's bleakest writing about the human condition, but despite some passages with a superficially autobiographical ring to them[29] it is essentially a formal exercise in the tradition of the rhetorical *memento mori*, of a sort that persisted on both sides of the Reformation divide throughout the early-modern period.[30] *The Wayes to Perfect Religion* is both more attractive and more interesting. The idiosyncratic conceit with which it opens, 'a comparison betweene the lyfe of Hunters, and the lyfe of religious persons', is not one of Fisher's most persuasive pieces of writing, but the work as a whole is a good example of what is arguably the most influential single genre in medieval English devotional writing, the treatise of counsel for a religious sister. The most famous representative of this genre is the *Ancren Riwle*, but other examples abound, notably in the works of Richard Rolle and Walter Hilton.[31] Fisher's work is closest in spirit to Rolle, and concludes with a series of short ejaculatory prayers to the name of Jesus, a devotion which for Fisher, as for many of his English contemporaries, had a special attraction, and whose main English source was Rolle himself. The work also contains Fisher's most eloquent and lyrical celebration of the beauty of Christ, and of the world that he has made – 'Behold the Rose, the Lillie, the Vyolet, beholde the Pecockes, the Feasaunt, the Popingaye: Behold all the other creatures of this world: All these were of his making, all there beautie and goodliness of hym they receyved it.'[32] Such sentiments should modify our perception of the 'life-denying' aspects of the tradition Fisher is held to represent.

Fisher's appropriation of the rich and varied tradition of late medieval piety is a creative one. If it is true that he is utterly at home in the devotional world he inherited, his deployment of its forms suggests not a plodding and dogged persistence in well-tried tracks, but a deliberate and confident redirection of

212

traditional materials: some of his best and most characteristic effects are achieved by manipulating classic and even hackneyed devotional topoi. The Good Friday sermon on the crucifix, one of his most moving works, is a sustained demonstration of this. Affective devotion to the passion of Christ, to the crucifix, the *imago pietatis* and related emblems stood at the heart of late-medieval religion. In his sermon Fisher presses almost every form of this devotion into service in what remains nevertheless a carefully controlled and shapely 'spiritual' exegesis of Ezekiel's scroll, written with 'lamentation and song and woe'. The central conceit is that Christ is the scroll, that the crucifix is a book, of which the upright and cross-bar are the boards, Christ's flesh and skin the parchment, the scourge-marks and thorn-pricks the writing, his five wounds the illuminated capitals, and so on. The conceit has a venerable ancestry in English devotion, ranging from the ubiquitous notion that images in general are 'laymen's books', to more specific precedents such as the Middle English combinations of devotional verses and symbolic passion images known as the 'Charters of Christ',[33] or such devotional writings as Rolle's *Meditations on the Passion* – 'More yit, sweet Ihesu, thy body is lyke a boke written al with rede ynke.'[34] Fisher daringly extends this image over the whole sermon, but prevents its fundamental artificiality from obtruding by ringing the changes continually on the ways in which the central image is unfolded. One of the most eloquent passages in the sermon invites the sinner to 'read' the message of the sufferings of Christ displayed in the crucifix.

Seest thou not his eyes, how they bee fylled with blood and bytter teares? Seest thou not his eares, how they be filled with blasphemous rebukes, and opprobrious wordes? Seest thou not his mouth, how in his dryghnesse they would have filled it with Asell and Gaule? . . . O most unkinde sinner, all this he suffred for thy sake . . .[35]

The details in this and similar passages are drawn from such compendia as Ludolph the Carthusian's *Vita Christi*, the pseudo-Bonaventuran *Meditationes Vitae Christi*, Nicholas Love's version of which was the most popular English book of the fifteenth century, and from the passion narrative in the *Legenda Aurea*. All three are ultimately indebted to St Bernard, and it was Bernard who originated the form which Fisher is using here, an adaptation of the *planctus Christi*, in which the sufferings of the crucified, usually placed in the mouth of the dying or dead Christ himself, are used to shame and urge hard-hearted sinners into repentance and compassion for the Lord who has endured so much for them.[36] The *planctus* dominated the passion piety of late-medieval English men and women, in such well-known lyrics as 'Wofully araid' and Hawes's 'Se ye be Kind'.[37] It had a direct liturgical source in the *Improperia* or 'reproaches' sung on Good Friday during the ceremony of 'creeping to the cross'. Fisher draws on all these resources, learned, devotional, and liturgical: much of the force of the sermon turns, for example, on his appeal to the visual impact of the crucifix which dominates the solemn liturgy of the day. Yet even these visual appeals to 'see' and 'behold' the crucifix, are filtered through the literary, devotional tradition. When, at the central point of the sermon, Fisher urges the fearful sinner to 'beholde earnestly the maner how thy saviour Iesu hanged on the Crosse', it is only at once to invoke a classic devotional passage from St Bernard:

Who may not be ravished to hope and confidence, if he consider the order of his body, his head bowing down to offer a kisse, hys armes spread to embrace us, hys handes bored thorow to make liberall giftes, his side opened to shewe unto us the love of his harte, his feete fastened with nayles, that he shall not starte away but abyde with us. And all his bodie stretched, forcesing him self to give it wholly unto us.[38]

This passage would have been familiar to most of Fisher's hearers, and to all of his readers. It occurs in countless devotional poems, in the passion narrative in the *Legenda Aurea*, and in such fifteenth-century treatises as *Dives and Pauper*. The passage was often used emotively rather than theologically – to arouse sympathy for and loving trust in Jesus. The appeal was to the will and emotions, rather than to the intellect. Fisher loses none of the emotional warmth implicit in the Bernardine exhortation, but, characteristically, he inserts some intellectual spine, and uses the text as the point of departure for an extended and theologically rich discussion of the atonement.[39]

The sermon similarly presses a whole range of highly charged popular devotional images into theological use, without sacrificing their emotional resonance. In every case the familiar image is developed beyond its predictable lines to force the hearer to enter more deeply into the meaning of the passion. The proximity to the cross of the Magdalene, conventional type of the convert prostitute, provides Fisher with an opportunity to reflect on the nakedness of Christ, and the way in which he takes on and absorbs the shame of human sexuality.[40] St Francis and his stigmata become a metaphor for the self-exploration of the converted sinner, and his assimilation to Christ, by reflection on the passion. And the special privilege of the saint in receiving the outward tokens of conformity to the crucified becomes the occasion for a striking and moving insistence on the universality of Christian discipleship. The stigmata, Fisher admits, are a 'singular gyfte', 'not common to be looked for of other persons'. But whoever will dwell on the meaning of the cross may, like Francis, come to a 'great knowledge of both Christ & of him selfe'.

A man may easily say and thinke with him selfe (beholding in his hart the Image of the Crucifixe) who art thou, and who am I. This everie person both ryche and poore, may thinke, not onely in the church here, but in every other place, and in hys businesse where about hee goeth. Thus the poore laborer maye thinke, when he is at plough earying his grounde, and when he goeth to hys pastures to see hys cattayle, or when hee is sittyng at home by his fire side, or els when he lyeth in hys bed waking and can not sleepe. Likewise the rich man may do in his business . . . and the poore women also . . . when they be spinning of their rooks, or serving of their pullens . . . It is an easy thynge for any man or woman to make these two questions wyth them selfe. O my Lord that wouldest dye for me upon a Crosse, how noble and excellent arte thou? & agayne, how wretched and myserable am I?[41]

That passage raises in an acute way the question of the extent of Fisher's 'medievalism' as opposed to his 'humanism' with which this paper began. The picture of farm labourers meditating on the passion at the plough, or of business men in their counting-houses and poor women at their spinning similarly engaged recalls the alert reader at once to one of the most familiar passages in Erasmus, that section of the *Paraclesis* where, quoting Jerome, Erasmus foresees the day when labourers at the plough will sing passages from scripture, and all, even the Turk, may have ready access to the word of God.[42] The similarities between the two passages point up the contrasts. Erasmus wants to distribute bibles: Fisher sees in the crucifix a more universal book, which can be read by those who are no clerks:

Thus who that list with a meeke harte, and a true fayth, to muse and to marvayle of this most wonderfull booke (I say of the crucifixe) hee shall come to more fruitefull knowledge, then many other which dayly study upon their common bookes. This booke may suffice for the studie of a true Christian man, all the dayes of his life.[43]

These sentiments would not be out of place in the first book of the *Imitation of Christ*, and indeed are by no means remote from Erasmus's own teaching. He too wanted men and women to meditate the cross, and long before Fisher's sermon was preached had devoted a section of his seminal work, the *Enchiridion Militis Christiani*, to saying so. But in that work he expressly repudiated as a way of doing this the very pattern of medieval passion piety which Fisher here so triumphantly celebrates and renews. We must 'exercise' ourselves in the cross, according to Erasmus,

not after the commune manner / as some men repete dayly the hystory of the passion of Chryst / or honour the ymage of the crosse . . . or at certayn houres so call to remembrance Chrystes punysshment that they may have compassyon and wepe for hym with natural affection / as they wolde for a man that is very iuste, and suffreth great wronge unworthely.

This, he insists, 'is not the true fruyte of that tree: nevertheless, let it in ye meane season be the mylke of ye soules, which be yongelynges and weyke in Chryst'.[44] On that note of condescension Erasmus waves away not only popular superstitions and more respectable para-liturgical devotion, but also the whole Bernardine and Bonaventuran tradition of passion piety, as 'mylke for yonglynges'. The dismissal is rooted, at least in part, in Erasmus's neoplatonic distrust of the physical and merely external. Its consequence, however, is the creation of a two-tier image of the church, in which there is a spiritual elite who experience true devotion, and 'yongelynges and weyke in Chryst' who grub about in the foothills. For all his undoubted clericalism, this stratification is completely absent in Fisher's devotional world. The crucifix speaks as eloquently, and as demandingly, to the unlettered and the simple as to scholar, prelate or clerk. As he says elsewhere,

let no creature thynke in hymselfe & saye, I am not within holy ordres, I am not professed to any religyon. All we be crysten people, take hede in what degre we stande, what state is it to be a crysten man or woman, the least crysten persone the poorest & moost lowe in degre is nygh in kynrede to almyghty god, he is his sone and his heyre of the kyndome of heven, broder unto Jhesu cryst aand bought with his precyous blode.[45]

This, of course, was Erasmus's view also, but in practice Erasmus's vision of the Church entailed an elitism of the educated. He viewed the popular religious culture as intrinsically crude and misleading, a jumble from which the spiritually discriminating would select only what is wholesome. Before this discriminating elite could become the Christian democracy, therefore, the elaborate and resonant symbol-system of late-medieval Catholicism needed to be stripped to something more austerely textual. Fisher would wholeheartedly have endorsed Erasmus's biblicism: his own preaching demonstrated his profound immersion in scripture, and it was to 'a little booke in his hande, which was a New Testament lying by him', that he turned for support and guidance in the last minutes of his life. But the scripture for Fisher was in no way at odds either with the tradition and ritual of the Church or with popular devotion. For Fisher the real sickness of the Church was not that it had a corrupt piety, but that it had not enough piety. He sought therefore not the stripping and simplification of Christian life by the critical use of the scriptures, but the increase of traditional piety by any means, including and above all scriptural preaching, but equally drawing on all the other resources of the symbolic and sacramental world of medieval Catholicism. Given the long-term problems of Tudor literacy, and the richness and vividness of Fisher's manipulation of that symbolic and sacramental system, it does not seem obvious that his was an intrinsically inferior or less hopeful religious strategy than that of Erasmus. Certainly we are not dealing here with any straightforward contrast between 'medieval' and 'Renaissance', but between a man who retains a commitment to and confidence in the symbolic structure of Catholicism, and one who does not. We shall return to this issue in due course.[46]

In arguing for the essentially positive and creative relation of Fisher to his religious inheritance I have of course been conceding and documenting Lewis's contention that he was a medieval figure. My point, however, is that to conceive that relationship as 'representative' is to obscure the dynamic element in Fisher's work: if he never challenges the bounds of the religious conventions of his day, he is rarely content simply to repeat what he has inherited. If he is 'medieval', he is so in the same sense that Hieronymus

Bosch is medieval, simultaneously original and a man of his time. Indeed, the comparison with Bosch can be pushed some way, for there is much in Fisher's writing that reminds us of the painter's work. The famous and terrifying vision at the opening of the sermon on Psalm 51, in which Fisher portrays the condition of mankind, perched in the rickety bucket of mortality over a pit of ravening demons, held up only by a thin cord in the hand of a God we have striven to make our enemy, could come straight out of a Bosch altarpiece. So too could the passage in which Fisher describes the man who has allowed himself to despair, and so has fallen into the 'depe pyt desperacyon', 'whose mouth is stopped up with a grete stone', and where he is gradually 'dygested & incorporate in to the substance of the devyll even as mete when it is dygested . . For amonges all synnes desperacyon is the thinge that moost maketh us devyllysche.' And, indeed, the Bosch-like image of the soul devoured and digested by despair allows us to see Fisher's imagination actually at work, weaving a vividly concrete and complex image out of simpler elements. The sermon on Psalm 129, Vulgate numbering, opens with an account of the whale devouring Jonah, develops by way of the devil in I Peter 5:8 seeking whom he may devour, and so produces the image of the sinner digested by the demonic sin of despair.[47]

There are, of course, ways in which Fisher's 'medievalism' narrows and limits him. For all the attractive human warmth of his portrayal of the piety of the dying Henry VII, it is impossible not to be struck by its characteristically late-medieval overdependence on *feeling*. True devotion must be tangible, felt along the pulse, it must give rise to sighs and weeping, whether of joy or of penitence. This sort of emotionalised piety was to be passed on into the Reformation by Cranmer and others in such writings as the General Confession in the *Book of Common Prayer*.[48] Its limitations are most obvious in a hysterical exponent like Margery Kempe, but they are uncomfortable even in so austere a figure as Fisher. The weakness is perhaps at its most striking in Fisher's Latin treatise, *De Necessitate Orandi*.[49] Once again this is a work in a clearly recognisable tradition and genre. Composed probably for a *dévot* readership, it is a treatise on mental prayer, drawing heavily on the English mystical tradition of Walter Hilton and the *Cloud of Unknowing*. Its basic teaching is that prayer at its highest is a convergence in wordless and imageless love on man's highest good, the God who draws us to himself, beyond the created order. Fisher is indebted, in phrase and thought, to Hilton, and to the teaching of the pseudo-Denys, in the warmed up and derationalised form in which it was current in medieval European devotion. The writings of the Victorines and of St Bernard also lie behind those passages in which Fisher uses the Song of Songs as the medium for his discussion of the soul's union with God. The work has rightly been praised by Surtz for its insistent emphasis on the prevenient grace of God, and the gratuitousness of salvation. Throughout it, Fisher stresses the overwhelming abundance of

God's love for us, stirring us to prayer before we even think of praying, enticing us to contemplate the splendour of his light, to taste his 'sweetness', and, in an erotic image rare in his English works but given extended scope here, to kiss the indescribable delights of his lips.[50] There is no doubting the depth of feeling in such passages, and the treatise gives us an unrivalled and rather startling insight into the nature of Fisher's own prayer. The fervid language of spiritual kisses, full of sweetness, ardour and delight, which is characteristic of this work is not, of course, the sign of personal aberration, but represents a convention deriving from Richard and William of St Victor, and above all from St Bernard. In English piety it can be traced back to the *Ancren Wisse*, but its chief English exponent was Richard Rolle of Hampole, the Yorkshire hermit and mystic whose cult was such a powerful force in England in the fourteenth and fifteenth centuries.[51] Rolle's works and influence were propagated in Fisher's day chiefly by the Carthusian order, with which Fisher, like More, had close connections, and in this treatise he draws heavily on his fellow-Yorkshireman's teaching. But it is here that a disturbing limitation appears. Both Hilton and the author of the *Cloud* had criticised Rolle, or his disciples, for excessive reliance on feeling and emotion in prayer.[52] Fisher, in following Rolle, shows no awareness of these dangers. For him, the chief aim of prayer is to nourish and maintain the fervour of charity in the soul. By 'fervour' he seems to mean an emotionally experienced ardour and heat. This 'prayer of the heart' is worth more than any number of vocal prayers, though these have their place: anyone who feels such fervour in prayer should cast aside his vocal prayers and follow the promptings of the Spirit, '*with weeping and sighing*'. Moreover, since this fervour is the object of prayer, there is little point praying when it has fled. When this happens, for example through weariness, we should 'at once give over' our prayer, contenting ourselves with what we have already 'acquired' from it, and go about our other business.[53] Fisher is at pains to distinguish the sweetness of prayer from the sweetness of the senses: nevertheless, this unqualified linking of persistence in prayer with a particular mental and emotional state, and his apparent tendency to make the experience of these exalted feelings the pinnacle of prayer, contrasts dramatically with Hilton's more sober teaching that we should 'beware of fervours' and 'thou shalt never pray the less when grace of devotion is withdrawn . . . But then it is most acceptable and pleasing to God . . .'[54] Fisher's guidance is, by the standards of the fourteenth century masters, over-concerned with affective experience, even soft-centred. He has taken up the weakest part of Rolle's teaching and failed, in transmitting it, to register the warnings of Rolle's wiser successors. It is impossible, on this score, to acquit him of what a recent historian of medieval spirituality, with characteristic Dominican rigour, has branded as 'devotionalism'.[55]

But Fisher is rarely in this way the victim of his background: his use of medieval categories and devotional topoi almost invariably extends our perception both of them and of him. In Fisher the devotional repertoire of the late middle ages is alive and well, putting out new branches and bearing new fruit, and he is in no sense a backward-looking writer. Perhaps the most intriguing example of this vitality of old devotional motifs in Fisher's life and writing is that of the head of John the Baptist.

The Baptist is an obvious scriptural paradigm for the pious mind seeking to 'place' Fisher in the divine scheme. Name apart, the bishop of Rochester himself is a sufficiently Johannine figure, emaciated and clad in hair-cloth, calling a generation to penitence. Had there been no closer similarities than these, even a moderately imaginative biographer might have invoked the comparison. In fact Fisher himself was intensely conscious of rather more pressing parallels, and drew attention to them. In the section on marriage in his treatise in defence of Henry VIII's *Assertio Septem Sacramentorum* Fisher had declared how much the death of John the Baptist weighed with him to establish the sanctity of marriage. John had rebuked Herod for his adulterous and forbidden union with Herodias, showing that the violation of marriage was a worse sin than many more obvious potential targets of prophetic wrath.[56] This controversial point was thrown off in 1524 as no more than an aside. Within five years, however, it had begun to assume for Fisher a far more existential urgency. In June 1529 he spoke before Campeggio's legatine court in defence of the marriage between Catherine and Henry. He startled his hearers by declaring his readiness to die in defence of the marriage, as John the Baptist had lain down his life, for that saint 'regarded it as impossible for him to die more gloriously than in the cause of marriage'.[57] There was more to this remark than met the eye; the king's supporters thought they detected an insulting comparison between Henry and Herod, and the king himself deeply resented the implication of Fisher's speech.[58]

The subsequent confrontation between bishop and king, and Fisher's ultimate fate, made the elaboration of the biblical comparison inevitable. Fisher's earliest biographer devotes much space to it, and in one of the earliest revisions of that early life of Fisher it is claimed that Anne Boleyn, playing both Herodias and Salome to Fisher's John the Baptist, sent for his head after his execution, and mocked and abused it, cutting her hand on one of the teeth, a wound which, of course, never healed.[59] The story is patently false, and might have been left there had not Fr Bridgett, Fisher's first modern biographer, noticed a curious item on the inventory of Fisher's belongings made by the king's commissioners in 1534. In the long gallery of Fisher's palace the commissioners noted 'A St John's head standing at the end of the altar'.[60] Bridgett was excited by this object. We know Fisher customarily to have placed a skull before him when he said mass or sat at table. Had this head of John the Baptist taken the place of that skull? 'This emblem of royal tyranny and saintly constancy Fisher kept ever before him when offering the Holy Sacrifice. Had God given him any presentiment of the kind of death by which he should glorify him?'[61] We need not suppose so. Carved and painted heads of St John the Baptist, usually in alabaster, and normally including, below the head on its salver, a small representation of Christ as Man of Sorrows or Lamb of God, were almost certainly the most common devotional objects in fifteenth-century England, far more so than crucifixes or images of the Virgin.[62] Their precise symbolism is obscure, but it was probably in part eucharistic, and a number of Corpus Christi guilds used them as emblems.[63] But they were already old-fashioned by the 1520s, occurring less and less frequently in the inventories of the goods of pious lay folk in this period. Fisher's retention of one on his altar shows a characteristic conservatism rather than a visionary precognition of his martyrdom, though clearly the crisis of the divorce may well have sharpened his sense of the appositeness of the old image.[64] However that may be, there is one final piece of evidence which prevents us from dismissing as mere pious fancy the idea that the motif of John the Baptist provides an aid to understanding the mind of Fisher. The evidence is at first sight unrelated to the divorce, since it long pre-dates it, but it does bear directly on Fisher's perception of Henry, and throws at least a sideways light onto the meaning of the Baptist's image for Fisher. It occurs in Fisher's sermon on the Field of the Cloth of Gold, preached on All Saints Day 1520, but unpublished till 1532.

The sermon is justly famous for its magnificent treatment of a favourite Tudor theme, the vanity of human glory and greatness. Fisher is therefore showing once again his mastery of a traditional mode, and the sermon is indeed unrivalled in the building up of its effects.[65] The treatment of the Field of the Cloth of Gold begins colloquially, and proceeds to magnificence:

I doubte not but ye have herde of many goodly syghtes which were shewed of late beyond the see, with moche Ioy and pleasure worldly. Was it not a great thynge within so shorte a space, to se three great Prynces of this worlde? I mean the Emperour, and the kyng our mayster, and the Frenche king. And eche of these thre in so great honour, shewing theyr royalty, shewyng theyr rychesse, shewyng theyr power; with eche of theyr noblesse appoynted and apparrayled in ryche clothes, in sylkes, velvettes, clothes of golde, & such other precyouse arayments . . . such daunsynges, such armonyes, such dalyaunce, and so many pleasaunt pastimes . . . soo ryche and goodly tentys, such Iustynges, such tournays, and such feats of warre.[66]

But at length, Fisher tells us, many 'had a lothsomes and a fastydyousnes' of such pleasures, and longed to be at home, for, 'by the reason of them, great money was spent, many great mennes coffers were emptyed, & many were brought to a great ebbe of poverty'. Covetousness and envy were the moral fruits of sumptuousness, and many 'for these pleasures were the worse, bothe in their bodyes & in their soules'. This generalised moralising about the courts of kings is given unforgettable particularity and vividness by Fisher in his well-known description of the dust storms that enveloped the parched

English camp and enshrouded all its finery.[67] For the glory of humanity is counterfeit, borrowed from other creatures to cover 'the wounde of shame'. Take away the 'glystering garment, take away the clothe of golde . . . & what dyfference is betwyxt an Emperour and another pore man?'[68] This begins to be trenchant, and unlikely to please a king to hear or read, but Fisher pushes it further. Kings are not merely mortal as other 'pore men'; they are in perpetual danger of dazzling themselves to damnation. It is at this point that we begin to hear resonances of the Baptist theme, for now Fisher introduces King Herod:

> The Actes of the Apostels tellyth of Kyng Herode, that he in ryche apparrell shewed hym self upon a tyme unto the people & they for his glystering apparrell & goodly arncyon, magnyfyed & praysed hym soveraynely as though he had been a god: but . . . almyghty god . . . stroke hym with a sore sykenesse, whereupon he dyed . . . Kynges & Emperours, all be but men, all be but mortall.[69]

The introduction of the figure of King Herod into a discourse on the fragility and vanity of human glory is by no means arbitrary: the surprising of a boastful and vainglorious tyrant Herod by sudden death is the theme of one of the most vivid of the *Ludus Coventriae* cycle of mystery plays. The Herod being referred to here, however, is not John the Baptist's Herod, but Herod Agrippa, the third of the Herods mentioned in the New Testament. Fisher no doubt would have been aware of this, but the three Herods, all of whom feature as enemies of Christ and his Church, were commonly conflated (as the three Mary's of *De Unica Magdalena* were), and Fisher is certainly here drawing on that common fund of imagery.[70] Yet the image of Herod in his sermon has a pointedness lacking from even the vividest occurrences of the theme in the medieval tradition as a whole, for Fisher is not talking about kings in general, but 'I mean the Emperour, and the kyng our mayster, and the Frenche kynge'. And lest anyone should fail to notice, Fisher now develops his sermon in a startlingly blunt way. The whole discourse to this point had concentrated on contrasting the transient glories of earth with the eternal glory of heaven. From things, Fisher now turns to persons. In heaven, among the saints, we shall see a more glorious court than that of the Field of the Cloth of Gold. Above all, we shall see

> the excellency of that Gloryous Trynytye, the Father, the Son, and the holy Ghoost . . . These thre, though they be thre dyvers persons yet they be but one God perfytely knyt togyder in a perfyte amytye, in one love, in one wyll, in one wysdom, in one power inseparably. The thre Prynces of whom we spake of before, were nat so: but they had dyvers wylles, dyvers councels, & no perdurable amyty, as after that dyd well appere. These Prynces were mortall and unstable, and so theyr wylles dyd chaunge & nat abyde.[71]

The directness with which the political manoeuvrings of Henry and his fellow monarchs are made the anti-type of the wisdom and 'amytye' of heaven adds a dramatic prophetic aspect to the introduction of the figure of Herod which would otherwise be lacking. The whole sermon breathes a profound distrust of the framework of human politics which in Fisher goes beyond moralising generalities to attach itself concretely to named individuals. Here already is the genesis of the identification of Henry with Herod, and, by extension, of himself with the Baptist: the subconscious movement towards a full identification of his role with that of the Baptist during the divorce crisis becomes more explicable. Indeed, it is possible that we have here more than the subconscious origins of the parallel, but actually its fullest public expression. This sermon was preached in the autumn of 1520. It was not published, however, till 1532, when it was printed by William Rastell, who was Thomas More's nephew and publisher, and like his uncle a staunchly pro-papal Catholic. The sermon therefore has the appearance of an opposition publication. For why did Fisher publish a sermon preached a dozen years before at this juncture? The inevitable outcome of the divorce proceedings was by now evident to all, and the king's onslaught on the Church, which Fisher prominently resisted, well under way. Elsewhere in this volume, Professor Scarisbrick draws attention to the vigour of Fisher's attempts in 1532 to mount a theological critique of Henry's anti-clerical measures, as well as to encourage political opposition. The Nun of Kent was at the height of her influence, and had long since been predicting the king's death or dethronement if he divorced Catherine and remarried. Fisher had undoubted sympathy for the Nun, and had at least an open mind about her prophecies. It is difficult to believe that these facts were irrelevant to his decision to permit the publication of this sermon against the presumption of earthly kings, with its story of the grisly end of Herod, who had set himself over against the Church and usurped the place of God. The sermon shows signs of revision: but even if the outspoken criticism of monarchs, and the Herod passage, were there in 1520, their publication at this precise point can hardly have been anything but deliberate. Thus a series of medieval devotional commonplaces on the theme of transience and the vanity of earthly rulers has been drawn into an unforgettable and complex cluster, in which Fisher's own self-perception, and the crisis confronting the English Church in the early 1530s, play a concealed but real part. The resulting work is different in power and quality from the conventional materials out of which it is made.[72]

It has been the principal contention of this paper that if we are to describe Fisher's spirituality as 'medieval', it is vital not to allow that label to conceal from us the breadth of vision and imaginative creativity with which it is imbued. Whatever Fisher's limitations as a spiritual guide, his religion was not the played-out and backward-looking thing that the term might be taken to imply. His religion gives no grounds for regarding its replacement by a more dynamic and 'modern' protestantism as inevitable. In that sense it is provincialism to see Fisher's religion as a thing of the middle ages, for most of its central emphases had a long and vigorous future ahead of them in the Counter-Reformation. And, if we can point to his tendency towards 'devotionalism' as a weakness of the late medieval tradition, that very tendency to 'emotionalise' piety was not done away by the reformers, but was entrenched by them in the charter document of the English Reformation, the *Book of Common Prayer*. If Fisher is to be judged medieval, so, for example, must Cranmer.[73]

But even this statement of the case does not take us far enough. We may call Fisher 'medieval', provided that we do not imagine that in doing so we rule out his claim to be also a Renaissance figure. In a recent discussion of the spiritual patrimony of Thomas More, Professor McConica has reminded us of the rootedness of More's personal religious outlook in the devotional atmosphere represented by the Charterhouses of London and Sheen, and by the Bridgettine house of Syon.[74] At Sheen the English tradition of Rolle and Hilton was dominant. The monks at Syon were deeply schooled in a corpus of fourteenth- and fifteenth-century spiritual classics which included some works by Rolle and Hilton, but was more notable for the many continental influences such as the *Dialogues* of St Catherine of Siena, and the *Imitation of Christ* and other works of the *Devotio Moderna*. In the early sixteenth century the community at Syon in particular was dedicated to making this essentially monastic and ascetical piety available to a wider audience of devout lay people. The monks chiefly involved, John Fewterer, Richard Whytford, William Bonde, and Richard Reynolds, were graduates, theologians and linguists, and all of them well acquainted with the new learning. The libraries they brought with them to Syon contained not only the medieval devotional classics – Ludolf the Carthusian, Bernard, Bonaventura, and the rest – but also a wide range of Renaissance writings and translations. Works by Ficino, Valla, Erasmus, Poggio, Platina, Pico della Mirandola, Petrarch, Lefèvre, Reuchlin, Savonarola, Linacre, Colet, More himself, were there, as well as a comprehensive range of Greek and Latin Fathers and pagan classics in recent editions.[75]

The spirituality of these men was precisely that of More, and of Fisher, whose friends they were; like them they were to be prominent in opposition to the king's religious policies, most famously Reynolds, the martyred 'Angel of Syon'. The majority of them were Cambridge graduates and former fellows of colleges. Most were from Pembroke, but there were products of Fisher's colleges, John's, Christ's and Queens' too. Their reading closely matches that represented by the explicit citations and the influences evident in Fisher's works. Like him they held together a loyalty to the affective piety of the middle ages with an openness to the resources of the new learning, and a concern for religious reform and lay religious formation. Their religion, like that of Fisher, was unselfconsciously traditional, yet they laid

223

out many of the lines along which later Tudor devotion, Catholic or protestant, would develop. Their most recent historian has argued both for their 'modernity of outlook' and 'fervently humanistic' scholarship, and, at the same time, for their pronounced theological and devotional traditionalism. Perhaps the most characteristic member of this group was Richard Whytford, the 'poor wretch of Syon', certainly the most important Tudor devotional writer before Becon.[76] Whytford, a product of Queens' and friend of Erasmus, was the protégé of Fisher's friend and former patron, Richard Fox, who had founded the first humanist establishment at Oxford, Corpus Christi College. It is entirely of a piece with the devotional attitudes of this group that so explicitly humanistic a venture as Corpus should take its name from the liturgical mystery which lay at the heart of medieval piety. Whytford's publications include translations of the rule of St Augustine and of St Bernard's *De Praecepto*: they also include a treatise which in both title and content anticipated much of the essence of later English devotional developments. *Werke for Housholders* was a manual for lay folk designed to provide a piety suited to others than 'such persones as ben solytary and done lye alone by them selfe'. Its method and its tone were to be taken up and developed further by the reformers, more specifically by puritan devotional writers.[77]

It would not be difficult to present these men as essentially 'medieval' figures. William Bonde's *Pylgrimage of Perfection* (1526), John Fewterer's *Glasse or Myrrour of Christes Passion* (1534), and Whytford's *Pype or Tonne of the Lyfe of Perfection* (1532) are all attempts to distil the essence of the affective and ascetic tradition of monastic devotion: they are as full of devotional topoi and conventional imagery as the works of Fisher which we have examined. And just as much as Fisher they resisted the tide of religious change. Whytford was deeply troubled by the spread of heresy, and polemic against the Reformation invades even the most tranquil of his devotional writing.[78]

Yet this is only half the story. If these monastic conservatives were deeply committed to the transmission of the sacramental, churchly and ascetic piety of the late middle ages, it was also their intention to transmit it to an ever widening lay audience, using all the resources of the press, and in the vernacular. They were concerned not merely with the transmission of the tradition, but with its renewal. And just as much as Erasmus and Colet they were conscious of the ills of the church; their monastery was famed for its reformed and austerely observant character. Fisher wholly shared this reformist outlook, and an important and too little recognised element in his writings is his scarifying and pessimistic assessment of the moral and spiritual state of the Church of his own times. A number of writers on Fisher have drawn attention to the passage in which he contrasts the patristic period, when there were 'no chalyses of golde, but . . . many golden preestes', with the modern age, when things are reversed. It is, of course, a commonplace, taken from Gratian, furiously debated between More and Tyndale, and used, as Fisher used it, to castigate and lament the state of the contemporary Church, by Savonarola, a figure in whom Fisher was interested, and with whom he had much in common.[79] It is only one of many passages in which Fisher, like Savonarola and like Colet, lamented the decay of piety and the corruptions of the clergy. One such passage, in which Fisher denounced the spread of hypocrisy and 'feigned piety' in the Church, was considered too disturbing for a lay readership a hundred years on into the Counter-Reformation, and was omitted from the 1640 translation of the *De Necessitate Orandi*.[80]

In such a reformist yet traditionalist context, Fisher's educational foundations with the Lady Margaret, and his openness to the work of men like Reuchlin and Erasmus, need not be seen as in any sense at odds with his conservative and churchly piety. A correct perception of the importance of this Bridgettine circle liberates us from the crude polarities of 'medieval' and 'Renaissance', 'traditionalist' and 'reforming'. Neither protestants nor 'Erasmians', they were nevertheless participants in a new stirring within Tudor Catholicism. McConica has rightly contrasted the piety and the anthropology of More and the Bridgettines on the one hand with that of Erasmus on the other. Their vision of humanity and the Church was less optimistic, more deeply Augustinian than his, and, maybe, more cloistered. The regimen of hair-shirt and discipline, even when toned down and vernacularised by publicists like Whytford, would never have attracted large numbers of practitioners. Yet every bit as much as that of Erasmus, the religious vision and the practical piety of these men has a claim to be considered a manifestation of Renaissance, for they too, and Fisher along with them, sought the renewal of the church and of a more vital lay piety with the aid of biblical preaching, new learning and the press. The imposition of an 'Erasmian' strait-jacket as the only legitimate wear for any figure claiming humanist credentials serves unnecessarily to narrow the meaning of humanism, and to confuse analysis.[81] And, indeed, if one of the principal marks of Christian humanism was its concern to renew the faith of the Christian people as a whole, it could be argued without excessive paradox that on this matter at least Fisher's credentials can claim comparison with those of Erasmus. For, whatever the limitations of his ascetical austerity as a popular piety, Fisher's instinctive and creative empathy with the symbolic world of early-sixteenth-century Catholicism gives to his work a depth and resonance, and a multitude of points of contact with the piety of the simple and unlettered, about which Erasmus wrote much, but understood very little.

Notes

1 In addition to my co-editor, Brendan Bradshaw, I am grateful to Dr Geoffrey Nuttall, Professor John Stevens, and Mr Richard Rex, who all read and commented

helpfully on an earlier draft of this paper. C. S. Lewis, *English Literature in the Sixteenth Century, Excluding Drama* (Oxford, 1954), pp. 161–5.

2 See, for example, the recent writings surveyed in Brendan Bradshaw, 'The Controversial Sir Thomas More', *Journal of Ecclesiastical History*, 36 (1985), 535–69; see also the pertinent remarks by J. McConica, 'The Patrimony of Thomas More', in H. Lloyd Jones, Valerie Pearl and Blair Worden (eds.), *History and Imagination: Essays in Honour of H. R. Trevor Roper* (London 1981), pp. 56–71, esp. pp. 64ff; J. McConica, 'Northern Humanists before the Reformation', in Cheslyn Jones, Geoffrey Wainwright and Edward Yarnold (eds.), *The Study of Spirituality* (London, 1986), pp. 338–41; there is an excellent discussion of the relation of Fisher's biblical exegesis to the 'old learning' in J. W. Blench, *Preaching in England in the Late Fifteenth and Early Sixteenth Centuries* (Oxford, 1964), pp. 11–20.

3 See his revealing remarks on More's *De IV Novissimis*: 'The colours are too dark. *In the true late medieval manner* More forgets that to paint all black is much the same as not to paint at all. What was intended to be a rebuke of sin degenerates almost into a libel upon life . . .' (emphasis mine), Lewis, *English Literature*, p. 176.

4 T. E. Bridgett, *Life of Blessed John Fisher* (London, 1888), p. 15; *Life*, XII, 208, 194.

5 *Life*, X, 220–1. The obvious English Baroque comparison is with John Donne, and the funeral effigy he had made of himself in his shroud. Geoffrey Nuttall comments that it is perhaps characteristic of the difference between the two men themselves, and of their respective periods, that in choosing a *memento mori*, Fisher should prefer an emblem of the universality of death, Donne that of *himself* dead. There are a number of other revealing points of comparison between Donne and Fisher: Donne's *Devotions upon Emergent Occasions* are perhaps the closest parallel in English to Fisher's one literary exercise in the *memento mori* tradition, the *Spiritual Consolation* written for his half-sister, Elizabeth White (for which, see below p. 212), probably Fisher's least satisfactory work, and certainly his least consoling.

6 *Life*, XII, 169–70.

7 *EW*, pp. 358, 64; The key writings on this aspect of More are by Geoffrey Elton and Alistair Fox. Elton's principal contributions are 'Sir Thomas More and the Opposition to Henry VIII' (1968), *Studies in Tudor and Stuart Politics and Government* (Cambridge, 1974), I, 155–72; 'Thomas More, Councillor' (1972), *Studies*, I, 129–54; 'The Real Thomas More' (1980), *Studies*, III (1983), 344–55. Fox's interpretation is in *Thomas More: History and Providence* (Oxford, 1982). See Bradshaw, 'Controversial Sir Thomas More', pp. 535–6, 540–1; Lewis, *English Literature*, p. 163.

8 Lewis, *English Literature*, pp. 163–4; Blench, *Preaching*, p. 236.

9 Sears Jayne, *John Colet and Marsilio Ficino* (Oxford, 1963); Leland Miles, *John Colet and the Platonic Tradition* (London, 1962); J. B. Trapp, 'An English Late Medieval Cleric and Italian Thought: The Case of John Colet, Dean of St Paul's', in G. Kratzmauss and J. Simpson (eds.), *Medieval English Religious and Ethical Literature* (D. S. Brewer, Cambridge, 1986), pp. 233–50; Harry Porter, 'The Gloomy Dean and the Law; John Colet, 1466–1519', in G. V. Bennett and J. D.

Walsh (eds.), *Essays in Modern Church History in Memory of Norman Sykes* (London, 1966), pp. 18–43. On pessimism in Renaissance anthropology, see C. Trinkaus, 'Themes for a Renaissance Anthropology', in A. Chastel *et al., The Renaissance* (London, 1982), pp. 83–125, especially pp. 96–7.

10 *The Writings of John Bradford*, ed. Aubrey Townsend (Parker Society, Cambridge, 1848), p. 273.

11 Ibid., p. 334.

12 *EW*, pp. 127, 109–10.

13 Ibid., pp. 28–9.

14 Ibid., pp. 24–5, 28.

15 *Two Fruytfull Sermons of St John Fisher*, ed. Sr Marie Denise Sullivan (Notre Dame, Ind., Ph.D. thesis, 1961), p. 67.

16 *EW*, pp. 37–8, 97–8, 100–1.

17 Ibid., pp. 283, 29, 25–6.

18 Ibid., p. 43.

19 Ibid., pp. 113, 167–9.

20 Ibid., p. 99; on tears and late-medieval piety, see C. W. Atkinson, *Mystic and Pilgrim* (New York, 1983), pp. 58ff. Cf. Blench, *Preaching*, p. 247; and see also John Longland, *Sermones Ioannis Longlandi* (London, 1518) (*STC* 16797), fo. 68, on the ideal confession – 'sit completa, sit humilis atque *lacrymabilis*' (my emphasis). The texts of the mass for the gift of tears are in *Missale ad Usum Insignis et Praeclarae Ecclesiae SARUM*, ed. F. H. Dickinson (Burntisland, 1883; Gregg reprint 1969), p. 819*; for Fisher's tears at mass, *Life*, X, 220. But this is a devotional habit by no means confined to the middle ages – both Ignatius Loyola and Philip Neri were noted for their weeping at mass.

21 *Opera*, cols. 1456–7. And for Fisher's doctrine of penance, and the importance of the Magdalene for it, see Richard Rex, 'The polemical theologian', above, pp. 119–20. See also Rex's remarks on the role of private revelations in Fisher's thought, ibid., p. 116.

22 *EW*, pp. 182, 283; cf. G. Ryan & H. Ripperger (eds.) *The Golden Legend* (Salem, 1969), pp. 62, 99–102, 480–1.

23 Wynken de Worde printed seven editions before 1529; see H. S. Bennett, *English Books and Readers, 1475 to 1557* (Cambridge, 1970), p. 250. On the contents of the Primers, Helen C. White, *The Tudor Books of Private Devotion* (Wisconsin, 1951), pp. 52ff.

24 Savonarola's sermon on Psalm 51 is printed in *Three Primers*, ed. E. Burton (Oxford, 1834), pp. 130–66. This is a 'reforming' Primer of 1535: White, *Tudor Books*, pp. 91, 96. For Longland's sermons, Blench, *Preaching*, pp. 23ff.

25 A comparison of Longland's sermons with Fisher's is instructive. They share the traditional medieval exegesis – see, for a typical example, their exposition of the meaning of the four rivers of paradise: Longland, *Sermones*, fos. 85b–86a; *EW*, p. 34. Longland's doctrine of purgatory is at least as severe as Fisher's, and Longland supports it with reference both to Thomas Aquinas and St Bonaventura: *Sermones*, fos. 6–7b; *EW*, p. 10. Longland uses the penitential psalms, as Fisher does, as an opportunity to expound the penitential teaching of the Church, with no more sense of anachronism: *Sermones*, fos. 55–9. However, he is much less restrained than Fisher in introducing a whole range of Catholic teaching into his exegesis

of the texts, as in the excursus on indulgences (fos. 61ff), and relics (fos. 406ff). And there is nothing in Fisher to match the sheer horror and panic of Longland's treatment of hell – 'O palpabiles tenebras, o tenebras intolerabiles ignis aeterni . . . Cruciabuntur enim die ac nocte in saecula saeculorum' (fos. 3a–6).

26 *EW*, pp. 272–5. Compare this picture of Henry's devotion to the Blessed Sacrament with what is said of Fisher's own in Rex, 'The polemical theologian', above, pp. 00–00. Rex also discusses the role of the sacraments as sources of assurance, above, pp. 00.

27 The funeral sermon, in emphasising Henry's penitence, implicitly underlines his guilt, and Fisher specifically discusses, for example, Henry's resolve to effect a 'true reformacyon of al them that were offycers & mynystres of his lawes', so that '*from hens forward*' (my emphasis) justice might be done, *EW*, p. 271. See also, below, pp. 221–2. For a rather different sort of discussion of the historical implications of Fisher's account of Henry's repentance, see Geoffrey Elton, 'Henry VII: Rapacity and Remorse', in *Studies in Tudor and Stuart Politics and Government* (Cambridge, 1974), I, 45–65.

28 *EW*, pp. 298–309.

29 Notably the passage in which he asserts the futility of 'buylding of Colleges' and 'makyng of Sermons' for those who have not made spiritual provision for the hour of death, *EW*, p. 362. But the speaker's repeated insistence on his own total unpreparedness contradicts everything we know about Fisher's daily piety, and seems different in kind from the sense of unworthiness in the presence of a holy God which we would expect from a saint, and which can be seen in the manuscript prayer by Fisher preserved in the Public Record Office, and printed as an appendix to E. E. Reynolds, *St John Fisher* (London, 1955).

30 A. C. Southern, *Elizabethan Recusant Prose 1559–1582* (London, 1950), pp. 190–3. See above, note 5, for reference to the best-known seventeenth-century example, Donne's *Devotions upon Emergent Occasions*.

31 The classic treatment is R. W. Chambers, *On the Continuity of English Prose from Alfred to More and his School* (Early English Text Society, original series, no. 191a, Oxford, 1932).

32 It is worth comparing Fisher's work with Rolle's *Ego Dormio et Cor Meum*, in *Selected Works of Richard Rolle*, ed. G. H. Heseltine (London, 1930), pp. 89–100, which concludes with a similar series of petitions in the form of a 'song' to the Holy Name. For Fisher's devotion to the Holy Name of Jesus, see *Life*, X, 221; for the passage cited in the text, see *EW*, p. 376.

33 R. Woolf, *The English Religious Lyric in the Middle Ages* (Oxford, 1968), pp. 210–11.

34 *English Writings of Richard Rolle*, ed. Hope Emily Allen (Oxford, 1931), p. 36.

35 *EW*, pp. 400–1.

36 J. A. W. Bennett, *The Poetry of the Passion* (Oxford, 1982), pp. 32–61. Fisher explicitly invokes Bernard and the *planctus* tradition, *EW*, p. 401. See also Douglas Gray, *Themes and Images in the Medieval English Religious Lyric* (London, 1972), pp. 18–30, 122–45.

37 R. T. Davies, *Medieval English Lyrics: A Critical Anthology* (London, 1966), nos. 106, 152.

38 *EW*, p. 411. Bennett discusses the origin of the passage, *Poetry of the Passion*, pp. 46–7.

39 *Dives and Pauper*, ed. P. H. Barnum (Early English Text Society, original series, no. 275, Oxford, 1976), vol. I (1), 84–5; Longland also uses this passage, *Sermones*, fo. 19a.

40 *EW*, pp. 416–17.

41 Ibid., pp. 391–2.

42 *Christian Humanism and the Reformation: Desiderius Erasmus, Selected Writings*, ed. and trans. J. C. Olin (New York, 1965), pp. 96–7.

43 *EW*, p. 390.

44 Erasmus, *Enchiridion Militis Christiani. An English Version* (the 1534 English translation), ed. A. M. O'Donnell (Early English Text Society, original series, no. 282, Oxford, 1981), p. 178.

45 *EW*, p. 159.

46 *Life*, XII, 192–3.

47 *EW*, pp. 90–1. Fisher used the same image of the soul suspended over a pit, but without the vividness or menace, in *De Necessitate Orandi, Opera*, col. 1708; *EW*, p. 207.

48 Below, n. 73.

49 I have worked from the text in *Opera* (above, n. 23), and have referred to the English translation produced at Paris in 1640, *A Treatise of Prayer and of the Fruits and Manner of Prayer. By the Most Reverend Father in God IOHN FISHER . . . translated into English by R.A.B.* The translation of 1560 was not available to me.

50 Edward Surtz, *The Works and Days of John Fisher* (Cambridge, Mass., 1967), p. 295; *Opera*, col. 1712. Fisher's teaching in this treatise should be compared with that of Walter Hilton, *The Scale of Perfection*, ed. E. Underhill (London, 1923), pp. 55–82.

51 Wolfgang Riehle, *The Middle English Mystics* (London, 1981), p. 39, and chs. 3 and 5 *passim*.

52 David Knowles, *The English Mystical Tradition* (London, 1964), pp. 96, 107–9.

53 *Opera*, col. 1728, my emphasis.

54 *Minor Works of Walter Hilton*, ed. D. Jones (London, 1929), pp. 82–90.

55 Simon Tugwell, OP, *Ways of Imperfection* (London, 1984), pp. 107–10, 152–69.

56 *Opera*, col. 262.

57 Bridgett, *Fisher*, p. 170.

58 Ibid., p. 174.

59 *Life*, XII, 198–9, 226–32.

60 *LP*, VII, no. 557 (27 April 1534), 221–2; Bridgett, *Fisher*, pp. 63, 176.

61 Ibid., p. 176.

62 Francis Cheetham, *English Medieval Alabasters* (Oxford, 1984), pp. 28f.

63 W. H. St J. Hope, 'On the Sculptured Alabaster Tablets Called St John's Heads', *Archaelogia*, 52 (1890), 669–708.

64 Susan Foister, 'Paintings and Other Works of Art in 16th Century English Inventories', *The Burlington Magazine*, 113 (1981), 275.

65 See, for example, Blench's comments on its fine writing, *Preaching*, p. 135.

66 *Two Fruytfull Sermons* (above, n. 15), pp. 4–6: the passage is quoted *in extenso* in Blench, *Preaching*, p. 135.

67 *Two Fruytfull Sermons*, pp. 11–12: Blench, *Preaching*, p. 136.

68 *Two Fruytfull Sermons*, pp. 14–15.

69 Ibid., pp. 15–16.
70 The play of the Death of Herod is printed, with helpful comments, in *English Mystery Plays*, ed. Peter Happe (Harmondsworth, 1975), pp. 332–42.
71 *Two Fruytfull Sermons*, pp. 17–18.
72 J. J. Scarsbrick, 'Fisher, Henry VIII and the Reformation crisis', above, pp. 155–68.
73 The case for the reformers' devotional medievalism was made by Gregory Dix, *The Shape of the Liturgy* (London, 1945), pp. 605ff. An even more entertaining, if somewhat less secure, case against Cranmer's 'emotionalised' piety, was made by Harry Williams, 'Unchristian Liturgy', *Theology*, 61 (1958), 401–4.
74 McConica, 'The Patrimony of Thomas More', *passim*.
75 On Syon see D. Knowles, *The Religious Orders in England*, Volume III, *The Tudor Age* (Cambridge, 1961), pp. 212–21. On the devotional ethos of the Syon and Carthusian circles at this time, see Roger Lovatt, 'The *Imitation of Christ* in Late Medieval England', *Transactions of the Royal Historical Society*, n.s., 18 (1968), 97–121, and M. G. Sargent, 'The Transmission by the English Carthusians of Some Late Medieval Spiritual Writings', *Journal of Ecclesiastical History*, 27 (1976), 225–40; the most authoritative treatment of Syon is now M. B. Tait, 'The Bridgettine Monastery of Syon (Middlesex)', Oxford D.Phil. thesis 1975. The list in the text is derived from an examination of M. Bateson, *Catalogue of the Library of Syon Monastery, Isleworth* (Cambridge, 1898), and Tait, 'Syon', chs. 7 and 8. The most comprehensive guide to the character and content of early Tudor devotional literature as a whole remains Dr Jan Rhodes's unpublished 1974 Durham Ph.D. thesis, 'Private Devotion in England on the Eve of the Reformation'.
76 On Whytford see White, *The Tudor Books of Private Devotion*, (Wisconsin, 1951), pp. 153–61; Rhodes, 'Private Devotion', pp. 176–94, 318f, 498; and Tait, 'Syon', p. 275–96.
77 The point is generally made in accounts of Whytford, but for a specific example see the treatment of the commandment to keep the Sabbath holy, anticipating many later 'protestant' and 'puritan' concerns, in *Werke for Housholders* (London, 1537) (*STC* 25413), sigs. D–D ii v. See also Tait, 'Syon', p. 292.
78 *STC* 3277, 14553, and 25421 respectively. Their work is discussed by Tait, 'Syon', ch. 7.
79 On the 'golden chalices, wooden priests' theme, see E. Ruth Harvey, 'The Image of Love', in *The Complete Works of St Thomas More*, VI (2), ed. T. M. C. Lawler, Germain Marc'hadour, and Richard C. Marius (New Haven and London), 729–59. Its source in Gratian is in *Decretum*, III, ed. E. A. Friedberg (Leipzig, 1879–81), I, 1305–6. For Savonarola's use of the same material, P. Villari, *Life and Times of Girolamo Savonarola* (London, 1889), I, 184, and see also below, n. 80. (I owe the Villari reference to Richard Rex.) For Fisher's interest in Savonarola, *Opera*, cols. 109, 637–8.
80 *Opera*, cols. 1715–16; the passage in question is quoted by Bridgett, *Fisher*, p. 435. Once again, there are striking similarities with Savonarola: cf. Villari, *Savonarola*, II, 58–9.
81 See for example, the confusing usage of Daniel Kinney in referring to More's 'Erasmian' writings in his otherwise excellent introduction to the collection of More's earlier writings that comprise volume 15 of the Yale *Complete Works* (New Haven and London, 1986). Kinney is concerned to differentiate between More's

humanism and that of Erasmus, yet nevertheless persists in calling More's humanist letters 'Erasmian'. On the range and variety of opinion and devotional temper in early Henrician England, and on the elements of continuity and tradition in English humanism, see Rhodes, 'Private Devotion', pp. 9, 199, and *passim*.

APPENDIX 1

Chancellors of the University of Cambridge, *c.* 1415–1535

Christopher N. L. Brooke

This list is based on Emden, *Cambridge*; detailed references to sources are given only for Rotherham and his successors. I ignore the details given in *VCH Cambs*, III, 331–3, based on *The Historical Register of the University of Cambridge*, ed. J. R. Tanner (Cambridge, 1917), which in its turn owed much ultimately to lists by John Caius and in British Library Cotton MS Faustina C. iii, fos. 81–102 (79–100) – from 289 to 1598, continued to 1605 – printed in R. Parker, *The History and Antiquities of the University of Cambridge* (London, n.d.), pp. 188–99, as of no critical value. The abbreviation occ. is used for 'occurs'.

John Rickinghall, occ. 1415, 1422; master of Gonville Hall, *c.* 1416–26; confessor of the duke of Bedford, 1426; bishop of Chichester, 1426–9 (Emden, *Cambridge*, p. 480; C. Hall and C. Brooke, 'The Masters of Gonville Hall', in *The Caian* (1983), p. 46; J. Le Neve, *Fasti Ecclesiae Anglicanae 1300–1541*, VII, (London, 1964), 2).

Robert Fitzhugh, occ. April 1423; again November 1428; bishop of London, 1431–6 (Emden, *Cambridge*, p. 232; Le Neve, *Fasti*, V, 3).

Marmaduke Lumley, occ. June 1425, 1427; bishop of Carlisle, 1429–50; of Lincoln 1450 (Emden, *Cambridge*, p. 377; Le Neve, *Fasti*, I, 2; VI, 98).

John Holbroke, occ. November 1429; 1430; master of Peterhouse, 1421–*c.* 1437 (Emden, p. 309).

William Lascelles, occ. February 1432 (Emden, *Cambridge*, pp. 353–4); died 22 August 1453 ('1423', Emden, *Cambridge*: cf. F. Peck, *Desiderata Curiosa*, II (London, 1735), VIII. 10).

Richard Cawdray, occ. December 1433; December 1435 (Emden, *Cambridge*, pp. 126–7).

John Langton, chancellor, 1436–47; master of Pembroke, 1428–47; bishop of St Davids, 1447 (Emden, *Cambridge*, pp. 351–2; Le Neve, *Fasti*, XI, 54–5).

Robert Ayscogh, occ. November 1447–1448x9 (dead by 20 February 1449: Emden, *Cambridge*, p. 27).

Nicholas Close, occ. July 1449; bishop of Carlisle, 1450–2, of Lichfield and Coventry, 1452 (Emden, *Cambridge*, p. 142; Le Neve, *Fasti*, VI, 98; X, 2).

William Percy (son of Henry, earl of Northumberland), occ. 1452, 1455; bishop of Carlisle, 1452–62; died 1462 (Emden, *Cambridge*, p. 450; Le Neve, *Fasti*, VI, 98).

Lawrence Booth (Bothe), occ. February 1457, December 1458 (Emden, *Cambridge*, p. 78); master of Pembroke, 1450–80; bishop of Durham, 1457–76; archbishop of York, 1476–80 (Emden, *Cambridge*, pp. 78–9; Le Neve, *Fasti*, VI, 5, 108–9).

Robert Wodelarke, occ. 1458–9, again 1462–3; provost of King's, 1452–79 (Emden, *Cambridge*, p. 645; cf. *Grace Book A*, p. 18).

Richard Scrope, occ. June 1461, March 1462; bishop of Carlisle, 1464–8 (Emden, *Cambridge*, pp. 514–15; Le Neve, *Fasti*, VI, 99).

John Booth (nephew of Lawrence Booth), chancellor 1463–4; admitted Oct. 1463; occ. February 1464; bishop of Exeter, 1465–78 (Emden, *Cambridge*, pp. 77–8; Le Neve, *Fasti*, IX, 2–3).

William Wylflete, occ. January 1465, May 1466 (Emden, *Cambridge*, p. 657).

Thomas Rotherham, chancellor, 1469–71; occ. (2nd term) 1473, 1480–1, 1483, 1492; bishop of Rochester, 1468–72, of Lincoln, 1472–80; archbishop of York, 1480–1500; master of Pembroke, 1480–8 (Emden, *Cambridge*, pp. 489–90; *Grace Book A*, pp. 98, 157–9, 172, 175–6; *Grace Book B*, I, 44, 50; etc.; Le Neve, *Fasti*, I, 3; IV, 39; VI, 5).

Edward Story, occ. January 1471; master of Michaelhouse, occ. 1466–74; bishop of Chichester, 1478–1503 (Emden, *Cambridge*, pp. 560–1; Le Neve, *Fasti*, VII, 3).

John Blythe, occ. as chancellor 1496, 1497, November 1498; bishop of Salisbury, 1493–9; died August 1499 (Emden, *Cambridge*, p. 68; *Grace Book B*, I, 68(?), [1] 92, 98, 106; *Calendar of Patent Rolls 1494–1509*, p. 47; Le Neve, *Fasti*, III, 3).

Richard Fox, elected chancellor 1498x9; succeeded by 1500; referred to as chancellor elect, bishop of Durham, 1498x9; as bishop of Durham, not called chancellor, 1499x1500 – in the same proctor's account Morton seems to be chancellor (Emden, *Cambridge*, p. 240; Emden, *Oxford*, II, 715–19; *Grace Book B*, I, 121, 136–7). He was bishop of Exeter, 1487–92, of Bath and Wells, 1492–4, of Durham, 1494–1501, of Winchester, 1501–28 (Le Neve, *Fasti*, IV, 47; VI, 109; VIII, 3; IX, 3).

John Morton, Cardinal, archbishop of Canterbury, 1486–1500, and also chancellor of Oxford University. The proctors' accounts for 1499–1500 refer to letters sent 'ad dominum cardinalem summum justiciarium nostrum cancellarium M. Rede et M. Braye', which seems to show Morton (or just possibly Fox) as chancellor in 1499x1500; he died 15 September 1500 (Emden, *Cambridge*, pp. 412–13; *Grace Book B*, I, 137).

George FitzHugh, occ. in Easter term 1502 ('magistro Fitzhuge cancellario universitatis'; *Grace Book B*, I, 170 (cf. pp. xxvii, 171); Emden, *Cambridge*, p. 231. He was the only FitzHugh known at the time who was a master).

William Sever, bishop of Durham, 1502–5, occ. 1502x3 as 'episcopum Dunelmensem cancellarium electum' (*Grace Book B*, I, 184): but this is not Ruthall (as Emden, *Cambridge*, p. 497), but William Sever (Le Neve, *Fasti*, VI, 109). Sever had no other known connection with Cambridge, and it is just possible that this refers to Fox, who had been translated to Winchester in 1501.

John Fisher, elected chancellor 1504x5: 'cancellarium electum episcopum Roffensem' (*Grace Book B*, I, 203) probably means 'chancellor-elect' rather than bishop-elect (see above under Sever). The marginal note in a later hand 'mense octobris anno 1504' may refer to his provision to the bishopric of Rochester (Le Neve, *Fasti*, IV, 39; cf. *Grace Book B*, I, 275 (Index); Emden, *Cambridge*, p. 229). The *Life* (X, 215) sets his election as chancellor immediately after he was made bishop. He resigned as chancellor in 1514, and the chancellorship was offered to Wolsey, who declined: Fisher was then asked to resume it, and Fisher seems to have remained chancellor and bishop till his death (Lewis, *Fisher*, II, 282–6).

1 In 1494 John Fisher lunched 'apud dominam matrem regis' at Greenwich, and the same day 'cenatum est cum domino cancellario' – possibly Rotherham or Blythe, possibly the royal chancellor, John Morton.

APPENDIX 2

Fisher's career and itinerary, c. 1469–1535

Christopher N. L. Brooke, Richard Rex, Stephen Thompson and Malcolm Underwood

A Early career

c. 1469–70		Born in Beverley[1]
mid 1480s		Cambridge: probable arrival[2]
1488	1 March	Cambridge, questionist
1490–1		Cambridge, incepted in arts, and elected fellow of Michaelhouse
1494–5		Cambridge, senior proctor (*Grace Book B*, I, 67–78: see above pp. 57, 60)
c. 1500		Appointment as the lady Margaret's confessor[3]
1501	5 July	Cambridge, incepted in theology (as D.Th.: *Grace Book B*, I, 162)
	15 July	Cambridge, elected vice-chancellor (ibid.);
1501–2		Cambridge, vice-chancellor (*Grace Book B*, I, 156–9; *T*, pp. 1, 11)
1502	8 September	Cambridge, appointed the Lady Margaret's reader (Emden, *Cambridge*, p. 229, citing BL Lansdowne MS 441, fo. 37v).

Notes

1 His indulgence to be ordained priest, dated 14 June 1491, gives as ground that he has to be a priest within a year of his election as fellow of Michaelhouse, and that his age was 'in vigesimo secundo vel circa tue etatis anno', which if literally true suggests *c.* 1469–70 for his birth (Vatican Archives, Reg. lat. 908, fo. 70 r-v; we owe this reference to Dr Miri Rubin and Dr Peter Linehan: cf. summary in *Calendar of . . . Papal Letters*, 15, no. 739). He must have been under 24 or no indulgence would have been needed: *Dict. de droit canonique*, ed. R. Naz, I (Paris, 1935), cols. 340–1. Since most of the indulgences of this kind over the previous 20 years or so give the recipient's age as 22 this may have been a bureaucratic convention, and it would be unwise to lay much stress on the words of the document, but 22 or thereabouts fits well what we know of his early career: cf. *Calendar of . . . Papal Letters*, XII, 93, 383, 536, 670; XIII, 200, 426, 581, 610, 708; XV, nos. 137, 347, 713; XII, 536 and XIII, 426 give the age as 23; the rest as 22. We owe help in this region to Dr Patrick Zutshi.
2 For his academic career see details in Emden, *Cambridge*, p. 229 (who, however, by a slip dates his inception in theology to 1510), based on *Grace Book A*, pp. 211, 215; *B*, I, 18, 22–6, 142–3, 145, 147, 162. For his election at Michaelhouse see above, note 1; for his alleged mastership there, above pp. 49, 62.
3 Fitzjames was still confessor as bishop of Rochester (1497–1503), and Fisher was well established before his consecration in 1504: see esp. St John's Archives C7.11, fos. 45v, 47, ed. C. H. Cooper, *The Lady Margaret* (Cambridge, 1874), pp. 95–7.

B Itinerary as bishop, 1504–35

References are to his Register (Maidstone, Kent Archives Office, DRc/R7), fos. 6/40–182v, unless otherwise stated. 'Ordination' means an ordination performed (or presumably performed) by Fisher himself. Dates in brackets are those of parliament, Convocation, etc., of which Fisher was a member. We cannot tell in detail for how much of these he was present. Halling and Bromley are sometimes 'manerium suum de' etc.; Lambeth Marsh 'mansum' – these details are not noted; but 'palatium' and 'capella' are distinguished as follows: c = *capella*, chapel; p = *palatium*, palace.

Dates of parliaments, convocations and councils are from E. B. Fryde *et al.* (eds.), *Handbook of British Chronology*, 3rd edn (London, 1986), abbrev. as *HBC*, pp. 534–5, 564–5.

1504		Provided to the see of Rochester by Bull of 14 October (fo. 40; John Le Neve, *Fasti Ecclesiae Anglicanae, 1300–1541*, 12 vols., rev. edn, London, 1962–7, IV, 39)
	24–5 November	Lambeth, St Catherine's c. Consecration; return of spiritualities; profession (fo. 40)
	26 November	London, Coldharbour (fo. 40v)
	15, 17 December	Bromley (fo. 40v)
1504–5		First visit to Queens' College as president (W. G. Searle, *History of Queens' College* (Cambridge, 1867–71), I, 135; see above, p. 58)
1505	8 March	Bromley, c. of St Blaise. Ordination (fo. 41)
	24 April	(By proxy) Rochester cathedral. Enthronement (fo. 42r-v)
	15 May	Rochester cathedral. Opening of first visitation (fos. 44v, 42v)
	17 May	Rochester cathedral (fo. 41v)
	20, 28 May	Bromley (fo. 42r-v)
	22 August	Bromley (fo. 42v)
	28 October	Malling, nuns' church. Professions (fo. 42v)
	20 December	Bromley, c of St Blaise. Ordination (fo. 43)
1506	18 January	Bromley (fo. 43)
	2 February	Windsor. Carried the cross at mass for Archbishop Warham during the meeting of Henry VII and Philip of Castile (St John's College Archives, D105.162)
	4 March	Rochester p (fo. 43)
	22–3 April	Cambridge, with Henry VII (see above, pp. 58, 65; Queens' Coll. Muniments Book I, fo. 194v; C. H. Cooper, *Annals of Cambridge*, I (Cambridge, 1842), p. 281)
	8 May	Bromley (fo. 43v)
	6 June	Bromley c. Ordination (fo. 43v)
	9, 14 June	Bromley (fo. 43v)
	20 July	Hatfield (fo. 44)

	10 August	Bromley (fo. 44)
	18, 26 September	Hatfield (fo. 44)
	8 October	Bromley (fo. 44)
1507	20 January	Strood Hospital (evidently St Mary's: fo. 44)
	26 January	Higham (fo. 44)
	27 January	Rochester cathedral, chapter house (fos. 44v–45)
	10 February	Bromley (fo. 45v)
	19 February	Rochester p (fo. 45v)
	27 February	Rochester p c (fo. 45v)
	22 March	Rochester p (fo. 45v)
	26 March	Higham, nuns' church. Professions (fo. 44)
	26, 28 April	Hatfield (fo. 45v)
	June–July	Cambridge (see p. 43 n.22. Clare College Muniments, Safe C 1/7, fo. 53; cf. Searle, *Hist. of Queens'*, I, 136)
	18 September	Hatfield c. Ordination (by licence of the bishop of Lincoln: fo. 46v)
	6 October	Malling, nuns' convent (fo. 46v)
	12 November	Bromley (fo. 46v)
	5 December	Bromley church (fo. 47)
	18 December	Bromley c of St Blaise (fo. 48)
1508	18 March	Rochester p c. Ordination (fo. 50)
	8 April	Rochester p c. Ordination (fo. 50)
	12 April	Rochester p c (fo. 50)
	22 April	Rochester (fo. 50)
	25 May	Rochester cathedral. Opening of visitation (fo. 49v)
	28 May	Rochester (fo. 49v)
	30 May	Rochester c (fo. 50)
	5, 7, 20 July	Bromley (fo. 50v)
	c. August–September	Sermons on the Penitential Psalms before the Lady Margaret published June 1509, and evidently delivered the year before; the third – on Psalm 38 – is dated 8 Sept. (*EW*, pp. 1–267, esp. 1–2, 44, 267, and cf. p. ix)
	29 November	Bromley (fo. 51: and, somewhat later, Rochester p, ibid.)
	8 December	Bromley (fo. 51)
1509	28 January	Bromley (fo. 51)
	21 March	Higham, nuns' church. Profession (fo. 51)
	21 March (*also*)	Rochester p (fo. 51)
	24 March	Rochester p c. Ordination (fo. 52)
	4 May	Richmond. Sang mass for Henry VII's soul (*LP*, I, 1, no. 20, pp. 19–20)
	8 May	n.p. (fo. 52)
	10 May	London, St Paul's. Sermon at requiem for Henry VII (*EW*, p. 268; Lewis, *Fisher*, I, 29, citing Hall)
	5 June	Bromley (fo. 52)

29 June	Death of the Lady Margaret, followed by burial at Westminster (Lewis, *Fisher*, I, 33ff.: see below, *c.* 29 July)
20 July	Lambeth Marsh (fo. 52)
c. 29 July	?Westminster 'mornynge remembrance had at the moneth mynde' of the Lady Margaret (*EW*, pp. 289–310)
30 July	Greenwich (fo. 53)
31 July	Lambeth Marsh (fo. 52)
29 August	Hanworth. Signed notarial attestation (*LP*, I (1), no. 153)
31 October ('28' corrected)	Lambeth Marsh (fo. 52)
(12 November, corr. to 31 July	Lambeth Marsh, fo. 52)
22 December	Bromley. Ordination in Bromley parish church (fo. 55v)
1510 (21 Jan.–23 Feb.	Parliament, Westminster)
(26 Jan.–15 Feb.	Convocation, St Paul's – dates from *HBC*, pp. 535, 564–5 – summons, fos. 52, 52v–53)
January–March	London, Master Dowman's place at St Paul's. Meeting of bishops of Rochester, Ely and Winchester (St John's College, Archives D56.182)
7, 18, 21 February	Lambeth Marsh (fo. 53v)
30 March	Rochester p c. Ordination (fo. 54)
2 April	Gravesend. Consecration of chapel of St George (fo. 54)
3 April	Gravesend. Consecration of parish church (fo. 54)
4 April	Woldingham. Consecration of parochial chapel (fo. 54)
21 April	Beckenham, in parish church (fo. 54)
21 April (? – said to be same day)	Lambeth Marsh (fo. 54v)
6 May	Strood. Reconciliation of church and cemetery (fo. 54v)
16 May	Lambeth Marsh (fo. 54v)
14 August	Bromley (fo. 54v)
19 August	Lambeth Marsh (fo. 55)
4, 5 October	Bromley (fo. 55)
14, 15, 29 October	Lambeth Marsh (fo. 55)
8, 27 November	Lambeth Marsh (fo. 55r–v)
5 December	Richmond. Signed Privy Council warrant (*LP*, I (1), no. 651(7))
1511 4, 12 March	Greenwich. Signed Privy Council warrants (*LP*, I (1), nos. 731 (7, 20))
15 March[1]	Lambeth Marsh c. Ordination (fo. 55v)
30 March, 3 April	Greenwich. Signed Privy Council warrants (*LP*, I (1), nos. 731(52), 749(3))
6 April	Lambeth Marsh (fo. 55v)
7, 12 April	Greenwich. Signed Privy Council warrants (*LP*, I, (1), no. 749 (16, 24))
19 April	Rochester cathedral. Ordination (fo. 55v)

	23 April	Malling (fo. 55v)
	25 April	Bromley (fo. 55v)
	13 May	Lambeth Marsh (this year he built a wall round his manor house at Lambeth Marsh, etc.: fo. 55v)
	22 May	Rochester cathedral. Opening of visitation (fo. 56)
	31 May	Greenwich. Signed Privy Council warrant (*LP*, I (1), no. 784 (56))
	May–June	London. Letters sent by Fisher about St John's College (St John's Coll. Archives, D56.1–2)
	1 June	Lambeth Marsh (fo. 56)
	30 June	Greenwich. Signed Privy Council warrant (*LP*, I (1), no. 804 (49))
	20 September	Halling. Ordination in c (fo. 57v)
	1 October	Halling (fo. 57v)
	20 December	Halling. Ordination (fo. 57v)
	28 December	Halling (fo. 57v)
1512	(4 Feb.–30 March	Parliament, Westminster)
	(6 Feb.–?17 Dec.	Convocation, London, St Paul's)
	15 March	Lambeth Marsh (fo. 59)
	18 March	Westminster. Signed Privy Council warrant (*LP*, I (1), no. 1123 (45))
	10 April	Rochester p c. Ordination (fo. 59)
	23 May	Lambeth (Marsh) (fo. 59)
	26 May	Halling (fo. 59)
	8 June	Halling (fo. 60)
	8 June (also)	Rochester, chapter house (fo. 60r–v)
	18 June	Lambeth Marsh (fo. 61v)
	21 October	Lambeth Marsh (fo. 61v)
	(4 Nov.–20 Dec.	Parliament, Westminster. Convocation continued at London, St Paul's)
	14 November	Bromley (fo. 61)
	26 November	Lambeth Marsh (fo. 61v)
1513	28 February	Lessness abbey (fo. 61v)
	5 March	Halling c (fo. 62; cf. *Grace Book B*, II, 11)
	12 March	Halling c. Ordination (fo. 62)
	4 April	Rochester p (fo. 62v)
		In 1513 he prepared to go the Lateran Council in Rome, but was stopped *en route* (*Life*, X, 254n.)
	27 June	Lambeth Marsh (fo. 68)
	26 July	Bromley (fo. 70)
	2(?), 20 August	Bromley (fo. 69v)
	8 September	Richmond. Signed Privy Council warrant (*LP*, I(2), no. 2243)
	1, 7, 20 October	Bromley (fo. 70r–v)
1514	(23 Jan.–4 March	Parliament, Westminster)
	1 February	Lambeth Marsh (fo. 71)

14 February	Lambeth. Signed Privy Council warrant (*LP*, I (2), no. 2684 (64))
31 March	Rochester cathedral. Start of visitation (fo. 71)
15 April (Easter Eve)	Rochester p. Ordination (fo. 71)
20 April	Bromley (fo. 72)
11 May	Bromley (fo. 71v)
12 May	Letter from the duke of Norfolk, the marquis of Dorset and the bishops of Winchester and Durham, to Fisher, about arrangements for him and others to receive the pope's ambassador at a place between Sittingbourne and Rochester (St John's Archives D105.98).
22 May	Rochester, chapter house (fo. 71v)
26 May	London (Lewis, *Fisher*, II, 283–4)
(22 June – 1 July and 6 Nov. – 20 or 23 Dec.	Convocation, London, St Paul's)
13, 14 November	Lambeth Marsh (fo. 72)
26 November	Rochester cathedral. Professions (fo. 72)
2, 15 December	Halling (fo. 72v)

1515

(5 February – 5 April	Parliament, Westminster; 9 Feb. – 26 March, Convocation, London, St Paul's. The bishop of Ely appointed Fisher and the bishops of Winchester and Norwich his proctors (dated 1 Feb. – no year, but ?1515: St John's Archives D105.86))
February – March	He prepared to go to Rome (see 1513) but was again stopped (*Life*, X, 254n.); St John's College Archives, D57.175, dated 10 March at Lambeth Marsh)
10 March	Lambeth Marsh (see above, Feb.–March)
23 April	Halling (fo. 72v)
1 June	Halling (fo. 73)
18 June	Lambeth Marsh (fo. 73)
27, 29 July	Halling (fo. 73)
2 August	Halling (fo. 73)
7 August	Rochester p (fo. 73)
17 September	Wateringbury. Reconciliation of parish church (fo. 73)
2 October	Rochester p (fo. 73)
7 October	Lambeth (joined in consecration of bishop of Ely, W. Stubbs, *Registrum Sacrum Anglicanum*, 2nd edn (Oxford, 1897), p. 97)
12 November	Lambeth Marsh (fo. 73v)
18 November	Westminster Abbey. Carried the cross for Warham at Wolsey's investiture as cardinal (*LP*, II (1), no. 1153)
(12 Nov. – 22 Dec.	Parliament, Westminster; 13 Nov. – 26 December, Convocation, London, St Paul's)

1516[2]	11 February	Lambeth Marsh (fo. 73v)
	26 February	Rochester p (fo. 73v)
	13 March	?London, Bath Place. Baptised Henry, son of duke of Suffolk (*LP*, II (1), no. 1652; Bath Place was Suffolk's London house)
	22 March	Rochester p c. Ordination (fo. 73v)
	7 May	Rochester p c (fo. 74)
	17 May	Rochester p c. Ordination (fo. 74)
	6, 7 June	Rochester p (fo. 74)
	13 July	Rochester p c (fo. 74v)
	July	Cambridge. For the opening of St John's: the bishop of Ely's licence to Fisher to consecrate the chapel dated 26 July (T. Baker, *History of St John's College*, ed. J. E. B. Mayor (Cambridge, 1869), I, 76); the instrument for the opening is dated 29 July (St John's College Archives, D56.196)
	c. 16–26 August	Rochester. Visited by Erasmus (cf. *Erasmi Epistolae*, ed. P. S. Allen, II (Oxford, 1910), nos. 452, 455–6)
	10 September	Rochester (fo. 74v)
	18 October	Rochester p (fo. 74v)
	2 December	Rochester p (Mayor, *Statutes*, p. 395)
	8 December	Rochester p (fo. 74v)
1517	19 March	Rochester cathedral. Opening of visitation (fo. 74v)
	11, 29 April	Rochester p (fo. 74v–5)
	16, 23, 26 May	Rochester p (fo. 75)
	6 June	Rochester p (fo. 75)
	5 July	Greenwich. Signed notarial attestation of treaty (*LP*, II (2), no. 3437 (6))
	19 July	Rochester p (fo. 75v)
	25, 27 October	Rochester p (fo. 75v)
	20 November	Rochester p (fo. 76)
	24 November	Rochester, Chapter House (fo. 76r–v)
	17 December	Rochester p (fo. 76v)
1518	4 February	Rochester p (fo. 76v)
	27 February	Rochester p c (fo. 76v)
	20 March	Rochester p (c). Ordination (fo. 77)
	10 July	Woldingham ('Woldeham') (fo. 77)
	24–7 July	Canterbury (*LP*, II (2), nos. 4333, 4348)
	27 July	Rochester (ibid.)
	25 August	Lambeth Marsh (fo. 77)
	10 September	Lambeth Marsh (fo. 77)
	24 September	Sutton (fo. 77v)
	7 October	Rochester cathedral synod (fo. 77v)
	16, 24 October	Lambeth Marsh (fo. 77v)
	8, 12, 20 November	Rochester p (fo. 77v)
	5 December	Rochester p c (fo. 78)
	18 December	Rochester p (c). Ordination (fo. 78)

1519   3, 26 January   Rochester p (fo. 78)
10, 16, 28 February Rochester p (fos. 78v–9)
(14 March   ?Legatine council, Westminster)
22 May   Rochester p (fo. 87)
1 June   Halling (fo. 79)
14 July   Halling ('in magna camera sua infra manerium suum de Hallyng') (fo. 79)
12 August   Halling (fo. 87)
3, 11, 17 October Rochester p (fo. 87)
6 November   Oxford. Joined in consecration of bishop of Exeter (Stubbs, *Registrum Sacrum Anglicanum*, p. 98)
12 November   Rochester p (fos. 95, 100)
9 December   Rochester p (fo. 100)

1520   21 January   Rochester p (fo. 101v)
18 February   Rochester (fo. 101v)
(26 February   English legatine council, Westminster)
1 March   Lambeth Marsh. Visitation announced (fo. 102)
16 April   Rochester p (fo. 102)
9 May   Strood Hospital (fo. 103)
30 May – 24 June
or later   France. In attendance on the king to the Field of the Cloth of Gold (for the Field, S. Anglo, *Spectacle, Pageantry and Early Tudor Policy* (Oxford, 1969), pp. 137–69). Fisher's sermon on the Field makes clear he was present (*A Critical Edition of 'Two Fruytfull Sermons' of Saint John Fisher, Bishop of Rochester*, ed. Sister Marie Denise Sullivan (Notre Dame, Ind. 1961), pp. 2–43). Fisher's name is on the lists of those attending or intending to attend (*LP*, III, 236, 240 (nos. 703–4)), but not named in the contemporary description, which refers to 'five or six bishops' (ibid., p. 308). He was not with the king at Gravelines on 10 July (ibid., 325–6, no. 906) nor with Wolsey at Bruges in August (ibid., 616, no. 1499; cf. 609–16, esp. nos. 1482, 1493).
15 August   Halling (fo. 103v)
22 September   Halling c. Ordination (fo. 104)
22 December   Rochester p c. Ordination (fo. 106v)

1521   23 February   Rochester p (fo. 106v)
10 March   Rochester – (fo. 106v)
16 March[3]   Rochester p. Ordination (fo. 106v)
– (not dated,
possibly late March) Lambeth Marsh (fo. 106v)
5 May   Lambeth. Joined in consecration of bishop of Lincoln (Stubbs, *Registrum Sacrum Anglicanum*, p. 98)
12 May[4]   St Paul's Cross Sermon against Luther (*EW*, p. 311; *LP*, III (1), 485, nos. 1273–4).
c. May–June   Cambridge (above, p. 59)

	4, 23 June	Halling (fo. 107v, fo. 107)
	1, 9, 13, 27 July	Halling (fo. 107)
	19 August	Halling (Cambridge, St John's College Archives, D10.12.14)
	31 August	Halling (fo. 107)
	23 September, 26 October	Halling (fo. 107v)
	2 November	Halling (fo. 107v)
	12 December	Halling (fo. 108)
1522	19 January	Rochester cathedral. Solemn mass and profession (fo. 108)
	10, 21 February	Rochester p (fo. 108)
	2 March	West Malling, nuns' church. Solemn mass and profession (fo. 108)
	9, 10 May	Rochester p (fo. 108v)
	27 May	Canterbury at reception of emperor (*LP*, III (2), no. 2288)
	2 June[5]	Rochester p (Cambridge, St John's College Archives, D105.53)
	1 July	Rochester p (fo. 108v)
	13 September	Rochester p (fo. 108v)
	19 October	London. Joined in consecration of bishop of London (Stubbs, *Registrum Sacrum Anglicanum*, p. 98)
	20 November	Rochester p (fo. 108v)
	20 December	Rochester p. Ordination (fo. 109)
	23 December	Rochester p (fo. 109)
1523	26 February	Rochester p (fo. 109v)
	21 March[6]	Rochester p. Ordination (fo. 109)
	4 April	Rochester p. Ordination (fo. 109v)
	6 April	London. Letter to Nicholas Metcalfe, staying with Fisher in London (St John's Archives D.105.246)
	(15 Apr.–21 May, 10 June–29 July, 31 July–13 Aug.	Parliament, London, Blackfriars. Summons (fo. 109))
	(20 Apr. – 14 Aug.	London, St Paul's. Convocation: summons (fo. 110))
	17 April	Lambeth Marsh (fo. 109v)
	26 April	Lambeth. Joined in consecration of bishop of St Davids (Stubbs, *Registrum Sacrum Anglicanum*, p. 98)
	12 May	Lambeth Marsh (fo. 109v)
	5 July	Lambeth Marsh (fo. 110v)
	20 August	Rochester p (fo. 110v)
	September	Rochester. Lord Morley was his guest *en route* for Antwerp, which he reached 20 Sept. (*LP*, III (2), no. 3373)
1524	5 January	Rochester p (fos. 110v–11)
	4, 16 February	Rochester p (fo. 111)
	15 March	Rochester p. Election of Abbess of Malling (fo. 111v)
	20 May	Rochester p (fo. 113v)

	24 July	Rochester p c (Mayor, *Statutes*, pp. 341–2)
	26 July	Rochester p (fo. 113)
	1 September	Canterbury (*LP*, IV (1), no. 614)
	23 September	Rochester p (fo. 114)
	1 October	Rochester p. Election of abbess of Malling (fo. 120)
	5 October	Rochester p c (fo. 115)
	8 October	Rochester p (fo. 116)
	24 October	Malling, nuns' convent (fo. 114)
	8 November	Rochester p (fo. 114v)
	8 December	Rochester p (fo. 114v)
1525	3, 14, 24 February	Rochester p (14th just Rochester; fos. 123v, 125)
	3, 20 April	Rochester p (fo. 129r–v)
	6 June	Rochester p (fo. 129v)
	18 June	Rochester p c (fo. 130)
	7 July	Rochester (fo. 130v)
	28 July	Rochester p (fo. 130v)
	21 August	Rochester (T. E. Bridgett, *Life of Blessed John Fisher* (London, 1888), pp. 114–16)
	20 September	Rochester p (fo. 130v)
	6, 27 October	Rochester p (fo. 131r–v)
	4, 29 November	Rochester p (fo. 132v)
1526	20 January	Rochester p (fo. 132v)
	8 February	Lambeth Marsh (fo. 133)
	?11 February[7]	St Paul's Cross. Sermon against Luther (E. Hall, *Henry VIII*, ed. C. Whibley (London, 1904), II, 57–8)
	16 March	Rochester cathedral. Opening of Visitation (fo. 133v)
	26 May	Rochester p c. Ordination (fo. 133)
	24 July	Woldingham, 'in rectoria de Woldeham' because of plague in Rochester (fo. 133v)
	15 August	Lessness abbey (*LP*, IV (2), no. 2396: Fisher will be at Lessness on the morrow of the Assumption)
	15 September	Halling (fo. 134v)
	5, 12 October	Halling (fo. 134v)
	13, 28 December	Halling (fo. 136)
1527	25 February	Rochester p (fo. 136v)
	5 April	Rochester p (fo. 136v)
	8 May	Rochester p (fo. 137)
	4 June	Rochester p (fo. 137)
	30 July	Rochester p (fo. 137)
	8 October	Rochester, chapter house. Sermon and Synod (fo. 138v)
	19 November	Lambeth Marsh (fo. 138v)
	27 November	Westminster Abbey, chapter house (Foxe, *Acts and Monuments*, ed. G. Townsend (London, 1846), IV, 621)
	28 November, 2 December	London, Bishop of Norwich's house (Foxe, *Acts and Monuments*, IV, 622)

	4, 5, 7 December	Westminster Abbey, chapter house (Foxe, *Acts and Monuments*, IV, 631–2)
	22 December	Rochester cathedral (fo. 138v)
1528	13 June	Rochester p (fo. 139)
	12 July	Rochester p (fo. 139v)
	2, 6 October	Rochester p (fos. 141v–3)
	25 October	London (*LP*, IV (2), no. 4875)
	7 November	Bridewell, London (*LP*, *IV* (3), App. no. 211; 'Philalethes Hyperboreus', *Parasceve* (1533), fos. D.5–6)
	14, 30 November	Lambeth Marsh (fo. 143v)
	6 December	Lambeth Marsh (fo. 143v)
1529	10, 16 February	Rochester p (fo. 143v–4; cf. *Grace Book B*, II, 152)
	12 March	Rochester p (fos. 148–9)
	26 March	Rochester p (fo. 145v)
	5 April	Rochester, chapter house. Opening of visitation (fo. 145v)
	9–10 April	Rochester, chapter house (fos. 146–8)
	27 April	Rochester p (fos. 146–8)
	31 May, 28 June	Sessions of Queen's trial (For Fisher's speech on 28 June, see Virginia Murphy (see below, note 8), p. 62, citing *LP* IV (3), no. 5732; S. Ehses, *Römische Dokumente zur Geschichte der Ehescheidung Heinrichs VIII. von England* (Paderborn, 1893), pp. 116–17; cf. *LP* IV (3), no. 5734, etc.[8]
	4 June	Lambeth Marsh (fo. 150v)
	16 June	London, Baynard's Castle, Catherine of Aragon's appeal to Rome (H. A. Kelly, *The Matrimonial Trials of Henry VIII* (Stanford, 1976), pp. 78–9)
	20 June	Lambeth Marsh (fo. 150v)
	22, 28 June	London, Blackfriars (Kelly, pp. 87, 92)
	1 July	Lambeth Marsh (fo. 150v)
	5 July	London, Blackfriars (Kelly, p. 101)
	1 August	Rochester (fo. 150v)
	16 August	Malling, nuns' convent (fo. 151)
	30 August	Rochester p (fo. 151)
	7 October	Rochester p (fo. 152)
	(4 Nov. – 17 Dec. 1529	Parliament, Westminster (cf. Edward Hall, *The Triumphant Reigne of Kyng Henry VIII*, ed. C. Whibley (London, 1904), II, 167) – Fisher was active in this session of parliament)
	5 Nov. – 24 Dec.	London, St Paul's. Convocation; summons (fos. 151v–2)
1530	14, 21 April	Rochester (fo. 153v; fo. 158)
	(29 April – ?,	London, St Paul's. Convocation)
	2 May	Rochester (fo. 158)
	20 May	Rochester p (fo. 158v)

	5, 20 July and probably 29 July (see below, 29 Oct.)	Woldingham ('Woldeham sue diocesis') (fo. 158v; 159; Mayor, *Statutes*, p. 258: 11 July)
	31 July	Rochester p (fo. 159)
	24 September	Rochester p c. Ordination (fo. 159)
	30 September	Rochester p (fo. 159)
	9 October	Rochester (fo. 159r–v)
	12 October	Rochester p c (fo. 159v)
	29 October	(corrected from 29 July, Woldingham) Rochester p (fo. 159)
	9, 22 December	Rochester p (fos. 159v, 160)
1531	7 January	Rochester p (fo. 160)
	11 January	'recessit a palacio suo Roffensi ad parliamentum tentum in civitate London' (fo. 160)
	?12 January	London (Chapuys refers to a debate planned for 12 Jan. in *Calendar of State Papers, Spanish*, IV (1), no. 547)
	(16 Jan. – 31 March	Parliament, Westminster)
	21 Jan. – 16 October	Westminster. Convocation (cf. *Life*, X, 351)
	Jan. – Feb.	London (Chapuys refers to conversations with Fisher in letters of 23 Jan., 21 Feb.; and on 1 March to his imminent departure for Rochester: *Calendar of State Papers, Spanish*, IV (2), nos. 615, 641, 646)
	13, 15, 17 March	Rochester p (fo. 160v, fo. 159, fo. 161)
	15 April	Rochester p (fo. 161)
	25 April	Rochester p c (fo. 161)
	1 May	Rochester p (fo. 161)
	3 June	Rochester p c (fo. 162)
	8 June	Rochester p (fo. 162)
	7 August	Rochester p (fo. 162)
	15 November	Rochester p (fo. 162v)
	7 December	Rochester p (fo. 162v)
1532	12 January	Rochester p c (fo. 162v)
	22 January	London. Chapuys wrote that Fisher was in London, but not summoned to parliament (*Calendar of State Papers, Spanish*, IV (2), no. 888)
	(15 Jan. – 28 March, 10 April – 14 May	Westminster parliament)
	(16 Jan. – 15 May	Westminster. Convocation)
	(23 February	Archbishop of Armagh ordained on behalf of JF (fo. 163v))
	11 March	Lambeth Marsh (fo. 156r–v)
	16 May	Lambeth Marsh (fo. 164)
	25 May[9]	Rochester p c. Ordination (fo. 164)

	11 June	Rochester p (fo. 164)
	1 July	Halling (fos. 168v–169v)
	3 August	Halling (fo. 166v)
	9 October	Halling (fo. 172v)
	21 October	Rochester, chapter house (fo. 173)
	11, 12 November	Halling (fo. 174)
	14 November	Rochester p (fo. 174v)
	13 December	Rochester p (fo. 174v)
1533	12 January	Rochester (fo. 174v)
	(4 Feb. – 7 April	Westminster, parliament)
	(5 – 11 Feb.	Westminster, Convocation)
	4 March	Lambeth Marsh (fo. 177)
	11, 18 March	Lambeth (fo. 177)
	(17 March – 7 June	London, St Paul's, Convocation)
	7, 10 April[10]	Lambeth Marsh (fo. 177v)
	5 May	Lambeth Marsh (fo. 177v)
	2 June	Rochester (fo. 178)
	5 June	Rochester (fo. 178)
	7 June	Rochester p c. Ordination (fo. 178)
	10 June	Rochester (fo. 178)
	17, 25, 26 July	Rochester p (fo. 178v)
	21 August	Rochester p (fo. 178v)
	30 September	Rochester p (fo. 178)
	(4 November	London, St Paul's, Convocation)
	12 November	Rochester p (fo. 179v)
	17 December	Rochester p c (fo. 179v)
	20 December	Bishop's c, presumably Rochester p c (fo. 180v)
1534	13 January	Rochester p (fo. 180v)
	Early 1534	Apparently ill in Rochester: cf. letter to Cromwell of 28 January, saying he had been ill for 6 weeks, and of Henry VIII dated 27 February, evidently 1534 (*LP*, VI, no. 116, cf. no. 136 of 31 Jan.; Lewis, *Fisher*, II, 336–9; *LP*, VII, 98–9, no. 239)
	(15 Jan. – 30 March, and later.	Parliament, Westminster)
	(16 Jan. – 19 Dec.	Convocation, London, St Paul's (cf. *Life*, XII, 107))
	28 February	Rochester (fo. 180v)
	After 30 March[11]	Last journey to London via Shooter's Hill (described in *Life*, XII, 127–30)
	13, 21 April	Lambeth. Sessions before commissioners – lodging in Lambeth Marsh meanwhile (*Correspondence of Sir Thomas More*, ed. E. F. Rogers (Princeton, 1947), p. 504; cf. p. 501; cf. *Life*, XII, 130–2)
	21 April, Tuesday	Committed to Tower of London (*Life*, XII, 137)[12]

(24 July	Reg., fo. 181, notes that the bishop was out of the diocese; fo. 182r–v gives his successor's election, Aug. 1535)
1535 17 June, Thursday	Trial at Westminster (*LP*, VIII, 350–1, no. 886; *Life*, XII, 170; Lewis, *Fisher*, II, 180–1, gives 27 June by a slip) – otherwise in the Tower till 22 June
22 June	Execution (*Life*, XII, 263; Le Neve, *Fasti*, IV, 39, citing H. Wharton, *Anglia Sacra* (London, 1691), I, 383)

Notes

1 Ember Saturday: '9th' in MS, but that was a Sunday; the nearest Ember Saturday was the 15th.

2 St John's Archives, D105.100, has a note of Fisher's appointment to meet the emperor's ambassadors at Dover; this may belong to 1516 or 1520 (see below).

3 '17' March, but Saturday *Sitientes*, i.e. the Saturday before Passion Sunday, 16 March in 1521.

4 Dated within the octaves of the Ascension, i.e. 9–16 May; 12 May was the Sunday, and *Calendar of State Papers, Venetian*, III, nos. 210, 213, date it to the Sunday (see also *LP*, III (2), no. 1274). The woodcut opposite p. 311 confirms that it was at St Paul's Cross.

5 From a letter dated 2 June (no year) referring to a visit by Henry VIII while escorting the emperor – this must be 1522 since Fisher was in France in 1520. For 1 July cf. the letters written on Fisher's behalf printed by G. J. Gray, *The Library*, 3rd series, 14 (1913), 133–45: no. 4 (p. 142) is dated Rochester, 1 July, and may well have been written in 1522. No. 1 (pp. 134–5) is dated Rochester, 20 October (the editor suggests a date after 1517; 1518 seems impossible; 1519 is possible, or a later date). No. 2 (p. 136) is undated. No. 3 (p. 139) is 'from Sellyng on Friday' (possibly one should read 'Halling' and the year may be 1521). No. 4: see above. No. 5 (pp. 143–4) is dated Rochester, 11 July (the editor suggests 1522 or 1523: 1522 seems more likely, since he was probably in London in July 1523).

6 '20' March, but Saturday *Sitientes*, i.e. 21 March.

7 *EW*, pp. 429–76, prints a sermon 'at Paulis' by Fisher at the cardinal's command, on Quinquagesima Sunday (the day is referred to also on p. 436), 'concernynge certayne heretickes, which than were abiured for holdynge the heresies of Martyn Luther . . . and for the keping and reteynyng of his bokes agaynst the ordinance of the bulle of Pope Leo the tenthe' (p. 529). This was presumably the sermon referred to by Hall.

8 See Virginia Murphy, 'The Debate over Henry VIII's First Divorce: An Analysis of the Contemporary Treatises', Ph.D. thesis, Cambridge, 1984, p. 62; and pp. 53–5 for a discussion of Fisher's movements in 1527–8, which cannot however be closely dated.

9 '21' May in MS, but the 25th was the Ember Saturday.

10 According to Chapuys and Capello, Fisher spoke out for Catherine on 6 April and was arrested, and Capello alleges he was put in Gardiner's custody – presumably at Winchester House, Southwark – but allowed to return to Lambeth Marsh on 'the third day': *Diarii di M. Santo*, LVIII (Venice, 1903), p. 144; *Calendar of State Papers, Spanish*, IV (2), no. 1058. In a letter of 16 June, Chapuys records his release within the last three days: *Calendar . . . Spanish*, IV (2), no. 1081; one suspects that the letter is misdated, as the Register shows him to have been at Rochester since 2 June at latest.

11 Said in Le Neve, *Fasti*, IV, 39 to have been formally deprived of his see 7–25 March 1534: the editor cites *LP*, IX, no. 236 (13) which belongs to Aug. 1535; the source seems rather to be *LP* VII, no. 373, a report by Chapuys dated 25 March 1534, which says that the bishop

of Rochester 'has been . . . condemned to confiscation of body and goods' on account of the nun of Kent. This must have anticipated in some measure; no attempt seems to have been made to fill his see till after his death: *LP* IX, 79–80, no. 236 (5, 13).

12 Letters of 16 and 17 April refer to his being already in custody. On the 16th Chapuys reports he had been sent to the Tower that morning; on the 17th John Husee refers to him as in Cranmer's charge, presumably at Lambeth: *Calendar . . . Spanish*, V (1), no. 44; *Lisle Letters*, ed. M. St C. Byrne (London, 1981), no. 168, pp. 126–7.

APPENDIX 3

Statistics of episcopal residence *c.* 1486–1535

Stephen Thompson

Bishop	Diocese	Dates	% of time resident
Alcock	Ely[1]	1486–1500	80
Nykke	Norwich[2]	1501–35	75
Savage	York[3]	1501–7	90
Audley	Salisbury[4]	1502–24	95
Warham	Canterbury[5]	1504–32	33
Mayew	Hereford[6]	1505–16	90
Oldham	Exeter[7]	1505–19	75
Fitzjames	London[8]	1506–22	100
Bainbridge	York	1508–14	0
West	Ely[9]	1515–33	*c.* 75

Notes

1 Cambridge UL, Ely Diocesan Records, G/1/6.
2 Norfolk and Norwich Record Office, Bishops' Registers, XIII–XVI.
3 Borthwick Institute, York, Archbishop's Registers, XXV, XXVIII.
4 Wiltshire Record Office, Register of Bishop Audley.
5 Bodleian Library, Oxford, MSS Film 1386 (Lambeth Palace Library, Reg. Warham).
6 *Registrum Ricardi Mayeur*, ed. A. T. Bannister, Canterbury and York Society, 27 (1920), *passim*.
7 Devon Record Office, Bishop's Register, XIII.
8 Guildhall, London, MS 9531/9.
9 J. J. Scarisbrick, 'The Conservative Episcopate in England, 1529–1535', unpublished Ph.D. thesis, Cambridge, 1956, appendix.

APPENDIX 4

Parochial Patronage and the episcopate, c. 1520

Stephen Thompson

Diocese	No. of parishes in diocese	No. in bishop's gift a) total	No. in bishop's gift b) in own diocese	% parochial patronage held by bishop in own diocese	Proportion of patronage based on parishes (%) (i.e. not prebends masterships etc.)	Approximate value of parochial patronage to incumbents (total)	Comments
Canterbury[1]	239	190	107	42	90	£4,750	Includes: 88 rectories, 19 vicarages
Chichester[2]	274	28	28	10	45	£300	Includes: 28 rectories, and vicarages
Durham[3]	108	29	29	26	45	£800	Includes: 17 rectories, 12 vicarages
Hereford[4]	254	19	18	16	31	£165	Includes: 12 rectories, 3 vicarages, 4 chantries
London[5]	573	68	52	12	63	£680	Includes: 23 rectories, 29 vicarages, 3 chapels, 14 chantries
Rochester[6]	122	30	21	20	96	£475	
Salisbury[7]	607	24	24	4	40	£300	
York[8]	694	c. 50	4	5	42	£260	Includes: 21 rectories, and vicarages

Notes

1 M. J. Kelly, 'Canterbury Jurisdiction and influence during the episcopate of William Warham, 1503–32', unpublished Ph.D. thesis, Cambridge 1963, pp. 10–12.
2 H. Cole, *King Henry the Eighth's Scheme of Bishopricks* (London, 1838), p. 32.
3 The Registers of Bishops Tunstal and Pilkington, Surtees Society, 161 (1946), pp. 1–3.
4 *Registrum Ricardis Mayew, 1504–16*, ed. A. J. Bannister (London, 1921), pp. 234–6.
5 Guildhall, London, MSS 9531/7/8/9/10/11/12.
6 Kent County Archives, Diocesan Records, b. 4, Register of John Fisher, fo. 49v.
7 I. T. Shield, 'The Reformation in the Diocese of Salisbury', unpublished B.Litt. thesis, Oxford, 1960, p. 75; Wilts Record Office, Register of Bishop Audley, *passim*.
8 Borthwick, Archbishops' Registers, nos. 25, 26, 27, 28, 29, *passim*.

APPENDIX 5

The episcopate and ordinations c. 1487–1546

Stephen Thompson

Diocese	Bishop	Dates	Total no. of ordination ceremonies	Ceremonies performed by diocesan bishop	Total of all priests ordained	Average nos. per ordination
Canterbury	Morton[1]	1487–99	18	14	117	6–7
Coventry and Lichfield	Blythe[2]	1503–31	113	17	3,200	28
Ely	Alcock	1487–99	44	44	352	8
	West[3]	1516–20	14	14	112	8
Exeter	Oldham	1505–19	73	17	949	13
	Veysey[4]	1519–47	126	7	825	7
Hereford	Mayew	1504–16	53	39	382	7
	Bothe[5]	1517–32	38	25	546	14
Lincoln	Smith	1498–1513	104	15	4,170	30
	Longland[6]	1521–46	130	3	c. 2,220	15
London	Fitzjames	1506–22	94	39	840	10
	Tunstal[7]	1522–30	42	2	302	7
Rochester	Fisher[8]	1505–34	42	39	44	1
Salisbury	Audley[9]	1502–21	78	14	977	12–13
York	Savage	1501–7	35	0	1,234	35–6
	Bainbridge[10]	1508–13	29	0	1,336	46
	Wolsey[10]	1514–30	77	0	c. 3,000	40

Notes

1 Bodleian Library, Oxford, MSS Film 1385 (Lambeth Palace Library, Reg. Morton, II), fos. 137ff.
2 Lichfield Joint Record Office, Episcopal Register, 14 (i) (unfoliated), *passim.*
3 Cambridge UL, Ely Dioc. Recs.. G/1/6, fos. 223ff; G/1/7, fos. 80ff.
4 Devon Record Office, Bishop's Register, XIII fos. 147ff. D. Pill 'The Administration of the Diocese of Exeter under Bishop Veysey', *Devonshire Association Report and Transactions*, 98 (1966), 262–81.
5 *Reg. Mayew*, pp. 237–72; *Registrum Caroli Bothe, 1516–35*, ed. A. J. Bannister (London, 1921), pp. 304–30.
6 Lincoln Record Office, Ep. Reg., XXIV, fos. 1–94, XXV, fos. 7–12, 111–37, XXVI, fos. 1ff; M. Bowker, *The Secular Clergy in the Diocese of Lincoln, 1495–1520* (Cambridge, 1968), p. 39; M. Bowker, *The Henrician Reformation, The Diocese of Lincoln under John Longland, 1521–1547* (Cambridge, 1981), pp. 40, 125.
7 Guildhall, London, MS 9531/8, fos. 20ff; /9, fos. 156ff; /10, fos. 160ff; /11, fos. 72v ff; /12, fos. 98ff; MS 9535/1, fos. 1–80v.
8 Kent County Archives, DRb, Ep. Reg. 4, *passim.*
9 Wilts Record Office, Register Bishop Audley, fos. 2–47v.
10 Borthwick, Archbishops' Registers, nos. 25, fos. 108B ff; 26, fos. 99ff; 27, fos. 166ff; 28, fos. 185v ff. See also J. A. Hoeppner Moran, 'Clerical Recruitment in the Diocese of York, 1340–1530, Data and Commentary', *Journal of Ecclesiastical History*, 34 (1983), 19–54 *passim.*

Index

DATE DUE			